Feeling Modern

Feeling Modern

The Eccentricities
of Public Life

JUSTUS NIELAND

UNIVERSITY OF ILLINOIS PRESS
Urbana and Chicago

∞ This book is printed on acid-free paper.

Library of Congress Cataloging-in-Publication Data
Nieland, Justus.
Feeling modern : the eccentricities of public life / Justus Nieland.
p.   cm.
Includes bibliographical references and index.
ISBN-13 978-0-252-03337-7 (cloth : alk. paper)
ISBN-10 0-252-03337-X (cloth : alk. paper)
ISBN-13 978-0-252-07546-9 (pbk. : alk. paper)
ISBN-10 0-252-07546-3 (pbk. : alk. paper)
1. Social history—20th century. 2. Eccentrics and eccentricities.
I. Title.
HN16b.N47   2008
306.4'8401—dc22   2007037241

For Sarah

Contents

List of Illustrations   viii

Acknowledgments   ix

Abbreviations   xi

Introduction: Eccentric Feeling   1

Part 1: Sympathy

   1. Tough Crowds   33

   2. Eccentric Types   67

Part 2: Intimacy

   3. Kumraderie   103

   4. Light Figures   133

   5. Tenderness   163

Part 3: Comedy

   6. Dead Pan   195

   7. The Passion to Be a Person   219

      Epilogue: Charlie Chaplin and the Revenge
      of the Eccentric   251

      Notes   267

      Index   303

Illustrations

1. *Harry Lauder* by Marius de Zayas 43
2. *Gertrude Vanderbilt* by Marius de Zayas 44
3. *Cecelia Loftus* by Marius de Zayas 47
4. *Eva Tanguay* by Marius de Zayas 48
5. "Rank Theatricality" (*Strike*) 82
6. "Grotesque Animation" (*Strike*) 87
7. "Animal Agents" (*Strike*) 88
8. "Magnetic Personality." Zip, the What Is It? 104
9. *The Mountain* by Gaston Lachaise 110
10. *Standing Woman (Elevation)* by Gaston Lachaise 113
11. *The Warriors* by Marsden Hartley 138
12. *Portrait of a German Officer* by Marsden Hartley 140
13. *Painting No. 47, Berlin* by Marsden Hartley 141
14. "Public Intimacy," from unidentified publication in Hartley's files on "Elephants and Rhinestones" 157
15. "The Dead End of Love." Detail, from unidentified publication in Hartley's files on "Elephants and Rhinestones" 158
16. *Sustained Comedy* by Marsden Hartley 160
17. *A Dressing Room for Gilles* by Joseph Cornell 165
18. "Size Matters" (*The Children's Party*) 186
19. "Being Amazed" (*The Children's Party*) 190
20. "Chaplin Changes! Can You?" Publicity poster for *Monsieur Verdoux* 265

Acknowledgments

I owe this book to the many kindnesses of others. Thanks first to Jim Naremore, who taught me to care about modernism and who supported this project at every stage. I feel lucky to have been a steady beneficiary of his wisdom and good judgment, and now I'm grateful for his friendship. I would also like to thank Jonathan Elmer, who always embraced the quirks of the project and read everything with characteristic brilliance and rigor. His good company and great wit also helped to make my last few years in Bloomington a pleasure. Thanks also to Judith Roof, who pushed me to ask better questions and to think differently.

I owe a lot to Michigan State University for providing the leave time and research grants needed to complete the book and for generally being an exciting place to begin a career. To the students in my Feeling Modern and Modernism's Visual Culture graduate seminars, thanks for the lively conversations; our semesters together sharpened my thinking about this book. I am grateful to the following colleagues for their thoughtful responses to portions of this book: Zarena Aslami, Sandra Logan, Ellen McCallum, Karl Schoonover, and Judith Stoddart.

Along the way, Nancy Armstrong, Judith Brown, Jonathan Greenberg, Todd Kuchta, Richard Higgins, Jordana Mendelson, Tyrus Miller, and Paul Morrison gave generously of their time and expertise to read parts of the manuscript, and I thank them for their insights. I would also like to acknowledge the staff at the Yale Collection of American Literature at the Beinecke Rare Book and Manuscript Library for their help with the unpublished Marsden Hartley material. At the University of Illinois Press, Joan Catapano has been a terrific editor, finding extremely helpful anonymous readers for my manuscript. I thank these readers for their encouragement and sound advice. Portions of chapters 4 and 6 appeared in *Modernism/Modernity* and *Novel: A Forum on Fiction,* respectively. I am grateful to Johns Hopkins University Press and Novel Corporation for permission to republish these essays here.

Then there are those who, on a more fundamental level, keep you going and forever in their debt. Jen Fay, Scott Juengel, and Pat O'Donnell have been the best colleagues a guy could ask for. Everything good about my time at MSU has been so mostly because of their hospitality, friendship, and intellectual generosity. My profound thanks to Ed Comentale, a real pal and my favorite person to talk to about modernism, Dylan, and pretty much everything else. This book wouldn't be what it is without Ed's challenges and provocations. For their constant love and support, I extend my heartfelt gratitude to my family: my parents, Maury and Sue Erickson Nieland, and my brothers, Andrew and James. Writing this book was often made bearable by the companionship of Oliver and Orson, who saw us through a sad time and whom we miss. Finishing the book was kept in perspective by Lila, who came to us at just the right time.

I notice I have slipped into the first-person plural in these last few lines. This is only right, since what matters most in my emotional life, and in everything else, I share with Sarah Elizabeth Wohlford. This book, every word of which she read with great intelligence and love, is equally hers. I dedicate it to her.

Abbreviations

ABH André Breton, *Anthology of Black Humor*, trans. Mark Polizzotti (San Francisco: City Lights Books, 1997)

ABR Wyndham Lewis, *The Art of Being Ruled*, ed. Reed Way Dasenbrock (Santa Rosa: Black Sparrow Press, 1989)

AE Wilhelm Worringer, *Abstraction and Empathy: A Contribution to the Psychology of Style*, trans. Michael Bullock (Chicago: Elephant Paperbacks, 1997)

AIA Marsden Hartley, *Adventures in the Arts: Informal Chapters on Painters, Vaudeville, and Poets* (New York: Hacker Art Books, 1972)

AM J. Arthur Bleackley, *The Art of Mimicry* (New York: Samuel French, 1911)

AT Jacques Derrida, "The Animal That Therefore I Am (More to Follow)," trans. David Willis, *Critical Inquiry* 28 (Winter 2002): 381

BB Miriam Hansen, *Babel and Babylon: Spectatorship in American Silent Film* (Cambridge: Harvard University Press, 1991)

CC André Bazin, "Charlie Chaplin," in *What Is Cinema? Volume 1*, ed. and trans. Hugh Gray (Berkeley: University of California Press, 1967)

CK Sergei Eisenstein, "Charlie the Kid," in *Film Essays, with a Lecture*, ed. and trans. Jay Leyda (London: Dennis Dobson, 1968)

C1 Marsden Hartley, "Circus," Yale Collection of American Literature, Beinecke Rare Book and Manuscript Library, Yale University, New Haven, Connecticut

C2 Marsden Hartley, "Elephants and Rhinestones," Yale Collection of

	American Literature, Beinecke Rare Book and Manuscript Library, Yale University, New Haven, Connecticut
CWB	Wyndham Lewis, *The Complete Wild Body,* ed. Bernard Lafourcade (Santa Rosa: Black Sparrow Press, 1982)
D	Max Nordau, *Degeneration,* trans. George L. Mosse (Lincoln: University of Nebraska Press, 1993)
DR	Gilles Deleuze, *Difference and Repetition,* trans. Paul Patton (New York: Columbia University Press, 1994)
DS	Walter Benjamin, "The Formula in which the Dialectical Structure of Film Finds Expression," in *Walter Benjamin: Selected Writings, Vol. 3, 1935–1938,* ed. Michael W. Jennings, Howard Eiland, and Gary Smith, trans. Rodney Livingstone et al. (Cambridge: Harvard University Press, 2002)
EC	Mary Ann Doane, *The Emergence of Cinematic Time: Modernity, Contingency, the Archive* (Cambridge, Mass.: Harvard University Press, 2002)
ED	Sergei Eisenstein, *Eisenstein on Disney,* ed. Jay Leyda, trans. Alan Upchurch (Calcutta: Seagull Books, 1986)
EM	Jane Bennett, *The Enchantment of Modern Life: Attachments, Crossings, Ethics* (Princeton: Princeton University Press, 2001)
EM	Sergei Eisenstein and Sergei Tretyakov, "Expressive Movement," in *Meyerhold, Eisenstein, and Biomechanics: Actor Training in Revolutionary Russia,* ed. Alma Law and Mel Gordon (Jefferson, N.C.: McFarland, 1996)
ER	E. E. Cummings, *The Enormous Room,* typescript ed. (New York: Liveright, 1978)
FFF	Ian Christie and John Gillett, eds., *Futurism/Formalism/FEKS: "Eccentrism" and Soviet Cinema, 1918–36* (London: British Film Institute, 1978)
GP	Sigmund Freud, *Group Psychology and the Analysis of the Ego,* trans. and ed. James Strachey (New York: W. W. Norton, 1959)
GSE	Marsden Hartley, "The Greatest Show on Earth," *Vanity Fair* 22.6 (August 1924)
HC	Hannah Arendt, *The Human Condition* (Chicago: University of Chicago Press, 1958)
JB	Janet Lyon, "Josephine Baker's Hothouse," in *Modernism, Inc.: Body, Memory, Capital,* ed. Jani Scandura and Michael Thurston (New York: New York University Press, 2001)

L   Henri Bergson, "Laughter," in *Comedy,* ed. Wylie Sypher (Baltimore: Johns Hopkins University Press, 1980)

LB   Sergei Eisenstein, "Lecture on Biomechanics," in *Meyerhold, Eisenstein, and Biomechanics: Actor Training in Revolutionary Russia,* ed. Alma Law and Mel Gordon (Jefferson, N.C.: McFarland, 1996)

ME   Giorgio Agamben, *Means without End: Notes on Politics,* trans. Vincenzo Binetti and Cesare Casarino (Minneapolis: University of Minnesota Press, 2000)

M8   Sergei Eisenstein, "Montage 1938," in *S. M. Eisenstein: Selected Works, Vol. II, Towards a Theory of Montage,* ed. Michael Glenny and Richard Taylor, trans. Michael Glenny (London: British Film Institute, 1991)

MFA   Sergei Eisenstein, "The Montage of Film Attractions," in *The Eisenstein Reader,* ed. Richard Taylor (London: British Film Institute, 1998)

MH   Townsend Ludington, *Marsden Hartley: The Biography of an American Artist* (Ithaca: Cornell University Press, 1998)

ML   T. S. Eliot, "Marie Lloyd," in *Selected Essays of T. S. Eliot,* ed. Frank Kermode (London: Faber and Faber, 1932)

ML   Nathanael West, *Miss Lonelyhearts,* in *Nathanael West: Novels and Other Writings,* ed. Sacvan Bercovitch (New York: Library of America, 1997)

MR   *E. E. Cummings: A Miscellany Revised,* ed. George J. Firmage (New York: October House, 1965)

M7   Sergei Eisenstein, "Montage 1937," in *S. M. Eisenstein: Selected Works, Vol. II, Towards a Theory of Montage,* ed. Michael Glenny and Richard Taylor, trans. Michael Glenny (London: British Film Institute, 1991)

MU   Bill Brown, *The Material Unconscious: American Amusement, Stephen Crane, and the Economies of Play* (Cambridge, Mass.: Harvard University Press, 1996)

N   Djuna Barnes, *Nightwood* (New York: New Directions, 1937)

NE   R. P. Blackmur, "Notes on E. E. Cummings' Language," originally published in *Hound & Horn* 4 (1931): 163–92, reprinted in *Critical Essays on E. E. Cummings,* ed. Guy Rotella (Boston: G. K. Hall, 1984)

NY   Djuna Barnes, *New York,* ed. Alice Barry (London: Virago Press, 1990)

OP André Bazin, "The Ontology of the Photographic Image," in *What Is Cinema? Volume 1*, ed. and trans. Hugh Gray (Berkeley: University of California Press, 1967)

PGCT Marcia Brennan, *Painting Gender, Constructing Theory: The Alfred Stieglitz Circle and American Formalist Aesthetics* (Cambridge, Mass.: MIT Press, 2001)

PMA Sergei Eisenstein, "The Problem of the Materialist Approach to Form," in *The Eisenstein Reader*, ed. Richard Taylor (London: British Film Institute, 1998)

PR Charles Altieri, *The Particulars of Rapture: An Aesthetics of the Affects* (Ithaca: Cornell University Press, 2004)

PV Brian Massumi, *Parables for the Virtual: Movement, Affect, Sensation* (Durham: Duke University Press, 2002)

RA Wyndham Lewis, *Rude Assignment: An Intellectual Autobiography*, ed. Toby Foshay (Santa Barbara: Black Sparrow Press, 1984)

RT Georg Lukács, *Realism in Our Time: Literature and the Class Struggle*, trans. John Mander and Necke Mander (New York: Harper and Row, 1964)

S Georg Simmel, "The Stranger," in *The Sociology of Georg Simmel*, trans. and ed. Kurt H. Wolff (Glencoe, Ill.: Free Press, 1950)

SE *Selected Essays by T. S. Eliot*, ed. Frank Kermode (London: Faber and Faber, 1932)

SEC Jacques Derrida, "Signature, Event, Context," in *Limited Inc* (Evanston, Ill.: Northwestern University Press, 1993)

SF Wyndham Lewis, *Satire and Fiction* (London: Arthur Press, 1930)

SP *Somehow a Past: The Autobiography of Marsden Hartley*, ed. Susan Elizabeth Ryan (Cambridge, Mass.: MIT Press, 1997)

SV Jonathan Weinberg, *Speaking for Vice: Homosexuality in the Art of Charles Demuth, Marsden Hartley, and the First American Avant-Garde* (New Haven: Yale University Press, 1993)

T Laura U. Marks, *Touch: Sensuous Theory and Multisensory Media* (Minneapolis: University of Minnesota Press, 2002)

TA Teresa Brennan, *The Transmission of Affect* (Ithaca: Cornell University Press, 2004)

TC Sergei Eisenstein, "Through Theatre to Cinema," in *Film Form: Essays in Film Theory*, ed. and trans. Jay Leyda (San Diego: Harcourt Brace, 1949)

TM *Joseph Cornell's Theater of the Mind: Selected Diaries, Letters, and Files*, ed. Mary Ann Caws (New York: Thames and Hudson, 1993)

TM   Roland Barthes, "The Third Meaning," in *Image/Music/Text,* trans. Stephen Heath (New York: Hill and Wang, 1977)

TWM   Wyndham Lewis, *Time and Western Man,* ed. Paul Edwards (Santa Rosa: Black Sparrow Press, 1993)

UG   Judith Butler, *Undoing Gender* (New York: Routledge, 2004)

V   Caroline Caffin, *Vaudeville* (New York: Mitchell Kennerly, 1914)

WA   Walter Benjamin, "The Work of Art in the Age of Its Technological Reproducibility: The Second Version," in *Walter Benjamin: Selected Writings, Vol. 3, 1935–1938,* ed. Michael W. Jennings, Howard Eiland, and Gary Smith, trans. Rodney Livingstone et al. (Cambridge: Harvard University Press, 2002)

WG   Lawrence Grossberg, *we gotta get out of this place: Popular Conservatism and Postmodern Culture* (New York: Routledge, 1992)

WM   Henry Jenkins, *What Made Pistachio Nuts? Early Sound Comedy and the Vaudeville Aesthetic* (New York: Columbia University Press, 1992)

Feeling Modern

Introduction:
Eccentric Feeling

This is a book about the relationship between human feeling and the experience of modernity's public world during the modernist period, an era whose protagonists had nothing short of revolutionary designs on emotion. Like all revolutions bound by the temporal logic of the modern, modernism's affective upheavals mark both a rupture and a return. Modernist feeling is thus often understood as either a flat rejection of emotion as conventionally experienced and expressed, one that takes the form of an inhuman antagonism to sentimentality and rhetoric, or as some late and lamentable revival of romanticism, one of modernism's many forms of spilled religion. As a result, modernist feeling in the critical imagination is still rather like fairy-tale porridge: bluntly interpreted as either too hot (the gushing reservoir of Romantic inwardness) or too cold (the impersonal stuff of Eliotic poetics or the steely externality of satire). In what follows, I hope to freshen this stale offering by rethinking modernist emotion through a more capacious notion of modernist publicness.

Publicness is a quirky word. Students of modernism may be more comfortable with "publicity" or "the public sphere." "Publicity" conjures the effects of industrial-commercial media technologies, from the banalities of the press to the sublimity of stardom, while "the public sphere" summons sober, Habermasian forums of rational-critical debate.[1] In this book, though, I generally use the term "publicness" to describe a range of modernism's encounters with public life in the early twentieth century and to recover their experiential, embodied, and affective dimensions. This, because modernist public*ness,* like the word, is often awkward and tremulous, gesturing toward an elusive set of qualities thought to define the experience of being in public, an experience mediated by emotion. The explosion of modernist studies over the past decade has, thankfully, put paid to the longstanding clichés about modernism's mandarin disdain for the commonplaces of public life evident in its more authoritarian strains—its disgust for the public and, by extension, for the democratic, the masses, the feminine, the quotidian, the ordinary. But the thunderous volley of calls to materialize modernism, to underscore, for example, its appropriation of or capitulation to the *business* of publicity—whether the enterprise is understood as bourgeois professionalism, middlebrow bad faith, or instrumental aggression—has virtually stilled the sensual pulse of public life throbbing at the heart of modernism. This is unfortunate, since the moderns were also thrilled by the quickening of that pulse in the early decades of the twentieth century and, while surely invested in bourgeois publicity despite themselves, were stirred by the emotional and erotic solicitations of public life spilling forever into their so-called inwardness, despoiling their sense of what might make or unmake a self. The moderns discussed in this book were enchanted by the joyous hum of public being, physically undone by collective scenes of sympathy, and ever-attentive to intimate potential of public spaces, finding new homes for feeling in uncanny places. If the word "publicness" is unsatisfying, then, let it be an erethism that provokes a more unruly poetics of public life.

My attention to modernist encounters with publicness suggests, first, that we ask how it *feels* to be in public, how publicness manifests itself, how it happens. How, I ask, did modernism understand the demands placed on emotional life by the new, and increasingly mass-mediated, forms of early-twentieth-century public life? What collective satisfactions and what kinds of intimacy were nourished or held in abeyance by modernism's awareness that the life of the feelings in modernity would be necessarily negotiated in public? What uniquely modernist technologies of inwardness and exteriority follow from feeling's circulation within a social horizon at once structured by restrictive norms of recognition, stultifying expressive codes, and forceful calls to identification, but also repeatedly undone by the very *wildness* of feeling? Herein lies feeling's modern eccentricity: in its noninstrumental refusal of bourgeois utility, morality, and typical sociality, in its defamiliarization of the emotional protocols through which human beings find public recognition, and in its more artful fashioning of experiences in which the feelings would live a different kind of public life, leaving the monadic subject behind.

To approach this experiential terrain we might begin, again, with Walter Benjamin, whose dialectical optimism was particularly sensitive to modernity's second chances, its unredeemed possibilities, and its less violent futures. Consider the implicit fantasy of publicly mediated affect at the heart of the most utopian version of his most famous essay, "The Work of Art in the Age of Its Technological Reproducibility" (1936).[2] The concept that anchors this fantasy is "innervation," a properly physiological term for nervous excitation that Benjamin, following Sigmund Freud, extends to conceptualize a technological public sphere surging with liberatory affective energies. Drawing an important distinction between premodern and modern relationships to technology, Benjamin argues that while the "first technology" sought to dominate nature through ritual and magical practice, the "second technology" of the modern must aim for "an interplay between nature and humanity" (WA 107). Rehearsing this interplay is not just the "primary social function of art" but the special capacity of film, whose function is *to train human beings in the apperceptions and reactions needed to deal with a vast apparatus whose role in their lives is expanding almost daily"* (107, 108, emphasis in original). Here, film's exhibition context becomes a public arena of experiential correlation, where human beings adapt themselves to the "new productive forces" freed by second technology (108). It is the goal of revolutions, Benjamin notes, to accelerate this adaptation: "Revolutions are innervations of the collective—or more precisely, efforts at innervation on the part of a new, historically unique collective which has its organs in the new technology" (124).

Innervation, in this suggestive account, is the theory of affective transmission that grounds film's public pedagogy, its function as an experiential training ground that enables the collective to adapt playfully to the opportunities of human nature transfigured by technology. The ludic language is crucial and follows from Benjamin's historical claim that "what is lost in the withering of semblance and the decay of the aura of art is matched by a huge gain in the scope for play [*Spielraum*]" (127). Put simply, innervation is the way humanity—playfully, mimetically—learns its way around this "vast and unsuspected field of action" opened by technology and most famously by the heretofore explored realms of human experience revealed by cinema's optical unconscious (117). As Benjamin's most insightful critics observe, his concept of innervation is thus rather more dynamic than Freud's.[3] Whereas Freud understands innervation as the internal transfer of nervous energy from sensory perception to motor activity, Benjamin, influenced by contemporary developments in perceptual psychology and acting theory, opens affect to more erratic flows. Affect travels from psyche to soma but also from motoric energy outside the organism inward; thus, affect moves from the riotous movements of the publicly mediated body on film to the perceiving spectator. Importantly, then, innervation requires performing bodies, public figures through which the collective learns how it feels to have its organs in the new technology. Consider Benjamin's own examples: "American slapstick comedies and Disney films trigger a therapeutic release of unconscious energies. Their forerunner was the figure of the eccentric. He was the first to inhabit the new fields of action opened up by the film—the first occupant of the newly built house. This is the context in which Chaplin takes on historical significance" (118).

The performing body of the "eccentric," a Russian term for circus performer, becomes for Benjamin the inaugural player in the *Spielraum* of second technology, a squatter amidst the celluloid architecture of experience. His ontology is reproducibility. And his apotheosis is Charlie Chaplin, whose dislocated gestures "[dissect] the expressive movements of human beings into a series of minute innervations," marking the internalization of fundamental discontinuity of both the production process of the assembly line and cinematic technology itself.[4] The significance for the masses of Chaplin, a model of mediated human being, "lies in the fact that, in his work, the human being is integrated into the film image by way of his gestures"; his performance "applies the law of the cinematic image sequence to human motorial functions" (DS 94). As an eccentric body, Chaplin's utopian function is twofold: he is an allegory of a human being with technological organs, and his jerky movements, circulating in the public medium of film, provide emotional therapy for his audience, whose laughter is its means of coming to grips with its own experiential reorganization.

Innervation, we might say, is an exemplary modernist fantasy—a particularly hopeful, but hardly isolated, way of conceiving the emotional circuits of mass-mediated publicness. In these circuits, perception becomes apperception as alienated humanity sees the changed nature of experience and lays claim to such experience as its own. It recognizes itself outside itself, *ec-statically*. I have in mind here the place of ecstasy in Judith Butler's recent argument for the primary sociality of embodied life.[5] For Butler, human existence is fundamentally ec-static insofar as the norms of recognition that delimit and condition human life are constituted outside the self in a contingent historical world that both precedes and always exceeds the "I." Film, for Benjamin, is just such a public horizon of human self-recognition, schooling spectators in modernity's new normal. Within this medium, the limits of the human are reconceived and ecstatically remade and the terms of public and collective life constantly reimagined through emotion—in this instance, through film's capacity for innervation. One way to read this book, then, is as a series of adventures in modernist innervation, meditations on the crossing of affect and embodied publicness, on the co-evolution of modernist affectivity and the shifting historical shape of modernity's public world. This requires understanding innervation here not in its strictly Benjaminian sense but more expansively as the mutual implication of emotion and publicness in the modernist imagination: the ways modernist emotion, rather than interiorized, is always publicly mediated; and conversely, the ways modernist publicness, rather than narrowly instrumental and rational, is enacted by the crafting, stylization, and poetic positing of specific kinds of feelings that, as a nod to Benjamin, I call eccentric. This book's central claim is that modernism's eccentric feelings expand the range of public experience articulated within the modernist period. They also enhance our estimation of modernism's particular conceptual resources for responding emotionally to the possible and, at times, impossible forms of public life in the early twentieth century. In the ecstasies of the public, we see the potential for modernism's public world to unsettle and rearticulate itself. To continue Benjamin's conceit, the domicile of publicness is not just freshly fashioned in modernity but in fact always under construction.

The Potential of Publicness

Critical understandings of modernism's relationship to "the public" have taken shape as part of the healthy infusion of cultural studies methodologies into a literary-historical terrain long assumed to be the arid province of leisure-class aesthetes. As a result, recent approaches to modernist publicness have been pitched alongside critical exhortations to embed modernist aesthetic practice in the prosaic institutions and everyday discursive contexts of modernity. Given its familiar artistic doctrines of impersonality, autonomy, and mythic transcendence, modernism's sublunary relocation has seemed particularly pressing to critics and has rewarded them amply with the tasty ironies attending this rebirth into telluric context. Revising the image of modernism as primarily a coterie affair, these contextual labors have demonstrated quite convincingly the co-implication of modernist aesthetic practice and the formal institutions of late-nineteenth- and early-twentieth-century publicity. Modernist publicness, in these accounts, is a function of its participation—through little magazines, manifestos, and in its tireless campaigns of self-promotion and deft use of mass media—in a range of recognizable public and semipublic institutions. Modernism's public face is typical.[6]

More often than not, such accounts work to ironize modernism's histori-cal agon with bourgeois publicity, underscoring how modernism's dissident self-fashioning is mired in a middlebrow marketing logic, or how the rhe-torically oppositional public spheres created through avant-garde manifestos ultimately honor the bourgeois discourse they attack. Materializing modern-ism thus entails bringing it into some kind of bad company: for example, the defrocked Habermasian ideal of a universal political subject at once critiqued and invoked by the manifesto; or those institutions that, at least in Jürgen Habermas's account of the public sphere's modern transformation, replace critical publicity with manipulative publicity, supplanting a "culture-debat-ing" public with a "culture-consuming" one.[7] In these readings, modernism's rhetorical opposition to modern institutions of industrial-commercial pub-licness (mass-market magazines, advertising, newspapers, and so on) masks more complex modes of accommodation to, and technical poachings of, its formal idioms and promotional logics. The most determinative context of modernist publicness, and thus the site of modernism's most ignoble em-bedding, is the modern consumer economy itself, which coincides with the historical formation and explosive growth of mass media in the last two de-cades of the nineteenth century. In the critical game of ironizing modernist publicness, professionalism is the ultimate trump card. So, we are told with increasing frequency, modernism is ordinary, a day job dependent like any other on the creation of markets, the promotion of salable brands and trade-mark styles, and the savvy management of an economy of scarcity and ge-nius.[8] Brought firmly into the ambit of bourgeois professionalism, modernist publicness is material in its institutional embedding and flatly instrumental in its assimilation to the bourgeois publicity of advertising and public rela-tions.

My concern is that this important recovery of modernism's material net-works of publicity is too persuasive, its ironic frisson giving way to a perva-sive boredom with modernism's public work. The ensuing spirit of critical disenchantment—alas, modernism is so much business as usual—ultimately reifies the very totality of the bourgeois public sphere. To me, this picture of materialist publicity assumes rather anemic definitions of its two cen-tral terms, materiality and publicity: where the former signals the degree of participation in bourgeois institutions and the latter denotes their familiar operation within rational, and rationalizing, industrial-commercial circuits. Can we make a bid to complicate and diversify this notion of modernist publicness—and its materialist dimensions—without, on the one hand, de-nying modernism's implication in instrumental publicity or, on the other, underestimating modernism's capacity for figuring public worlds irreducible to instrumental reason, for positing not-yet-typical publics?

I hope to do so in this book by describing a more promiscuous variety of modernist publicness. By "publicness," then, I generally mean embodied public experience, a sensual and affective manner of encountering modernity's public worlds in which the terms of this encounter—actual and imagined, present and futural—are mediated by emotion, specifically, by the eccentric feelings I describe in more detail below. Publicness here is not primarily a product of industrial-commercial publicity (though embodied publicness is surely mass-mediated) but, better, *a tentative phenomenology of the public world.* As such, this account of modernist publicness means necessarily accounting for the ontological and epistemological dimensions of public experience. I attempt then to describe modernism's various ways of being-in-public, and I explore how such modes depend upon and produce knowledge about public life in modernity in a way that places into question both what constitutes a public (its terms of inclusion, its claim-making capacity, its manner of coalescence) and what constitutes an experience (its sensual and affective dimensions, its presumed immediacy, its potential to worry the boundaries of a self-contained, self-identical subject). Modernity, critics note with increasing urgency, is a sensational affair, bringing in its wake new sensory and perceptual regimes, new structures of feeling and modes of embodied knowledge, new technologies for the emotional organization of everyday life. As a global phenomenon with proximate effects and with local arenas of contestation, modernity now seems, in Arjun Appadurai's words, "more practical and less pedagogic, more experiential and less disciplinary" than it did even a decade ago.[9] And yet the experiential and affective registers of modern publicness have been overlooked in calls to materialize modernism, though these registers are precisely where the effects of modernization are localized, where the institutional and discursive contexts of modernity are most intimately, albeit disjunctively, felt, and where matter, as the bedrock of sensation, seems most dubiously pre-ideological and natural.

If the publicness described in this book is primarily a phenomenology— embodied and emotional—then popular performance is where this phenomenology happens: its mediating stage or scene. Put another way, popular performance, for the modernist artists and intellectuals I discuss in this book, is a quotidian theater of eccentric feeling: a space where various modes of modern publicness—and their attendant emotional demands and resources—are encountered, conceived, and performed. Throughout this study, I will use the phrase "popular performance" rather than "popular culture," and I should explain why. I do not seek to make an argument about cultural value hierarchies in the modernist period. I am not interested in using modernism's investment in the popular to trouble the putative "great divide" between modernism and mass culture, one long since erased by critics. Nor do I wish to describe, as work in a Birmingham cultural studies tradition or a Bordieuian framework does, how modernism participates in the discursive construction of "the popular" to delimit and distinguish an arena of professional expertise and authority.[10] Indeed, I readily acknowledge that modernism and mass culture are in and of the tissue of modernity and that modernism's popular investments are often structured by elitist self-interest or professional self-legitimation. What I wish to signal, however, are the limited ways of understanding how popular performance is supposed to work for modernism, the underestimation of modernism's capacity to think publicness and affect through popular performance, and the specific conceptual resources of performance itself, a famously unstable context, as a site for encountering and imagining the emotional varieties of public experience.

There are many good reasons why popular performance becomes a privileged space for the conceptual alignment of publicness and affect, reasons I explore in detail in the local contexts of individual chapters, but it seems worth setting down at the outset three more general, and related, explanations. The first has to do with popular performance as an emotionally charged reflective occasion for modernists, a manner of recollecting past public worlds, actual and imagined. The second entails popular performance as a physical arena of heightened affectivity and sensation, making emotional demands on modernists in their present. And the third, oriented toward the future, considers performance as a labile conceptual site where publicness itself becomes performative, a form of non-constative speech. The first two explanations place popular performance into the sociohistorical and discursive contexts that shape modernism's normative publics, that make them typical. The final one makes the case for modernist publicness itself as performative and draws attention to modernism's poetic decontextualization of modernity's forms of public life. The temporal frames of these explanations are important because, as I will show, central to the activity of modernism's eccentric feelings are both its role in the mimetic reproduction of past public worlds into the future and its more critical marking of disjunctive modes of publicness to come. Eccentric feelings, we might say, operate on the seam between two seemingly incommensurate fantasies of modernity, as discursive mastery and as the rupture with normativity.

Contextual explanations first. Perhaps the most evident one is the struc-

ture of feeling produced by the particular historical location of popular performance in the modernist imagination, by the promise of a certain kind of
public sphere held out by such performances and its inevitable betrayal. Why,
for example, does Benjamin turn to the eccentric circus performer on film
as the figure for the transformation of human experience? One of the unifying threads within my rather eclectic archive of primary texts (encompassing experimental and commercial film, film theory, nonfictional accounts of
performance, and the more traditionally literary domains of the novels, plays,
stories, essays, and diaries) is their relationship to the tradition of "variety"
performance. In the early twentieth century, "variety" was a baggy term for
a range of entertainments structured by a diverse series of performances or
turns—including the circus, vaudeville, the music hall, and burlesque, as well
as cinematic approximations of these properly pre-cinematic divertissements.
As a reflective occasion, popular variety performance, for modernists, is particularly freighted with emotional attachments, the site of some of their more
intense longings, their fiercest nationalism, their most nostalgic reveries. Here,
we need only recall the powerful, affective tenor of T. S. Eliot's eulogy of British music-hall singer Marie Lloyd, whose "invariably sympathetic" relationship with her audience made her the embodiment of a kind of collaborative,
working-class popular performance threatened with extinction by bourgeois
public culture and its "cheap and rapid-breeding cinema."[11] The historical
avant-garde, by contrast, celebrated variety's antisentimentality, emphasiz-
ing not its sympathetic capacity but rather its externality, physicality, and
expressive gestures—its radical detachment from the domain of bourgeois
interiority. One thinks immediately of F. T. Marinetti's paean to "The Variety
Theatre" (1913), which for the futurist opposes "body madness [*fisicofollia*]" to
the conventional theater's "stupid analyses of feelings," exalting "action, heroism, life in the open air, dexterity, the authority of instinct and intuition" over
bourgeois psychology, that "dirty thing and dirty word."[12] However incompatible Eliot's and Marinetti's modernisms, both turn to variety performance
to air their beefs with bourgeois emotional protocols, even as they supplant
them with radically different structures of feeling. Modernist thought about
popular performance is tightly bound to modernism's reinvention of the life
of the feelings, and this is so, in part, because of the historicity of the variety
form itself.

In her influential theory of early cinematic spectatorship, Miriam Hansen
has gestured toward this strange historical spot, arguing for the progressive dimension of the variety format in which films were exhibited during
cinema's founding moments. The alternative potential of early cinema, she

argues, was "an accidental effect of overlapping types of public sphere": one, "the more local, ethnically conscious public sphere" of the variety format and its plebian lineage (the variety theater, the circus, and the road show), and the other, "the more comprehensive, all-American public sphere of mass and consumer culture."[13] The variety format, Hansen continues,

> not only inhibited any prolonged absorption into the fictional world on screen, but the alternation of films and nonfilmic acts preserved a perceptual contin-uum between fictional space and theater space. A sense of theatrical presence was also maintained by nonfilmic activities that accompanied the projected moving image and were essential to its meaning and effect upon the viewer—lectures, sound effects, and above all, live music. Such exhibition practices lent the show the immediacy and singularity of a one-time performance, as opposed to an event that was repeated in more or less same fashion every-where and whenever the films were shown. Hence the meanings transacted were contingent upon *local* conditions and constellations, leaving reception at the mercy of relatively *unpredictable*, aleatory processes. (*BB* 93–94)

We need all of this quotation because it condenses nearly every prized concept underlying the modernist celebration of popular performance and so helps to explain its emotional attraction by virtue of its proximity to these embattled values: direct address, presence, vitality, immediacy, locality, con-tingency, unpredictability, and the like. Indicating the vestiges of the pre-modern within the modern, variety performance occupies that particular temporal-spatial category that Ernst Bloch calls the "non-synchronous." In this Marxist formulation of uneven cultural development, history is "no entity advancing along a single line, in which capitalism, for instance, as the final stage, has resolved all the previous ones; but is a *polyrhythmic and multi-spatial entity, with enough unmastered and as yet by no means revealed and resolved corners.*"[14] And variety, in the modernist imagination, is one such locus of undomesticated and unresolved premodernity.

When Hansen declares that vaudeville was "in so many respects a model for the institution of cinema," she has in mind the way the gentrification or refinement of vaudeville—its transformation, beginning in the 1880s, from a masculine working-class cultural form to a massified brand of bourgeois leisure—paralleled the cinema's own domestication of its plebian roots, and with it, a more open and variable, less ideologically suspect model of specta-torship (*BB* 115). The British music hall underwent a similar transition around the same time. Mirroring the changes of its transatlantic counterpart as well as the expansion of the Parisian *café-chantant*, and with the emergence of the suburban variety theater, the London music hall was, by the late 1880s, "on the verge of losing its exclusive working-class character and gaining a new, more upscale market demographic."[15] The increasing massification, refinement, and perceived contamination of the British music hall as it went global around the turn of the century (importing French revues, American song and dance forms, Russian ballet, and the like) spawned the genre one critic has recently dubbed "the music-hall lament,"[16] which begins in the early 1890s and achieves its melancholic apex in Eliot's "Marie Lloyd" essay. Even the circus succumbed. No matter how insistently its many modern admirers figured it as a site of allotemporal authenticity, as a trans- or ahistorical repository of primitive presence and brute soma, it had already begun its own massification, signaled most obviously with the 1881 debut of P. T. Barnum's traveling three-ring circus, a baroque masterpiece of industrial production, publicity, and distribution.

While it is not my goal to offer another history of these cultural forms per se, my study depends in an important way on variety's historical situation amid "nonsynchronous layers of cultural organization" (*BB* 93). This historical site—at once reified and authentic, mechanical and vital, the site of experiential lack and modernity's heterogeneous socius—was, I argue, a provocative, imaginative reservoir for modernists grappling with a modernity's public world. And it is this placement that generates the conceptual terms—experiential plenitude, particularity, contingency—through which the phenomenologies of modernist publicness are established and challenged, and often in a way critical of the fantasies of immediacy and self-presence that mark a phenomenology traditionally conceived. Variety's emotional appeal thus hinges in part on what Mary Ann Doane has recently called the lures of contingency and singularity, those fantasies of the "free and undetermined moment, which holds out the promise of newness itself" in a capitalist modernity bent on the "increasing rationalization and systematization of time."[17] As a testament to pervasiveness of this fantasy in modernity, consider this flicker of optimism from Max Horkheimer and Theodor W. Adorno's *Dialectic of Enlightenment*:

> Traces of something better persist in those features of the culture industry by which it resembles the circus—in the stubbornly purposeless expertise of riders, acrobats, and clowns, in the "defense and justification of physical as against intellectual art." But the hiding places of mindless artistry, which represents what is human against the social mechanism, are being relentlessly ferreted out by organizational reason, which forces everything to justify itself in terms of meaning and effect. It is causing meaninglessness to disappear at the lowest level of art just as radically as meaning is disappearing at the highest.[18]

Liberated from the tyrannical logic of means and ends, Horkheimer and Adorno's acrobats are singular figures of the nonpurposive—mindless, nonsensical, and thus still truly human. This formulation, nostalgic as it is, nicely captures the broader field of implication of variety performance. Positioned as the dialectical outside of instrumental reason—that is, as the very possibility of difference within a public world seemingly predicated on the replication of the same—variety became a trope for the experiential heterogeneity of modern life, barely visible in the crepuscular light of minimal human being. Put bluntly, performance is an overdetermined site of retrospective investment for modernists. Its accompanying affect is often tantamount to the kind of intense enjoyment offered by symbolic objects that, embodying a mythical fullness, take the place of an impossible social totality.

Beyond its existence as a product of symbolic investment, the affective dimension of popular performance is understood by modernists as a decidedly more immediate affair. Here, the popular stage is a proximate arena awash with emotional currents and rife with sensorial stimulation, a physical space giving rise—or failing to give rise—to feeling in public and, indeed, to characterizations of the social world predicated on its capacity to feel. Consider this blunt appraisal of American vaudeville in a 1911 Russell Sage Foundation Survey:

> As to Vaudeville, its most striking characteristic is simple stupidity. . . . It may be described as a succession of acts whose stimulus depends usually upon an artificial rather than upon a natural, human, and developing interest; these acts having no necessary and as a rule no actual connection. This description, be it noted, also fits the experience afforded by a street-car ride, or by any active day in a crowded city. Vaudeville is adapted in many ways to cosmopolitan audiences, whose members have few common sentiments, or common ideas, to which a regular drama will make a universal appeal. Like the succession of city occurrences, vaudeville is stimulating but disintegrating. . . . Both represent hyper-stimulus, and lead to neurasthenia, the antithesis of rest or Nirvana.[19]

This canny jeremiad exemplifies how the sensory environment of urban modernity was often linked to the emergence of sensational amusements (as intellectuals like Benjamin and Siegfried Kracauer would often point out), positioning them in relation to an increasingly heterogeneous social outside, to a "cosmopolitan audience" sharing neither ideas nor sentiments. That relation, here, is a tight fit in the form of a structuring homology between formal, perceptual-experiential, and social orders: vaudeville's organizational

stupidity—the crude arbitrariness of its variety format, a series of disconnected stimuli without logical origin or telos—fits the disaggregated happenings of urban experience and befits, in turn, modernity's disintegrated social
world. Vaudeville's *stupidity* inheres, much as the circus did for Horkheimer
and Adorno, in its departure from instrumental rationality. Only here this
nonsense indicates not the last refuge of the human but an arbitrary assault
on the stuff of genuine human interest: a crass deployment of fake stimuli
that betrays the apparent absence of a common humanity that would be
ratified in public by universal, and naturally developed, sentiments.

While it may seem idiosyncratic, this formulation—which sees in the perceptual regime of the variety format the falsification of the human sensorium
and the disaggregation of the social world—is central to modernist understandings of publicness. As I explain in chapter 1, Wyndham Lewis's critique
of reification depends on a similar notion: that modernity's public world, produced by the fetishistic, discontinuous world of modern consumer capitalism
and abetted by its visual technologies, especially advertising and the cinema,
has grown stupid and nonsensical. In Lewis's reactionary narrative, vision itself is transformed in modernity into a radically "private organ," one that participates in "the cutting up of the ideal, public, *one*, exterior reality of human
tradition into manifold spaces and times."[20] The hypnotic sensual rhythms of
public spectacle falsify the will, producing instead a massive failure of reason
and purposive agency—here in the form of an involuntary mimesis of social
behavior, in Lewis's terms, the aimless volition of modernity's mass publics.
In these conservative formulations, the scene of public performance is doubly stupid—both in its sensual and social disintegration and in the way this
pervasive discontinuity, this absence of a common ground of traditions and
feelings, is understood to enable artificial forms of affective manipulation
and control in public. Put in a way that begins to introduce the terminology
of the first section of the book, the stupidity of popular performance names
a public alternatively characterized by the absence of sympathy and more
increasingly subject to technologies of sympathetic manufacture.

While I try to remain attentive to the historical contexts in which popular
performance would become such a fraught site of emotional investment for
modernists, and in which modernism might be led to consider the physical
scene of performance as one particularly charged with affects giving rise to
stupid or sympathetic publics, I also want to make a plea for the conceptual
variety of the publics imagined and enacted through popular performance.
This requires an understanding of publicness itself as a performative endeavor, as a break with the reproduction of the same, as the positing of modes

of being-in-public that would operate in atypical ways, refusing the rational emotional protocols of bourgeois publicity. Students of modernism are only too willing to enumerate modernism's various linguistic revolutions and to explore its capacious avenues of experimentation with aesthetic form. And yet it is as if these vast resources for poetic speech, for new ways to say, narrate, and present, are achieved at the cost of a reduced faculty for limning the parameters of public words, an impoverishment most obvious in the reification of modernist publicness within the instrumental domains of advertising and public relations. We need, in other words, a descriptive vocabulary for the forms of modernist publicness as rich and various as those for other modernist forms, and one that takes seriously the *anti-descriptivist* production of publicness.[21] This means conceiving of social entities that modernism calls publics as constituted by acts of performative naming, rather than always as expressions of preexisting conceptual entities abrim with positive features. We need more attention to modernist publicness as deviant predications, without content, as feats of virtuosity.

I owe the term "virtuosity," and its related understanding of publicness, in part to Hannah Arendt and to recent returns to the performative dimensions of her political philosophy. While I do not wish to rehearse fully the terms of this account, or its embattled return to the scene of contemporary political theory, I think it useful to extricate a few threads from its dense fabric. For Arendt, publicness is not bound to particular institutions but is, rather, the very space of appearance of the political. This space is created by the human faculties of action and speech in the presence of others, by an audience-oriented activity that aligns politics to performance: "The performing arts . . . have indeed a strong affinity with politics. Performing artists—dancers, play-actors, musicians, and the like—need an audience to show their virtuosity, just as acting men and women need the presence of others before whom they can appear; both need a publicly organized space for their work, and both depend upon others for the performance itself."[22] Arendt's analogy between politics and performance is backed by the complex notion of publicness she develops in her suggestive take on the public/private divide in *The Human Condition*. Arendt understands publicness, first, as the phenomenological condition of appearance: the experience of "being seen and heard by others as well as by ourselves" and the constitutive exteriority of human being that constitutes the reality of the world.[23] Therefore, the public realm is also the site of "the common," by which she means the primary plurality of shared human existence. For Arendt, this irreducible worldly diversity, this "simultaneous presence of innumerable perspectives and aspects in which the common world presents itself and for which no common measurement or denominator can ever be devised," only ends "when it is seen only under one aspect and is permitted to present itself in only one perspective" (*HC* 57, 58). Notably, then, Arendt encourages us to understand publicness as also a *potentiality*: "Wherever people gather together, it is potentially there, but only potentially, not necessarily and not forever" (199). Indeed, it is this dimension that marks the "peculiarity of the public realm, which, because it ultimately resides on action and speech, never altogether loses its potential character" (200). Because the potential character of publicness "precedes all formal constitution of the public realm . . . unlike the spaces which are the work of our hands, it does not survive the actuality of the moment which brought it into being" (199).

There are several important implications of this elusive formulation. Because Arendt defines publicness as a performative political arena brought into being by action and speech, she points to an understanding of publicness as at once noninstrumental and non-teleological. In fact, Arendt makes clear that the specific achievement of publicness-as-politics "lies altogether outside the category of means and ends": as in "the performance of the dancer or play-actor, the 'product' is identical with the performing act itself" (*HC* 207). Because political activity does not reify or harden—like the product of work does—into a finished object or end, it is contingent and resistant to closure. Thus, Arendt's publicness is non-normative, an interruptive naming of a new social reality.[24] The specificity of political action, as distinguished from mere behavior, just *is* the faculty of beginning, the human capacity "to start new unprecedented processes whose outcome remains uncertain and unpredictable" (231–32).

It may seem, on the face of it, odd to argue for the particular relevance of Arendt's idiosyncratic definition of the public realm for the rethinking of modernist publicness and affect I propose in this book. To the contrary, I find Arendt's story of publicness—bound as it is to her understanding of action and the political—uniquely poised to illuminate modernism's public world and its spectrum of eccentric feelings. First, Arendt makes a crucial distinction between her idealized public as a space of appearance and what she calls the modern "rise of the social," by which she means modernity's political space of normativity, characterized by the dominance of behaviorist social sciences, statistical uniformity, and instrumental reason, as well as the rise of administrative and mass society (HC 38). In doing so, she seconds much of modernism's distaste for bourgeois social forms dominated by instrumentality and its particular dissatisfaction with the social replication of the family form "under conditions of mass society or mass hysteria, where we see all people suddenly behave as if they were members of one family, each multiplying and prolonging the perspective of their neighbor" (58). In her belief that action in public is fueled, in Bonnie Honig's terms, by an agonistic struggle for the emergence of a "self that is never exhausted by the (sociological, psychological, and juridical) categories that seek to define and fix it," Arendt thus shares modernism's anxious apprehension of a mimetic social horizon with ever-increasing technologies of normalization.[25] But for Arendt, to champion this struggle is never to defend modern individualism or the Romantic redefinition of private, intimate life as "the radical subjectivism of [one's] emotional life" (HC 39). Instead, Arendt understands such feelings as a compensatory response to the leveling effect of the social, as the emotional side effects of public deprivation.

Perhaps most important for my purposes, Arendt's notion of publicness-as-potentiality suggests that we reimagine modernism's public world as a capacity—a virtual framework out of which emerge varieties of publicness that, once performed, may or may not become workable, actualized. These feats of performative virtuosity unfold on two levels: on one, the performing figures through which modernism imagines publicness are virtuosos (for example, Disney's cartoons for Sergei Eisenstein, Josephine Baker for E. E. Cummings, the acrobat Alfredo Codona for Marsden Hartley, the slapstick comic for Nathanael West); on another, the forms of publicness that modernism conceives though such performances are themselves virtuosic actions, political enactments of public being and feeling. Some of them, to some eyes, may seem unworkable, irrational, aimless, or downright stupid, if by "stupidity" one means a departure from instrumentality, rationality, or institutional operation. To other eyes, the very impossibility or normative impropriety of a posited public world might signal a more critical dissatisfaction with the ossification of public business as usual. One person's stupidity, we might say, is another person's ecstasy. As a conceptual swarm of tendencies toward the common in Arendt's sense, modernism's capacity for publicness is only exhausted by the emotional protocols attending inwardness—modernism's most familiar subject of feeling. There, "imprisoned in the subjectivity of [its] own singular experience," the feeling subject forsakes the primary power of human existence, the "potentiality in being together" (HC 58, 201). This potentiality has its own affective register, and it is my belief that we can recover modernism's promiscuous publicness if we are more attentive to its most eccentric feelings, to that range of affects that contraindicate radically isolated inwardness, that accompany its phenomenologies of publicness. It is to these feelings that I now turn.

Feeling Outside the Monad

In this book, I use the phrase "eccentric feelings" to capture the interaction between two registers of feeling that, together, shape modernism's creative deformations of public life. Within one register, eccentric feelings are broadly epistemic, content-based ways of feeling *about* preexisting social entities that modernists understood as "the public." They are what affect theorists would call "ideational" feelings: that is, they are formed by specific beliefs, they motivate action, and they assume a reasonable agent with discernible desires and steady intentionality. For example, because we know Wyndham Lewis's proto-fascist beliefs (he was only too happy to publicize them), we can rationalize his deep revulsion toward Charlie Chaplin's adoring public, whose fondness for this small, childish personality would betray that public's longing to submit to modernity's proliferative systems for domesticating real greatness. In another and more dynamic register, eccentric feelings are the labile and nonidentitarian modes of affect *occasioned by* and *enacted within* public performance, affects that fuel alternative stories of public being and feeling. While it is important to keep in mind how modernism's various, hortatory, and occasionally shrill declarations of belief (attitudes codified and stylized in manifestos, diaries, essays, and theoretical writings) shape its feelings about the public worlds of the modern and produce the illusion of subjective orientation, this tooling of emotion by belief should not be confused with the easy circumscription of already existing attitudes about already existing forms of publicness. To my way of thinking, modernism's public relations—its processes of positing forms of public life—are most refreshing when the affective energies associated with publicness call into question what modernism means by both the public and the subject who feels (or does not feel) a part of it. Recovering the potential of modernism's eccentric feelings, then, demands attention to such affects' capacity for the fitful disorientation of personhood and the ecstatic de-reification of public worlds. And this entails feeling outside the monad: ex-centric feeling.

I have in mind here Fredric Jameson's now-famous story of modernist affectivity and inwardness. To capitalist modernity's abstraction of sensual experience, effected both through technological mediation and rationalization's ruthless dismantling of all natural unities, *including* the senses and mental functions, aesthetic modernism responds with a sensory regime at once autonomous and fragmented, both a symptom of reification and its utopian compensation. In Jameson's powerful Marxist narrative, Joseph Conrad's impressionist recoding of the world in terms of "perception as a semi-autonomous activity," or Jamesian experiments with point of view, are "desperate myths of the self," modes of acclimation to the specializations and divisions of life within the market system.[26] But they are also ways of creating "a life space in which the opposite and the negation of such rationalization can be, at least imaginatively, experienced."[27] The social fragmentation, alienation, and solitude that are, for Jameson, aesthetic modernism's hallmarks find canonical expression in Edvard Munch's *The Scream,* a painting that comes to embody the modernist metaphysics of expressivity itself, in which the subject is conceived as a "monadlike container, within which things felt are then expressed by projection outward."[28] This is the modernist subject as alienated monad, forged by the sociohistorical conditions of modernity but rich with emotional compensation. On the other side of the strong affects lifted from the absconded depths of modernist inwardness are the "free-floating and impersonal" intensities of the postmodern, where affect can only wane because "there is no longer a self present to do the feeling."[29]

What is objectionable in this formulation is not the way modernist affectivity is posited as a reaction to a reified public world—indeed, central to this book's argument about eccentric feeling is its promiscuous circulation within a mediated public sphere—but rather its reduction to the singular subjective model of the expressive monad in an attempt to make a tenuous distinction between modernist and postmodern structures of feeling. To be sure, modernity yields fantasies of monadic inwardness—and the strong kinds of affect and centered kinds of subjects that accompany it—but it also abets various conceptualizations of precisely those "free-floating and impersonal" affects that, for Jameson, constitute the euphoric terrain of the postmodern. This means that the monad is only one of a number of formal crystallizations of modernist subjectivity. Moreover, as a possible but not necessary inscription of interiority, the monad is achieved over and against modernism's underacknowledged investment in eccentric feeling, a broad range of affects that worry the stable confines, and attendant metaphysics, of modernist inwardness. This emotional terrain, which I navigate in the chapters that follow, includes affects of depersonalization or pre-personalization; emotions of ecstasy, mood, or sensual mimesis in the anthropological inflection given it by the Frankfurt School; and the public dimension of what Freud called the properly "social feelings" that ground modernist understandings of collective life. In fact, given the frequency with which the public sphere is imagined as a scene of impersonal and abstract affective energies giving shape to all kinds of personhood, one might marvel at the sheer rhetorical force necessary to make the monadic model, with all its impermeability and self-sufficiency, convincing in the first place. The closer one examines the public life of modern feeling, the more it becomes clear how modernist affectivity is often *already* conceived of as nonidentitarian rather than the probative expression of a centered but alienated subject. Indeed, modernism's eccentric feelings are often incompatible with—and, in fact, immanently critical of—certain coercive determinations of personhood, as well as certain ossified models of subjectivity, sociality, and public belonging.

If the category of "eccentric feelings" thus exerts some critical pressure on one influential theoretical model of modernism's feeling subject, the phrase also captures a central paradox in the public feelings under consideration in this book: the way they are imagined as at once abstract, typical, worrying the boundaries of the self's most intimate interiors, and at the same time experientially singular, refusing typological organization. On the one hand, as Benjamin's fantasy of an innervated public sphere makes clear, modernists are anxiously aware of feelings' delirious potential for abstraction: their circulation beyond, their provenance outside of, or their conceptual violence to a self-contained subject. Eccentric feeling names affect's diffused public existence as impersonal, typical, or vagrant intensities that can be mechanically transmitted or externally manufactured in sites of public performance. Eccentric feeling thus gives the lie to, as it seemingly expropriates, the self's most intimate interior, betraying instead its social production: *my feeling is typical.* On the other hand, feeling's eccentricity is understood as precisely its non-abstractability, marking in various ways the particularities of feeling occluded in normative models of publicness. Here, eccentric feeling denotes the desires for publics inflected with local affect: *my feeling is atypical.* On both sides of this paradox, then, lies a more radical notion of affect as a form of sensual responsiveness that eludes structure: as either the free-floating affective energies preceding the instrumentalization of publics and persons or the experiential remainder of normative or coercive publics.

To couch this more fully in the register of contemporary affect theory, we could say that the paradox of eccentric feeling marks modernism's vacillating understanding of emotion as, at one extreme, discursively structured—an increasingly powerful public production, subject to ever more powerful technologies of sociolinguistic organization—and at the other, radically pre-discursive. Here I wish to position eccentric feeling between the long shadow of Michel Foucault and the wide range of more recent, poststructuralist work on affect. Foucault, of course, offers the most powerful account of modern affect—indeed, of the whole modernist mythology of interiority—as a discursive inscription within a modernity bent on the typological determinations and disciplining of persons.[30] Dismissing the existence of pre-discursive affect as always a dubious ideology of "true" feeling, Foucault underscores how affect is used to naturalize certain bodies and subjectivities within the domain of the private. In so doing, affect bolsters a domestic ideology predicated on the separation of spheres and reifies privacy as both exterior to the market and the sign of an authentic and natural self.[31]

By contrast, the work of Larry Grossberg and Brian Massumi has attempted to loosen the coercive grip of modernity's technologies of the self by introducing an important distinction between affect and emotion. The former is unqualified, a-signifying, and pre-discursive, "pre-personal intensity" in Grossberg's terms; whereas emotion, as Massumi puts it, is "subjective content, the sociolinguistic fixing of the quality of an experience which is from that point onward defined as personal. . . . It is intensity owned and recognized."[32] Grossberg's work is especially useful for this project because of the centrality of the popular in his formulation of unstructured affect as "plane or mechanism of belonging and identification." An arena of discursivization, popular culture is in fact "the primary space where affective relationships are articulated" (*WG* 84, 85). For Grossberg, this conception of affect is thoroughly ambivalent: the organization of affect makes the world matter in particular ways; it "gives color, tone, and texture to the lived," enabling powerful investments and liberating modes of belonging; and yet the structuring of affect as a plane of intensity is also essential to the operation of ideology (88). Affect, in this sense, is the emotional lubrication that explains the power and ease with which ideology is internalized and naturalized.

The modernists I consider in this book share a similarly ambivalent appraisal of the relationship between affect and discourse. Feeling is both too structured and never structured enough. One way to understand modernism's oft-remarked anxiety about emotion is as a particularly sensitive barometer for measuring the speed and force of affect's conversion into discourse. These concerns are perhaps most evident in its gendered anxieties about a public sphere dominated by compulsive sympathy and the contagious mimesis of social behavior, and in its nervous witnessing of affect's swift circumscription within modernity's systems of subjective legibility, its increasing saturation with *types* of personhood. So too in its various theorizations of those rapacious mechanisms of identification that propel affect so quickly from intimate to abstract collectivity, coterie feeling to crowd behavior, immanent community to anomic society, modernism finds itself unable to separate affect from the public determinations of the individual. At the same time, modernism is captivated by the forms of collective and political life—by their mythic resonances, their centripetal cultural force, their erotic satisfactions, their plaintive rejoinders to a modernity seemingly hostile to the grounds of traditional community—and seeks to turn its own aesthetic innovations into rival technologies for shaping and structuring collective affects, instrumentalizing emotion through form. While this ambivalence about structured affect threatens to reproduce the modernist subject's more familiar, and desperate, gambits—for example, as the paranoid achievement of an inviolate, self-determining individual whose affects are impervious to discourse, or as the masochistic yielding to a larger collectivity—it also may, when considered more dialectically, point to modernism's reckoning with unstructured affects less easily put to work.

So, while we should keep in mind modernism's pronounced discomfort with unstructured affect (here we might recall Eliot's appeal for "*significant* emotion," or Ezra Pound's formulation of the image as "an emotional and *intellectual* complex" soldered by temporal instantaneity), we need not let this blind us to modernism's acute attentiveness to the potential of unstructured feeling.[33] Modernism, I hope to show in this book, is marked by a demonstrable concern with the power of affective states irreducible to reason, with affects that actively unsettle belief rather than embody preexisting values. It is obsessed with the kinds of eccentric feelings that worry the boundaries of identity and their reification in bourgeois social forms predicated on possessive individualism and its attendant claims on association—fixity, rational expediency, and acquisitiveness. We need, in other words, to retain modernism's unique resources for thinking of affect and publicness in a noninstrumental fashion.

Part of the difficulty here lies in distinguishing noninstrumental affect from its conventional and easily dismissed associations with aestheticism, for which emotion, to the eyes of more unsympathetic readers, works to seal private aesthetic experience against the means-end logic of bourgeois utility and to remove the aesthetic from the praxis of everyday life. In more recent, and largely Foucauldian, approaches to the modernist sensorium, critics like Sara Danius and Karen Jacobs have drawn our attention to modernist visuality as a response to the scientific appropriation—via photography and other imaging technologies—of the epistemic privileges of the human senses.[34] Modernism, invested as it is in crafting subjective, embodied, and local ways of seeing, thus opposes the instrumentalization of the senses with one hand, rejecting naive positivism. But with the other hand, it puts the subjectivized sensorium to work, relocating truths to the province of interior depths, thereby justifying modernist authority and creating the market for a uniquely modernist mode of expertise. In this way does modernity's gap between scientific/abstract and visionary/embodied perceptual modes fuel modernism's own professional self-fashioning.

Notice how we are back to the business of ironizing modernism's putative separation from the space of bourgeois utility, which means reading all modernist attempts to separate affect from instrumentality as acts of bad faith. To understand modernism's construction of its affects, sensations, and feelingful interiors as one mode of professional self-legitimation among others is no doubt helpful but risks overlooking this range of work (conceptual and otherwise) such affects perform. This is not to make a naive claim for the exceptionalism of modernist affectivity but rather to plead for its particular capacities for diagnosing existing publics and for imagining future ones. Modernist affect is always active, true, but it does different kinds of work, much of it directly inimical to instrumentality. In this sense, this book shares Charles Altieri's recent assertion that modernism—with its allergy to positivism and its heightened self-reflexivity about the conventionality of emotion, its stultifying rhetoricity—is uniquely equipped to critique the dominant cognitivist approach to the emotions that sees them, in instrumental fashion, as means through which agents sort information, appraise action, and "guide reason toward possible modes of compassion and sensitive judgment."[35] Modernism's phenomenological vitality, for Altieri, thus inheres in its "intricate efforts to make the nondiscursive and nonepistemic dimensions of art wield the same level of cultural force as did scientific and utilitarian argument" (PR 33). While I find much to admire in Altieri's fine descriptions of the phenomenologies of affective engagement made available by painting and poetry (being affected by art, he proves, is a complex thing indeed), his uncoupling of affect from discourse threatens to remove modernism from the plane of history itself. Altieri simply has no truck with the post-Foucauldian work on emotions that "treats them as if they were deeply flawed social constructs to be interpreted and resisted in their current forms" and that therefore makes "no effort to reconstruct what might be desirable or necessary or even changeable in our ways of experiencing these emotions" (262). And, as a result, he is unwilling to register fully how the noninstrumentality of modernist affect is always working dialectically within the discursive horizons that bind it to the mimetic reproduction of the same: normative publics, restrictive political formations, totalitarian models of identity. It makes no sense to separate affect's discursive shaping from its noninstrumentality; the intersection of these levels constitutes the terrain of the specific affective fantasies I call eccentric feelings. As the affective reflex of a reified public sphere, modernism's eccentric feelings thus mediate the ambivalence of mass publicness: the pleasures and horrors of abstract affects, the fantasies of collectivity, sociability, and intimacy they enable and preclude.

The Form of Things to Come

I pursue this argument through the book's tripartite structure, itself indebted to three interconnected affective registers—sympathy, intimacy, and comedy—that animate modernism's investments in popular performance. Part 1, "Sympathy," grounds my study in the context of modernist fellow-feeling's uneasy relationship to the broader humanist discourse of moral and ethical behavior. In the first two chapters, I explain how the emotional scene of public performance, pervaded by free-floating affects, is paradoxically imagined not just as the abstraction and typification of the self's emotional contours but also as a matrix of modern community that bridges gaps between alienated subjects in a modernity of pronounced social asymmetries. Defining what I call a "mimetic-sympathetic public sphere," I argue that the capacity of popular performance to become electrified with sympathetic currents at once vital and artificial is predicated, in the early twentieth century, on a modernist understanding of publicness as the space of the contagious, mechanical reproduction of feeling, one whose dual and mutually reinforcing mechanisms are mimesis and sight. This understanding is energized both by the residual force within the modernist period of Romantic theories of crowd behavior and group psychology as well as by developments within the fields of experimental psychology and psychophysiology. In this phenomenology of publicness, the willful, rational sympathy that, for Habermas, prepares the bourgeois individual for the abstraction and public feeling demanded by the bourgeois public sphere gets stupid—becomes a kind of delirious disorientation. To be in public, and to be within the space of popular performance, is to be subject to involuntary sympathy, contagious mimicry, hypnotic political identifications, all galvanized by vision.

Chapter 1 provides a political anatomy of modernity's mimetic-sympathetic publicness by reading the imitative gestures of popular performance in the context of a broader concern with mimetic politics in the work of thinkers like Benjamin, Roger Caillois, Adorno, Gabriel Tarde, Gustave Le Bon, William James, and Freud. Within this milieu, I situate a study of vaudeville written in 1914 by Caroline Caffin, art critic for Alfred Stieglitz's journal *Camera Work,* and the professional treatise of British music-hall mimic J. Arthur Bleackley, *The Art of Mimicry* (1911), before offering a discussion of popular mimetic performance in the work of modernist gadfly Wyndham Lewis. I read the evolution of Lewis's "Wild Body" stories (1909–27) as symptomatic of a broader movement in his career from an early investment in the sympathetic ecstasies of public performance to a theatrical typecasting that mimes to disrupt a public narcotized by sympathy. Placing Lewisian mimesis in dialogue with Caffin's and Bleackley's own, I show how the radical embrace of reification that defines Lewis's avant-gardism echoes the immanent logic of the variety stage, at once awash with vital sympathetic currents and a spectacle of emotional and political manipulation.

In chapter 2, I turn to the political promise of a mimetic-sympathetic public sphere in the work and thought of the radical Soviet filmmaker and theorist Sergei Eisenstein. Like Lewis, Eisenstein thinks that the reproduction of politics, and the binding of typical publics, requires the structuring of eccentric feeling through mimesis. In fact, Eisenstein's early theories of montage and performance are energized by his relationship to Eccentrism, an overlooked Soviet avant-garde of the early 1920s modeled on circus stunts and the frenetic pace of American melodramas and detective thrillers. Eccentricity's wider resonance for Eisenstein lies in the way it signifies the threat and promise of both the contingent event—erupting *within* a rationalized world—and the recalcitrant particularity, coded as erotic deviance, that frustrates the smooth engineering of public feeling. In these terms, Eisenstein's reckoning with eccentricity yields an alternative mode of mimesis adequate to contingency and figured as a delirious openness to ecstasy, an erotic liberation from type. Thus, while Lewis's and Eisenstein's politics could hardly be more dissimilar, they both embrace depersonalization as a tool for disrupting the typical work of mimetic-sympathetic publicness: Lewis, with an aggressive externality steeled against the violence of Romantic sympathy; Eisenstein, by championing non-instrumental, ecstatic feelings that restore the political—and the affects and attachments thought to structure politics—to a queer space of potential.

The book's second part, "Intimacy," considers how eccentric feeling fuels alternative formulations of publicly mediated intimacy in the work of three sentimental male modernists—E. E. Cummings, Marsden Hartley, and Joseph Cornell. These particular moderns not only complicate persistent claims about male modernists' supposed antisentimentality but do so in a fashion that frees modernist inwardness from the Romantic well of pure experience, of raw nature unsullied by culture. In their work, intimacy depends on the depersonalizing eccentric feelings of modernity's mass-mediated public sphere, on its constitutive confusions between nature and technological second nature, nearness and farness, recognition and unknowability. These figures thus help me write a new chapter in the curious marriage of intimate feeling and impersonality long seen as one of modern sociality's more peculiar eccentricities in the sociological tradition extending from Georg Simmel, Erving Goffman, and Anthony Giddens to more recent theorists of "stranger intimacy" like Mark Seltzer, Michael Warner, Lauren Berlant, and Michael Trask.[36] This section argues that we reconsider our tendency to understand modernism's depersonalizing detachment as arch disdain, sexist, or proto-fascist and ask instead: From what restrictive discursive order is one detaching? Into what relationship to the public world, and to erotic or political life, does such detachment bring the self? And what does this self, disorganized as it is by eccentric feeling, look like? If, as the book's first part establishes, a central threat of the mimetic-sympathetic public sphere is depersonalization-as-typicality (the standardization of the self's emotional contours, reproducibility as a mode of being, involuntary imitations of social behavior), then chapters 3 through 5 explore more fully what emerges, in dialectical fashion, as a latent insight in the formulations of Lewis and Eisenstein: eccentric feeling's abstract potential as freedom from "type-life," alternatively understood as modernity's ossified political formations, or its proliferating categories or personhood, or its routinization of everyday experience. Eccentric feeling, in these more sanguine terms, is the affective register of depersonalization: feeling's irreducibility to identity, its pre-discursive status, its openness to contingency and change.

In the case of Cummings, charted in chapter 3, all intimacies are dangerous insofar as they are but germinal collectivities, abstracting forms of comradeship. Indebted to Freud's formulation of group identifications as those stemming from more intimate, erotic emotional ties, the threat of intimate affect in Cummings's work is encouraged and controlled by "tactile self-orchestration," an emotional fantasy of sensual self-identity that hopes to sever aesthetic sensation from libidinal desire. Indeed, whether Cummings is appraising the sculpture of Gaston Lachaise, or the spectacle of Josephine Baker at the Folies Bergère, or the "magnetic personalities" of his World

War I novel *The Enormous Room* (1922), embodied publicness entails both a haptic opening to social plurality and an opportunity for the distinction of a monstrous singularity. For Cummings, then, public ecstasy is thoroughly ambivalent: it indicates the capacity of public space for the emotional currents of comradeship but also its potential for anonymity and radical inaccessibility, for the sensual thrill of nonrelational being that Cummings associates with the aesthetic, and explicitly racialized, spectacles of popular performance.

Shifting from Cummings's monstrous publicity and toward modernism's progressive investment in eccentric feeling, chapters 4 and 5 explore, respectively, the mediated public sphere's potential for erotic depersonalization and its capacity to refuse typological order and thus remain eventful. Chapter 4 reads Hartley's misty-eyed attachment to acrobats as a matter of queer desire and its negotiation, an attempt to theorize a form of public intimacy through light figures, corporeal and linguistic. Hartley's ideal intimacy is premised neither on a plummy fantasy of unmediated connection, nor the solidification of the purely personal, but rather on a kind of subjective detachment produced by public spectacle, which becomes the site of transient but tractable emotional attachments. In fact, in his unpublished manuscript on the circus, "Elephants and Rhinestones" (circa 1945), Hartley's sentimental iconophilia departs from a dominant modernist gambit linking vision, authenticity, and privatized interiority: rather than penetrating, his erotic vision disperses; rather than implicating the spectator, it finds no subject, only a fleeting attachment that Hartley secures by losing himself. Chapter 5 explores the emotional energies of Joseph Cornell's experimental filmmaking to revise the critical picture of Cornell as an uncomplicated Romantic, a melancholic modern haunted by the aesthetic mediation of experience. I do so by arguing that Cornell's filmmaking, specifically his anarchic, variety-themed cinematic trilogy—*Cotillion, The Midnight Party,* and *The Children's Party* (circa 1938–69)—be understood as phenomenology of public experience: specifically, of a messy and inexhaustible everyday in which experiential poverty is combated through the *extensive* affects of sensual mimesis and mood. Through these films, Cornell extrapolates a playful definition of experiential richness *as* variety that, in his diaries, he dubs "extension." The wonder of extensive modern experience is its ability to remain eventful: futural, contingent, and, like the tender subject of Cornellian experience, open to infinite transformation. Cornell's cinematic tenderness is thus a mode of ethical and emotional disposition toward a public sphere that resists totalization.

In the final part of the book, "Comedy," I turn from the eccentric activity of intimate public affects in the work of modernism's more misunderstood Romantics to the very frustration of public feeling—its operational failures, slips, or glitches—in the work of Nathanael West and Djuna Barnes, two of modernism's most infamous externalists. Comedy specifically reminds us that laughter, following Freud, is a preeminently social feeling. But in the peculiar conjunction of dark humor and radical depersonalization I consider here, comic affect is decidedly inhuman. In the philosophical tradition stretching from Aristotle to Henri Bergson and beyond, laughter has long been seen as the sign of the properly human being, as a capacity that separates the self-reflective expressivity of human experience from the unreflective immediacy of animals and thingly nature. For this reason, laughter's modernist inhumanity is charged with the critical force of eccentric feeling: the modernist laugh mocks of the propriety of human feeling and, beyond that, calls attention to the failure of the human itself as a restrictive form of life. Thus do modernism's comedies of depersonalization register most forcefully what has been implicit in the rest of the book—the eccentric circulation of inhuman affective intensities irreducible to type or quality and the concomitant breakdown of public feeling conceived in the terms of humanist universalism.

Chapter 6 illuminates the critical potential of feeling's unworking, of its failure to cement community and to secure the lineaments of human personality, through the odd slapstick of Nathanael West's late modernism. I read West's *Miss Lonelyhearts* (1932) as a critique of the logics of emotion and interiority that structure both the Enlightenment heritage of the public sphere and recent critical approaches to the reified horizon of modern publicity. Drawing on André Breton, Bergson, and Charles Baudelaire, as well as on vaudeville joke writers and comic performers like Bert Williams, Lou Weber, and Joe Fields, I argue that West's peculiar slapstick neither attempts to transcend the heterogeneous social world of the novel—as in the antisentimental, elite *humour noir* of the surrealist avant-garde—nor does it assume, as does the popular rhetoric surrounding slapstick performance, that laughter reifies a universal affective current and thereby proves that we all experience our bodies in the same way. Instead, West argues that when public horizons are affective, they are constitutively violent, collapsing experiential difference into sameness; further, he rejects the notion that affect does the emotional work of self-preservation, generating laughter, instead, from subjective undoing.

My final chapter considers the impersonal laughter of Djuna Barnes's *Nightwood* (1936) in the contexts of modernist theories of impersonality and the resurgent philosophical interest in the question of the animal—specifically, in the animal's capacity for those affects, like laughter, thought to constitute persons. Exploring the novel's surfeit of animal expressivity, I argue that the failure of emotion to secure what is proper to the human personality in the novel results in the comic passions of animal life. Issuing from the members of what Barnes calls her "disqualified" publics are the eccentric feelings of a people beyond the public norms of human recognition. The novel's animal laughter brings its characters to an awareness of their fundamental deprivation of privacy—their impossible public being—and in so doing asks its readers to acknowledge the shared finitude of animal life. In this fashion, Barnes's interest in the intensity of animal affect as the limit of recognizably human experience allows me to explain how the interruptions in the public circulation of human feeling—breaks alternatively feared and desired by modernism—are repeatedly enacted through depersonalization, through forms of studied inhumanity. In the comic dehumanization of Barnes and West, then, lies the continued relevance of their work: both its critical exposure of the limits of publicness traditionally conceived and its gestures toward potential publics that modernity had yet to realize.

Eccentric feelings like these urge us to rethink the relationship between modernist emotion and the private/public distinction that has proved so central to critical appraisals of modernism, and indeed to the modern's own self-understanding. Instead of looking to the strong affects of alienation and anomie that issue from modernist privacy in its modern inflection as inwardness, as the repository for the meager compensations of freedom and authenticity, what if we turned our attention to those affects imagined by the moderns as means of redressing privacy in the original sense restored to it by Arendt—as the *privation* of a publicness whose value lies precisely in its lack of positive, abiding content and thus in its capacity for the establishment of new social relations? Conceived as a response to such deprivation, modernism's eccentric feelings would surely reproduce familiar fantasies of submission to or orchestration by the technicians of public sentiment (to borrow an Eisensteinian phrase). But they also afford us an emotional vocabulary for better describing the conditions of being deprived of the legibility and recognition of the public world. Because this is a modernist grammar, after all, it will be intricate, necessarily speculative, and, I hope, surprising. The strange, public life of modernist feeling is a poetry of virtuosity, crafting the forms of erotic attachment, sociability, and political affiliation that make public life ever worth living.

1
Sympathy

1

Tough Crowds

It is this quality of translating by his own body, voice, and actions, the impressions received, just as action of the light on the sensitized plate translates the objects before it, which is the medium of expression of the imitator. . . . And when every characteristic has been absorbed, the imitator must be able to add to the reproduction the feeling of the original. For the time being he must feel like the subject that he is portraying and he must be able to impress this feeling on his audience.

—Caroline Caffin, *Vaudeville*

In Caroline Caffin's landmark study *Vaudeville* (1914)[1], the stage mimic is the very catalyst of sociality, a somatic medium charged with the task of promoting sympathy first by feeling like others and then by making the audience feel like them as well. Since Caffin was closely affiliated with Alfred Stieglitz's *Camera Work,* it is not surprising that her description figures the imitator's work of registering and reproducing impressions as a kind of intersubjective photography, one in which merely mechanical reproduction is supplemented by human feeling. More curious, though, is the way Caffin's language, both here and throughout her book, resuscitates a sympathetic idiom ill-suited to the Taylorized vaudeville stage, belonging more properly to Adam Smith, David Hume, and Bernard Mandeville and to eighteenth- and nineteenth-century discourses of moral and social behavior. Recall the mimetic terms of Smith's account of sympathy in *The Theory of Moral Sentiments* (1759):

As we have no immediate experience of what other men feel, we can form no idea of the manner in which they are affected, but by conceiving what we ourselves should feel in the like situation. . . . [I]t is by the imagination only that we can form any conception of what are his sensations. . . . It is the impressions of our senses only, not those of his, which our imaginations copy. By the imagination we place ourselves in his situation. . . . [W]e enter as it were into his body, and become in some measure the same person with him.[2]

In Smith's skeptical epistemology, sympathy as fellow-feeling is assumed but only experienced through an imaginative fiction in which the subject imitates the impressions of his *own* senses. If Smith is correct, Caffin's mimic is quite literally twice as impressive: he must "feel like the subject he is portraying, and he must be able to impress this feeling on his audience" (*V* 135).

The theatricality of Smith's theory implies that sympathy requires a scene, a visual staging of affect. But if the popular stage for modernists is routinely imagined to be a public scene swirling with emotional currents, the particular relationship between vision, affectivity, and imitation is more often than not understood as involuntary, compulsive, indeed mechanical, as embodied in Caffin's photographic mimic. We might say that the sympathetic dynamics of popular performance in the late nineteenth and early twentieth centuries operate less along the lines of Smith's formulation, in which sympathy is imaginative and willed—an ethical act—than of Hume's, wherein sympathy approximates a quasi-automatic physiological "propensity to company and society" that stems from the "very imitative nature" of the human mind, a disposition that in turn "makes us enter deeply into each other's sentiments, and causes like passions and inclinations to run, as it were, by contagion, through the whole club or knot of companions."[3] For Hume, and for Caffin, the logic of mimetic-sympathetic contagion presupposes a *visual economy* for the reception and transfer of affect, a model mediated by the putative immediacy of the "impression," through which emotion circulates seamlessly from the perceptual sign of one's passion to its emergence in another: "When any affection is infus'd by sympathy, *it is at first known only by its effects, and by those external signs in the countenance and conversation,* which convey an idea of it. This idea is presently converted into an impression, and acquires such a degree of force and vivacity, as to become the very passion itself, and produce an equal emotion, as any original affection."[4] The anachronistic echoes of moral philosophy in modernist vaudeville criticism begin to suggest how the modernist interest in public performance's capacity for sympathy points not to the ethical-political potential of a self-contained subject, of modernist subjectivity as a "monadlike container" in Fredric Jameson's formulation, but rather places just that kind of bounded inwardness in question.[5] To gauge the capacity of the popular stage to be sympathetic is thus to measure the threats and promises of eccentric feeling, of a self that experiences in public the expropriation, circulation, and typicality of its emotional property. The sympathetic self of Caffin's mime is a figure of eccentric feeling's capacity for abstraction: its ability to be rendered into impersonal or vagrant intensities and thereby mechanically provoked, transmitted, or mimed in groups, crowds, and public places.

In this chapter, I explore how modernist thinkers gauged the public operation of such eccentric feeling in their connoisseurship of performers who would model the very *typicality* of modern personality, performances I call "typage" to anticipate my discussion of Sergei Eisenstein in chapter 2.[6] I track this concern in popular accounts of variety performance like Caffin's *Vaudeville* and music-hall mimic J. Arthur Bleackley's treatise *The Art of Mimicry* before turning to a more sustained discussion of mimetic performance in the decidedly unpopular work of Wyndham Lewis. Regarding these first two figures, we know precious little. Caffin was closely connected to *Camera Work* through her husband, Charles, a prominent New York art critic, a close friend of Stieglitz, and a regular contributor to his journal. In addition to writing *Vaudeville,* whose illustrations were provided by Marius de Zayas, a fellow traveler in the Stieglitz group, Caffin transcribed all of her husband's published writings; co-wrote with him a lengthy study of modern dance, *Dancers and Dancing of Today* (1912); participated actively in the women's suffrage movement; and was affiliated with Greenwich Village's radical feminist group "Heterodoxy." Less is known about Bleackley: he concludes *The Art of Mimicry* with press blurbs (including a 1904 rave by Max Beerbohm in the *Saturday Review*) that indicate he was a regular performer in London theaters and music halls in the early 1900s, and he appears to be the only professional music-hall mimic to publish a book on his art.[7] Lewis's case is, by contrast, much more familiar to modernists, though in light of Caffin and Bleackley's work, his anxieties seem less uncommon, if not exactly typical. In the final section of this chapter, I read the evolution of Lewis's "Wild Body" stories as indicative of a turn in his career from an atypical investment in the emotional excesses of so-called big being to a mimesis built to interrupt public flows of affect. Placing Lewisian mimesis in dialogue with Caffin's and Bleackley's own, I show how Lewis's grotesque aesthetic of externality thus not only thinks of modernity's reified public sphere dialectically (the proximity to the poison is the cure) but does so through a critique of the logic of expressivity that defines the propriety of modernism's hermetic subject of public feeling.

The Mimetic-Sympathetic Public Sphere

One of this book's guiding assumptions is that the particularly labile conception of emotion that Teresa Brennan has recently called "the transmission of affect," which understands affects as "social in origin but biological or physical in effect" and which holds that "the 'atmosphere' or the environment literally gets into the individual," receives an especially thorough hearing in modernism, as critics of the period's more reactionary strains have long pointed out.[8] And yet the idiom of sympathy attending modernism's phenomenologies of public being often exceeds the moderns' familiar, and reactionary, defense of affective "self-containment" and in fact comes to underwrite the moderns' more ecstatic modes of publicness (*TA* 2). In other words, modernism's understanding of the mediated public sphere as a site of nonidentitarian and potentially liberatory eccentric affects—as an arena for imagining the particular models of publicness, sociality, and intimacy such affects enable—is doubled by a more anxious awareness of a sympathetic public sphere. This mimetic mode of modernist publicness thus departs significantly from the Habermasian model that, as I have argued, still dominates the instrumental accounts of modernism's relationship to its public worlds. For Jürgen Habermas, remember, the experience of willful, rational, imaginative sympathy provided by epistolary conventions and the protocols of the domestic novel is a training tool for proper bourgeois subjectivity—effectively teaching the isolate individual to experience his subjectivity as "always already oriented towards an audience" and thus preparing the private reader for the abstraction and public feeling demanded by the bourgeois public sphere.[9] But modernist sympathy provides no such gentle rituals of inculcation. The willful openness to rational, abstract public being and feeling that Habermas calls "audience-oriented subjectivity" becomes, for Caffin, Bleackley, and Lewis, a kind of delirious disorientation of purpose, a drive to mime at once primitive and thoroughly mechanical, *photographic*. To be in public is to be subject to involuntary sympathy, contagious mimicry, hypnotic political identifications, all galvanized by vision.[10]

There are several explanations for the currency of this idea in the work of the writers and thinkers I examine. The first is the residual force within the modernist period of Romantic theories of crowd behavior and group psychology, beginning with Gustave Le Bon's *The Crowd: A Study of the Popular Mind* (1895) and continuing through Wilfred Trotter's *Instincts of the Herd in Peace and War* (1916), William McDougall's *The Group Mind* (1920), and Freud's own *Group Psychology and the Analysis of the Ego* (1921). In this, his critique of Le Bon and others for their failure to specify satisfactorily the mechanism whereby people, in "the heightening of affectivity" in groups, sacrifice their individuality in favor of a common mind, Freud himself observes the relationship between vision, affect, and imitation in one such explanation—what McDougall calls "the primitive sympathetic response":

> The manner in which individuals are thus carried away by a common impulse is explained by McDougall by means of what he calls the "principle of direct induction of emotion by way of the primitive sympathetic response," that is, by means of the emotional contagion with which we are already familiar [as postulated by Le Bon]. The fact is that the perception of *the signs* of an affective state is calculated automatically to arouse the same affect in the person who perceives them. The greater the number of people in whom the same affect can be simultaneously *observed,* the stronger does this automatic compulsion grow. (Freud qtd. in *TA* 56, Brennan's emphasis)

While Freud admits that "something exists in us which, when we become aware of the signs of an emotion in someone else, tends to make us fall into the same emotion," he ultimately replaces this dubious explanation for social feeling, what he derisively dubs "the magic word—suggestion," with his own theory of the libidinal identifications that bind the constitution of groups.[11] We will return to Freud's discussion of the erotic dynamics of group ties in chapter 3. For now, I simply want to note how the formulation of sympathy as a compulsive reproduction of public feeling through visual mimesis, which Freud dismisses as insufficiently scientific in the work of early-twentieth-century group psychology, in fact dovetails with similar notions in the fields of experimental psychology and psychophysiology, themselves energized by two of the nineteenth century's greatest inventions, biology and the unconscious. Indeed, from midcentury on, these fields were preoccupied with what Rae Beth Gordon calls the "radical division between the higher and the lower faculties (reason, judgment, and will as opposed to sensation, motor response, instinct, and automatisms)" and increasingly understood perception as rooted in a corporeal unconscious dominated by the forces of instinct and involuntary imitation.[12] Further, the domains of psychophysics and physiological aesthetics begin to converge in the 1880s and 1890s around the notion that perception entails unconscious corporeal mimesis, that "perceiving the aesthetic object not only produces specific sensations but also corporeal reactions that retrace the form and movement of that object," a line of thought that produces the influential, mechanical James-Lange theory of emotion and culminates—as chapter 2 shows—in

Eisenstein's wish to turn the public stage and movie theater into a sphere of "imitative, mimical infectiousness."[13]

Most important for my purposes is the way modernist sympathy and its attendant mimetic imperatives spawn a range of radical theories of modern publicness and sociality, theories joined by the convergence of imitation and eccentric feeling but that place very different values on the sympathetic subject and the mimetic socius it indicates. At one utopian extreme, one might locate the Benjaminian understanding of eccentric affect's potential for mimetic innervation, a revolutionary capacity I discuss in more detail in chapters 2 and 5. As Miriam Hansen has shown, Walter Benjamin adopts the conception of "innervation" from its Freudian signification as a physiological process that "mediates between internal and external, psychic and motoric, human and mechanical registers."[14] But where Freud tended to see this process as a unidirectional conversion of energy from interiorized affect to somatic manifestation, Benjamin pins his hopes on innervation's reverse movement within a mediated public sphere: the possibility that the external, corporeal stimulation provided by a body on film might allow its viewing collective to recover liberatory mimetic affects and energies, a notion thoroughly in keeping with developments in psychophysiology.

More normative, though also compensatory, was the mimetic model of sociality offered by French sociologist Gabriel Tarde in *The Laws of Imitation* (1890), which described "the social man as a veritable somnambulist. . . . *Society is imitation and imitation is a kind of somnambulism.*"[15] Tarde's theory, which also shaped Le Bon's attempt to understand the contagious imitation of crowd behavior, defined social mimicry as a kind of distance photography, the "action at a distance of one mind upon another," an "interpsychical photography" operating both actively and passively, with or without the volition of the miming subject.[16] As Ruth Leys has demonstrated, Tarde's "imitation-suggestion" theory appealed to American sociologists looking to explain how a heterogeneous society could manufacture social fellow-feeling and political consensus, since, for Tarde, imitation's result "is always one thing: similarity or an increase therein, between two or more individuals. . . . Increase of similarity . . . is a social goal."[17] At the same time, Tarde's argument, in positing imitation as an "affective identification that precedes the very difference between self and other," implied a plasticity of identity and the hypnotic production of the same, thereby threatening notions of individual autonomy and a self-determining, self-identical subject.[18]

At another, equally radical extreme, the compulsive identification that characterizes modernism's sympathetic publicness was less the hallmark of a desirable socialization (as in Tarde's formulation) or the avenue for a liberatory recovery of collective affects (as in Benjaminian "innervation") than a pathological assimilation of subject and environment, the deathly indistinction of a thoroughly reified public sphere. In his remarkable essay "Mimicry and Legendary Psychasthenia," published in the surrealist journal *Minotaure* in 1935, sociologist Roger Caillois suggested that such imitation was not simply an overidentification with others but an overidentification between personality and place in which the subject "feels himself becoming space, *dark space where things cannot be put*. He is similar, not similar to something, but just *similar*."[19] Ultimately, Caillois translated the lack of distinction between the organism and its surroundings that he identified in the insect world into a terrifying model of the subject in a rationalized socius: in its seduction to milieu, *"life takes a step backwards."*[20] Indeed, one wonders if all of these understandings of mimetic-sympathetic publicness—as emotional renewal, as compensatory fellow-feeling within a differentiated socius, and as the self's unnerving susceptibility to sensation, suggestion, and typicality—aren't playing within the pliant body and labile expressivity of Caffin's vaudeville mimic. If this is plausible, then the mime's ability to absorb every characteristic of his model, looked at differently, portends a vision of the modernist self's very characteristicness, which is to say, its complete typicality and affective openness to mass identification. Considered in this light, the mimic's plastic embodiment, to borrow Mark Selzer's language, "typifies typicality, the becoming abstract and general of the individuality of the individual" that marks the type of person proper to mass-mediated public culture.[21] But for Caffin, Bleackley, and Lewis, coming to terms with this body means grappling with a reified public sphere in which abstraction just as easily provides an occasion for ecstatic community as leads to serial violence, and in which a certain performance of typicality might, paradoxically enough, preserve the eccentricity of inner experience.

What the Public Wants

> When the body has completely become an object, a beautiful thing, it can foreshadow a new happiness. In suffering the most extreme reification man triumphs over reification. The artistry of the beautiful body, its effortless agility and relaxation, which can be displayed today only in the circus, vaudeville, and burlesque, herald the joy to which men will attain in being liberated from the [affirmative] ideal, once mankind, having become a true subject, succeeds in the mastery of matter.[22]

Here, near the conclusion of his well-known essay "The Affirmative Character of Culture" (1937), Herbert Marcuse singles out certain variety attractions as unique bearers of a utopian, "anticipatory memory." This is a strange passage, to be sure, and perhaps the most emancipatory moment in an otherwise dire assessment of the status of art in bourgeois society. The dialectical force of the logic is clear: only through the body's total objectification—here meaning both its reification and its spectacular display in the mutable sensuousness of the objective world—can authentic subjectivity be achieved. There is, it would seem, no way out of reification, but through it. And thus, for Marcuse, modernity's most thoroughly reified entertainments—where the repetitive, mechanical display of human performance is the product—may also be its most vital.

Marcuse's point about variety's ambiguity as a cultural form was almost unanimously shared by its critics and performers, who could never definitely establish whether its attractions were matrices of modern community and public being, ruthlessly Taylorized and commodified entertainments, or worse, spectacles of affective manipulation. This uncertainty is, in fact, the structural ambivalence both of Bleackley's treatise *The Art of Mimicry* and Caffin's study *Vaudeville.* In 1914, Caffin noticed the vaudevillian's drive to "spice his offering with novelty, more novelty and always novelty," attributing the strategy to an underlying change in "public appetite," a shift Henry Jenkins has identified as vaudeville's ultimate message: "the pleasure of infinite diversity in infinite combinations."[23] This message was thoroughly in synch with both the texture of modern life and the market imperatives of commodified leisure, which began its transition to mass culture in the waning decades of the nineteenth century, when American vaudeville was born. Unlike its progenitor—the nineteenth-century music-hall and saloon tradition, which catered to mostly male working-class audiences in both Europe and America—the consolidated national network of American vaudeville "forged a mass audience: a heterogeneous crowd of white men and women of different classes and ethnic groups."[24] The domestication and massification of variety theater in America and Europe, then, demanded a heterogeneity of content and form to match its diverse audience. Such a heterogeneous audience posed a real challenge to vaudeville performers looking to "kill" and demanded a mastery of affective immediacy—a dynamic and participatory relationship between themselves and their crowd. As Caffin explains, "So little time is allowed to each performer that their appeal is necessarily frankly direct. It hides itself behind no subtleties but is personal and unashamed. It looks its audience straight in the face and says, in effect, 'Look at ME! I am going to astonish you!' It makes no claim to aloofness or impersonality, but comes right down to the footlights and faces the crowd and tells it 'All for your Delight *We* are—here [*sic*]'" (10). Caffin's emphasis on the authentic, frank, and personal self-exposure of the performer's address recalls the terms of T. S. Eliot's famous 1923 obituary of legendary British music-hall performer Marie Lloyd, whose art was distinct to the extent that her audiences "were invariably sympathetic."[25] And "it was through this sympathy that she controlled them. . . . It was her understanding of the people . . . and the people's recognition of the fact that she embodied the virtues which they genuinely respected most in private life, that raised her to the position she occupied at her death" (ML 458). For Eliot, Lloyd's perfect sympathy with her audience made her "the expressive figure of the lower classes" and the embodiment of a dying kind of popular culture that generates "that collaboration of the audience with the artist which is necessary in all art" (458).

While Eliot mourned Lloyd's death and the lack in the bourgeois imaginary it revealed, his romanticizing about Lloyd's vital attunement to the audience assumes (as does Caffin's) a mutual receptivity between performer and spectator belied by his own language to describe Lloyd's total control. In the massified modern version of variety theater that is the object of Caffin's study, the desired expressive identity between performer and audience was as difficult to secure as the distinction between emotional fellow-feeling and affective manipulation. Indeed, as Jenkins has shown, an entire emotional typology, a "pseudoscience of 'affective mechanics,'" emerged in early-twentieth-century show business to level the differences in taste of a diverse public. Making reference to the developing science of reflexology, George M. Cohan and George J. Nathan argued in 1913 that the "emotional lives of all men follow a fixed norm, precisely as do their physical lives. . . . If we are normal, we all cry at the same things, laugh at the same things, and are thrilled by the same things" (qtd. in *WM* 33–34). Through deft deployment of a basic repertoire of surefire laugh-getters and tearjerkers, any performer could draw from his audience the desired response. And to further expedite emotional impact, vaudes buttressed their typology of affect with an extensive social shorthand of stock costumes, facial characteristics, and accents to convey social, ethnic, and racial types—the Irishman, the Jew, the "coon," the East-Ender, the urban dandy—as efficiently as possible. In doing so, of course, vaudeville depended on the familiarity of these types to the audience and thus, as Caffin argued, reassured spectators of the legibility of a differentiated urban society. If on any given night a performer's affective mechanics short-circuited, or his typology proved unconvincing, he had only the sheer force of his personality, the virtuoso performance of his individualism, to fall back on. More than any other skill, this ability to "project a unique personality that transcended stock roles" was the vaude's hottest commodity (*WM* 71). It is precisely in this sort of performance—one that trades in the very nontypicality of personality—that Caffin's study locates the hope for the social sympathy Eliot had found in Lloyd: "We find it is ever the strong personality and the ability to get it across the footlights and impress it upon the audience that distinguish the popular performer" (*V* 26).

Caffin concedes that a fragile logic underpins the success of such strategic typage, which must balance the desire for an authentic, eccentric personality and for a generality of personhood subtending social legibility. Consider her chapter "The Appeal of Character Study," a paean to the exuberant vitality of character comedians intent on "reproducing the human characteristics and spiritual nature of the originals," including Albert Chevalier's London coster, Harry Lauder's Scottish peasant (see figure 1), and Lilian Shaw's German mother and young Parisienne (*V* 60). Caffin wants to argue that the successful imitation of a type can be considered authentic if it is imbued with humanity and not overly distorted. Grotesque exaggeration, which precludes affective transmission, must therefore be studiously avoided.[26] But the spiritual authenticity of the type, for example, Gerty Vanderbilt's "typical American girl" (see figure 2), is also secured by its social saturation: her "long straight limbs" and her "free and unafraid carriage of the head" are true because "they may be duplicated many times any fine winter afternoon on Fifth Avenue or the main thoroughfare of almost any city in the Union" (V 30). By this reasoning, then, the imitation is human and authentic if recognizable, particularized, and not grotesque—but it is only recognizable to the extent that it is reproduced often enough to be considered universal. It is true because it is duplicated. This paradoxical logic—whereby human authenticity is communicated through the performance of abstract types, individuality through social duplication—eventually prompts Caffin to admit that what vaudeville's typology really offers is an attractive fiction of social legibility: "So the portrayer of character who will show to us types sufficiently unusual to pique our interest and curiosity, but human enough for us to recognize the essential characteristics, not only amuses us with his emphasis on the humor of his study but flatters us by making us feel how thoroughly we understand human nature. Of course we don't, not even the wisest of us" (43). This admission—we don't understand human nature—forces Caffin to speculate that the art of a performer like Harry Lauder is not to embody social sympathy (like Lloyd) but to mask its absence—to "set us thinking of . . . the throbbing heart of man" in "such a way as to make us forget we were one of a crowded audience of miscellaneous individualities" (54).

HARRY LAUDER

Figure 1. "Actual Human Character." Marius de Zayas, *Harry Lauder,* in Caroline Caffin, *Vaudeville* (New York: Mitchell Kennerly, 1914).

Faced with the dispiriting reality of a differentiated public sphere, Caffin's popular performer offers sympathetic compensation: his aim is ever "to seek the chord which shall evoke an answering vibration in his audience and to attune his offering in a key which, in spite of modulations and varying harmonies, shall strike consistently on that string" (V 9). Playing to the audience, the "artist's sympathy informs each [appeal] with the spirit of the occasion and robs it of mechanical artifice" (27).[27] Caffin's text returns insistently to

Figure 2. "Typical American Girl." Marius de Zayas, *Gertrude Van-derbilt*, c. 1908. Indian ink on board, mat opening, $17\frac{1}{8} \times 11\frac{1}{8}$ in. Courtesy of Francis M. Naumann Fine Art.

this vital, "sympathetic current" (64), either to applaud its deft production or to decry its absence, as in the case of those jaded moderns who refuse to be thrilled by the feats of acrobats. Here, Caffin implores her readers to return to the sensory intensity of youth, to that moment when, "after a first visit to a show of some kind, this new world of hazard and daring opened up" before them (169). Ransacking "the storehouse of memories belonging to each of us," Caffin proposes a "sympathetic viewing of acrobats," whereby the spectator realizes "for one's self the sensation, say, of jumping for a trapeze bar . . . or any other quite elementary exercises, and [uses] the memory of these sensations to help you to feel the movements of acrobats with your own senses; then, so far from complaining of boredom, you are more likely to find their feats too thrilling" (169–71). Note how Caffin's prescription for the sympathetic viewing of acrobats operates along the mimetic lines of a Benjaminian innervation—stimulating movement produces in the miming public spectator the liberatory recovery of lost collective affects—yet Caffin remains convinced that this sort of innervation could just as easily produce salutary sensation or "vicarious pain" as pleasure: "It would be wholesome and invigorating for them to feel that sympathetic thrill . . . and insure them from the enervating sensationalism that comes of watching the danger of others in which we ourselves have no share" (180, 186).[28]

Caffin thus locates the potential for vital, eccentric feeling in both the public stage's capacity for mimetic innervation and in certain performances of typicality that together secure the sympathetic current coursing through the variety stage. But Caffin remains ambivalent about whether the vaudeville audience is insufficiently receptive, or dangerously so, an uncertainty that—like mimetic plasticity—is also troped through the photographic plate: "Did you ever look into the faces of an audience and catch sight of one in which the expressions of the actors on the stage was mirrored, one after another, with no consciousness on the part of the face's owner? It would seem as though such a face must be a sort of sensitized plate, *obliged to reproduce whatever came within the angle of its vision*" (V 135, my emphasis). Considering the likeness between Caffin's metaphor and Tarde's formulation of mimetic intersubjectivity as "a quasi-photographic reproduction of a cerebral image upon the sensitive plate of another brain," we might say that Caffin's attitude toward the mimetic-sympathetic public sphere oscillates between utopianism and despair, since a public capable of the mimetic innervation of feeling is equally susceptible to emotion's mesmeric manipulation.[29]

Ultimately, it is this same quality of somnambulistic reproduction that Caffin cannot but associate with the mimic, no matter how attractive the performer's craft. For Caffin, mimics like Cecelia "Cissy" Loftus (see figure 3) and Elsie Janis are appealing to the extent that they model a plasticity of identity: "all lissomeness and pliability," they "melt" from one "soft, diaphanous personality" to the next, giving themselves up entirely to each succeeding portrait, so that "for the time being there is nothing left of [their] own individuality" (V 138). The plastic and responsive body, as I suggested earlier, is the precondition of Caffin's idealized social sympathy; at the same time, the mesmerizing impersonality of the mimic, or the galvanizing personality of the vaude, that might guarantee the authenticity of a mimetic-sympathetic public sphere nevertheless falsifies it.[30] Caffin elaborates this fear in her chapter "The Force of Personality" by reference to Eva Tanguay (see figure 4), "a Song and Dance Artist who does not dance, cannot sing, is not beautiful, witty or graceful, but who dominates her audience more entirely than anyone on the Vaudeville stage" (35–36). The mystery of Tanguay's captivating but talentless performance, Caffin argues, is the way she radiates "her intense vitality . . . through this raffish aureole, setting the surrounding atmosphere agog with vivacity," making the audience love her without ever appealing to them directly. Instead, she offers a "saucy, impudent grin. 'I don't care' she seems to say; 'this is my stunt—like it or not, it's fun to do it, so I don't care!'" (37–38). The answer Caffin proposes is one that Karl Marx might admire:

> I wonder if the secret, after all, is that she is the epitome of that strong force of modern civilization—advertising. . . . Again and again we are reminded that money is flowing in on her. Again and again we are informed that she is unique. And this reiteration, so forcibly and believably uttered, with an assurance that we really are interested, hypnotizes us into a belief that we are. The public likes it, it is the secret of the success of advertising and here is that success embodied. . . . Behold the end desired by the cult of self— Advertisement! (39–40)

As with Eliot, for Caffin the potential for a sympathetic exchange is structured by a conviction that the performance draws the audience into a reassuring (and narcissistic) spectacle of itself: "For these figures you see on the stage are but a reflection of what YOU, their creators, want" (*V* 226). While Eliot asserts that "what is called the lower class" finds in Marie Lloyd "the expression and dignity of their own lives," Caffin concludes that the imitative performances of vaudeville confront the audience with models of vital sympathy as well as the spectacular image of its reification—the forgery of sympathy under the phony spell of the mimic's aura (ML 456, 458). The mimic is either "the Circe of the Force of Advertising," or she has "caught something of the elemental dynamic buoyancy that enables mankind to over-ride disaster and, having caught it, is radiating it upon a nerve-wracked world" (*V* 41, 42). Unlike Marcuse or Benjamin, Caffin did not see how the vaude could be both at once.

British imitator J. Arthur Bleackley was also convinced that mimicry was nervy business; but while Caffin longs for a sympathetic current between imitator and audience, Bleackley mimes to secure his artistic uniqueness

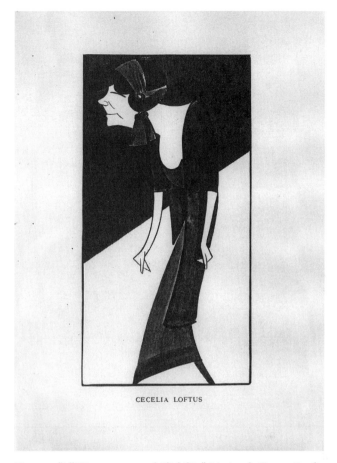

CECELIA LOFTUS

Figure 3. "All Lissomeness and Pliability." Marius de Zayas, *Cecelia Loftus*, in Caroline Caffin, *Vaudeville* (New York: Mitchell Kennerly, 1914).

over and against the mass. The artistry of the plastic body was, for Bleackley, the product of painstaking study and subject to defilement by a cruel and unwashed audience. His treatise, what he calls a "practical method for would-be mimics, whose talent is latent and undeveloped," consists mainly of advice for the aspiring professional imitator: "study the art of acting first"; "get in the habit of noticing everything"; "develop your senses"; "observe the 'mimicry of nature'"; "keep in good physical condition"; "master the art of respiration"; "be forever humble"; and avoid "voice lozenges, raw eggs, or stimulants."[31] Bleackley's rules are remarkable in many respects

EVA TANGUAY

Figure 4. "Circe of the Force of Advertising." Marius de Zayas, *Eva Tanguay,* in Caroline Caffin, *Vaudeville* (New York: Mitchell Kennerly, 1914).

but most of all in their foundational conviction that a heightened sensory acuity—observational powers, a retentive memory, the sense of hearing—that will guarantee successful mimicry is a matter of *cultivation,* of practiced attunement to the objective world: "You have surrounded yourself with appropriate books, pictures and people. You are gradually training your senses. . . . Make the world and human nature your incessant study on the lines that I have indicated" (*AM* 64).

The paradox of Bleackley's argument—that the distinction of mimetic originality can be conferred upon *anyone* surrounded by the appropriate environmental stimuli—is never addressed. Instead, Bleackley continues to maintain that only through sustained sensory training can the mimic's imitation become original art. Thus, like other mimics, Bleackley asserts the superiority of his art to acting, an argument that failed to persuade a critic like Caffin.[32] For Bleackley, this means repudiating the externalist logic of Meyerholdian typage for a quasi-Stanislavskian naturalism: the actor, Bleackley explains, imitates "types," while the mimic imitates "individuals"; thus, the "actor's art is only a modified form of mimicry, and it is not so creative. His province is 'to hold the mirror up to nature,' whereas the province of the mimic is to dispense with a mirror altogether and present an original effect" (*AM* 19). Bleackley's celebration of creative, humanistic mimicry legitimates his craft and differentiates it from the "false, counterfeit school of mimicry, which is to be avoided" (12). Stoically resisting the presumed social ubiquity of this school—a "parrot-like, phonographic school of mimicry" defined by a "mechanical reproduction of voice and gesture"—Bleackley's art is infused with the power of imagination and a distinguished sensibility: the true mimic develops "creative and individual" impressions, the "very antithesis of reproduction or servile copy. You have no wish to degenerate into a parrot, a mocking bird, or mere buffoon. Then stimulate this subtle imaginative faculty, if you wish to develop into a great artist" (14, 10, 12, 71).

As he piles on mechanical metaphors to define "false" mimicry, Bleackley betrays an acute anxiety about the encroachment of mimetic technologies on the auratic vitality of his art. But his idiom of degeneracy and servility also registers the lurking menace of social similitude. If Bleackley's treatise seemed an innocent fantasy of the mimic's sympathy with the environment, a capacity extending to any "would-be mimic" prepared to immerse himself in the environment, it eventually becomes a defensive arrogation of aesthetic and social sensibility: "Those who are altogether devoid of art, who are awkward and *gauche,* who never succeed at anything but making money, and browbeating their neighbour, condemn the followers of an art which they are singularly incapable of pursuing themselves; on account perhaps of their limited powers of analysis, sense perception, and imagination" (*AM* 52). Quoting J. H. Newman's *Apologia,* Bleackley proceeds to shore up the mimic's unique receptivity by denying it a certain intersubjective sympathy: "'Minds in different states and circumstances cannot understand one another.' . . . There are people of matter-of-fact, prosaic minds, who cannot take in the fancies of poets; and others, of shallow, inaccurate minds, who cannot take in the ideas of philosophical inquirers" (52). Bleackley's project in *The Art of*

Mimicry is to divide actors from mimics and "true" mimics from false ones, but he is also at pains to differentiate the cultivated sensibility of the "great artist" from the dulled sensorium of society at large: "A habit of observation is necessary, however, and this habit is what many individuals are too lazy to form, going as they do through life with their eyes sealed up, as it were, in a bag" (55). Not surprisingly, the model of the mimic's artistry is avant-garde "Bohemia," where "imagination and ability" and "talent and originality prevail"; in "Society, the social club, the Park," on the other hand, one may look for such artistry "in vain" (73).

Eliotic in its appraisal of modernity's dissociated sensibility, Lewisian in its antipathy to vulgar philistinism, Bleackley's aestheticist typage is nearly choked with resentment for modern society and its metonymic stand-in, the audience: "It is useless to try to be subtle in a large music hall; you will only succeed in being unintelligible, which may 'go down' in the case of a great artiste; for the public follows public opinion as a rule, like a flock of sheep; and whether they understand or not, they usually applaud a star" (AM 31). But while his quest for sensory cultivation was thoroughly decadent (Bleackley may indeed have owned a pet turtle), his longing for refined sensibility did not, as it did for Des Esseintes, turn him against nature, or even against the public. Much as Bleackley might have liked to refine his aesthetic sensibility and liken it to the avant-garde, he was "engaged in business," and so he "must cultivate business instincts" (90), even though it meant subjecting his art to the caprice of the herd:

> Don't be too technical; the general public will not understand you. Your great desire and object must be to please and play up to your various audiences. *Try to adapt yourself to various coteries.* The more artistic and idealistic your work, the less it will be appreciated by the ordinary members of society. Artistes will appreciate you, but you wish to appeal to a wider class; besides artistes are not always too charitable. Therefore, *discriminate and adapt yourself to your surroundings,* and try to present a repertoire of "impressions" that will appeal to all. (74, my emphasis)

Like many of modernism's great "artistes," Bleackley sees his artistic vitality menaced by an aggressive, materialist public indifferent to art. In such a world, Bleackley's art of mimicry is not a sensuous merging with the social, nor does it entail, as Beerbohm himself once put it, a narrowing of the scope of the "quest for emotion," a simple "unswitching" of the self from its surroundings.[33] To survive, the mimic must join the battle with this aggressive and vulgar public, if for no other reason than to confirm his own individuality.

And Bleackley learned this trick not from Beerbohm but from a "celebrated" music-hall artist who once instructed him to "come onto the platform, lean leisurely on the piano with extended arms, look defiantly at the audience as much as to say: 'Banish your skepticism! Here I am, you can't get away from the fact. I am here, you are there. Who are you? Look at me! Now, you've got to listen to me whether you like it or not!" (*AM* 94). And yet, as in Caffin's account, where the strength of singular personality is doubled by the aura of advertising, Bleackley's strategy is similarly confounded by the dynamics of a mimetic-sympathetic public sphere, in which to make a unique public impression—or, in Bleackley's own telling language, "to present an original effect"—always entails the uncanny recognition of the self's secondariness, of its being impressed by the general public. "Mimicry is nervous, exacting work," Bleackley avers, and only an aggressive performance of individuality that is also a mimetic adaptation to the environment may "save you many a nerve-destroying shock!" (103, 94).

The Garments of Strangeness

It is not impossible that, during his many trips to the London music halls in the prewar period and into the early 1920s, Wyndham Lewis caught Bleackley's act. Had Lewis stalled his ferocious blasting of Victorian vampires long enough to read Bleackley's treatise, he would have found exquisite comedy in the mime's humanist presumption that true mimicry is the display of a "distinct individuality" and never a mere "mechanical reproduction of voice and gesture" (*AM* 10). Consider Lewis's well-known reversal of the humanist terms of Bergsonian laughter in "The Meaning of the Wild Body" (1927): "The root of the Comic is to be sought in the sensations resulting from the observations of a *thing* behaving like a person."[34] What could be more ludicrous than a pop-cultural imitator who mistakes his corporeal plasticity for human vitality, his paid inauthenticity for productive power? Always eager to presage the portentous in the quotidian, Lewis might have found the vaude's celebration of creative imitation a fecund example of how consumer capitalism had (in his characteristically paranoid formulation) forced imitative desire into all spheres of modern life, fomenting in people "the will to *instal[l] themselves inside* things, a kind of thirst to sexually invade everything—to violate any intimacy [*sic*], and mix themselves in the most intimate recesses of the being of everything met."[35]

This is the Lewis who "hate[s] the movement that blurs lines"; the Lewis for whom typage is both a survival strategy for an ego threatened by external flux (the fluid, the feminine, the masses, and so on) and, even more perniciously, a prosthetic, proto-fascist mode that facilitates the total mobilization of the self.[36] This unsympathetic Lewis, who becomes typical as a defense against a ridiculously sympathetic modernity and its too-imitative social relations, is one of modernism's more notorious characters and, too often, an easily dismissed caricature. Less familiar is the young Lewis, who in his first critical essay, "Our Wild Body" (1910), lamented the "vast, Anglo-Saxon conspiracy against the body" and the decline of "physical sympathy" in Victorian culture and who, instead, expressed a receptivity to "the French idea of hospitality—the hospitality of the body—making another at home in one's body, so to speak, courteously throwing open the fleshy doors that lead to apartments usually regarded as private" (*CWB* 251). In fact, Lewis's earliest published writings—stories, observations, and quasi-ethnographic studies of primitive Brittany—are suffused with a surprising vitalism not unlike Caffin's: a longing for corporeal sympathy that finds expression in such ritualized public scenes of primitive theater as pensions, bars, fairs, fetes, and circuses.

Although in his autobiography, *Rude Assignment,* Lewis would emphasize his career's unimpeded evolution from vitalist sympathy to formalist detachment, these modes were already entangled in a complex way in the "Wild Body" stories.[37] The imaginative origin of these stories was Lewis's "Breton Journal," a rough diary of his travels to Brittany, whose first entry on 17 August 1908 finds Lewis observing the aftermath of a local Pardon (a primitive carnival or fair) where four or five "hideous topers" are "deep in desperate and interminable conversations" in a deserted town square (*CWB* 193). The fete concluded, the orgy of amusement complete, the men have achieved the fullness of fellow-feeling: "They enjoy'd their self voluptuously, they enjoy'd the enjoyment that others had in them, and with that enjoyment [*sic*]. It is not always the same that men get together in each successive gathering. These people have learnt the secret of finding a complete world, a synthesis of beings, always a small number that satisfy sympathetically" (193–94). Lewis argues that the "chief use" of these peasant fetes is "the gathering together of a vast and orderless concourse of people," not to make one "vast society" but to "make one of a society of ten souls" (194). The tight circle of sympathy occasioned by the popular amusements—which are, Lewis continues, "essentially *orgies*"—allows the peasants to experience communally their "rebellion against life, fate, routine," even while they sacrifice it in a "supreme tribute to Fate":

But while the smoke of all of this is going up, and their sacrifices are accomplish'd unconsciously amid the clamours of their crowds, certain of their emanations strain to each other as they perish; that theatre "debordant" [outflowing] in each nature,—that that [*sic*] is most delicate, most inspir'd in each nature, and for that reason to be sacrificed as superfluous, as it were a spirit, catches at some other, before its life is extinct, and is thrill'd in this bitter companionship. Many in these fêtes, in the society of their comrades or of some one met there, know the sweetness of union and a melancholy at this death,—this dissipation, this gross throwing away of something born to the ideal, without knowing the cause of either. (194)

In this orgy of sympathy, the peasant shares and then kills what is most intimate to his nature because it is superfluous to—and may in fact interfere with—his daily existence. Put in a way more resonant with Lewis's later screeds, the peasant trades his individuality for the ecstasy of fellow-feeling, the depersonalizing rapture of abstract typicality. There is a wistful appreciation in Lewis's tone here, a keen admiration for the peasants' expenditure, for the way they "leave themselves bare, make a bonfire of what the intelligence tells us is most precious." But even more insistent is his claim that the artist, in his "defiance of Fate," cannot brook this exposure and must remain "the enemy of such orgiac participation of life," though it means living "without knowing this emotion felt in the midst of its wastefulness" (CWB 194–95).

This sentiment, which trades on, but ultimately forgoes, the primal authenticity and sympathetic receptivity of the peasant, is a familiar one in modernism, and fundamentally Romantic.[38] But the assumptions that underlie its romanticism—about the peasants' motives, the utility of the fete, and, finally, the difference between the peasant's blind immersion in eccentric feeling and the artist's refusal of identification—are already under erasure here. For Lewis is careful to define the almost postcoital state in which he finds the spent revelers not as (as we might expect) a communion of self-exposure but by mutual estrangement: "Each man [is] still robed, physically and spiritually in the garment of strangeness or rather in the *nakedness* of strangeness—for after a day's companionship with a man he will succeed in hiding his real self from you for ever,—the strangeness essential to all perfect relationships between men" (CWB 193). As the outflowing current of the "theatre 'debordant'" turns inward, the ritual of fellow-feeling has preserved rather than eliminated the self's opacity, and the spectacular self-exposure has become a more ambivalent—though no less serious—dialectic of expression and concealment, proximity and distance, identity and masquerade.

Depersonalizing ecstasy, in Lewis's paradoxical formulation, preserves the strangeness of singularity.

In "A Breton Journal," at least, Lewis makes no attempt to reconcile his rhetoric of expenditure and expression with his no-less-insistent idiom of conservation and restraint. However, in "Les Saltimbanques," his first complete circus story (published originally in the August 1909 version of the *English Review*), he offers a more subtle anatomy of public feeling, here training his attention not on the affective bonds between participants but rather on the emotional dynamic between the performers and their public, which now includes the narrator as well as the peasants. The story begins as the narrator—seemingly indistinguishable from the young Lewis—encounters "a strolling circus troupe from Arles" on the road to its next performance (*CWB* 237). The show, just finished, has gone poorly, and the troupe's leaders, the *cornac* (French for "mahout" or "guide") and his wife, gripe bitterly of their inhospitable audience:

> [The performers'] spirits became sorer and sorer at the recreation and amusement that the public got out of their miserable existence. Its ignorance as to their true sentiments helped to swell their disgust. They looked upon the public as a vast beast, with a very simple but perverse character, differing from any separate man's, the important trait of which was an insatiable longing for their performances. For what man would ever go *alone* to see their circus, they might have argued? . . . The brute in us always awakens at the contact of a mob of people. When they set up their tent in a town, and opened to its multitudinous form this tabernacle dedicated to "the many-headed beast," they felt their anger gnawing through their reserve, like a dog under lock and key, yet maddened by this other brutal presence. . . . Whenever they met one of these monsters—which was on average twice a day—their only means of escape was by charming it with their pipes, which never failed to render it harmless and satisfied. Then they would hurry on, until they met another, when they would again play to it and flee away. (237–38)

It is tempting here to conflate the performers' contemptuous attitude toward "their long pilgrimage through this world inhabited by the public" with the narrator's, and thus with Lewis's own (CWB 237). But Lewis complicates a simple equivalence early on by signaling his narrator's recognition of the public's motives, which elude the circus troupe itself:

> The reflection that all these people parted with their sous for so little would be the only bright spot in the gloomy Adrien Brower of their minds. They that felt they were getting the better of them in some way. That the public

was paying for an idea, *for something that it gave itself,* did not occur to them, but that it was paying for the performance as seen and appreciated by them, the performers. For it is most difficult to realize the charm of something we possess. (238, my emphasis)

Keeping in mind the description of the orgies of fellow-feeling in the "Breton Journal," we might posit that the performers' narcissism blinds them from the crowd's investment in the show, which is, as Caffin hoped, the auratic spectacle of its own solidarity—the charming something it gave itself and which arises from its own energies.

The narrator's initial assuredness about the crowd's motives (and, thus, the performers' self-delusion) encourages sympathy with the cornac, who labors to get the crowd to take their seats. This frustrated effort, as the narrator sees it, stems from an utter miscalculation of feeling between performer and crowd, "they just as incomprehensible to him as he was to them" (CWB 239). While the showman's face is marred by "an expression of the bitterest disgust with his audience," they watched him with "glee and pride. . . . When he scowled, they gaped delightedly; when he coaxed they became grave and sympathetic" (238–39). So, the misfiring of sympathy between the showman and the public, in fact, generates another sympathetic exchange between the showman and the narrator. The more spectacularly the cornac, "fuming to entertain" the public, fails, the more the performer's authentic self, the "outraged expression that was the expression of his soul," becomes superficially legible for the narrator (239). This dynamic continues until, abruptly, a clown bursts through a wall of people and trips over the cornac's foot, causing the seats to fill "as by magic" (239). For the narrator, even more surprising than the crowd's receptivity to the Pierrot is the "truly astonishing" change in the cornac, whose once "lugubrious personage had woken to the sudden violence of a figure set in motion." Remarking on this abrupt metamorphosis, the narrator explains: "His nature is evidently subject to great extremes" (239).

An equally plausible explanation, and one the narrator can only countenance in passing, is that the performer's face is less a window to his soul than a mask that withholds or conceals his most intimate self. In fact, the narrator insists on the cornac's authenticity even while observing him "absorbed in briefly rehearsing to himself . . . the part he was to play" (CWB 239). Similarly, while he expresses throughout a familiarity with circus traditions, the narrator will nonetheless argue for the cornac's heroic abrogation of convention. Although he has ostensibly assumed the role of the "man who invents posers for the clown, wrangles with him, and against whom the laugh is always turned," the cornac's wild self-abandon allows him to respond to the clown's "stock wit" and "ready-made quips" with a "strange but genuine hilarity" and an "unmanageable vitality." During "the whole of the evening," the narrator rhapsodizes, "he was rather 'hors de son assiette'—hardly master of himself" (240–41). This showman, for the narrator, is a real eccentric. But the more the narrator asserts the showman's vital authenticity, the more Lewis hints at the opposite—that this self-expression is mere posturing. In this way, the cornac's nature is not riven by "extremes" that are publicly and pathetically exposed but rather (like the "hideous topers" at the Pardon) clothed in an elaborate typage, a system of codified roles with which the public is intimately familiar. Such a ritualistic typology would adopt any number of "garments of strangeness" (to borrow Lewis's language from "A Breton Journal") to better hide the real self from a ravenous public (193).

What Lewis juggles quite deftly in this story is his simultaneous attraction to the self-exposed physical sympathy and ecstatic communal feelings of Breton culture and his concern that such emotional abandon threatens the artist's integrity. He does so by creating, in the figure of the cornac, a showman artist whose public performance of typicality both encourages and checks sympathy; his mimesis shifts between distance and "a humorously aggressive participation in social ritual at the level of *surface* only."[39] The clear loser in Lewis's reformulation of the circus's economy of sympathy is the public, which is stripped of all traces of vitality but retains all of its stultifying mechanism. The problem with the public in "Les Saltimbanques" is not, as it is in "A Breton Journal," an "orgaic" participation in life that would risk subjective annihilation in an effusion of sympathy (for this is, at least, a reasoned volition) but rather its inability to "readily dissociate reality from appearance" and its mechanical, self-defeating submission to "the narrowest convention of habit" (CWB 241, 245). Thus, if "the clown and the manager consulted in an audible voice before cracking each joke, concocted it, in fact, in their hearing, they would laugh at it with the same fervour. . . . It would be a revolt against fate to criticize the amusements that Fate had provided for them, and it would be a sign of imminent anarchy in all things if they looked solemn while the clown was cracking a joke" (246).

And yet, it is from the crowd, "spiritually herded to their amusements as prisoners are served out their daily soup," that, in the story's final pages, a critical consciousness emerges, here in the form of a young boy in the front row who, near the conclusion of the performance, begins to jeer at the proprietor (CWB 245). This boy, who, the narrator avers, "had probably never thought comically before," was now experiencing "a sudden awakening, as though the comedy of existence had burst in upon his active young brain without warning, and, in the form and nature of this awkward showman, was now raging within him like a heady wine" (246–47). This is, to put it mildly, a strange place for such an epiphany—the boy's laugh, "apparently a spontaneous and personal action," countermands Lewis's critique of amusement as the typification and mechanization of vital human impulses (246). Is the showman's typage, then, merely the occasion for the mystical emergence of a critical voice, or, in fact, its most vital catalyst? Lewis's syntax in describing the boy's awakening suggests the latter—that something about the "form and nature" of the "awkward showman," bodying forth the comedy of existence, both forces itself into the boy's brain and demands to be mimed: a strategy of typage whereby character is externalized to defend interiority. This transfer of sensibility between showman and boy is only briefly acknowledged, but the language used to describe it connotes sensuous contact and possession even as it demands distance: the boy "had of a sudden opened his lips among the people and begun covering this man with his mockery. The showman prowled about the enclosure, grinning, and casting sidelong glances at his poet. His vanity was in some very profound and strange way tickled" (247). And yet, as soon as the mask drops (if it ever did), another one supplants it: "But his face would suddenly darken and he would make a rush at the inexplicable boy." Here, within the public scene of imitation, Lewis replaces the blind, centrifugal energies of eccentric feeling with the more guarded transmission of typage as a critical faculty. Now, two typecasters play with each other but remain mutually inexplicable.

Lewis's conceptual trick in these stories, then, is to domesticate eccentric feeling, or better, to square a certain mode of abstract being and feeling with an even more inalienable, individual eccentricity. Like "A Breton Journal," in which Lewis reconciles the typical pleasure of ecstasy with the strangeness of singularity, "Les Saltimbanques" bears out Lewis's early conviction that the "conventional, civilized abstraction of social life" in modernity had minted a form of sympathetic currency (*CWB* 224). In "Some Innkeepers and Bestre" (1909), Lewis analyzes this "kind of abstract factor in [man's] mind and self that is the equivalent of money, a kind of conventional, nondescript, and mongrel energy, that can at any moment be launched towards a friend and flood him up to the scuppers, as one might cram his pockets with gold" (223). This "artificial and characterless go-between, this common energy," is of keen interest to Lewis because it brokers a certain fellow-feeling while keeping "man's individual nature all the more inviolable and unmodified": "This is the modern man's ideal of realizing himself in others; that is, the *degree* of himself, and not the specific character, which is inalienable" (224). As Peter Nicholls has noted, with Lewis's celebration of this "characterless, subtle, protean social self of the modern man" whose "wit" and sympathies" are "the moneys of the mind" (*CWB* 224) comes a mimicry of "self-conscious play," but never self-expression.[40] The price of such feeling—made possible by reification under an abstracted socius—is a regrettable foreclosure of an intersubjectivity of "very self to very self": "Civilization has resulted in the modern man becoming, in his inaccessibility, more savage than his ancestors of the Stone Age" (*CWB* 224).

At the risk of understating matters, I want to stress that between the early publication of these stories and their revision in *The Wild Body* of 1927, the once-inviolable modern man had become, in Lewis's estimation, all too vulnerable. Threatened by the incursion of imitative desire into all spheres of modern life—in mass politics, sexual relations, consumer capitalism, advertising, fashion, and artistic radicalism—Lewis was forced to redefine not just the terms of sympathetic publicness and mimetic play but of his own avant-gardism. Following his devastating experience in World War I and the virtual cessation of his artistic production since the publication of *Tarr* (1918), Lewis disinterred himself in 1926, returning to London's literary and artistic scene with a series of infamous screeds, including *The Art of Being Ruled,* "Paleface," "The Revolutionary Simpleton," and *Time and Western Man.* In *The Art of Being Ruled,* Lewis savaged the "What the Public Wants Doctrine" of England's liberal democracy, which, in lockstep with the demands of scientific and capitalist progress, had turned people into mimetic machines who "ask nothing better than to be 'performing mice'" or "*types*—occupational types, social types, functional types of any sort" (*ABR* 127, 151). "Absence of responsibility, an automatic and stereotyped rhythm, is what men most desire for themselves," Lewis huffed, and they find this rhythm in their "group" or "type" life (class, sex, or racial affiliations), which they mistake for democratic self-expression:

> If a hundred [people] were observed "expressing" their "personality," all together and at the same time, it would be found that they all "expressed" this inalienable, mysterious "personality" in the same way. In short, it would be patent at once that they only had *one* personality between them to "express."
> ... It would be *a group personality* that they were "expressing"—a pattern imposed on them by means of education and the hypnotism of cinema, wireless, and the press. (130, 148, emphasis in original)

In Lewis's view, the goal of these proliferating group identities—and the various revolutions to which they are committed (the "sex war," "class war," "age war," and so on)—is to "standardize" and render docile the individual, "to get him to rub off (in the process of the 'expression') any rough edges that may remain from his untaught, spontaneous days" (149).[41] As Lewis surveyed a social field saturated with revolutionary rhetoric ("Every one today, in everything, is committed to revolution"), he became increasingly suspicious of all ideology and political action (17): the "social arena," Lewis felt, "would increasingly be filled with combatants, locked in continuous struggle," and effecting one "total but no less static Great War like the one in which Lewis had suffered a decade earlier."[42]

Again, in *Time and Western Man*, Lewis assailed these type identities for producing a rapturous fellow-feeling at the expense of the individual's erasure; gone is the former sense that collective energy might confirm the self (as in "A Breton Journal") under the garments of strangeness: "But no artist can ever love democracy or its doctrinaire and more primitive relative, communism. The emotionally-excited, closely-packed, heavily-standardized mass-units, acting in a blind ecstatic unison, as though in response to the throbbing of some unseen music—of the sovietic of fourierist fancy—would be the last thing . . . for the free democratic West to aim at" (26). In a related change of tack, if the "Wild Body" stories sentimentalized the imbrication of commerce and romance for producing liberating social sympathies, in "The Revolutionary Simpleton" and *Time and Western Man* "the moneys of the mind" had lost their animistic charm. In these blistering attacks on the cultural incursion of an infantile romanticism, Lewis recoiled from capitalism's romance of industry, which found its "pure expression" in the narcissistic self-enclosure of Advertisement: "The world in which Advertisement dwells is a one-day world. It is necessarily a plane universe, without depth. Upon this Time lays down discontinuous entities, side by side; each day each temporal entity, complete in itself, with no perspectives, no fundamental exterior reference at all" (*TWM* 12). Much to Lewis's horror, this romantic "time-mind"—spawned by Henri Bergson's "time-obsessed" philosophy and the timelessness of Einsteinian physics—had caught on and was thoroughly infecting not just advertising and science but modernism's most fashionable artists, including Charlie Chaplin, Anita Loos, Gertrude Stein, and James Joyce. In this social context, defined by the public saturation of typicality and the falsification of sympathy, Lewis goes back to the circus.

In "The Cornac and His Wife," Lewis's 1927 revision of "Les Saltimbanques," a dynamic of competition has firmly supplanted the more uncertain play of mimicry. Consider the following addition to the revision, whose narrator, Ker-Orr (now firmly aligned with the author himself), summarizes Lewis's changing appreciation of mimetic performance:

> I have described the nature of my own humour—how, as I said, it went over into everything, making a drama of mock-violence of every social relationship. Why should it be so *violent*—so mock-violent—you may at the time have been disposed to enquire? Everywhere it has seemed to be compelled to go into some frame that was always a simulacrum of mortal combat. Sometimes it resembled a dilution of the Wild West film, chaplinesque in its violence. Why always *violence*? . . . For my reply here I should go to the modern Circus or to the Italian Comedy, or to Punch. Violence is the essence of *laughter* (as distinguished of course from smiling wit): it is merely the inversion or failure of *force*. To put it another way, it is the *grin* upon the Deathshead. It must be extremely primitive in origin, though of course its function in civilized life is to keep the primitive at bay. But it hoists the primitive with its own explosive. It is a realistic firework, reminiscent of war. (*CWB* 101, emphasis in original)

Like Lewis's decision in the revised story to write "the Showman" and "the Public" with a capital S and P, this passage bespeaks the revision's incorporation into a more systematic theoretical frame, and one consistent with the tenor of his polemics of the late 1920s, which regularly metaphorized the modern as savage, the primitive as mechanical. Though Lewis will claim that this story, and all those in the "Wild Body" collection, are "studies of rather primitive peoples," the violent comedy of the savage body—as the references above to the "modern Circus," Charlie Chaplin, and Hollywood Westerns suggest—is also the anatomy of a reified modernity that has erased the distinction between the mechanical and the organic. The fascinating ambivalence of the showman's performance in "Les Saltimbanques" and the dialectic of self-exposure and concealment that his strategic role-playing embodied have been eliminated. Now, the strolling player illustrates Lewis's notion of a comic type, which in the theoretical essay "Inferior Religions" (1927) he defines as "a failure of a considerable energy, an imitation and standardizing of self, suggesting the existence of a uniform humanity,—creating, that is, a little host as like nine-pins; instead of one synthetic and various ego" (*CWB* 150–51). The cornac's "death struggle with his 'Public'" exemplifies one of modernity's "inferior religions": an elaborate civilized ritual that imposes a pattern on human existence, producing in its mechanical rhythm "the staid, everyday drunkenness of the normal real" (149).

The cornac's performance is not only newly moribund but a thoroughly economic exchange between performer and public loaded with sadism and mutual dread; these "little circuses" mark the degeneration of dialogue between performer and audience into a "dialogue between mimes, representing employer and employee" (*CWB* 96). Before mysterious and playful, the showman's "insane contortions" are now all work, as routinized and slavish to Fate as the peasants' consumption (91). Moreover, the feral struggle between producer and consumer of entertainment has short-circuited the ambivalent affective economy of the earlier version, severing the narrator from the showman. A "fierce reproach to the onlooker" (91), the cornac's role-playing is "the most unaccountable freak of personality" and his impromptu acrobatics less provocative: "I thought it appropriate to applaud" (97, 98). And, in perhaps the most remarkable revision, the cornac's contortions are figured as the contemptuous display of opacity, of a newly rigid boundary between self and Other: "The drama this time was an *internal* one, therefore.... We were invited to concentrate our minds upon what was going on *inside*. We had to visualize a colony of much-twisted, sorely-tried intestines, screwed this way and that, as they had never been screwed before. It was an anatomical piece. The unfortunate part was that that public could not *see* these intestines as they could see a figure in the air, and liable to crash" (99).

The showman's defiant self-exposure (if so it can be called) is another attempt to perform the nontypicality of personality within a mimetic-sympathetic public sphere that bedevils such singular acts, one that recalls both the impudent address of Eva Tanguay's mimetic performance for Caffin (secured by the commodity aura) as well as Bleackley's aggressive engagement with the music-hall herd ("I am here, you are there.... Look at me!"). As I have argued, such scenes tend to be marked by a confusion between being singularly impressive and being typically impressed, between auratic uniqueness and reproducibility as a mode of being that finds a likely analogy in the mechanical mimesis of visual technologies, themselves—in Benjamin's famous formulation—"the signature of a perception whose 'sense for sameness in the world' has so increased that, by means of reproduction, it extracts sameness even from what is unique" (WA 105). In Lewis's case, this scene of showmanship is similarly fraught with implication. It references his critique of the romantic "abdominal consciousness" of D. H. Lawrence in "Paleface": "'*The consciousness in the abdomen*' removes the vital centre into the viscera, and takes the privilege of leadership away from the hated 'mind' or 'intellect,' established up above the head."[43] It renews the terms of his famous definition of art in *Tarr*: "This is another condition of art; *to have no inside,* nothing you cannot see."[44] It anticipates the elaboration of his satirical method in *Apes of God* (1930): "The ossature is my favorite part of a living animal organism, not its intestines. . . . It is easier to achieve those polished and resistant surfaces of a great *externalist* art in Satire."[45] And, straining under the weight of its theoretical burden, the passage indicts the public's inability to see (its "tendency to shut the eyes to what is unpleasant, in favour of things arbitrarily chosen for their flattering pleasantness"), which the story attributes to the sensory degradations of routinized amusement in a fashion that marks Lewis's rethinking of the relationship between singularity of person, visuality, and mimesis (*TWM* 10).

For the peasant's blind intoxication with *the surface of things* is what finally differentiates him from the vision of "true social revolutionary": the peasant "looks at everything from the outside, reads the labels, and what he *sees* is what he has been told to see, that is to say, what he expects. . . . His contact with the quickest, most vivid, reality, if he is averagely endowed, is muffled, and his touch upon it strangely insensitive; he is surrounded by signs, not things" (*CWB* 102). Lewis's language of sensory depletion here makes clear that the theory of publicness elaborated in the circus story's revision is now fully in line with his trenchant anatomy of modernity's mimetic-sympathetic public sphere in *Time and Western Man,* in which visuality has become complicit with the reified rhythms of type-life. The "plane universe" of advertising and modern consumer capitalism—fetishistic, discontinuous, oblivious—has, for Lewis, dethroned the "crowning human sense, the visual sense" that alone produces "the sensation of overwhelming *reality*"; as a result, "our ideal, objective, world, which was wrought into a unity—the common ground of imaginative reality on which we all meet—is being destroyed in favor of a fastidious egoism, based on a disintegration of the complex unit of the senses, and a granting of unique privileges to vision, in its raw immediate and sensational sense" (392, 394). Further, what Lewis sees as the eye's modern transformation into a radically "*private* organ," one that participates in "the cutting up of the ideal, public, *one,* exterior, reality of human tradition, into manifold times and spaces," is aided and abetted by the visual technology of the cinematograph, "through which people are to be trained from infancy to regard the world as a *moving* picture. In this no 'object' would appear, but only states of an object": discontinuous, "direct, sensations, unassociated with any component of memory" (393, 394, 383, 384).[46]

In this theory of reified publicness—a reactionary formulation that anticipates, as it inverts, the utopian terms of Benjamin's "Artwork" essay—cinematographic perception, egoistic and sensational, is tantamount to blindness, a mockery of true subjectivity. Similarly, the hypnotic rhythms of public spectacle falsify the will, producing instead an involuntary mimesis of social behavior, an "aimless," "nonsensical" volition, the always-static "picture of a Will that just goes on for some reason 'objectifying' itself, resulting in the endless rigmarole in which we participate, and of which (*qua* Will) we are witness" (*TWM* 312). The early Lewis's investments in moments of eccentric feeling and potentially liberating collectivity—his sense that "we all shed our small skin periodically or are apt to sometime, and are purged in big being"—are now in lockstep with the more conservative formulations of modernist crowd psychology.[47] Thus, his curiosity about "mongrel social energy" is supplanted by anxiety about the unconscious "mob of the senses" of the crowd; primitive openness to ecstasy becomes inseparable from involuntary—because unseeing—identifications of mass politics, from "the blind ecstatic unisons" of democracy or communism (26). In short, the refurbished subject of Lewis' mass-mediated public sphere is now built along the lines of what Mark Seltzer calls the "mass in person," whose "inner experience" is marked by "the complete fusion with the mass at the expense of the individual."[48]

Against the blindness of reified sensation that defines the mimetic-sympathetic public sphere, Lewis will oppose a detached, intellectual vision that is also an alternative mode of publicness. Lewis underscores this distinction between the integrated sensory acuity of the detached observer and the "muffled" perception of insensitive mass in a crucial addition to the conclusion of "The Cornac and His Wife," which now ends: "There had been *two* Publics, however, this time. It had been a good show" (CWB 104). The "Two Publics," as he explains in *Rude Assignment,* are the low-brow "Majority Public" and the high-brow intellectual minority, those who "[persist] in employing their critical faculties" (*RA* 17). And the schism between them, which Lewis elsewhere lays "at the door of monopoly-capital and mass-production," as well as the generally "low quality of the herd," is troped in the cornac's anatomical piece, his final performance of typicality (23). Though Lewis would undoubtedly resent the connection, his circus showman's opacity to a public anesthetized by vulgar entertainment recalls D. H. Lawrence's judgment about circus spectatorship in the contemporaneous poem "When I Went to the Circus": "When modern people see the carnal body," and "displaying no personality, / modern people are depressed," there is "no gushing response, as there is at the film."[49] The difference, and it is crucial, is that Lewis's circus showman is illegible because the public is unable *truly* to see, while Lawrence's public can *only* see. Lewis's freakish acrobat is unsympathetic not because of his carnal interior, too vital for contemporary spectators, but for his deathly externality.

This public performance entails a bit of grotesquerie that Caffin would no doubt have found distasteful, disrupting as it does the vital currents of eccentric feeling. Lewis's showman is now against identification, his visceral center of sympathy steeled, his typage the deathly mimicry of Lewisian satire—an aesthetic of hardness, surface, and detachment that checks sympathy and assimilation, enacting a comedic aggression toward its object. There is, of course, a fair amount of self-loathing and self-pity in Lewis's increasingly pathetic mimic, whose intestines, however mangled, will not be publicly exposed. And yet what Lewis's narrator laments in the passage—even as it adumbrates the idiom of Lewis's external method—is not the public's ravenous consumption of the showman's interiority but rather its inability to get inside. Quite surprisingly, Lewis hangs onto the longing for corporeal sympathy that had marked his earliest sketches on Breton culture. And so, Lewis refuses to forsake entirely the narrative of critical awakening that reappears again in the person of the jeering boy. But where this transformation before took the form of an undeniable conversion (with showman as agent), here there is no hint of a sympathetic transfer between the boy and the showman; the awakening is more tentative, dubious, indeed, "unaccountable" (*CWB* 103).

To ascribe Lewis's fear of eccentric feeling and the nondifferentiation it entails to fascist paranoia, aristocratic disdain, or the hysteria of one of modernism's many besieged masculinities is a powerful temptation and no doubt merited in part. Such claims, though, risk overlooking Lewis's prescient hunch that eccentric feeling is, finally, the affective reflex of a mediated public sphere and its transformations of the human personality. Modernist romanticism, Lewis teaches us to recall, is always a mass-mediated romanticism. This is borne out in the way the emotional satisfactions and abstract pleasures of big being (the "monies of the mind") that Lewis enjoys in his vitalist phase are uncannily doubled by the broader abstraction of social life that is synonymous with capitalist modernity, or in the way "primitive" ecstasy is later understood as itself a production of the visual technologies of the modern that expropriate the self's emotional core, bending affect toward the reified discursive rhythms of modern life.

Of course, Lewis is not alone in this insight, although he sharpens it to the razor's edge of satire. With Caffin and Bleackley, Lewis offers an anatomy of mass-mediated publicness whose ecstatic operations I describe in the following chapters. If, as I have suggested, their work provides a tentative phenomenology of the social world, it is one that consistently troubles the jargon of expressivity that still dominates our understanding of modernism's monadic subject of feeling. This happens most obviously in this phenomenology's challenge to the notion of modern personality as an expressive or auratic uniqueness. Attempts to perform publicly the eccentricity of the self are instead confronted with its secondariness, with the self's infinite strangeness to itself that is at the heart of the photographic experience.[50] We see this in Caffin's and Lewis's awareness that the singular projection of modern personality is doubled by the romantic aura of advertising and in Bleackley's description of authentic mimicry as the presentation of an originality effect. Even more generally, we observe this in the way the mimetic performances described in this chapter—the manipulation of types of social persons—become more profound encounters with the condition of mass visuality, where the authenticity of personality is ratified over and against a differential system of images through which modern persons identify themselves within the expanding typologies of an increasingly heterogeneous social world.[51] In this world, as Lewis knew, the singularity of person is true because it is duplicated.

More subtly, this phenomenology challenges expressivity as a logic of the constitution of social, public, and political life and points to the more rhetorical, performative, and poetic dimensions of publicness I examine in this book. When Eliot calls Marie Lloyd an "expressive figure" of the lower class, or when Caffin explains that the plastic mimics are "but an expression" of what their creators want, or when Lewis sees his showman's public charmed by the spectacle of its own unity, they imply how such virtuosic figures in fact *constitute* the spectacular unity of the people rather than express some essence that preexists the moment of that public's coalescence. In this sense, behind Lewis's snide observation that groups of modern people "expressing their personality" are really expressing a "pattern imposed on them" by "the hypnotism of the cinema, the wireless, and the press" is a rather radical insight about the discursive production of popular identities through public (but empty) images of solidarity, a unity soldered by visual technology as well as the sympathetic currents coursing through the modern public sphere.[52] Free-floating affect—Lewis's "mongrel social energy" or Caffin's sympathetic vibrations—is the public itinerary of emotion that swirls around the perceived lacks in modernism's social world. This is politicized emotion insofar as it ministers to the political itself as, in Ernesto Laclau's terms, "the alienation of the essence of the social bond."[53] The phenomenologies of public life in the chapters that follow thus, in various ways, challenge expressivity as both a fiction of interiority and a lie about the immanence of communitarian being. Modernism's eccentric feelings, like its public worlds, are fundamentally improper, ecstatic at heart. In this fashion, mediated affect is the very fuel of modernism's poetic forms of public life, which, because they are never inevitable, are always changeable.

For Lewis, reified deadness is an engine of change. Like the strategies of imitation commented upon by Caffin and Bleackley, Lewisian typage responds directly to the sensory estrangement of the modern, one brought about, in Lewis's account, by capitalism's disintegration of unity of the senses. But whereas Caffin's humanism placed faith in the mime's sympathetic typology to revitalize an estranged sensorium, and Bleackley's aestheticism preached mimicry as a pedagogy of the senses that would distinguish and shield the mimic from an insensitive public, Lewisian typage, as it is transformed into the external method of satire and parody in the late 1920s, is doggedly inhuman, forgoing sympathetic mush. Like the body of his circus showman, it becomes sculptural, classical, cold: "There is a stiffening of Satire in everything good, of 'the grotesque' which is the same—the non-human outlook must be there (beneath the fluff and pulp which is all that is seen by the majority) to correct our soft conceit" (*SF* 48). As one critic has put it, if Lewis believed that dehumanization was the "chief diagnostic" of modern regimes of consumerism, abstraction, and reification, it was also "the chief remedy for Lewis: if the modern is to survive its own dehumanization, it must dehumanize further; it must take 'strangeness, surprise, and primitive detachment' to the limit."[54] This logic—no way out but through—returns us to Marcuse's celebration of the reified bodies of vaudeville, the circus, and burlesque. Lacking Marcuse's dialectical faith in the liberatory teleology instantiated by these thingly bodies, Lewis will aggressively reshape the social order, casting grotesque types "very near to the everyday aspect of things" but distorted enough to disrupt and expose the frozen complacency of daily life (*SF* 48). This mimetic excess, Lewis believes, will only appear "'grotesque' or 'distorted' . . . to those accustomed to regard the things of everyday, and everyday persons, through spectacles couleur-de-rose" (48). And those puppets, at least from Lewis, will get no sympathy.

2
Eccentric Types

WE ARE ECCENTRISM IN ACTION

1) Presentation—rhythmic wracking of the nerves
2) The high-point—the trick
3) The author—an inventor-discoverer
4) The actor—mechanized movement, not buskins but roller skates, not a mark but a nose on fire. Acting—not movement but a wriggle, not mimicry but a grimace, not speech but shouts. *We prefer Charlie's arse to Eleonora Duse's hands!*
5) The play—an accumulation of tricks. The speed of 1000 horse power. Chase, persecution, flight. Form—a divertissement.
6) Humped backs, distended stomachs, wigs of stiff red hair—the beginning of a new style of stage costume. The foundation—continuous transformation.
7) Horns, shots, typewriters, whistles, sirens—Eccentric Music. The tap-dance—start of a new rhythm.[1]

In *Time and Western Man,* Wyndham Lewis described the movement of his ideal political unit as "eccentric." By this he meant "unemotional" and "individualist," "a unit looser and more accidental, moving more freely than the ubiquitous drum-throb" of mass politics. This eccentric rhythm, Lewis hoped, would oppose the "method of mass-suggestion" of modernity's mimetic-sympathetic public sphere, where temporal sameness masqueraded as revolutionary novelty in the deathly rhythms joining capitalist industry, democracy, and communism (26). But, as the manifesto above suggests, eccentricity also names the pulse of Americanization as it is experienced disjunctively and on a global scale. For "eccentric" is a term of art for Russian circus performers, a synonym for the artists' "trick" (*tryuk*), and "Eccentrism" the *nomme de guerre* of an overlooked Soviet avant-garde of the early 1920s that promoted an illogical performance style modeled on the physicality of circus stunts, the frenetic rhythm of American melodramas and detective thrillers, and the cultural irreverence of Chaplin's ass. In 1921, the original eccentrics—Grigory Kozintsev, Leonid Trauberg, Sergei Yutkevich, and Georgi Kryzhitsky—founded FEKS, the "factory of the eccentric actor," a theater workshop in Petrograd devoted to cultivating a gag-based mode of performance suited to the erratic tempo of modernity: "For the actor—from emotion to the machine, from anguish to the trick. The technique—circus. The psychology—head over heels. For the director—a maximum of devices, a record number of inventions, a turbine of rhythms."[2] Mixing the modernolatry of the futurists' "Variety Theatre" manifesto with a Formalist assault on automatized perception and its naturalistic props, Eccentrism's embrace of popular performance exemplified the Soviet avant-garde's "cult of Americanism": its enthusiastic response to Taylorist strategies of industrial organization in the postrevolutionary drive toward economic stability sparked by the New Economic Policy.[3] If, as another manifesto concludes, "the Americanisation of the Theatre in Russian means ECCentriSM," then this process would mean a chancy philosophy of modernity.[4] For the Eccentrists and others, modernity was not simply disenchanted or, in Lewis's narrative, the deadly reification of sensation but primarily physical, exteriorized, and maximally eventful. To exploit modernity's eccentricity means to see it as a bag of tricks, to pull a gag against the routinization of modern experience and specifically against the somber interiority of bourgeois psychology.

For the young Sergei Eisenstein, then in the thrall of Vsevolod Meyerhold, Eccentrism's externalizing approach to emotion fit nicely with Meyerhold's own biomechanical acting technique, itself built on the rationalized scientific principles of Taylorist labor management and the participatory theatricality of the circus and the commedia dell'arte. Eisenstein was introduced to FEKS by Yutkevich, whom he met at Meyerhold's acting workshops. In the summer of 1922, according to Trauberg, Eisenstein "belonged" to the group, and with Yutkevich, Eisenstein formulated his first major theoretical work, "The Montage of Attractions" (1923), published while he was working on *The Wiseman,* his highly Eccentrist Proletkult stage adaptation of A. N. Ostrovsky's classic Russian drama *Enough Simplicity in Every Wise Man* (1868). Here, Eisenstein would famously define the "attraction" as *"any aggressive movement in theatre, i.e., any element of it that submits the audience to emotional or psychological influence, verified by experience and mathemati-*

cally calculated to produce specific emotional shocks in the spectator in their proper order within the whole. These shocks provide the only opportunity of perceiving the ideological aspect of what is being shown, the final ideological conclusion."[5] The attraction, in this formulation, serves to maximize the affective eventfulness of the theatrical and, later, the cinematic experience. Yet Eisenstein insists that the attraction "has nothing in common with the stunt" or "the trick." Indeed, he believes it is "high time that this much abused term was returned to its rightful place": the trick is "only one kind of attraction," and "in so far as the trick is absolute and complete *within itself* it means the direct opposite of the attraction, which is based exclusively on something relative, the reactions of the audience."[6] In this distinction between the attraction and the eccentric trick lies the terms of Eisenstein's dissent from both Eccentrism and Formalism. While for Viktor Shklovsky, the eccentric trick is in fact the primary material of cinema, the ground of its function as a medium of defamiliarization, for Eisenstein, the trick's singular eventfulness is complemented by the structure of the attraction, which relates it to the audience and bends its affects toward their proper order within the ideological whole.[7] The attraction's discursively oriented emotional force, we might say, tames the trick's raw affect. The attraction is domesticated eccentricity, structured contingency.

Eccentricity, in the context of Americanization, is thus a potent figure of what Mary Ann Doane has recently dubbed the "lure of contingency" in capitalistic modernity—the possibility of "a resistance to system, to structure, to meaning," the promise, and threatening nonsense, of rationalization's outside troped above by Charlie's backside.[8] Doane claims that this lure waxes with the "vicissitudes of the affective," in which figures of contingency, promising "a vast reservoir of freedom and free play," become "highly cathected sites of both pleasure and anxiety."[9] Anticipating this argument is Walter Benjamin's utopian description of the eccentric's emotional work, which dislocates feeling from monadic inwardness through a kind of "negative expressionism": "Eccentrics—clown and natural peoples—overcoming of inner impulses and the body centre. New unity of clothes, tattoos and body. Promiscuity of clothing of man and woman, of arms and legs. Dislocation of shame. Expression of true feeling: desperation, dis-location. Consequential search for deep possibilities for expression: the man, who has the chair he is sitting on pulled away from him, and stays sitting—Genderlessness, complete disintegration of vanity."[10]

The investments of Benjamin and Eisenstein make for an odd pair here since the filmmaker is generally understood to have no truck with the sort of dislocated, ungendered affect celebrated in the passage above. In fact, Eisenstein's very modernism inheres, so the story goes, in the capacity of his montage technique to tool emotion into revolutionary activity with ever greater systematicity and control. In this chapter, I argue that Eisenstein's interest in the kind of undomesticated feeling described by Benjamin and Doane has been overshadowed—like most of the filmmaker's erotic investments—by his critical reputation as a tactician of totality, a technician of public sentiment, pummeling the masses into orchestrated action with every blow of his cine-fist. To recover this more *eccentric* Eisenstein—playful, excessive, and erotically undone by emotion—I consider the wider resonance of eccentric feeling in Eisenstein's mimetic politics. My argument, in short, is that while Eisenstein's work and thought is surely invested in a dogmatic form of political organization predicated on the mechanical reproduction of feeling, and with it of an organic political order, we can also discern a nonpurposive mode of understanding emotion that unlinks affect from predetermined modes of social and political organization. While the more familiar work of Eisenstein's mimetic politics domesticates chance, the more eccentric activity I track turns to ecstasy to imagine a politics of contingency and potential, an erotic politics that is central to Eisenstein's queerness.

I pursue this argument in what follows by placing eccentricity in a broader relationship with the idea of abstraction in the filmmaker's thinking of emotion: in his early mechanistic theories of performance; in *Strike* (1925), his first film; and in the broader evolution of his typological thought—his complex investment in the affective and political potential of generalizability and abstraction. In this sense, I explore Eisenstein's promiscuous typological imagination as a counterexample to the mimetic politics of Wyndham Lewis, whose late response to the imperatives of public sphere was aggressive ossification, an unfeeling adaptation to modernity's reified public world. By contrast, the engine of Eisenstein's politics throbs with emotional fuel. But his early work is uniquely dependent upon the same principles of mimetic-sympathetic contagion and on the manipulation of affect's visual transmission as a technology of political interpellation. In fact, Eisenstein is perhaps modernism's best theorist of the same mechanistic visual economy that so disturbs Lewis and is embodied, for him, in "the blind ecstatic" unions of communist mass politics. Moreover, the success or failure of Eisenstein's mimetic politics—the ability of film and theater both to bind political affiliation through affect and to imagine the formal contours of political belonging itself—depends on a relationship between eccentricity and abstraction, particularity and typicality, that shifts alongside his conception of mimesis.

Eccentricity is a tricky figure at the crossing of political, erotic, and formal domains: it signifies both the contingency that destabilizes organic political unity and the undomesticated particularity, repeatedly coded as erotic deviance, that frustrates the smooth reproduction of public feeling.

The utopian potential of eccentric feeling in Eisenstein's thought is always bound to the problem of emotion's mimesis, to what Benjamin called affect's potential for mimetic innervation.[11] And here, for Benjamin, lies the redemptive potential of modernity's quintessential eccentric, Charlie Chaplin, whose dislocated movement "dissects the expressive movement of human beings into a series of minute innervations."[12] In doing so, Chaplin both internalizes the very eventfulness—the trick structure—of the cinematic medium itself and offers an allegory of an enabling mimetic incorporation of modern technology. Hansen observes the conceptual debt that Benjamin's "two-way" notion of innervation owes to Soviet acting theory, specifically to Eisenstein's theories of biomechanics and expressive movement, which hope to produce spectatorial affect through the motoric stimulation of the actor. Yet the linchpin for emotion's mimesis in Eisenstein's early career is not the eccentric's dislocated eventfulness but rather the abstracting force of organic typage, the "attractionness of movements," which entails the actor's deft management of expressive eccentricity. Throughout this chapter, I mean to expand the definition of typage—the Soviet avant-garde's term for an external, stylized, and easily recognizable form of characterization designed to challenge bourgeois individualism while concretizing abstract social practice—to encompass the broader theoretical place of abstraction and generalization in Eisenstein's thought. It is only after Eisenstein reformulates typage, later in his career, as a kind of sensual mimesis that a truly ex-centric form of innervation emerges: here, emphatically *not* in Chaplin's moralizing sentimentality but in the eccentric's ecstatic "overcoming of inner impulses and body centre" in a radical, noninstrumental model of affect liberated from the rigid types of political and erotic being and at play within the technological horizon of Americanization.

Expressive Movements, Mimetic Theater

The early shape of Eisenstein's typological thinking emerges in the theories of performance he developed while immersed in the radical Soviet theater of the early 1920s. From Meyerhold, master of the Left theater and Eisenstein's avowed "second father," the young montageur inherited not just a love of the circus and the commedia dell'arte but also his mentor's biomechanical system of actor training. In his "Notes on Biomechanics," Eisenstein describes Meyerhold's technique in these dichotomous terms: "Stanislavsky . . . followed the psychological teachings of the vitalists. Meyerhold followed the teachings of the mechanists-materialists. Biomechanics was earlier considered in connection with man's spiritual life. Only later did it remain exclusively as the training of man's physical life."[13] Presumably, then, Meyerhold's system is "materialist" because it shares what Joseph Roach describes as the governing ideological assumption of Soviet behaviorism: that "external conditions determine human nature and that objectively controlled manipulation of the physical environment will alter the inward man."[14] In this sense, as Alma Law and Mel Gordon have it, biomechanics was one of many "systematic approaches to train the actor in [a] new eccentric, Constructivist theatre," a description that nicely encapsulates biomechanics' counterintuitive merger of expressive vitality and psycho-physiological control, eccentricity and technique.[15]

On one level, of course, this union is by now familiar insofar as "Eccentrism" itself operated in postrevolutionary Russia as a potent metaphor for the performative possibilities heralded by Americanization and Taylorism: "From emotion to the machine, from anguish to the trick. The technique—circus. The psychology—head over heels" (FFF 10). At the same time, the performance theories Eisenstein elaborates from a Meyerholdian model occasionally reflect an odd tension between will and instinct that troubles their materialist origins. Moreover, this tension, which threatens to compromise a behaviorist model of affect that would move unproblematically from the outside inward, from corporeal movement to mechanically provoked emotion, is only finally controlled by more technique—here in a theory of affective mimesis that hinges on a typology of movement designed to manage, rather than enable, expressive eccentricity.

Consider, in particular, the related series of loosely Meyerholdian essays that coalesce under Eisenstein's theoretical rubric "expressive movement": "Expressive Movement" (1923), co-authored with Sergei Tretyakov; "The Montage of Film Attractions" (1924); and his later "Lecture on Biomechanics" (1935).[16] As a concept, expressive movement allows Eisenstein to surpass Meyerhold's insufficiently theorized biomechanical model by systematizing the "attractionness" of physical movements, that is, the "quality of these movements to evoke in the spectator a predetermined reaction, to create an impression (the attraction potential of movements)" (EM 184). Importantly, the "attractionness" of an expressive movement increases in direct proportion to its organic nature: "[T]he most expressive, the most attractive moment is one which flows according to natural and organic norms" (LB 206). To be an "attraction," an actor's movement must simultaneously be organic, stemming therefore from an inner, unwilled affect, "respond[ing] to the tendency of instinct," as well as thoroughly constructed, "achieved by the artificial mechanical setting in motion of the body as a whole and must in no way result from the emotional state of the performer."[17] Put another way, the success of expressive movement depends on the actor feeling both inside and outside at once, or, more precisely, of experiencing an affect instinctual enough to produce organic movement but not so interiorized as to constitute an "emotional state." In this relentlessly externalizing performative system, movement's affect burns clean; swiftly converted to organic movement, it leaves no distasteful emotional residue for the audience to experience.

The engine of this non-experiential affective system is mimesis, as filtered through William James's and Theodor Lipps's physiological accounts of emotion and empathy, respectively. As a form of affective mimicry, in which the spectator's physiological imitation of the actor's (organically correct) motion produces the desired emotion, expressive movement's aim is, Eisenstein insists, "not for the 'sincerity' of an actor's movement, but for its imitative, mimical infectiousness" (EM 187).[18] Here, the space of public performance becomes a site of mimetic contagion, a notion that depends not just on physiological theories of affect but also on Eisenstein's familiarity with group psychology's accounts of the emotional susceptibility of crowds: "In the first place, in collective work there is present an infective emotional interaction. . . . The more participants in an exercise, the stronger is the manifestation of individuality. . . . The effect of a mass of people on each performer increases the organic resistance to conscious impulse" (184–85). But rather than threatening to subsume individuality within the mass, the surrender to instinct within a crowded theater is, for Eisenstein, the very trigger of "individuality" understood as the surfacing of an underlying organic unity, itself secured by the contagiousness of public, expressive movement.

Given such an understanding of movement's mimicry, Eisenstein continues, "there is no more need for an actor's emotional experiencing of type, image, character, feeling, situation, since as the result of expressive movement by the actor, the emotional experiencing is transferred where it belongs, specifically to the auditorium" (EM 185). Thus, Eisenstein takes issue not with the *fact* of emotional experience exactly but with its *site,* which should be properly public, visualized rather than interiorized: "For the actor, there remains the work, completely analogous to the work of the circus performer or the athlete . . . and the objective is expressive movement as a factor of *vi-*

sually perceived emotion" (187, my emphasis). And as the actor's montage of "purely organic" movements produces "the *visual* effect of the emotion apparently experienced," this visualizing of emotion aims not for the audience's analysis of affect (as in the Brechtian gestus) but for its compulsive, physiological mimicry within the public scene. Thus, the performative scene of mimesis amounts to a constructivist processing, the actor's "*real, primarily physical* work on their material—the audience," and is not to be confused with the "really shameful methods of experiential schools of acting" (MFA 51, emphasis in original).

In sum, at this stage in Eisenstein's thinking, the reproduction of emotion depends upon mimicry, which depends upon gestural or motor organicity, which in turn depends upon various models of performative typicality: or, to use the terminology of these essays, on whether the actor's movements are "characteristic," and whether the character presented is "convincing," that is, socially legible and predictable, or in Eisenstein's words, "a character one could meet" (LB 206). As a result, unorganized or otherwise "unorganic gestures," insofar as they threaten to short-circuit the public reproduction of emotion, are consistently devalued. Thus, Eisenstein's belief that "all forms of tics, convulsive twitchings, aimless movements invoke a feeling of revulsion"; thus, his warning that "exaggerated movements, ceasing to fit into an organic schema, would have the effect of pathological grimaces (precisely because of the inorganic character of their origin")" (EM 192; MFA 49–50). Insofar as organic movement always portends organic sociality—and conversely, insofar as inorganic gesture implicates a pathologically differentiated socius— the terms of Eisenstein's mimetic theater point to the limits of his mimetic politics, which entail both a repudiation of the Meyerholdian grotesque as a privileged figure for transformation and heterogeneity as well as a version of typage as relentless abstraction, the rigid management of expressive and motor eccentricity through the forceful application of the general organic rule. In other words, this theater, and this politics, can't face change, or better, can only see the unpredicted tic as an enervating grimace.

Eccentricity Happens

Strike, Eisenstein's first feature film, is also his most explicitly eccentric, a dazzling display of antic performance (circus clowning, expressive movement, and theatrical grotesquerie) and formal trickery (superimpositions, double-exposures, shifting frame dimensions, and hyperactive irises and dissolves).

Tonally eclectic, *Strike*'s formal playfulness and often comedic theatricality are marshalled toward the monumental actuality of revolutionary content and aims. Based on the 1903 strikes at Rostov-on-the-Don and conceptualized as part of a seven-part film cycle entitled Toward the Dictatorship of the Proletariat, *Strike* anatomizes the germination of collective action, its complex surveillance within modern networks of power, and its final, violent repression. Thus, part of *Strike*'s strangeness lies in its mixture of fantastic circus matériel and revolutionary material, an eccentric hybridity that blurs what Jay Leyda calls two broader "poles of attraction" in Eisenstein's career, "the discovery of reality and the appeal of the circus."[19] As Ivor Montagu puts it,

> these two aspects of his career are apparent in every foot of *Strike*. On the one hand, here and there, actual material is arranged with economy and laconism into a realism poignant in its universality; on the other, the fantastic clowning of the circus shows itself in detail everywhere, and in the exaggerated, even hypertrophied, treatment of particular episodes and the plot in general. The twisting of actual material, with an ironic air of naturalism, to express such fanciful, exaggerated, "propaganda-poster" ideas, works often with a confusing, indeed, shattering effect on the spectator that must have delighted the young Eisenstein.[20]

While Montagu aptly characterizes the bewildering affective yield of *Strike*'s experimentalism, his certainty about Eisenstein's presumed delight in it is puzzling. At this stage in his career, Eisenstein would seem to have no truck with emotional confusion or for the cognitive dispersal of "shattering effects." Rather, as Eisenstein insists in his theoretical essays roughly contemporaneous with the film, *Strike* marks the "first instance of revolutionary art where the form has turned out to be more revolutionary than the content"; and the desideratum of revolutionary form is not confusion but control.[21] A kind of strategic stuntwork, *Strike*'s formal theatricality aspires to the mimetic "magnetism of theatre, circus, and cinema"—it aims precisely for that constructivist processing of the audience theorized in the expressive movement essays (MFA 35). Here, through a newly cinematic "montage of film attractions"—that "series of blows to the consciousness and emotions of the audience"—Eisenstein will give the audience "*real* satisfaction (both physical and moral) as a result of *fictive* collaboration with what is being shown (through motor imitation of the action by those perceiving it and through psychological 'empathy')" (35). And the action *Strike* submits for mimetic reproduction is the "technique of the Bolshevik underground," properly "historical-revolutionary material" from the "*'manufactured' past* of contemporary revolutionary reality . . . for the first time treated from a correct *point of view:* its characteristic movements were investigated as stages in a single process from the point of view of its 'manufacturing' essence" (PMA 55, 53). Tellingly, Eisenstein tropes the very form of *Strike* as a filmic "expressive movement," a skillful play between the characteristic movements of the event and its organic essence. As in theatrical expressive movements, *Strike's* aims are at once affective, pedagogical, and mimetic: an emotional seizure of his audience that would communicate specific technologies of revolt and repression while producing a successful mimesis of revolutionary activity and its engine, unity.

Firmly located at the vexed convergence of modernist Formalism and documentary actuality, *Strike's* aesthetics anticipate the vital, dialectical movement between formal defamiliarization and the "priority of raw material"—"low" social contents—soon to be called for in Shklovsky's 1927 "Symposium on Soviet Documentary."[22] Yet they drift, as Eisenstein notes, toward an imbalance between form and actuality that subsumes the latter in deviant theater, a "flotsam of rank theatricality" as he put it in his later essay "Through Theatre to Cinema" (1934), written under the pressure of the reigning aesthetic of socialist realism.[23] In this sense, the terms of Eisenstein's retrospective dismissal of *Strike* in "Through Theatre to Cinema" resonate powerfully with the aesthetic theory of his Marxist contemporaries like Georg Lukács, for whom the eccentric particularity that joins naturalism and modernism is both pathological and perverse. Indeed, the language of Lukács's infamous screed "The Ideology of Modernism" (1958) suggests a way of reading Eisenstein's repudiation of eccentricity as a disavowal of the relationship between particularity and erotic deviance, even as it offers a means of understanding the erotics of distortion and abstraction in Eisenstein's work, the way Eisenstein will come to figure queer desire as an ecstatic liberation from the strictures of the realistic-typical. A late attempt to salvage socialist realism from degenerating into doctrinaire propaganda, Lukács's argument is structured by a central distinction between realism and modernism on the basis of the relationship between the eccentric detail and the socially typical: "In realist literature the descriptive detail is both *individual* and *typical.* Modern allegory and modernist ideology, however, deny the *typical.* By destroying the coherence of the world, they reduce detail to the level of mere particularity (once again, the connection between modernism and naturalism is plain)."[24] Modernist particularity, for Lukács, is a paltry thing: its *mere-ness* lies in its "arbitrariness," in the absence of a "hierarchy of significance," that "fusion of the particular and the general that is the essence of realist art" and that realism realizes in properly typical characters through whom the organic, evolutionary totality of history courses and is made concrete (*RT* 34, 45). For Lukács, then, the organicity of realist typicality entails the proper structuring of particularity without which history and human action are devoid of meaning.

Importantly, Lukács's critique of modernist detail is underwritten by a developmental heteronarrative, a story of human potentiality and change in which modernism's cultivated eccentricity is pathologically queer. Whereas the worldview of realism is "dynamic and developmental," reflecting the human's proper ontology as "*zoon politikon*," always located within his social and historical environment, modernism's is "static and sensational" (*RT* 19). Modernist man is an "ahistorical being," confined by an enervating subjectivism that mistakes "abstract potentiality"—Lukács's term for the imagined possibilities for action and being, hatched in the prison house of inwardness—for "concrete potentiality," the latter concerned with "the dialectic between the individual's subjectivity and objective reality" and the "interaction of character and environment" realized in the heroic action and choices of typical realist characters (21, 24). The "psychopathology" of modernist "stasis" and "impotence" is, for Lukács, most obvious in the characterological peculiarities of, to use Lukács's overdetermined example, Robert Musil's Moosbrugger, "a mentally-retarded sexual pervert with homicidal tendencies" (31). Realist individuals maintain a normative "polarity" between "the eccentric and the socially-average" that "serves to increase our understanding of social normality," while modernism's "fascination with morbid eccentricity"—and here Musil's Moosbrugger is typical—is held "to exhaust human potentiality" (31). Musil, like Henry de Motherlant, Samuel Beckett, and Gottfried Benn, adopt sexual "perversity and idiocy as types of the *condition humaine*," yoking perversity to primitivism and leading "straight to the glorification of the abnormal and to an undisguised anti-humanism" that culminates in a perverse vision of the world in terms of style (32):

> A typology limited in this way to the *homme moyen sensuel* and the idiot also opens the door to "experimental" stylistic distortion. Distortion becomes as inseparable a part of the portrayal of reality as the recourse to the pathological. But literature must have a concept of the normal if it is to place distortion correctly; that is to say, to see it *as* distortion. With such a typology this placing is impossible, since the normal is no longer the proper object of literary interest. Life under capitalism is, often rightly, presented as a distortion (a petrification or paralysis) of the human substance. But to present psychopathology as a way of escape from this distortion is itself a distortion. . . . Distortion becomes the normal condition of human existence; the proper study, the formative principle, of art and literature. (33)

In this paranoid vision of modernism, eccentric particularity, sexual perversity, imagination, and style become co-conspirators in a universal distortion of the human condition. Refusing to develop or to produce and reproduce in a fashion proper to the human substance, modernism is thus locked in a deathly stasis, forever failing to realize its concrete potentiality.

This is to say that for a highly influential strand of Marxist aesthetic theory, modernism's eccentricity is modernism's queerness, the excessive particularity of both refusing hierarchic structure, drifting toward meaninglessness, and worrying the organic course of human development. If Lukács's critique codifies the threat of eccentricity, the emblematic site of its perverse potential might be Roland Barthes's "The Third Meaning" (1970), an essay that turns to Eisenstein *because* of the filmmaker's putatively dogmatic semantics of revolution ("Eisensteinian meaning devastates ambiguity"), appropriating precisely those excessive details—revealed in the still—that Lukács disparages for their nondevelopmental particularity.[25] Dispatching the obvious meaning of the images bound to "Eisensteinian realism and decorativism," Barthes reads perversely, touchingly, fetishistically for the obtuse level of meaning that emerges in the "penetrating trait," the radical contingency of unstructured meaning freed in the interruption of narrative and ideological sequence, in the stalling of meaning's "complete system of destination" (TM 57, 54). This is, in Robert Ray's words, "fetishism as epistemology," a *détournement* of fetishism's more familiar guise in Karl Marx and Freud as "knowledge's opposite, as a means of false consciousness and disavowal," and a return to "its origins in passion."[26] In Barthes's terms, the "certain *emotion*" carried by the third meaning is doubly eccentric: highly particular, it "simply *designates* what one loves, what one wants to defend: an emotion-value, an evaluation," and it is marshalled in the service of erotic polysemy, of the pleasures of the signifier's "perpetual erethism, desire not finding issue in that spasm of the signified which normally brings the subject voluptuously back into the peace of nominations" (TM 59, 62, emphasis in original).

If, in Lukács, the lack of meaning embodied by the eccentric detail mocks action, Barthes's obtuse meaning cruises in erotic drift: "Opening out into the infinity of language," it "belongs to the family of pun, buffoonery, useless expenditure. Indifferent to moral or aesthetic categories (the trivial, the futile, the false, the pastiche), it is on the side of carnival" (TM 55). And such luxuriant expenditure, Barthes notes, "does not *yet* belong to today's politics but nevertheless *already* to tomorrow's," which is to say it is firmly linked to the politics of what Lukács calls abstract potentiality, of the possibilities for being and acting freed in the imaginative space of the signifier (62–63).

The burden of semantic and political reproduction lifted ("it does not copy anything"), the third meaning denatures and distorts realism, which is to say it camps, blurring "the limit separating expression from disguise, but also [allowing] that oscillation—an elliptic emphasis, if one can put it like that, a complex and extremely artful disposition" (57). If I am reading Barthes and Lukács too willfully here, I do so because they effectively demarcate the continuum of values born by "eccentricity" in Eisenstein's thought, linking it to vagrant eros and to contingency's perverse role in mimetic politics. Even *Strike,* as we'll see, is torn between the erotics of emotional and political control and the more chancy pleasures of disguise and distortion—the drifting and blunting of identity and its equally voluptuous release from political nomination. However latent in the film, this tendency, what we might call Eisenstein's erotics of incipience, is in fact central to the film's treatment of political potentiality, its ability to imagine and enact "a temporality," in Bill Nichols's words, "that is not linear in arrangement nor teleological in progression but contingent and transformative, rich with potential for excess that could be called *aufhebung,* or reality transforming."[27]

In this frame, the erotic trajectory of Eisenstein's developmental narrative, "Through Theater to Cinema," is positively Freudian. The essay's unfavorable appraisal of *Strike* hinges upon its central opposition between cinema and theater, one that entails a series of interlocking distinctions: between "'events' themselves," the domain of the "purely cinematographic element" secured by the shot's indexicality, and "'reactions to events'—which is a purely theatrical element" (TC 6); between theater's "illusionistic scenery" and cinema's realism; between "real doing" and "pictorial imagination"; between "material-practical and fictitious-descriptive principles" (8). The distinction is canny, allowing Eisenstein retrospectively to renarrate his career as a gradual, organic movement from the polymorphously perverse eddies of jejune style to the normative current of socialist realism. So, for example, his early work in Proletkult theater witnesses the incipient growth of the cinematographic element—the inclusion of the "actual-materialistic element" in theater not through "illusionary acting" but rather from "the physical fact of acrobatics" and the staging of factual events. And conversely, his work in film evinces a bending of the theatrical element toward cinematic factuality (7)—thus, Eisenstein's anxiety about the rank theatricality of a technique like typage and his insistence that "the typage tendency," which "may be rooted in theater," can grow "out of the theater into film . . . as an indicator of definite affinities to real life through the camera" (9).

For Eisenstein and others in the Soviet avant-garde, the theatricality of typage stemmed from its origins in the seven stock figures of the commedia dell'arte. Typage's theatricality, which is everywhere on display in *Strike's* stereotyped social world, can therefore be yoked to the real so long as it includes "a specific approach to the events embraced by the content of the film," so long as it adopts "the method of least interference with the natural course and combination of events" (TC 7–8).[28] Provided it does not distort, typage can be calibrated toward organicity. The enervating theatricality that Eisenstein now understands to be inorganic, lacking the "vital element" of story and plot, at the time "seemed natural," of a piece with the typological imperative itself:

> We brought collective and mass action onto the screen, in contrast to individualism and the "triangle" drama of the bourgeois cinema. Discarding the individualist conception of the bourgeois hero, our films of this period made an abrupt deviation—insisting on an understanding of the mass as hero.
>
> No screen had ever before reflected an image of collective action. . . . But our enthusiasm produced a one-sided representation of the masses and the collective; one-sided because collectivism means the maximum development of the individual within the collective, a conception irreconcilably opposed to bourgeois individualism. Our first mass films missed this deeper meaning. Still I am sure that for its period this deviation was not only natural but necessary. (TC 16–17)

The metaphorics of this crucial passage are striking. Naive typage—the presentation of the proletariat as a non-individuated collectivity posed against bourgeois interiority—is a one-sided deviation, a superficial swerve of the cinematic art's petulant youth. Mature typage is thus "typical" in the Lukácsian sense: it understands the development of the individual within the collective as a deeply meaningful, natural telos that retroactively subsumes all prior, wayward perversions as so many developmental necessities. Interestingly, this distinction demands certain adjustments to the concept of eccentricity itself. There are, it seems, two kinds of eccentricity: one, the enervating, distorting, queer eccentricity that monkeys with unity and political reproduction and is associated with *Strike's* "flotsam of rank theatricality"; the other, a properly innervating eccentricity that Eisenstein associates with the acuity of montage, in which one film fragment, joined with another, "suddenly acquires and conveys a sharper and quite different meaning than that planned" (TC 10). And so, "in the midst of the flood of eccentricity in [his stage production] *The Sage* . . . we can find the hints of a sharply expressed montage" in which what "was most interesting was *the extreme sharpness of the eccentricity not torn from the context of this part of the play;* it never became comical just for comedy's sake, but stuck to its theme, sharpened by its scenic embodiment" (9, 10, my emphasis).

Such eccentricity, it seems, just happens. But this happening, growing out of the seeds of Eisenstein's love of popular performance, is an event less of errant, unstructured contingency than organic need: "The music-hall element was obviously needed at the time for the emergence of a 'montage' form of thought. Harlequin's parti-colored costume grew and spread, first over the structure of the program, and finally into the method of the whole production" (TC 12). As Eisenstein's metaphors suggest, this is an eccentricity fully compatible with organic unity, and this "uninterrupted unity between the collective and the milieu that creates the collective" cannot be forced "by trickery or double-exposure or mechanical intersection," as it was in *Strike's* superimposition of "man onto images of buildings—all an attempt to interrelate man and milieu in a single complicated display" (14–15). Neither can it be finessed by theatrical mise-en-scène, which forever falls short of "fusing stage and audience in a developing pattern" (15). This fantastic formulation of eccentricity bears the clear markings of what David Bordwell calls Eisenstein's "epistemological shift," in which "a materialist dialectic yields to a more idealist one" and the conflicts of reflexological montage are synthesized into a harmonic, organic unity in which the artwork, now a "feelingful whole," affords "a glimpse of the future unity of the individual and the collective."[29] Bordwell dates the shift around 1930, but as my discussion of the expressive movement essays indicate, this organicism is already manifest in the early 1920s, where it is inextricably linked to a materialist, reflexological mimesis that must also domesticate eccentricity. As in the earlier essays, "Through Theatre to Cinema" attempts to square typage and organicity, thereby securing affective mimesis. Provided it does not distort, typage can become as organic as an eccentricity purged of its queer theatricality. A corollary logical assumption, then, is that *Strike* fails because its typage interferes—its eccentricity is of the enervating sort, maximizing distortion, and troubling the mimetic-organic work of the film's natural course.

For an especially rank example of such Eccentrism, consider Shklovsky's favorite moment in *Strike,* the barrel-graveyard scene, for him an event "completely improbable and implausible" and therefore paradigmatic of the film's "eccentric and unexpected effects."[30] As the strike drags on, the fifth reel, "Provocation to Disaster," opens on the outskirts of the city as a member of the tsarist police enters a seemingly abandoned settlement adorned with two dead cats hanging by their tails, stark emotional cues meant to trigger the spectator's revulsion toward the grotesquerie to come. But the "tsarist police," an intertitle announces, "are not squeamish." The policeman proceeds and is met by a dwarf, who springs from an overturned basket and promptly "announces" him to "The King," himself asleep at the wheel of an abandoned automobile. After a grotesque bathing ritual, this bedraggled hooligan, dressed in the tattered suit of a baggy-pants comedian, strikes what the intertitle calls a "shady deal" with the policeman and introduces him to his retinue, proclaiming, "My realms are limitless." A vast lumpen-proletariat underground housed in the Kovoshino cemetery, the King's hooligans emerge at his signal, ready for duty, from a host of large barrels sunk into the earth, open to the sky, and arranged in a gridlike pattern in a large field (see figure 5). One understands immediately Shklovsky's rave: this is beyond strange, a tour-de-force of eccentric *ostranie*.

Eisenstein's presentation of the lumpenproletariat in *Strike* makes clear that their eccentricity—of body, of movement, of social position—is of the enervating variety and in stark contrast to the privileged corporealities of the

Figure 5. "Rank Theatricality." *Strike*, dir. Sergei Eisenstein, 1925.

striking workers. Indeed, we should recall briefly that the preceding reels of the film teem with the properly organic expressive movements of the proletariat: in the first reel, as the workers plan for the strike, they are shot as graceful aerialists, perched on beams high above the factory floor, dancing across its rooftop, or deftly traversing the steely latticework of its bowels; when they strike in the second reel, their battle for control over the factory is modeled on the movements of acrobats, incorporating in the climatic struggle for the factory whistle a circus see-saw; in the fourth reel, especially, Eisenstein stages the increasingly strained domestic scenes within the workers' village according to principles of biomechanical "*raccourci*," the utilitarian movements of the "active, nonstable body in space," arranged "for maximum expressiveness" and toward the aim of acting dynamically on the spectator.[31] One early scene is especially telling: the strapping prols, conveniently conspiring in loincloths at the waterfront, are spied upon by the spindly "Owl." As the five "activists" swim out to an anchor suspended above the water, posing upon it in a sensual tableaux of unified muscularity, an intertitle declares the mission both of the workers and their organic movements: "Agitate everywhere." Meanwhile, bumbling "Owl" gets trapped in a wall of huge, horizontally arranged ropes, a visual rhyme of the worker's phallic prowess. Noticing the spy, whose inorganic movements betray him, the workers make a circuitous, spectacular escape, climbing from the suspended anchor to the roof of a nearby houseboat, from which they execute a series of acrobatic dives back into the water and away from the "Owl." Scenes like this clarify how *Strike* is structured by a crucial distinction between acrobats and clowns. If the corporeality of the proletariat thus hinges upon the former's physical facticity, that "actual-materialistic element" of theater that underwrites social organicity and the work of revolutionary agitation, the clowning, literally unproductive physicality of the King's retinue heralds a different kind of social material. Its vulnerable heterogeneity finds its most apt visual metaphor in the bizarre topography of the barrel graveyard, where the dwellings of the lumpenproletariat are at once overly particularized (each clown in a barrel unto himself) and dangerously open to exterior influence. Whereas the community of male workers is organically bound by a homoeroticism of "real doing," of the material-practical principle of concrete and heroic action and choice, the clowns' grotesque queerness is a function of their contingency, their abstract potential for future transformation, their location at the very emergence of politics: a site of unbinding prior to political nomination and rife with its own eroticism.[32]

In *Strike,* and in political thought more broadly, the lumpenproletariat are the equivalent of "random innervations" or "pathological grimaces" in the organic movement of the social body. The danger (and possibility) of these eccentric social elements lies in their vulnerability, their potential to be yoked to reactionary or revolutionary political movements. For the Marx of *The Eighteenth Brumaire* specifically, as Peter Stallybrass persuasively argues, the lumpen "seems to figure less as a class in any sense that one usually understands that term in Marxism than a group that is amenable to political articulation."[33] As a differentiated social mass lacking a stable identity of its own, the lumpen's malleable heterogeneity is thus not, Stallybrass asserts (following Georges Bataille), the "*antithesis* of political unification but the very condition of the possibility of unification" and thus "figures the political itself" understood as the power to "fashion classes out of radically heterogeneous groups."[34] In this sense, for Marx and for Eisenstein, the threat of the lumpen's heterogeneity lies in its potential complicity with hegemonic power, a relation that turns on such difference's paradoxically enabling relationship to social typage—the double movement whereby the *informe lumpen* at once frustrate social organicity and typological organization and, having thus raised the specter of an illegible socius, fuel ever more insistent and oppressive processes of social taxonomy, differentiation, and surveillance. Enervating eccentricity thus both short-circuits the social organicity facilitated by Eisenstein's cinematic typage and sparks a repressive countertypage whose totality structures the calamitous events of the film's final two reels. The eccentric's deviance, Eisenstein knows, is capricious—it can always swerve the other way.

Strike's fifth reel exemplifies precisely this dynamic, underscoring the relationship between the lumpen's political malleability and hegemonic power while offering a kind of parable of the workings of Eisenstein's mimetic theater. The King's gang of lumpenprols is hired by the police to compromise the unity of the striking workers, whose internal solidarity is already showing some signs of vulnerability in the fourth reel. Without their labor and thus without food, the workers' initially idyllic newfound rest appears increasingly restive, and their domestic life is marred by spousal bickering and the cries of unfed children. Presumably, then, this a perfect time for saboteurs: the police's plan calls for the lumpens to break into and set fire to a state liquor store and thereby incite the workers to fits of looting that would justify their swift liquidation. The plan's logic seems curious until we realize that it returns to the fundamentally mimetic assumptions of Eisenstein's materialist theater: the lumpens' riotous movements will draw a crowd and provoke in it a contagious imitation of their violence. In fact, Eisenstein structures the riot as a theatrical event, an impromptu street performance, crosscutting between a unified mass of workers in the street who, returning from a meeting, will play audience, and the frenzied movements of the King's gang "at 'work,'" as the ironic intertitle has it.

The lumpen goes about its business, looting, burning, and defenestrating with pathological glee. As the crowd gathers outside, it is directly called to mimesis by a visibly deranged female provocateur who climbs a tree amidst the audience and shouts "S-m-a-s-h it!" But the workers are unmoved; recognizing the King's boys' actions as "provocation" subsidized by the police, the crowds begin returning to their homes as the members of the gang are consumed in the fire, drinking greedily even as they perish. This is, in short, a story of innervation's enervation that underscores the principles of expressive movement (here in negative form: inorganic gesture precludes mimesis), the recalcitrant unity of the workers, and the failure of the lumpenproletariat to bind the workers in a reactionary political articulation. And yet this deft bit of mimetic pedagogy swiftly becomes a bracing lesson in the totality of tsarist power, as the firemen—at the urging of the police—turn their powerful hoses on the fleeing crowd in one of the film's most famous sequences. This dazzling montage, which witnesses the capture of one of the worker's leaders, culminates in a stunning series of medium-close shots of workers brutalized by powerful streams of water. Heroic, individuated bodies are progressively erased by the force of the water until, in the reel's final shot, the body disappears entirely within the spray. The grotesque mode of formal abstraction troped by the water is a direct instrument of Statist repression, and Eisenstein punningly names this figure of power's own typological violence with the sixth reel's title card, which immediately follows the disfigurement of the worker's body: "Liquidation."

Fluidity's violence to form here reminds us of how, in modernity, organic typage, as a fantasy of social legibility, is always haunted by its more nefarious incarnation, surveillance. In *Strike,* the police's animalistic spies, too, are liquid, as Eisenstein demonstrates in their ostentatious introduction early in the film. After a trick shot in which the spies leap into grotesque animation from the frames of their photographs in the secret police's archives (a leap that links the spies' contingency and the excessive particularity of photographic indexicality [see figure 6]), we cut to the intertitle "Preparations" and then iris into a pet shop where the spies are introduced by name—respectively, "Fox," "Owl," "Monkey," and "Bulldog." The names, and thus the inspiration for the setting, are culled from actual spy nicknames Eisenstein discovered in police archives. And the spies are presented through the same formal pattern: first a dissolve, for example, from a close-up of the face of an actual monkey to a matching close-up of "Monkey"'s face, whose expressions mimic his animal totem; then a cut to a naming intertitle, "Monkey"; then a flashy wipe to "Monkey," now disguised as an ice-cream vendor, eavesdropping on a worker's private conversations on the sidewalk. Surveillance is thus predicated upon typage as a system of social legibility and control, yet effective social discipline requires a certain liquidation of identity, and thus the spy's manipulative mimesis. So, the spies are at once narrowly typed by one-to-one relation between character and trait ("Owl" observes; "Fox" is sly) and are thoroughly plastic. In this fashion, it is hardly coincidental that the agents not only share the grotesque malleability of the lumpen but are routinely disguised as them; "Bulldog," we might note, leaves the pet shop after picking up a dancing bear and is next seen performing as an organ-grinder. As Yuri Tsivian notes, "Typically a police agent wouldn't pretend to be a worker, but rather a bum, a beggar, or a street musician with a tame animal, something that helps the spy melt into the street life."[35] Strike's social world thus refuses to stabilize under the pressure of typage. It is, as Eisenstein's later remarks intimate, a performative public sphere, a too-liquid flotsam of deviance and dissembling, bad for revolutionary organization.

If Strike's anatomy of modern surveillance thus requires Eisenstein to mimic the techniques of the power network he analyzes—to survey surveillance and type oppressive typage—then perhaps it requires a similarly ambivalent identification with the mimetic strategies of its animalistic agents who, at the campy erotic limit blurring expression and disguise, are themselves figures of abstract potentiality.[36] Here, we might recall Eisenstein's observation that the pure organics of expressive movement, distorted in postlapsarian modernity, "are not destroyed" in animals and children (EM 210). In this light, Eisenstein's subtle appropriation of the spies' animalistic plasticity is suggested in the echoes between their fluid transformations and the dissolves that technologically enable them. This formal mimicry of animal mimicry, I want to suggest, points to a premodern imitative faculty—a sensual mimesis of play and transformation—that remains the mimetic road not overtly taken in Strike (see figure 7). Michael Taussig has made a similar observation about Strike's "zoomorphic physiognomics" in this scene, reading the animalized agents as "double-men," figures of prehistory beneath the rationality of the modern state.[37] Drawing on what Max Horkheimer and Theodor W. Adorno call modernity's "organization of mimesis," Taussig sees the spies as indices of how "the mimetic prowess inherent to some Other 'prehistorical' time was not so much annulled by Enlightenment (read 'civilization') as repressed and reconfigured," appropriated by the state as "an instrument of deception in the struggle for power."[38] If, in this model, a repressed animality and a corresponding premodern mimesis return

Figure 6. "Grotesque Animation." *Strike,* dir. Sergei Eisenstein, 1925.

under the state's repressive rationality, then *Strike*'s pet shop demonstrates that "behind every bureaucrat lurks an alchemical hot line to prehistory."[39] If this notion seems fanciful, consider its direct enactment in the sixth reel, as the murderous infiltration of the workers' tenement by cossacks on horseback is crowned, in one shot, by two children, high above the street, playing with toy horses. In the context of the impending slaughter, this ironic act of mimicry borders on a perversion of sympathetic magic.

If premodern sensual mimesis remains only a repressed and distorted possibility in *Strike,* its latent presence anticipates Eisenstein's later thought, especially his strong preoccupation with premodern modes of cognition and affect: with a typage compatible with sensual thought and productive of affective states irreducible to "emotional infectiousness" in a public space. In fact, there are strong indications that such affective modes are the very yield of *Strike*'s antitypological world, its surfeit of grotesque plasticity. One contemporary reviewer noted that "the furious montage often makes a hash of the action" so that "it's not always clear what is going on on the screen";

Figure 7. "Animal Agents." *Strike*, dir. Sergei Eisenstein, 1925.

another worried that "the working class spectator" would not "accept *Strike* wholeheartedly," and "in some places he may simply find it incomprehensible."[40] Lev Kuleshov agreed: "The film was shot in the tradition of the theatrical grotesque, which was absolutely unsuited to the cinema"; there was simply "too much excess in it; the unified line of action is missing."[41]

The terms of Kuleshov's critique of *Strike* have resurfaced in contemporary cognitivist film theory, where the film has proved a reliable counterexample of proper cognitive orientation. For one theorist, *Strike* exemplifies a film whose chaotic visual style makes demands incompatible with the hardwired cognitive structures of our "emotion system": "The film contains a collection of cues (including the slapstick action sequence in which the foreman is knocked down by a wheel; the repulsive faces of grotesquely exaggerated actors) that could potentially have been coordinated into a highly effective signal to elicit an audience's emotional orientation, but these moments remain isolated and singular."[42] Emotional cues that remain singular would, of course, be the equivalent of eccentric affectivity, random innervations in the filmic mimetic work. Eschewing a cognitivist mandate that submits affectivity to the shaping of belief and action, these affective states are impervious to the "habit logic" Eisenstein will later deride. Such emotion is both tricky, stemming from stunts and a psychology "head over heels," and truly eventful, now in the sense of an unsystematizable contingency. This is what Montagu meant by *Strike*'s "confusing, indeed, shattering" effect on the spectator. In these bewildering affects, we find the rudiments of what he will later call "ecstasy"; here, they follow not from the "poignant universality of his realism" but from typage's dissolution amidst a welter of fanciful particulars.

Eisenstein on Ecstasy

Recovering the sensuousness of typage required a rethinking of mimesis itself. Such is the theoretical burden of Eisenstein's "Imitation as Mastery," his 1929 speech to the Congress of Independent Filmmakers at La Sarraz. The elusive talk turns on a fundamental distinction between two modes of imitation: the first, magic one "copies form"; the second, which Eisenstein calls the imitation of "principle," forsakes a slavish attachment to superficial, formal likeness and instead works at "penetrating matter . . . penetrating behind appearance into the principle of appearance" and, in so doing, mastering that principle.[43] Linking superficial form with the deceptions of the visible world itself, Eisenstein now understands mimesis not as, for example, the aping of the body's proportions but as the more fundamental investigation of its "design structure."[44] This "penetration" amounts to what Mikhail Yampolksy calls an "X-Ray 'autopsy' of the visible, the flesh": the "intuitively magic physiognomic disclosure of the line which lies concealed beneath the body of the object (or text)," the revelation of what Eisenstein dubs in another context the essential "bone-structure."[45] Eschewing naturalistic imitation, the magic of such mimesis depends instead on the discovery of a primal generalization that subtends the flux of the world of appearance, a penchant for sensuous, typological abstraction that Eisenstein would repeatedly associate with the intuitive prelogic of primitive cultures.

This formulation of mimesis as primitive abstraction exemplifies Eisenstein's insistence in the 1930s that the "affectiveness of a work of art is built upon" the "dual unity" of progressive, rational consciousness and "sensual thought" (or "inner speech")—those prelogical, primitive forms of cognition he saw preserved, in residual fashion, in modern aesthetic practice.[46] His theory of mimesis, then, owes a debt not only to the linguistic theory of anthropologists and ethnographers like Lucien Levy-Bruhl, Lev Vygotsky, and Jean Piaget, who located the origins of language in the mimetic behavior of primitives, but also to the aesthetic theory of Wilhelm Worringer. In *Abstraction and Empathy* (1908), Worringer conceptually linked the modern and the primitive through a similar distinction between "the pure imitation impulse, the playful delight in copying the natural model," and "the urge to abstraction," this last peculiar both to "the peoples at their most primitive cultural level" and to a powerful strand of modernist art.[47] In Worringer's account, the pleasure of naturalist mimesis lay in the primal psychic need Theodor Lipps called "empathy" (in-feeling), wherein "aesthetic enjoyment is objectified self-enjoyment" (*AE* 5). While for Lipps, empathetic enjoyment depends upon an object whose form inclines "toward the truths of organic life, that is, toward naturalism in the higher sense," Worringer's riposte is that inorganic, dehumanized abstraction answers to another psychic need: it results from an "immense spiritual dread of space," erupting when mankind has failed to secure "a relation of friendly confidence with the appearance of the outer world" (14, 15, 17). In such agoraphobic times, Worringer argues, the aesthetic pleasure of abstraction comes from the way it manages "the caprice of the organic": it is a defensive bid to "tear [the object] away from the course of happening," to lift it "out of the unending flux of being, to purify it of all its dependence on life, i.e., of everything about it that was arbitrary, to render it necessary and irrefragable, to approximate it to its *absolute* value" (20, 21, 17). In abstraction's absolutism, we might say, lies a mimesis that can putatively succeed where *Strike*'s typage failed—it is fully equipped to handle the fluid contingency of the external and the swerves of the organic.

Lest we turn Eisenstein into Wyndham Lewis, another admirer of Worringer's, we should note how dehumanized abstraction, for Eisenstein, is fleshed out by a thoroughly Romantic conception of the image in his montage essays of 1937 and 1938. Whereas Lewis's reading of Worringer emphasizes abstraction's anti-empathetic externality, in these essays Eisenstein will consider abstraction's sensuality—and its potential for a kind of community—by excavating the generalized image buried beneath the mendacious surface of things. In "Montage 1937," Eisenstein hopes to avoid two aesthetic excesses, "to reduce art to abstraction" and "to blindly subordinate oneself to nature," by redefining montage as the union of "depiction" and "image," the specific, literal "representation plus a generalization about the inner essence of what is represented."[48] So, montage in performance requires locating the "inner generalizing element" in the gesture of "aversion," to use one of Eisenstein's examples. While the performative "variety of expression is legion," the trick is "to extract the essential content of the emotion": "Its multiplicity is a set of variants on one basic scheme, which will permeate all instances and varieties" (M7 22–23). The human face, Eisenstein continues in a formulation Lewis might admire, is itself a machine of abstraction: "physiognomy generalizes, as it were, those mimetic features which are most peculiar to him. His habitual movements seem to be frozen in the permanent *character mask* of his face, his persona" (36). Thus, successful actors must recreate the "same duality within a single mimetic display: the persona (a generalization about the person, his character), and the mimetic expression which passes across it (the particular instance of the emotion experienced by that character)" (36). Just as the face's abstract mimicry freezes habitual movement and contingent emotion, the abstracting tendency of Chinese painting, in "freeing it from whatever is transitory and impermanent," reveals the static "linear skeleton" of "Real Form" (28). And this formal skeletal principle is also a social ideal: thus, the final carnival scene of *Que Viva Mexico!,* in which "people are dancing in death masks," exemplifies what Eisenstein calls "super-generalization"—the "falling away of the persona (the face) within the essential substance (the skull)." "Here are all racial groups, all levels and classes of society, workers, peons, men and women. . . . Behind their masks there are no smiling faces, indeed there are no faces at all: in place of the masks are real bony skulls" (46–47).

While Eisenstein assures his readers that "abstraction is nothing to be afraid of," elsewhere he cautiously observes those historical eras in which "generalisation—the 'idea'—begins to exists philosophically as the sole essential factor, which swallows up the particular, the 'random,' the transitory, even though it is the latter which actually lends flesh and blood and concrete objectivity to this 'idea' of the phenomenon" (M7, 34, 30). Similarly, his remarks on the grisly skull-and-bones society of *Que Viva Mexico!* lead him to the admission that "super-generalisation," if "taken too far, inevitably lapses into metaphysics and mysticism. . . . The result is inevitable whenever an author, carried away by the urge to generalise, loses touch with concrete reality and generalisation in its social—that is, primary, fundamental, and decisive—form, whether at a *realistic* or *philosophical* level. There is an element of self-criticism in this statement" (47). There is also, we should add, a criticism of Worringer here, of primeval abstraction's tendency to lift the thing from the flux of being. Abstraction's excess, Eisenstein realizes, is precisely its tendency to lose touch with the eccentric flesh of the world: particularized, random, eventful, and concrete. But this flesh is more than skin-deep: its *"true revelation"* requires "the immutable weapon of Marxism–Leninism, which is capable of tearing away every mask and of laying bare the very essence of a phenomenon beneath whatever 'appearances' it may assume" (50). An artist's capacity for imagistic generalizability depends upon the particular social structure in which he is embedded. For this reason, as Eisenstein explains elsewhere, the otherwise admirable montage techniques of an American filmmaker like D. W. Griffith will founder on his "inability to abstract a phenomena," to create a *"unified, powerful, generalized image."*[49]

The force of the generalized image, as Eisenstein explains in "Montage 1938," lies in the cognitive vitality of its "unifying principle."[50] The partial depictions of montage are now linked to "the single overall theme which in equal degree pervades all the sequences" and "evokes in the spectator's perception that *common essence* which generated each separate element and binds them together into a *whole,* and specifically into that generalized *image* through with the author (and after him the spectator) has experienced the theme in question" (M8, 299). As his related praise of a vital, experiential (indeed, Stanislavskian) model of acting elsewhere in the essay suggests, Eisenstein has, in 1938, thoroughly interiorized typage, that most theatrical of concepts. Typicality is now tantamount to the sounding of conceptual essence in the generalized image.[51] What's more, the image's very typicality—its common essence—becomes the sensuous vehicle of community between author/performer and the newly "creative" spectator: through the particular, highly interiorized associations evoked by montage ("every spectator in his own way"), the spectator is brought "inexorably" to the "same image that has been conceived by the author, but that image will also have been brought into being by a creative act on the part of the spectator" (310). In this sense, spectatorship is at once liberated and masterfully controlled: the spectator's "individual nature," Eisenstein insists, is not "enslaved to the individuality of the author but is deployed to the full by a fusion with the author's purpose" (309). Simultaneously "the author's image and—equally—*his own* image, which is alive and intimate," this imagistic fusion approaches a kind of embodied intersubjectivity as "the image conceived by the author has become flesh of the flesh of the spectator's image" (310). This bit of cinematic transubstantiation is modeled on the corporeal materialism of Marxist science, in which "truthful research is the truth dissected, the separated limbs of which are reunited in the result" (309). Co-participants in a truthful joinder, spectator and artist undergo the particular subjective state Eisenstein will later call "ecstasy," "the moment in which one experiences the feeling of unity in variety: the feeling of a single, generalizing law that extends through all the variety of single (apparently) accidental phenomena of nature, of reality, of history, of science."[52]

Given Eisenstein's remarks about the social conditioning of Griffith's imagistic impotence, it is striking that the privileged site of ecstatic performance in Eisenstein's late career is the animated world of Walt Disney, not just an American but the very embodiment of Americanism as standardized mass culture. If ecstasy is "a sensing and experience of the primal 'omnipotence'—the element of 'coming into being'—the 'plasmaticness' of existence, from which *everything* can arise," then "Disney pictures," Eisenstein raves, are "pure ecstasy."[53] Their animated forms are "plasmaticness" itself, the "rejection of once-and-forever allotted form, freedom from ossification, the ability to dynamically assume any form" (*ED* 21). The very plasticity of these "boneless elastic figures" portends a "departure from one's self, from once and forever prescribed norms of nomenclature, form, and behavior," a "world of complete freedom" only possible in a society that "had completely enslaved nature, namely, in America" (21, 10, 3). Eisenstein's understanding of Disney's primitive potential is resolutely dialectical: "America and the formal logic of standardization had to give birth to Disney as a natural reaction to the prelogical," and so "*metamorphosis* is a direct protest against the standardly immutable" (43). Disney exemplifies for Eisenstein a broader historical pattern in which figures of the humanized animal proliferate in inhuman social systems; just as the seventeenth century's "mathematical abstraction and metaphysics in philosophy" produced first the materialized animal of René Descartes and then the universal animism of Jean-Jacques Rousseau, so the animated cartoon emerges as the wish image of "American mechanization" (33). Disney thus marks the return, near the end of Eisenstein's career, of Eccentrism-as-Americanization. In Walt's plasmatic dream factory, the antitypological once again flourishes within a gray world of brutal abstraction. Typage is liquified.

Most striking for my purposes are the affects produced by plasmatic formlessness: "obliviousness," "mindlessness," and "intoxication" across "all nationalities, all races, all types of social systems" (*ED* 9, 6). Here, Eisenstein is careful to distinguish Disney's production of "obliviousness" from narcotizing distraction: "Obliviousness as a way of distracting thought from the real to the fantastic; obliviousness as a tool for disarming the struggle. This is not what Disney gives us" (9). Rather, Disney's affectivity is liberated from morality and ethics, from the "sermonizing" and "Quakerizing" of Chaplin: "Disney is simply 'beyond good and evil'" (9). It is "like an aroma given without a flower; a taste extracted from a fruit; sound as such; affect freed from any purpose" (10). The formulation is remarkable: *affect freed from any purpose*. The cinefist has turned to protoplasmic mush. We are far from the mimetic theater of expressive movements. Even imagistic ecstasy, however fleshy and communal, was always cognitively routed toward what Charles Altieri has dubbed the "belief-judgment nexus," the instrumentality of the author's purpose, here the unyielding skeleton of Marxist truth (*PR* 9). This ecstasy, importantly, is "*beyond* any image, *without* an image, *beyond* tangibility—like a pure sensation" (46).

Following Baruch Spinoza and Gilles Deleuze, Brian Massumi has recently drawn a relevant distinction between two levels of reception of every "image-event"—discursive qualification and affective intensity (*PV* 26). The former entails a conscious, sociolinguistic, and in many cases ideological fixing of the image-event; the latter marks the unconscious, sensual register of the event's phenomenological force. Emotion lies between these levels: it is "qualified intensity" and "subjective content, the sociolinguistic fixing of the quality of an experience which is from that point onward defined as personal"; affect, on the other hand, is something like unqualified sensory intensity, imma-nent—though not directly accessible—to experience (28). It is, in Eisenstein's terms, "beyond tangibility, like a pure sensation" (*ED* 46). Affect's autonomy, for Massumi, has a political importance insofar as it operates in a immanent realm prior to the reductions of will and consciousness; this dimension, which Massumi, following Deleuze, calls "the virtual," allows him to think of the body as a site of change, of becoming, and of constant dynamism—a formulation precluded in cultural studies approaches that read the body as a culturally fixed position on an ideological grid. Affect's potential thus lies in its ability to think movement as "qualitative transformation" (*PV* 3).

It would be hard to find a better description of animation's plasmatic potential for Eisenstein, that is, its function *as* potential ("pure coming into being") and change. In *Strike,* remember, it was the lumpen's grotesque plasticity that threatened the stability of Eisenstein's organic typage, just as the plasmatic transformation of the animalistic spies augured the hor-ror of a public sphere that was all potential. There, the heterogeneous un-predictability of the lumpens—and the principles of Eisenstein's mimetic theater—were demonstrated most forcefully in the fiery destruction of the state liquor store. Now Eisenstein is newly appreciative of pyromania, and fire itself is emblematic of the very "flowing diversity of forms" (*ED* 25). Capable of "assuming *all* possible guises," fire, like animation, embodies the "potentiality of the primal plasma . . . the principles of dialectics"; it functions to provoke "'unconscious' and 'impulsive' conditions—that is, of bringing 'sensuous thought' to the foreground, and forcing 'consciousness' into the background" (41, 45, 32–33).

Plasmaticness, then, is grotesquerie transvalued and opening onto a non-instrumental, "primitive" realm of sensation within the modern, and ruth-lessly rationalized, culture industry. The difference between the primitive and modern modes is, for the later Eisenstein, nugatory, a matter of the evolution of synecdoche: "The difference is that the primal, sensuous *pars pro toto* takes *any trait* in place of the whole, while at the higher stage of *pars pro toto,* the generalization . . . is the *unique trait* that completely embodies the principle of the whole (the *most important thing* about the whole)" (*ED* 83). I would argue, however, that this distinction in thinking the relationship between parts and wholes, which Eisenstein here minimizes to underscore the very penetration of sensual thinking, is crucial and in fact emblematic of a broader separation in Eisenstein's thought—not between "the primitive" and "the modern" but between two routes to ecstasy, one offered by plasmaticness, the other enabled by the generalized image. The image, as Eisenstein notes here and elsewhere, is a reduction to typological essence and fixity. It is a cogni-tive, albeit more "creative," path toward the reproduction of a preconceived image and emotion. It is a prepackaged event. Plasmaticness, on the other hand, is the liberation from the typological in a flowing diversity of form that hopelessly frustrates synechdochic operations. It returns to the dialectical potentiality of matter itself, removing affect from discourse, freeing it into the eventfulness of sensation.[54] If image freezes eccentricity, plasmaticness embodies it, no bones about it.

Occupying a prediscursive realm of affect liberated from type, instrumen-tal organization, and political nomination, plasmaticness becomes nothing less than a sensual figure of politics-as-potentiality; in its "flowing diversity of forms," plasmaticness tropes both a mutable subjectivity that refuses the stabile identity of bourgeois psychologism and models a liberating mode of social and erotic relation. The movement from bones to plasma, from con-trol to release, here and elsewhere throbs with erotic intensity; in this regard, consider Eisenstein's fantasy of a Mexican martyr, brutalized by the lash, re-leased into the ecstatic chaos of abstract form: "Thus the naked line shatters the illusion of space, thus the line makes its way through the colour, thus the law of harmony splits open the varied chaos of form. . . . The whips swish no more. The searing pain has given way to a state of warm numbness. The marks of the blows have lacerated the surface of the body, the wounds have opened up like so many poppies and the ruby blood has begun to flow. Thus the line has given birth to colour."[55] Like plasma, colour in Eisenstein is a site of erotic release, but it is also—as Barthes reminds us, citing the filmmaker's late lectures on *Ivan the Terrible*—a privileged formal technology of perpetual noncorrespondence, of denaturalization, of the eventful opening to a future released from the mimetic reproduction of the same:

> This dissociation has a de-naturing or at least a distancing effect with regard to the referent (to "reality" as nature, the realist instance). Eisenstein would probably have acknowledged this incongruity, this im-pertinence of the signifier, Eisenstein who tells us concerning sound and colour: "Art begins the moment the creaking of a boot on the sound-track occurs against a different visual shot and thus gives rise to corresponding associations. It is the same with colour: colour begins where it no longer corresponds to natural colouration . . ." Then, the signifier (the third meaning) is not filled out, it keeps a permanent state of *depletion*. (TM 61–62)

Thus does Barthes help us to see how Eisenstein's eccentric eros—like his politics—might remain in a state of nonphallic expectation; late in his career, Eisenstein's erections refuse to harden, to ossify into the phallic typicality of a Lewisian tyro. In the detumescence of plasma and color, then, lies the abstract potential for future erotic and political attachments. This is Eisenstein on ecstasy.

As students of modernism, we have been trained, perhaps with good reason, to be suspicious of ecstatic moderns. We understand excessive elation as complicit with fascist orchestration, as a form of unbinding that accompanies the even more dubious pleasures of totality or redemptive violence. We see in the limit-experiences of modernity a disreputable romanticism that finds, even as it colonizes, the world outside the self in the lucid violence of the Woolfian moment, or the expansive throb of a Lawrentian orgasm. Modernist ecstasy is thus still something of an embarrassment today: an affective reaction-formation to modernity's scene of disenchantment, or a displacement of the sacred that overcompensates for the experiential poverty of the modern with a fantasy of the self whose ossified contours are outstripped by its ability to be forever jolted out of the furrows of quotidian experience, forever surpassing normative ethical limits. Looked at more dialectically, though, the moderns' fantasies of enjoyment—however symptomatic—might also be one of modernity's more powerful technologies for disorientation and thus for calling into being an actuality commensurate with a changed subject. Such is one of the more provocative claims of Fredric Jameson's recent *A Singular Modernity*: "It is on the face of it perverse not to hear the great modernist evocations of subjectivity as so much longing for depersonalization, and very precisely for some new existence outside the self, in a world radically transformed and worthy of ecstasy."[56]

As a specifically desubjectivized mode of affect, ecstasy's potential lies in the way that Eisenstein, following Levy-Bruhl, understands animism as a transitional space between a primitive, pre-individuated world of nondifferentiation in which "the individual consciousness of every member of the group is and remains strictly solitary with the collective consciousness," experiencing "the uninterrupted feeling of participation," and a world where subjective consciousness is fully differentiated both from each other and from the objects of the material world (*ED* 97). In this space, as Eisenstein puts it, the subject-object relationship is "both one and not one. . . . The object continues to be regarded as independent of the 'I,' but not independent of the attributes of the 'I'; i.e., the same thing is considered to be present in it that you start to notice about yourself (hunger, emotions, etc.)" (97). Disney's animism, then, is emblematic not of the primitive "identification" (the "complete simultaneous identity" of subject and object) but rather of what Eisenstein calls "likening," whose "sensuous effect is obtained only when there is sensuous 'immersion' in the likened subject," the "immersion of *self* in nature and animals" (50–52, 42).[57]

In these terms, Eisensteinian mimesis—as nonphallic, plasmatic likening—finally shifts from a technology for reproducing a prestructured political feeling to an ecstatic mode of social being. If the itinerary of Lewis's anatomy of modernity's mimetic-sympathetic public sphere discussed in the previous chapter moves from an early, romantic interest in ecstatic collectivity, primitive sympathy, and sensual mimesis to a dehumanized typage that publicly mimes a reified socius, Eisenstein's popular investments take him in the other direction: from externalized typage as a tool for mechanically reproducing emotion to a romantic mimesis that offers liberation from the typological through the enchanted materialism of Disney. Taking alternative routes through a reified public sphere, both Eisenstein and Lewis eschew a nostalgic distinction between a premodern public sphere of primitive sensation and the mediated affectivity of mass culture. Instead, both are provoked—by popular performance and the divergent nature of their political commitments—to conceptualize feeling through modernity's regimes of abstraction: Lewis, through a critical, quasi-Adornean mimetic adaptation to the alienated that underscores the violence of an imperious sympathy; Eisenstein, by understanding Disney as the sign of freedom from mechanization, the liberation of affect from purpose, and the union of the self with the dialectical happening of things. In this sense, both turning away from and toward sympathy are forms of public life. But Eisensteinian mimesis rejects the typological violence whose critical potential Lewis finally appropriates, reveling instead in the unstructured erotic potential of ex-centric feeling: a noninstrumental, nonidentitarian realm of affect opening within Walt's plasmatic dream factory. As a playful model of sociality imagined on the horizon of the culture industry, such mimesis approximates the labile "sociological structure" that Georg Simmel called sociability, the curious satisfaction of abstract association itself: "a feeling for, by a satisfaction in, the very fact that one is associated with others and that the solitariness of the individual is resolved into togetherness, a union with others."[58] Impersonal, prior to emotion as personal content or passionate interest, this "play form of association" is indeed devoid of any end outside itself, "the pure, abstract play of form."[59] As such, plasmatic publicness cruises: it takes perverse enjoyment in affiliations that, like the affects that energize them, remain unstructured, in potential attachments that have yet to stabilize, that are always coming into being.

2
Intimacy

3

Kumraderie

For (in my opinion) happy is that writer, who, in the course of his lifetime, succeeds in making a dozen persons react to his personality as genuinely or vividly as millions react, each and every year, to the magnetic personality of Zip, the What-Is-It!
—E. E. Cummings, "The Adult, the Artist, and the Circus"

E. E. Cummings paean to "Zip," an African American microcephalic named William Johnson who became one of the early twentieth century's most famous freaks, begs the question: What exactly is the pleasure of public space, the particular frisson of being-in-public (see figure 8)?[1] A tentative answer emerges in the terms of R. P. Blackmur's devastating anatomy of Cummings's writing in "Notes on E. E. Cummings' Language" (1931). For Blackmur, what is so egregious, so *intolerable* about Cummings is the "impenetrable surface" of his language, the way he employs "only the outsides of words" that, thus, can "be made to surrender nothing actually to the senses."[2] The cultivated eccentricities of typography and punctuation, like his peculiarities of diction, produce a thinness of superficial *sensation,* but not real *feeling,* which requires attaching isolate sensation to "some central body of experience," the social dimension of "unanimity in our possible experience of words" (NE 116, 122). Cummings's words are bad citizens: their "sterile" particularity destroys the publicness of the word, "for in practice the character of a word (which is its sense) is manifest only in good society" (116). The pure exteriority of his language thus leaves his reader in "the realm of thrill," where the rush of sensation cocoons the word in "sentimental impenetrability," a strangeness that only intensifies the more it is examined (120). In this rather poetic reversal of the most famous, and infamously gendered, term of New Critical opprobrium, Cummings's "sentimentality" is intolerable not because it is unmanned, in Suzanne Clark's terms, by "everything that modernism must exclude" (the feminine, the conventional, the rhetorical, the domestic, the everyday, and so on), but because it so steadfastly refuses to surrender to the sensual horizon of sociality and normativity.[3] Pushing the implications of Blackmur's formulation a bit, we might say that Cummings's particular sentimentality lies not in feminized overemotionalism but rather in the thrill of nonrelational being. His feeling is freakish, magnetically fascinating yet repudiating intimate attachment and desire itself.

Figure 8. "Magnetic Personality." Zip, the What Is It?

Blackmur's suggestive distinction between thrill and feeling thus offers us a useful idiom to frame Cummings's attempts to square affect with publicity: here, more specifically, to define a phenomenology of publicness in which being demonstrably public might *not* entail being social, or social in any common sense. This style of publicness is framed by Cummings's various appropriations of the political aesthetics of popular performance in his writings on aesthetics and popular culture; in his first novel, *The Enormous Room* (1922); and in his first play, *Him* (1927). For Cummings, such publicness is first and foremost a repudiation of intimacy and the centrifugal current of intimate feeling that, for him, may begin with friendship but always ends in the more nefarious, systematizing abstractions of collective and political being. Maintaining this kind of publicness demands the eccentric feeling that is best approximated by Cummings's phrase "tactile self-orchestration," a curious formulation about which I'll say more below. For now, note how the term appropriates the sense of touch—one particularly given to erotic proximity, intimacy, and tender mutuality—in the service of tenuous fantasy of sensual self-identity that hopes to sever aesthetic sensation from libidinal desire, from what Susan Buck-Morss calls the originary field of aesthetics: "corporeal, material nature."[4] If aesthetics is a form of cognition "located at the surface of the body, the mediating boundary between inner and outer," then tactile knowing should be particularly meaty and mediatory.[5] But Cummings's brand will prove to be rather anesthetic, numbed by a potent modern myth of masculine autogenesis, where sublime self-sufficiency is secured by corporeal unresponsiveness and the abandonment of sensuality and sex. In, fact, Cummings's sentimentality is downright antisentimental, linking him to the Kantian tradition's turn against the prevailing, and strongly homoerotic, sensuality of the "Age of Sensibility." By turning to the paradoxical exteriority of Cummings's sentimentalism—centripetally self-contained, impervious to eros, and finally hostile to the material world itself—this chapter hopes to provide, first, a suggestive foil against which Marsden Hartley's and Joseph Cornell's explorations of the intimate, ecstatic potential of the modern public sphere emerge in chapters 4 and 5, and second, a way to explore further the collective politics of eccentric feeling, worried differently by Wyndham Lewis and Sergei Eisenstein in part 1 and now set in the key of American radical individualism.

In his early career, before he become a Cold Warrior and rabid McCarthy-ite, Cummings would paradoxically emphasize the radically democratic, collective nature of public performance and turn vernacular theater into the public proving ground for his intense subjectivism.[6] While his brand of romanticism is often linked to the high British tradition (Lord Byron, John Keats, Percy Bysshe Shelley, and the like) or to Emersonian transcendentalism, I place it in the vicinity of a powerful strand of American modernism that emerged from what Frank Lentricchia has called the "big bang of modernist American philosophy."[7] This period, which spanned roughly from 1890 to 1913, was energized by the stars of Harvard's philosophy department: George Santayana, Josiah Royce, and William James, a fin de siècle dream team who, according to Lentricchia, established a compelling intellectual and ideological matrix for the diverse projects of Gertrude Stein, Robert Frost, Wallace Stevens, T. S. Eliot, and (most important for Cummings) Ezra Pound. In this context flourished the "hedonists of modernist poetics," dissatisfied with the genteel tradition's fetish of purity—its "rigorous evacuation from poetry of sensuousness and the sensual, and of any tendencies to social representation."[8]

I insert Cummings in this milieu with an eye toward illuminating how his own form of being-in-public materializes more sharply within it, and in more specific relation to the modernisms of James and Pound, whose commitment to radical individualism entailed a sensitivity to the self's sensuous experience and to its social unfolding. When Cummings graduated from Harvard in 1915, James and company had either retired or were about to do so, and Pound was already blasting away in London. Nevertheless, the personal ties between the James and Cummings families were long-lasting: Cummings's father, a professor of sociology at Harvard before becoming a Unitarian minister, was a graduate student of William James's (James, in fact, introduced Cummings's parents to each other); and Cummings was a childhood playmate and lifelong friend of James's son, Billy. Cummings read Pound's work avidly in college, shared printed space with him in the June 1920 issue of the *Dial,* and finally met him in person in Paris in 1921, a rendezvous whose import he recounted in a breathless letter to his mother: "As you may know, I have for some years been an admirer of Pound's poetry: personally, he sometimes gives me a Father Complex."[9] But it was Cummings's publication of *Eimi* (1932), a searing denunciation of political collectivity based on his 1931 trip to the Soviet Union, that cemented their friendship while provoking what Cummings called "ye Spank Kumains movement" among the radical Left.[10] Despite or because of the general animus toward the novel, Pound adored the book, gave Cummings the ironic nickname "The Kumrad," and inaugurated the prolific correspondence between the two that lasted long after Pound was charged with treasonous acts against the United States during World War II, acts that Cummings was quick to defend in a gesture of "kumraderie."[11]

Cummings shared with James and the early Pound a liberal ideology of the autonomous self, of its absolutely inviolable nature, as well as the paradoxical fear that modernity's proliferating regimes of abstraction (from economics to the conceptual imperialism of Western philosophy) were positioned to wreak unprecedented havoc on the fortress of the individual.[12] In many ways, it was this allergy to system that motivated Cummings to write *Eimi* and that underwrote his hostility to all political collectives, to which, unlike Pound (and much to Pound's frustration), Cummings could never pledge allegiance. More interestingly for our purposes, Cummings's defense of subjectivism was linked to an insistence on the sensuous, perceptual dimensions of the self. Thus, Cummings celebrated Pound's imagism in 1915, indulging in its emphasis on the immediacy and physicality of the image as the vehicle of sensation, and would remark to his father in a letter of 1918, "I should think myself equally cheated if I allowed my humanly-sentimental-mind to interfere, *one iota*, with the sealed letters of sensation brought to my soul by these eyes, these ears, this nose & tongue."[13]

Here, though, in stressing a closed and unidirectional sensory circuit ("sealed letters of sensation" brought to the perceiving self by its senses), Cummings both anticipates the kinds of corporeal gestures he will privilege in popular performance and suggests how his hedonism might part company with Pound and James. As Lentricchia puts it, Pound's modernist image, as it develops from Santayana's aesthetics, is not just a form of perception but also "a form of expression which integrates feeling and object in a *public* medium," one that "operates as shuttle between, and binder of, subject and object" and "ought not to be an inducement to retreat into an incommunicable awkwardness."[14] That is, the aesthetic pleasure of the image entails a "teasing invitation to the social being," one Cummings's own aesthetic theory would repeatedly decline.[15] In its theoretical openness to the social as accessed through sensation, Pound's early concept of the image, as Cary Wolfe has argued, "rejected symbolist transcendence for the same reasons that James's empirical psychology rejected the claims of the philosophical Idea: Neither tradition could do justice to the self's heterogeneous experience of a complex world composed of 'innumerable unfortold particulars.'"[16] These connections—between the public sensation of the Poundian image and the more explicitly social feelings of Jamesian pluralism—encourage us to read Cummings's interest in the experiential dynamics of the individual being-in-public as a powerful index of modes of eccentric feeling capable of negotiating between autonomy and connectedness, individual difference and social multiplicity. In this sense, Cummings's work, like Pound's, speaks to a dilemma at the heart of American individualist ideology. For all its rhetoric of freedom, Cummings's individualism likewise "threatens to leave us in a stalemate between the private sphere of difference and the social, material sphere of all those features of modernity that promise to devour it."[17] Cummings, however, will work through this stalemate in public, turning his attention to ostensive bodies that demonstrate how an obscene externality might sustain, rather than threaten, a fantasy of sensual self-identity, of purely aesthetic sensation devoid of eros or intimacy.

Being Singular

Reckless exposure, and its debt to popular culture, provided the terms for the critical reception of Cummings's early work. In a review of *The Enormous Room* published in the *Dial* in 1922, John Dos Passos lionized his friend's book as the "sort of thing [that] knocks literature into a cocked hat. It has the raucous directness of a song and dance act in cheap vaudeville, the willingness to go the limit in expression and emotion of a negro dancing."[18] Mobilizing the subversive immediacy of popular art and the racialized expressivity of the folk, *The Enormous Room,* for his pal "Dos," ditches "the rubber raincoat of fiction" for an aesthetic of exposure, a sensual immediacy belonging more properly to the popular arts.[19] Accepting the risks that accompany such seminal production, *The Enormous Room* seems to Dos Passos "to be the book that nearest approached the mood of reckless adventure in which men will reach the white heat of imagination needed to fuse the soggy disjointed complexity of the industrial life about us into seething fluid of creation. There can be no more playing safe."[20] Dos Passos's sexual language here is fitting, signaling both the peculiar combination of exhibitionism, comedy, and obscenity that linked "burlesque" literary modernism and popular culture in the culture wars and censorship battles of the early 1920s while echoing a Poundian fantasy of phallic auto-productivity whose result, Dos Passos continues, is "a distinct conscious creation separate from anything else under heaven."[21] Indeed, this process of producing from the "disjointed complexity" of industrial modernity the "seething fluid of creation" was perhaps Cummings's most abiding aesthetic preoccupation. As he put it, "IT IS THE FUNCTION OF 'ART' TO RESTORE THIS WHOLENESS *INTEGRALITY*."[22] To use Dos Passos's language, art's wholeness is, for Cummings, a bulwark against modernity's recalcitrant complexity, which is also to say, now in a Jamesian register, that Cummings's aesthetic positions itself against the messy heterogeneity of the modern world that it must somehow "feel and express."

Cummings's aesthetic lexicon everywhere resonates with the central terms of James's late philosophy as it engages some of the most pressing dynamics of the modern socius—specifically, the relations between wholes and parts, singulars and plurals, and their translation from conceptual abstractions into material, sensory dynamics between the perceiving self and the social. In James's model of the pluralistic universe, contrary to what is often assumed, "totality" is indeed a goal, but the totality James is looking for is "neither variety nor unity taken singly."[23] Rather, he seeks a dynamic synthesis of variety and unity, independence and connection, a simultaneity linked in his mind to "the bergsonian [sic] point of view," which asks, "How can what is manifold be one? how can things get out of themselves? how be their own others? how be both distinct and connected?"[24] In this world, "each part hangs together with its very next neighbors in inextricable interfusion. . . . It is not a universal co-implication, or integration of all things," and thus represents a "definitely conceivable alternative to the through-and-through unity of all things at once, which is the type opposed to it by monism."[25] Thus, James's notion of unity, as Carrie Brammen points out, is always "partial, contingent, and dynamic"; governed by chance, his pluralistic universe is, James himself admits, rather grotesque: "A friend . . . once told me that the thought of my universe made him sick, like the sight of the horrible motion of a mass of maggots in their carrion bed."[26] But better this disjointed complexity, for James, than the truly gross violence of monism, which "insists that when you come down to reality as such, to the reality of realities, everything is present to *everything* else in one vast instantaneous co-implicated completeness—nothing can in *any* sense, functional or substantial, be really absent from anything else, all things interpenetrate and telescope together in the great total conflux."[27]

In its adjectival excess, James's caricature of monism ("one vast instantaneous co-implicated completeness") is nothing if not Cummings-esque. "Homogeneity," Cummings's privileged term for formal, perceptual, or cognitive integration, is also his most contradictory concept, one fraught with a series of ambivalences that defined his aesthetic project in the 1920s: Is homogeneity the end or origin of the ostensive body? Is this unity synthetic or essential? What is the affective relationship between this singularity and the heterogeneous, contingent presences that surround it? Does the integrated body encourage or check identification and intimacy? Is public, theatrical space that frames this body democratic or aristocratic, collective or singular?

As Cummings suggests in one of his paeans to "burlesk," a good place to understand the sensation of the extraordinary public body is Gaston Lachaise, that "lyric architect of the human form," as his friend Marsden Hartley once described him.[28] Consider the gendered terms with which

Cummings praises the French sculptor's female nude, *The Mountain* (see figure 9), in the *Dial* in 1920: "Surrounded by a gurly [*sic*] sea of interesting chromatic trash it lay, in colossal isolation: a new and sensual island" (*MR* 17). One implication here is that the nude's sensuous homogeneity is produced through the detritus of its surroundings—thus, its "completely integrated simplicity" (17). Yet elsewhere, Cummings suggests that the form's integration exists not because of the feminized "sea of chromatic trash," or even in spite of it, but rather defiantly *against* the heterogeneous gunk of the material world.[29] What distinguishes Lachaise's "genuine" naïveté from that of unnamed, "would-be primitives" is his "absolutely inherent desire" to "negate the myriad with the single, to annihilate the complicatedness and prettinesses and trivialities of Southern civilizations with the enormous, the solitary, the fundamental" (16). Here, the abstract pluralities and complexities to which the Jamesian self remains open are not just foreclosed but violently destroyed.

Figure 9. "Colossal Isolation." Gaston Lachaise, *The Mountain,* 1924. Bronze, 8/11, cast after 1964. 19.7 × 49 × 23.6 cm. Iris & B. Gerald Cantor Center for Visual Arts at Stanford University (1995.78). Gift of Jane Lathrop Stanford, by exchange with the Bowers Museum of Cultural Art.

At times, Cummings attempts to deliver the singular *Mountain* to the sensation of the myriad by celebrating Lachaise's unique treatment of form, "which completely expresses itself, form that perfectly tactilizes the beholder, as in the case of an electric machine which, being grasped, will not let the hand go" (15). Collapsing vision and touch, the sculpted body's self-expression opens the perceiver to touch and to a form of what Laura U. Marks has recently called "haptic visuality": in this "combination of tactile, kinesthetic, and proprioceptive functions," Marks argues, "the eyes themselves function like organs of touch," and the viewer's body becomes more intimately "involved in the process of seeing than is the case with optical visuality" (T 2, 3). Marks proposes haptic visuality as an alternative theoretical model to "the mastering, optical visuality that vision is more commonly understood to be": haptic vision presses up lovingly against the particularities of its objects of experience rather than controls them from a position of disembodied abstraction (xvii). As an affair of the surface, haptic perception, moreover, is at once erotic and ethical: it "tends to rest on the surface of its object rather than plunge into depth," producing a sensual relationship that at once brings the viewer and object into embodied proximity but "allows the [object] to maintain its unknowability" (8, 18).

But there is something disconcerting about Cummings's mechanical metaphor for haptic intimacy. Its electric violence disturbs any erotic mutuality between an imposing object and the body of the perceiving subject that it will not release. To return to Blackmur's terms, sensual perception is a surface of thrill and not, as Marks would have it, a space of quasi-Levinasian optical caress; here, to see the object is to be touched, but not to touch in return. This sensory imbalance between subject and object is made more explicit later when, dissenting from the critical consensus on another nude, the *Elevation* (see figure 10), Cummings closes the poised, solitary body off from reference, from its production, and from the vision of its beholder: "The Elevation is not a noun, not a 'modern statue', not a statue OF Something or Some One BY a man named Gaston Lachaise—but a complete tactile self-orchestration, a magnificent conjugation largeness, an IS. The Elevation may not be declined; it should not and cannot be seen; it must be heard: heard as a super-Wagnerian poem of flesh, a gracefully colossal music" (*MR* 21). At this elevation, the sculpture's sensual climate suffers from a coldness one might call Lewisian, were it not for a Romantic haze that envelops it. Here, tactility extends no invitation to the viewer to "dissolve his or her subjectivity in close and bodily contact" with the object but rather, as "tactile self-orchestration," galvanizes a subjective expressivity savaged by the likes of Lewis

(*T* 13). This autonomous body, to follow Cummings's linguistic pun on "decline," is mobile (it will not be still), deictically present (it may not be refused), yet removed into an ineffable beyond (it will not be seen). As such, *Elevation* becomes for Cummings what his own work was for Dos Passos: a testament to an achievement "which remains passionately and serenely itself—a marvel and a mystery: the spontaneous and inevitable expression of one fearlessly unique human being."[30]

Six years after the Lachaise essay, Cummings would describe the revue in terms nearly identical to (though considerably more freighted than) those used to read Lachaise's Wagnerian body-poems:

> The revue is not . . . a mammoth exhibition of boudoir-paintings-come-to-life and is not (as F. Ziegfeld, Jr., pretends to believe) a "glorification" of some type of female "beauty." By the laws of its own structure, which are the irrovocable [*sic*] laws of juxtaposition and contrast, the revue is the use of everything trivial or plural to intensify what is singular and fundamental. In the case of the *Folies Bergère,* the revue is the use of ideas, smells, colours, Irving Berlin, nudes, tactility, collapsible stairs, three dimensions and fire works to intensify Mlle. Josephine Baker. (*MR* 162–63)

Here, Cummings finds in the revue the same laws of juxtaposition and contrast that he also celebrated in the Freudian unconscious and in burlesque, where opposites—the ugly and the beautiful, the bad and the good—occur together and "*secretly or unconsciously* modify or enhance" each other (*MR* 128, emphasis in original). That is, the riotous heterogeneity of the burlesque show and the revue materializes in three-dimensional form, producing first a perceptual and then a cognitive unity that "enables us to (so to speak) *know around* a thing, character or situation" (127). As a formal ideal, this looks like Hegel-night at the National Winter Garden Theater, where the internal contradictions of a pluralistic theatrical universe are sublated into a synthetic unity. But again, as in the Lachaise essay, the unity is not actually produced, but intensified; the particularities of plurality exist not to be merged but to distinguish, intensify, or otherwise publicize an elemental singularity that must have been already there to begin with:

> In brief, the *Folies Bergère* permits Josephine Baker to appear—for the first time on any stage—as herself.
>   Herself is two perfectly fused things: an entirely beautiful body and a beautiful command of its entirety. . . . She enters the show twice: first—through a dense electric twilight, walking backwards, on hands and feet, legs and arms stiff, down a huge jungle tree—as a creature neither infrahuman nor super-

Figure 10. "Complete Tactile Self-Orchestration." Gaston Lachaise, *Standing Woman (Elevation)*, 1927. Bronze; H. 73⁷/₈, W. 32, D. 17³/₄ in. (185.1 × 81.3 × 45.1 cm). The Metropolitan Museum of Art, Bequest of Scofield Thayer, 1982 (1984.433.34). Image © The Metropolitan Museum of Art.

human, but somehow both; a mysteriously unkillable Something, equally nonprimitive and uncivilized or, beyond time in the sense that emotion is beyond arithmetic. . . . Cries of "disgusting" mingle with gasps of "how shocking!" and wails of "how perfectly disgusting!" Horrified ladies cover their faces or hasten from the polluted environs. Outraged gentlemen shout, stamp or wave their arms angrily. And still Josephine Baker dances—a dance neither of doom nor of desire, but altogether and inevitably of herself. (*MR* 163)

Conflating the black body and the feminine, the primitive and the modern, Josephine Baker's performing body, as Janet Lyon has recently argued, "had the desired effect of telescoping modernism's favorite fetishes into one figure" and became a privileged "object of the racialist modernist imaginary" in Germany, America, and France, where Cummings caught her show.[31] Lyon offers the provocative thesis that Baker's dancing, especially at her own Montmartre cabaret, Chez Josephine, worked as a self-reflexive deconstruction of modernist racial ideologies, effectively enacting an improvisational form of cosmopolitan otherness as "embodied identification" within the cultural multiplicity of her club (JB 42). The openness of Baker's performative cosmopolitanism, for Lyon, hinges on the formal grotesquerie of her dancing, its functional capacity as "a pure surface phenomenon, consisting of endless varieties of form," not unlike what I described as the appeal of Disney's "plasmaticness" for Eisenstein in chapter 2.[32] This improvisational, surface performance, Lyon submits, was doubly unintelligible, both to the protocols of modernist aesthetics that valued "formal complexity and imagistic depth" as well as to the "interpretive paradigms of colonialism," which would read her dance as expressive of a "'deep core' of race" (41). Instead, it operated like a Deleuzian rhizome, generating assemblages of desire—and thus "sociopolitical possibilities" for her and her audiences—through the particular intimacy of her performance, which Baker herself characterized in the following way: "Watch me when I dance in the middle of you. It is like that that I must dance, not against a backdrop but in the middle of a circle of clapping people forming around me, in the middle of men and women, on the same level, the same light, side by side" (qtd. in JB 42).

I rehearse Lyon's suggestive reading of Baker's dance because it so strikingly recuperates the terms—performative surface, formal grotesquerie, intimate contact, the suspension of familiar epistemological binaries—that, in Cummings's vision, enable the production of a monstrous, racialized singularity poised against liberating cosmopolitan identifications and, indeed, against identifications of any sort. While Cummings's ecstatic gaze betrays a libidinal investment in Baker's "infrahuman" sexuality, we should seriously consider his claim that her body is *most* appealing to him when it is *least* erotic, least given to a Deleuzian assemblage: that is, when her dance is "neither of doom nor of desire, but altogether and inevitably of herself." Thus removed from the plane of identification, desire, and material need itself, Baker's body attains the same magnificent self-orchestration of Lachaise's nude. Importantly, this mode of self-theatricalization, while elemental, is in fact accentuated by the theatrical accoutrements of the Folies, whose electric twilight and jungle foliage provide the spectacular ground against which this singularity, this "mysteriously unkillable Something," may emerge. Plurality, here and elsewhere in Cummings's work, becomes necessary trivia in an area of distinction, effectively reduced to a surface on which the singular realizes itself.

In this mode of inscription, the eros of haptic surface, where friction between the subject's touch and the object's texture muddles agency, gives way to a more violent relationship between figure and ground. Recall that in Aloïs Reigl's art-historical narrative, appropriated by Marks (and Gilles Deleuze and Félix Guattari before her) to describe nomadic art and space, a similar movement from surface tactility to the abstraction of figure from ground epitomizes a shift from the decline of haptic proximity to the rise of the distanced beholder of Renaissance perspective, whose increased distance from the object of perception "allows the beholder to imaginatively project him/herself into or onto the object" (*T* 5). By this logic, the emergence of figure from ground is what allows for the kind of identification (empathy, or "in-feeling") that subtends the modernist emergence of a psychological idea of space, of space not as a passive container of bodies but as charged, in Anthony Vidler's terms, with "all the dimensions of a relative, moving, dynamic entity."[33] In the context of such spatial theories, Cummings's conceptual trick is to produce a figure whose singular abstraction from theatrical ground courts no intimate identification, staying swaddled in thrill and being "perfectly disgusting." In Baker's case, as Cummings notes, it was this capacity for theatricalized intolerability in The Chocolate Dandies revue that made her a star and earned her a place in the Folies:

> As a member of the *Dandies* chorus, she resembled some tall, vital, incomparably fluid nightmare which crossed its eyes and warped its limbs in a purely unearthly manner—some vision which opened new avenues of fear, *which suggested nothing but itself and which, consequently, was strictly aesthetic.* It may seem preposterous that this terrifying nightmare should have become the most beautiful (and beautiful is what we mean) star of the Parisian stage.

Yet such is the case. The black star . . . has accomplished precisely this trans-formation, and at the tender age of twenty. (*MR* 160, my emphasis)

As the horrified reactions she provoked at the *Folies* make clear, Baker oc-casions a kind of ethnic sublimity that depends, as for Immanuel Kant, on an aestheticized self-containment: "To be sufficient to oneself and hence to have no need of society, yet without being unsociable, i.e., without shunning society, is something approaching the sublime, as is any case of setting aside our needs."[34] Cummings's idealization of Baker's racialized singularity is not primarily a mode of racist primitivism (though it is also that) but rather a po-tent figure for a kind of public being whose freakish nature attracts attention but nonetheless checks identification and desire. This is Baker's real monstros-ity: to be, in Kant's terms, an object of disgust, obtrusively "insist[ing] . . . on our enjoying it even though that is just what we are forcefully resisting."[35]

A Sole Chaos of Desire

Michael North has characterized *The Enormous Room* as Cummings's "ex-tended vaudeville turn," comic and indecent.[36] Actually, the war novel is more like a circus, recalling Cummings's description of that institution as a "*thrilling* experienc[e] of a life-or-death order," an affective jolt not unlike the "solemn visit of a seventy-five centimetre projectile and the frivolous propinquity of Shrapnel" (*MR* 113):

> For, at the very thought of "circus," a swarm of long-imprisoned desires breaks jail. Armed with beauty and demanding justice and everywhere threatening us with curiosity and Spring and childhood, this mob of forgotten wishes begins to storm the supposedly impregnable fortifications of our Present. We are caught off our guard—we must defend ourselves somehow: any weapon will do. We seize the idea that a circus is nothing but a big and colorful toy especially invented for the amusement of our underdeveloped or naif minds. With this idea and the idea that the theatre is an enlightened form of entertain-ment worthy of our mature intelligences, we lay about wildly; until—after a brave struggle—the motley horde retreats, abandoning its dead and wounded. But we ourselves are not unscathed: our wounds give us no peace; we must somehow forget them. Accordingly, we betake ourselves to a theatre or to the movies. There, under the influence of the powerful anaesthetic known as Pretend, we forget not only the circus but all our other sorrows, including the immortal dictum of that inexorable philosopher Krazy Kat: *It's what's behind me that I am.* (*MR* 109–11, emphasis in original)

A voracious, if idiosyncratic, reader of Freud, Cummings's circus is the site of the uncanny: its affective economy is both the occasion for psychic trauma, of being wounded by "forgotten wishes," but also a salve—its "outrageous intensity," Cummings avers, makes it "unique as a curative institution and endows [its] denizens" with "a fourth- or fifth-dimensional significance for the neuroses" (112).[37] As such, the association Cummings makes here between the ludic space of the circus and states of psychic unrest and compensation anticipates *The Enormous Room*'s specifically modernist psycho-spatiality, its understanding of space, in Vidler's terms, "as a projection of the subject, and thus, as a harbinger and repository of all the neuroses and phobias of that subject."[38] Permeating spatial form with the psychic rhythms and anxieties, Cummings's novel appropriates the spaces and bodies of public performance to negotiate the pressures placed upon being singular by the collective imperatives of the Great War itself, behind Cummings in 1925 but clearly not forgotten.

Cummings's war experience can be briefly summarized as follows: In April 1917, young Estlin, seeking the prestige of action and a modicum of risk, volunteers for duty with the Norton-Harjes Ambulance Service, a Red Cross unit working for the French army. In France, Cummings befriends William Slater Brown, a journalism student at Columbia who had joined the ambulance unit for similar reasons and who identifies with Cummings's raffish aestheticism. After being separated from their unit upon arriving in Paris, they are assigned to the front at the small village of Germaine (where they see little action), quickly alienate themselves from their group, and thus spend the bulk of their time in the company of eight Frenchman (mostly mechanics and cooks in the unit) with whom they speak French, gossip, and air their pacifist philosophies. Bored, Cummings and Brown write to French aviation officials, volunteering their services as airmen but expressing their reservation about killing Germans. These letters, and others, attract the attention of the French censors, and ultimately both young men are sent to La Ferté-Macé, a French holding camp and the primary setting of *The Enormous Room*.[39] The novel chronicles (in a highly experimental first-person narration) the events that precipitate the imprisonment of a loosely autobiographical "C"; his experiences in prison with his friend "B"; his eventual release; and, most important, those "startling identities" whose company he keeps, whose marvelous antics and bodies "C" renders in a flurry of breathless portraits (*ER* 45).

Such ostensive bodies, of course, attain heightened significance in the context of World War I, where the "propinquity of Shrapnel" would be anything but frivolous. As Johanna Bourke has pointed out, between "1914 and 1918, more and more bodies of young, healthy men were at risk of frighteningly new ordeals of mutilation."[40] New weaponry (pointed bullets, hand grenades, artillery fire, and the like) and the particularly infectious conditions of trench warfare wreaked havoc on men's bodies, which were now "*intended* to be mutilated." As a result, "psychological trauma was brought to a new level of visibility."[41] In *The Enormous Room,* such fears are displaced onto the prison guards (the *plantons*), who, consequently, are the most reliable targets of C's disdain. "Next to the lowest species of human organism," the plantons run the gamut of disfigurement, their "peculiarities of physique" incurred, we assume, in active duty at the front: "Every one of them had something the matter with him physically. . . . For instance, one planton had a large wooden hand. Another was possessed of a long unmanageable left leg made, as nearly as I could tell, of tin. A third had a huge glass eye" (*ER* 111).

Bodily infirmity and fragmentation mark the more troubling threat posed by La Ferté-Macé to the integrity of the individual, to the "mutilated personalities" of the camp's occupants, whose "little annoying habits of independent thought and action" have been deemed "treasonous" by the French government (ER 83). In this sense, the regimes of abstraction that are, for Cummings as for Pound and James, a hallmark of modernity find their corollary in the false totalities of the camp's authorities and, beyond that, in the more abstract institutions of the French government and the obscenity of modern warfare itself. This war machine grinds on, but the ideological "stasis" is disturbed by its own structural dynamism, which is, more precisely, the shock value of plurality (107). C explains: "Now the thing which above all things made death worth living and life worth dying at La Ferté-Macé was the kinetic aspect of that institution; the arrivals, singly or in groups, of nouveaux of sundry nationalities whereby our otherwise more or less simple existence was happily complicated, our putrescent placidity shaken by a fortunate violence" (107). "Everyone," C observes, "is here for something" (106), by which he means not just that all have been found guilty of treason but also that difference is useful—that the vortex of bodies and personalities that defines the institution in turn unifies it: "our society had been gladdened—or at any rate galvanized—by the biggest single contribution in its history, the arrival of six purely extraordinary persons" (152). And this galvanic work, for Cummings, is precisely the expansive, violent kinesis of the circus, whose "bigness becomes apparent when we perceive that it is never, for so much as the fraction of a second, motionless": "I say the bigness of the circus-show is *a kind of mobility.* Movement is the very stuff out of which this dream is made" (*MR* 112–13, emphasis in original).

Cummings's kinetic whole thus recalls the monism of which James was critical—the absolute idealism that, as Brammen points out, "represents the metaphysical embodiment of 'bigness,' operating according to the same logic of monopoly capital as an 'all-devouring' merger that ingests all of its excess."[42] As James himself declared, "I am against bigness and greatness in all their forms. . . . The bigger the unit you deal with, the hollower, the more brutal, the more mendacious is the life displayed."[43] Bigness's lie, for James, is in its imperious expansiveness and its potential violence to difference, and one would do well to retain a similar wariness toward the structural logic of *The Enormous Room:* an attempt to mimic the unifying kinesis of its circus "bigness" that, theoretically, would approximate the "vast instantaneous co-implicated completeness" of the social monad. And this homogeneous kinesis, as Cummings's references to circus's oneiric character suggest, is also the rhythm of the Freudian psyche. Thus, the fortunate violence of the camp's sundry nationalities serves to bind novel and narrator alike.[44] If Cummings attempts to secure a Jamesian dialectic of variety and unity, maintaining a binding homogeneity within his fictionalized circus-show is a sticky business. Its kinetic matter consists of bodies and subjectivities that, at times, Cummings wishes to be thoroughly individualized and, at others, joined in a fulsome collective. In fact, this wild mix is initially quite nightmarish for C, who finds his self-possession assailed as he lies down to sleep during his first night in the Enormous Room:

> But I did not close my eyes: for all about me there rose a sea of most extraordinary sound . . . the hitherto empty and minute room became suddenly enormous; weird cries, oaths, laughter, pulling it sideways and backward, extending it to inconceivable depth and width, telescoping it to frightful nearness. From all directions, by at least thirty voices in eleven languages (I counted as I lay Dutch, Belgian, Spanish, Turkish, Arabian, Polish, Russian, Swedish, German, French—and English) at distances varying from seventy feet to a few inches, for twenty minutes I was ferociously bombarded. (ER 42)

For the bewildered initiate, this is a heterotopia whose spatial parameters are warped and distended by its very heterogeneity.[45] On the one hand, capable of extending to impossible dimensions, it approaches the Romantic sublime, whose "characteristics of absolute height, depth, and breadth had," as Vidler notes, "emerged in the mid-twenties as the leitmotiv of idealistic modernism" in the work of Le Corbusier and others.[46] On the other, this ineffable space is collapsed into a "frightful" intimacy with the sounds of difference, a proximity of singular figure and heterogeneous ground that marks the failed suppression of claustrophobia and one of its signal fears—the fear of touching. Here, Cummings literalizes the horror of an international social monad as it goes about its business of processing particularity; to borrow James's language, "all things interpenetrate and telescope together in the great total conflux," though the horror of such abstraction lies not in its potential violence to the plural but in its menace to the first-person singular. Most suggestive in this regard is C's stunned reaction as the occupants of the Enormous Room are summoned to eat:

> Never did Circe herself cast upon men so bestial an enchantment. . . . Before the arbiter of their destinies some thirty creatures, hideous and authentic, poised, cohering in a sole chaos of desire; a fluent and numerous cluster of vital inhumanity. As I confronted this ferocious and uncouth miracle, this beautiful manifestation of the sinister alchemy of hunger, I felt that the last vestige of individualism was about utterly to disappear, wholly abolished in a gambolling and wallowing throb. (ER 65–66)

This transformation of the camp into a "sole chaos of desire," a plural menagerie at once vital and inhuman, authentic and deathly, for C "was uncanny, and not a little thrilling" (65). Emerging on the seam of intimate collectivity and singular isolation, the thrill of the uncanny is the affective index of the novel's ambivalence about sociality itself and, thus, about whether the social dynamism of the Enormous Room secures a haven of fraternal eros—a combinatory of vital libidinal energy—or the Freudian deathliness of binding repetitions.

Consider the relationship between desire and collectivity in Freud's own *Group Psychology and the Analysis of the Ego,* a contemporary attempt to grapple with the erotic dynamics of collective ties in the context of the Great War. Freud draws on the insights of Gustave Le Bon, William McDougall, and Wilfred Trotter, but he supplements their explanations of the formative mechanism of the group mind as a magical kind of primitive *suggestibility* with his own psychoanalytic "formula for libidinal constitution of groups," in which *"individuals put one and the same object in the place of their ego ideal and have consequently identified themselves with one another in their ego"* (GP 60–61, emphasis in original). Extending the insights of *Beyond the Pleasure Principle* (1920), in which he linked love instincts to a binding energy that, like Cummings's rhythmic circus, "combine[s] organic substances into ever larger unities," Freud explains that groups, too, are "held together by Eros, which holds together everything in the world" (GP 31).[47] Indeed, Freud explains, it is eros that meliorates the "sediment of feelings of aversion and hostility" that reside in "almost every intimate emotional relation between two people"; it is "love alone" that "acts as the civilizing factor in the sense that it brings [the] change from egoism to altruism" necessary for the kinds of libidinal ties constitutive of groups (42, 41, 44).

These special emotional ties, which Freud famously termed "identifications," anchor the affective operation that converts those negative affects (envy, hostility, and disgust) inherent in all intimacies into the eccentric feeling that Freud dubs "social feeling," which "is based upon the reversal of what was first a hostile feeling into a positively-toned tie in the nature of an identification" (GP 67). As libidinal ties in which "love instincts . . . have been diverted from their original aims," group identifications are thus forms of "desexualized, sublimated homosexual love for other men" (44). The more inhibited the erotic instincts that constitute groups, the stronger the ties that bind them; the more "directly sexual" the ties internal to groups, the more the group risks dissolution, the unbinding that accompanies the erotically self-satisfied individual or a couple consumed by *l'amour fou* (92). Thus, while Freud insists that "the Greek word 'Eros' . . . is in the end nothing more than a translation of our German world *Liebe* [love]" (31), his argument pivots, as Diana Fuss points out, "upon a curiously *un*Freudian conception of libido—a libido denuded of any kind of sexual drive."[48] This fuzzy distinction between eros and love in the context of group feeling stems from the deeper ambivalence in this text about the relationship between identification and desire and from Freud's related uncertainty—here and elsewhere—about whether homosexual desire is uniquely suited to social feeling or its chief antagonist.[49]

Freud's argument thus joins homosocial collectivity, desire, and identification in a way that allows us to better grasp the threat and appeal, for C, of the Enormous Room's affects. Freud's formulation—that the "social feeling" of groups depends on a binding homosocial eros that opens egotism to the positivity of identification—is one that Cummings will tentatively engage (drawn as he is, on occasion, to the fleshy pleasures of intimate consubstantiality) and finally reject. The Freudian group dynamic that links eros to organization and that attributes the disorganization of groups to the remotion of love is palatable—for C—only when the intimate emotional ties of comradeship can be domesticated, their potential for abstraction in the service of violent collectives curtailed. The cosmopolitan character of the Enormous Room only intensifies the centrifugal demands for identification, moving them outward, concentrically, to ever more abstract planes of emotional affiliation. In this context, the challenge of identificatory curtailment is signaled in Cummings's strained formulation "a sole chaos of desire," which hopes to capture linguistically the compatibility of singularity and abstract social feeling. Hence, *The Enormous Room* participates in, and distinguishes itself from, a broader cultural discourse about the impossible demands that the Great War placed on male friendship, a discourse stretching from Freud, through popular autobiographical accounts of the Great War, to the work of canonical British war poets like Wilfred Owen, Siegfried Sassoon, and Robert Nichols. Sarah Cole has described this crisis as one between two modes of male intimacy: personal "friendship" between individual males brought by combat into intimate proximity as individuals, and "comradeship," an impersonal belonging to abstract, corporate unity. This distinction, Cole argues, "signals the difference between a world organized around the individual and one in which human beings, rendered passive and indistinguishable, become fodder for a voracious war machine."[50]

The difference between Cummings's treatment of wartime masculine intimacy and the accounts Cole discusses is that he makes no distinction between personal, enabling intimacies and impersonal, enervating ones. For the Kumrad, all intimacies, insofar as they are but germinal collectivities, have the potential to either engulf or restore the body and the subject. Thus, when Pete the Hollander, later in the novel, emerges from solitary confinement as an "uncanny" ghost, C remarks that within "three days Pete discarded the immateriality which had constituted the exquisite definiteness of his advent, and donned the garb of flesh-and-blood," becoming as "physically transformed as I have never seen a human being transformed by food and friends" (*ER* 130). Elsewhere, though, intimate community is a kind of disembodiment. Recall that C's first day ends as he is "swallowed by the Enormous Room," the same sort of subsumption of the individual by the mass that C had witnessed as the men, called to dinner, became a menagerie (79). Only through an imaginative substitution does this digestion become more thrilling than repugnant; that is, in talking to the prisoners, C "exchange[s] . . . a considerable mass of two-legged beings for a number of extremely interesting individuals" (79). Cummings's gambit, we might say, is to convert massive being into "extremely interesting" being. To do so, he pushes public being past "suggestion," identification, and collective libido altogether and into a sublime public inaccessibility that, like Josephine Baker, suggests nothing but itself and is thus strictly aesthetic. If the emotion that accompanies this sublime singularity can be called a feeling, it is less like love and more like aversion or disgust, which is to say that Cummings's idealized public intimacy is suffused with the affects of negativity that, for Freud, are residual in all intimate emotional relations.

The logic, then, seems to be that the menace of the Enormous Room's collective affects can be nullified if the Enormous Room, like the Folies Bergère, can be turned into a theater of singularity—if C, like Josephine Baker or Zip!, can become a freak.

This transformation is facilitated by the novel's overweening idiom of play, which displaces the scene of war with a rhetoric of amusement and also, more crucially, draws on the ludic to fashion an alternate temporality and its attendant model of collective life. Cummings's playtime works as a sort of compensatory heterotopia: it struggles to articulate an international fraternity of *homo ludens* that is—impossibly—sensuously proximate and sublimely singular, a community only achieved outside of time and history itself.[51] Imagining this collectivity demands a special mode of presentation, which C engages through the extended simile that begins the second, and longest, section of the novel—the timeless period spanning the end of his first day to the moment of his departure:

> It is like a vast grey box in which are laid helter-skelter a great many toys, each of which is itself completely significant apart from the always unchanging temporal dimension which merely contains it along with the rest. . . . I do not purpose to inflict upon the reader a diary of my alternative aliveness and non-existence at La Ferté . . . because the diary or time method is a technique which cannot possibly do justice to timelessness. I shall (on the contrary) lift from their grey box at random certain (to me) more or less astonishing toys; which may or may not please the reader, but whose colours and shapes and textures are part of the actual Present—without future and past—whereof they alone are cognizant who—so to speak, have submitted to an amputation of the world. (ER 82–83)

Such play is a kind of autism, the novel's imagined readership a community of epistemological amputees who proceed like the abjected character Surplice, whose gift is being "utterly ignorant," whose face "radiates the pleasure upon being informed that people are killing people for nobody knows what reason, that boats go under water and fire six-foot long bullets at ships, that America is not really just outside this window" (188, 189). In *The Enormous Room*, this strategic infancy amounts to an impossible desire for authentic experience, a nostalgia for a condition prior to history and language: for Cummings's ideal infants, to experience "necessarily means to re-accede to infancy as history's transcendental place of origin," as Giorgio Agamben puts it; it is "always something he is in the act of falling from, into language and into speech."[52]

Cummings's toy box, which would summon collectivity, also shifts its terms: far from the raucous collective cohering in "a sole chaos of desire," this community is beyond desire as well as language—each toy-member will be presented as "itself," "completely significant," and "apart," each figure following the other on the stage of individuation. The popular principle of formal organization for the novel's social world thereby shifts from the kinetic bigness of the circus, which threatens an imperious violence to difference in the name of more abstract, collective unities, to the select society of freak show, which separates and spectacularizes difference in the service of an asocial singularity. In this theater of individuation, C plays the role of barker, ascending from the more or less interesting inhabitants to those most spectacular individuals, those whom Cummings, following John Bunyan, calls "The Delectable Mountains." Consider, for example, Surplice, who, taunted as "Syph'lis" by the camp, illustrates for C a dynamic of theatricalized abjection that is much like the cultural work of freaks, who have often functioned as "scapegoats onto which to project all otherness, and against which to fantasize . . . solidarity," here the camp's fraternity of sufferers, bound by a common object of amusement (*MU* 216). More important, though, Surplice, provoking spectacular disgust, achieves a position outside of knowledge, for C, an enviable spot: "And now take Surplice, whom I see and hear and smell and touch and whom I do not know" (*ER* 186). A public being at once proximate to the senses and utterly unknowable, both near and far, Surplice embodies—like all of Cummings's freaks—that particularly uncanny mode of intimate relation that, for Georg Simmel, characterizes "the stranger," in whom are uniquely organized "the unity of nearness and remoteness of every human relation," so that "distance means that he, who is close by, is far, and strangeness means that he, who also is far, is actually near."[53]

Stranger-relations entail, for Simmel, a special mode of wandering uniting nearness and farness, bringing together a liberation from space and a kind of fixity within it: the stranger is "fixed within a particular group," but "his position in that group is determined, essentially, by the fact that he has not belonged to it from the beginning, that he imports qualities into it, which do not and cannot stem from the group itself" (S 402). In Cummings's novel, such wandering finds a face (and a name) in the "exquisite personage" of Josef Demestre, "the Wanderer," whom we glimpse earlier in the novel:

> On moving a little I discovered a face—perhaps the handsomest face that I have
> ever seen. . . . This face contained a beauty and dignity which, as I first saw it,
> annihilated the surrounding tumult without an effort. Around the carefully

formed nostrils *there was something almost of contempt.* The cheeks had known suns of which I might not think. The feet had travelled nakedly in countries not easily imagined. *Seated gravely in the mud and the noise of the cour, under the pitiful and scraggly pommier ... behind the eyes lived a world of complete strangeness and silence.* The composure of the body was graceful and Jovelike. ... As it turned out, he was once of The Delectable Mountains; to discover which I had come a long and difficult way. (*ER* 73–74, my emphasis)

The resilient terms of Cummings's appraisal of Lachaise's nudes resurface forcefully in this passage. The Wanderer is situated firmly in the "gurly trash," yet his singularity, figured through his contemptuous physiognomy, preexists the group and, in fact, does violence to these banal environs. It is as if this face is charged with the forceful production of identity itself. "The aesthetic significance of the face," as Simmel remarks in a lesser-known essay from 1901, lies in its projection of "an unmistakable personality." The success of this projection is the "achievement ... in mirroring the soul," of perfectly united spirit and substance; and conversely, its failure effects a "despiritualization" that takes the form of the uncanny, shattered bodies strewn throughout C's adventure, "figures whose limbs appear to be in danger of breaking off ... repugnant because they disavow what is properly human."[54] However erotic and fetishistic the poetic yield of C's gaze, the Wanderer's achievement is his ability to exist in a spatio-temporal *beyond.* The Mountains' difference, however delectable, will not be consumed; much like disgust itself in Kantian aesthetics, it is the truly sublime other of taste.[55] The Wanderer's is a body at once publicly present and inaccessible, rapt in prelinguistic bliss, a world "of complete strangeness and silence" that finds metonymic expression in his beard, "Blacker than Africa. Than imagination" (*ER* 161).

Similarly strange is the Zulu, whose "perfectly extraordinary face" is "perfectly at once fluent and angular, expressionless and sensitive" (ER 183). Without speaking, his body is a semantic vessel of unerring precision. With his "innate and unlearnable control over all which one can only describe as the homogeneously tactile," the Zulu is capable of haptic intimacy with his comrades and perfect isolation, able to convert "his utterly plastic personality into an amorous machine for a few seconds," and then "in order entirely to suffer" he can keep his emotions "carefully and thoroughly ensconced behind his rigid and mobile eyes" (174, 183). Like Lachaise's *Elevation,* like Josephine Baker, the Zulu earns the designation "an IS," for Cummings the sine qua non of emotional self-possession—his equivalent of a Poundian *virtú.* And yet this emotion, like the intimacy it brokers, is oddly kinetic, as well as controlled. The

Zulu's machinic eros not only bears out the fundamental mobility of stranger intimacy (freed from "established ties of kinship, locality, and occupation") but greases the wheels of what is, finally, a *formally abstract relation* (S 404). The "similarity, harmony, and nearness" of stranger intimacy, Simmel notes, "are accompanied by the feeling that they are not really the unique property of this particular relationship: they are something more general, something which potentially prevails between the partners and an indeterminate number of others, and therefore gives the relation . . . no inner and exclusive necessity" (407). A matter of form rather than internal need, such intimacy's emotional tone is "an element of coolness, a feeling of the contingency of precisely *this* relation—the connecting forces have lost their specific and centripetal character" (406, emphasis in original). Rather than move inevitably toward the abstraction of collective belonging, the Zulu's eros, if such it can be called, preserves self-identity through the distance of formal contingency. Just as the Zulu's intimate is anyone properly positioned by his amorous machine, so are the Kumrad's freaks familiar with anyone or anything who will play ground to their figure, witness to their public self-production.

Considering the intense primitivism that courses through all of Cummings's paeans to extraordinary corporeality, it is perhaps inevitable that Jean le Nègre "swaggers" in C's memory as the prison's "finest" specimen (ER 198). Jean is the novel's most perfect, and most disturbing, conflation of the generational and the racial other. His ludic drive is irrepressible, but more fascinating for C is Jean's hypervisibility, his function in the novel as a constantly performing, oversexualized cynosure of vision. His arrival is a sensation and, like nearly everything he does, a public spectacle. It is announced that a "NIGGER" has joined the company of the Enormous Room, and as Jean enters the prison, C struggles to get a glimpse of him through an opening in the Room's walls that looks onto the yard, but "at least two dozen men were at the peep-hole, fighting and gesticulating and slapping each other's backs with joy" (197). In the yard, he is "the mecca of all female eyes"; his battle with the Fighting Sheehey draws a "five-deep ring of spectators" and ends with "Jean alone occupying the stage. . . . Blood spotted here and there the wonderful chocolate carpet of his skin, his whole body glistened with sweat. His shirt was in ribbons over his beautiful muscles" (200, 208).

In America's ignoble history of the black curiosity, as Bill Brown notes, there are "opposing strategies for generating racialized aberrance: one theatricalizes difference, the other the impending end of difference" (*MU* 208). C's freak show, animated by Cummings's dual commitment to a monstrous singularity and a binding homogeneity, is constantly torn between these two: the former insists that singularities be seen, made obtrusively present; the latter contains the threat that such difference might die in intimacy. His staging of the Delectable Mountains works to make difference visible, to insist these personalities remain radically strange, outside of knowledge.[56] Yet his presentation of this select society is troubled by the paradox whereby the repetitious insistence of such figures of uncommon being can only more forcefully manifest a type—a "delectable mountain," say, or a "freak." Like Simmel's strangers, whose every non-common element is only a sign of some other, more abstract commonness, so Cummings's freaks "are not really conceived as individuals, but as strangers of a particular type" (S 407). Thus, we might say that the freak show's organizing principle is the "eccentric type," a paradox that haunts Cummings's theater of singularity and prompts ever more violent performances of identity, in which formerly inconsumable personalities become grounds for new, and more sublimely self-identical, figures.

This is nowhere more manifest than in C's stunning reverie over Jean:

> And I think of Jean Le Nègre . . . you are something to dream over, Jean . . . you are a sudden and chocolate colored thing . . . and the flesh of your body is like the flesh of a very deep cigar. Which I am still and always quietly smoking: always and still I am inhaling its very fragrant and remarkable muscles [. . .]
> —Boy, Kid, Nigger with the strutting muscles—take me up into your mind once or twice before I die [. . .] Quickly take me up into the bright child of your mind, before we go suddenly all loose and silly (you know how it will feel). Take me up (carefully; as if I were a toy) and play carefully with me; once or twice before I and you go suddenly all limp and foolish. (*ER* 214)

The intensely homoerotic fellow-feeling Cummings imagines here returns us to the chaos of desire, seeming to second both Freud's insight that "desexualized, sublimated homosexual love for other men" constitutes the Kumraderie of group attachments as well as his anxiety about these ties' proximity to eroticism. In Cummings's fantastic union, intimate eros—like the intractable complex of identification and desire that enables it—is both conjured and dissolved. Jean's flesh is vaporized before it is consumed, the scene of intimacy staged not only in the space of the imagination but in an impossible space of ahistorical infancy that looks like death.

Like the "social feeling" it instantiates and the homoerotic eros it occasions, Jean's body is displaced in the production of C's newly liberated and spectacularized modernist "I." All others must be upstaged, or as C explains, "perfectly annihilated by that vast and painful process of Unthinking which may result in a minute bit of purely personal feeling. Which minute bit is

Art" (ER 224). Not coincidentally, this, the novel's most oft-quoted passage, occurs when C appears for the first time as a specifically aesthetic spectacle, collecting leaves in the yard with B to the befuddlement of their spectators: "[E]veryone did not know that by this exceedingly simple means we were effecting a study of colour itself, in relation to what is properly called 'abstract' and some-times 'non-representative' painting" (224). As for Baker at the revue, so too for Cummings in *The Enormous Room:* "Frequently I would discover so perfect a command over myself as to easily reduce la promenade to a recently invented mechanism; or to [. . .] the maimed and stupid dolls of my imagination. Once, I was sitting alone on the long beam of silent iron and suddenly had the gradual complete unique experience of death . . ." (225). Here emerges the modernist freak, who in reducing the Room's denizens to an aesthetic mechanism spectacularizes his singular self-command, one confirmed only in the bliss of infancy or death. This is narcissism, and it is a far cry from the anarchic, overflowing sort that Herbert Marcuse imagines in *Eros and Civilization,* wherein "the libidinal cathexis of the ego (one's own body) may become the source and reservoir for a new," and nonrepressive, "libidinal cathexis of the objective world—transforming this world into a new mode of being."[57] The material world, for C, has been lost to the senses, severed by play, and this amputation finds a visual analogue late in the novel as C sits, like an acrobat, atop an iron beam placed in the center of the yard to give prisoners a "taste of the gymnastic." And it is just here that C will place himself when he is finally played with, like a toy: "Of an afternoon I sat with Jean or Mexique or the Zulu on the long silent beam of silent iron, pondering very carefully nothing at all . . . I felt myself to be, at last, a doll—taken out and occasionally played with and put back into his house and told to go to sleep" (*ER* 231–32). The grammatical agency is slippery and ambiguous enough to suggest that what appears to be C's most passive moment ("I felt myself to be") is actually his most masterful ("I willed myself to be"). In public, and in the company of men, C finds himself alone. The dream of intimacy has been eclipsed by sublimity of purely personal feeling that, for Cummings and Freud, is the other side of eros, and C is left to play with himself.

Such a Perfect Acrobat!

A fitting coda to Cummings's investigation of being-in-public, and its attendant dialectics of singularity and social heterogeneity, intimacy and self-feeling, is *Him* (1927), the poet's first play. Part surrealist phantasmagoria, part Dada nonsense, part expressionist horror show, this experimental drama marks Cummings's attempt to participate in the "great future" he envisioned for the theater in 1926: "said 'future' being the circus" (*MR* 144). Its setting is the unconscious of "Me," who undergoes anesthesia as the play begins for (we learn later) the abortion of her child, conceived with her lover "Him," an artist and playwright. Him's struggle is to achieve the sort of singular self-command C experiences at the close of *The Enormous Room;* and the play itself could be considered an attempt to reduce the variegated social horizon of the Jazz Age to a idealistic invention. Here, this experiential authenticity is explicitly the acrobat's:

> Him (*To her*): But imagine a human being who balances three chairs, one on
>> top of another, on a wire, eighty feet in the air with no net underneath, and
>> then climbs into the top chair, sits down, and begins to swing. . . .
> Me (*Shudders*): I'm glad I never saw that—makes me dizzy just to think
>> of it.
> Him (*Quietly*): I never saw that either.
> Me: Because nobody can do it.
> Him: Because I am that. But in another way, it's all I ever see.
> Me: What is?
> Him (*Pacing up and down*): This: I feel only one thing, I have only one conviction; it sits on three chairs in Heaven. Sometimes I look at it, with terror: it
>> is such a perfect acrobat! The three chairs underneath are three facts—it will
>> quickly kick them out from under itself and will stand on air; and in that
>> moment (because everyone will be disappointed) everyone will applaud.
>> Meanwhile, some thousands of miles over everyone's head, over a billion
>> empty faces, it rocks carefully and smilingly on three things, on three facts,
>> on: I am an Artist, I am a Man, I am a Failure—it rocks and swings and it
>> smiles and it does not collapse tumble or die because it pays no attention
>> to anything except itself. (1.2.10–11)[58]

This scene transpires in the first of the play's four lyrical scenes between Him and Me, which unfold in the private space of a lover's discourse where they discuss their affair, their growing estrangement, Him's artistry, and, obliquely, their unborn baby. *Him*'s action is divided between these scenes and the nine fantastical ones of the second act, which comprise a vaudeville of satirical burlesques from Him's unfinished play, *Mr. O Him, the Man in the Mirror,* and take aim at a range of social issues: Jazz Age masculinity; the commercialization and hucksterism of the modern; Him's schismatic identity; the crusade against modernist obscenity launched by John Sumner and the Society for the Suppression of Vice; Freudianism; the vacuity of the booboisee; American tourism abroad; a homosexualized Italian fascism staged at the

Old Howard Burlesque House in Boston; and the impoverished, mobbish malcontents of postwar Europe. For contemporary critics, the play's chief failure was, as Edmund Wilson put it, that "the development of the love affair and the connection with it of the phantasmagoria are obscure even to the reader, and one would think that for a theater audience they must prove completely baffling."[59] And yet this divide is precisely the point, since Him's aesthetic ideal, which precipitates the deterioration of his relationship with Me, depends upon a radical, vertiginous separation between the spectacular performer and the public, the self and the world.

This acrobat is no doubt familiar. It induces the nightmare of Josephine Baker all over again. But while Baker and the Delectable Mountains thrilled with an uncanny strangeness, "homogeneously tactile," Him's acrobat is prized for its immateriality, its specular separation from the realm of the senses altogether. It stands on air, a pure figure without ground. In fact, until the final scene, the play conspicuously lacks those rapturous descriptions of physicality that, normally, strain the bounds of Cummings's speech. Instead, the play moves consistently from material corporeality with all its proximate demands on sovereign singularity and toward a vaporous insubstantiality not unlike that of Jean le Nègre, at least as C dismembers him. This departure from the body is signaled in the play's first scene, where Me experiences her operation as artificial, a funhouse embodiment. The stage directions explain that we see *"a flat surface on which is painted a DOCTOR anesthetizing a WOMAN. In this picture there are two holes corresponding to the heads of the physician and of the patient, and through these holes protrude the living heads of a man and a woman"* (1.1.1, emphasis in original).

Identities and bodies are more labile, more specular than spectacular, in this play, which is both a function of its Strindbergian oneiricism and its decidedly Freudian bent, as well as a signal of Cummings's shifting figuration of being-in-public. *Him*'s most insistent leitmotif is the mirror, which marks the growing insubstantiality of Him's imaginative acrobatics, what he later calls "the disappearance of [his] being," as well as its difference from the grounded production of Me's maternal body. Distinguishing Him's hermetic aestheticism from Me's vital earthiness, critics have noted Him's failure to reconcile his desire for a transcendent beauty that dances out of sight with the necessity of being-in-the-world.[60] Indeed, Him worries early on that his quest for vital beauty has only driven him from reality—"But seriously: the nearer something is, the more outside of me it seems"; and later, he exclaims bitterly to Me "that beauty has shut me from the truth; that beauty has walls—is like this room, in which we are together for the last time, whose walls shut us in from everything outside" (1.4.26; 3.6.124). According to these readings, Him's failure to engage with "everything outside" and thus participate in a truly vital production (say, of childbirth) turns nightmarish in the play's penultimate scene, where Me's doctor becomes a freak show barker. This "harmless magician" introduces eight monstrous specimens before pulling the curtain to reveal the ninth, Princess Anankay, a figure draped in white and holding a newborn babe in her arms: *"The crowd recoils. . . . The woman's figure proudly and gradually lifts its head: revealing the face of ME. HIM utters a cry of terror. Total darkness—confused ejaculations of rage dwindle swirlingly to entire silence"* (3.6.138). Me's reproduction, whether or not it is actually abortive, as the silence suggests, is at least true. And her truth is confirmed by her place in the aristocracy of the freak show—that final, privileged position on the theater of individuation occupied by C at the close of *The Enormous Room*. On the other hand, Him, the would-be acrobat, in the play's final scene peers through the invisible wall but cannot believe that the faces he sees compose an audience of real people. Thus, damning "everything but the circus," Him is hoisted with his own petard: he remains shut against the reality of the exterior *"because* this [outside] is true" (3.7.139, my emphasis).

These sorts of readings are persuasive, but in judging Him's failure against Me's victory (judgments that reproduce Cummings's naturalization of the maternal production), they miss the play's greatest trick. In his essay "Les Saltimbanques," Jean Genet saw in acrobatic performance a process of autogenesis whereby the artist replaces his body with his art, or with images of himself: "Death—the Death of which I speak—is not the death that will follow your fall, but the one which precedes your appearance on the wire."[61] *Him* witnesses a similar substitution that occurs as both Him and Me are subsumed within another acrobatic "I" that is the illimitable product of Cummings's language, which, as it often does in modernist texts, becomes a sort of prosthetic extension that "enables the writer to move from interiority to literary productivity, to mediate self and world."[62] In this way, the condition of exteriority has not been banished from the text but reasserts its familiar function as the public (but not social) horizon for the performance of mastery, here of a linguistic sort. Edmund Wilson, remarking on the ostensiveness of the play's poetic language, was particularly taken by Cummings's "astonishing faculty for mimicking and caricaturing the speech of a variety of kinds of people: his soap-box orator, his sideshow barker, and his American ladies in Paris."[63]

Yet as we have seen, heterogeneity for Cummings always feeds the production of singularity, and linguistic excreta is no exception. Put another way, Cummings's mimetic faculty is never a mode of sensual relation that brings the self into sensuous "likening" with alterity, as it seems to be for the late Eisenstein and as it will be for Cornell (chapter 5). Instead, his mimesis serves the speculative dialectic of absolute idealism, turning all negativity into positive being. And thus its ventriloquism is a Derridean "metaphysical mimetologism," the imitation of the same within a closed performative stage of higher reconciliation, where the will to identity is now manifest both in the performing body and in logos itself.[64] This shift is nowhere more manifest than in the concluding freak show, where what is on display is not the monstrous bodies of the strange people per se but Cummings's masterful rendering of them in the barker's speech: "Nex we have, upun uh speciully design reinforce concrete platform wich travuls wid her wereever she goes duh knee plus ultry uv affectionut obesity duh indolent acmy uv amorous adisposity duh mountain uv libidinous ee-quilibrium Miss Eva Smith bettur known tuh uh legiun uv admirurs as Lidl Eva" (3.9.133). This is very much in keeping with the play's general shift of focus from somatic materiality of the body to the narcissistic embodiment of language whose every gesture outside the self is really just more of the same: "Metaphors are what comfort and astonish us, which are the projected brightness of ourselves" (1.4.27). If in *The Enormous Room* Cummings courts the uncanny heterogeneity of the outside only to publicize his own singular being, *Him*'s play of language finds Cummings more content to bask in the private refulgence of his own fictions, more shielded from the self's material and social contingencies, and purged of its uncanny doubleness, its ecstatic non-self-coincidence. This "PLAY," Cummings explained, "isn't 'about,' it simply 'is.'"[65] If the play ends in hermetic stillness and death, this is the welcome silence of the strictly aesthetic, its sensual substance destroyed by idealism's dream-pistol. Acrobatic speech falls silent in the rare air of pure experience. It is an idiom of colossal isolation and not, as Hartley will figure it, a tentative grammar of intimacy.

4

Light Figures

Indulge me in this undernarrated episode in the long history of modernist caprice. During the summer of 1943, Marsden Hartley made a visit to Madison Square Garden to catch "Spangles," a one-ring circus mounted by the Ringling Brothers. In early August, he wrote to his young friend Richard Sisson, an army sergeant stationed in New York, asking him if he had seen this "darling show" with a white horse that looked like "a page out of Wm. Blake's prophetic books."[1] Hartley, who would die just a month later, also explained that he was putting the finishing touches on his circus book, titled first "Circus" and later, more showily, "Elephants and Rhinestones: A Book of Circus Values." In this unfinished project, the aging Hartley would fulfill a longstanding desire to develop "the idea of acrobatics" and to "make [himself] historian for these . . . esthetes of muscular melody" for whom "life is but one long day in which to make beautiful their bodies, and make joyful the eyes of those who love to look at them!"[2] And so, sixty-six years old, with sore joints and an ailing heart, Hartley returns to the place under the big top where his eyes can best get their fill: "I make the awful ascent by the stairways, alas no elevators in the circus, and when I have achieved this exhausting feat, I am thoroughly at home."[3] This, the habitué's accustomed seat ("section twenty five or six"), is the very apex of pleasure: "I always have wanted to be opposite the flying trapeze," he claims, because "this is the act of all acts that I care for most. . . . [I]t is these artists who have always given me the most" (C2, 2; C1, 1).

The precise nature of the acrobat's gift is elusive but of crucial import for our understanding of modernism's broad repertoire of feeling in the public sphere, as well as of the political asymmetries informing such affective modes. Hartley's work not only troubles still-current gendered truisms about "(masculine) modernism's programmatic antisentimentalism, its ironic detachment from love," but urges us to consider the eccentric structuring of modernist affects within and across a dynamic and reflexive public sphere: here, for example, through the spectacular performances that so fascinated the modernists.[4] Indeed, Hartley's misty-eyed attachment to acrobats is not *just* feeling but theory, a matter of desire and its negotiation, an attempt to think a form of public intimacy ("the idea of acrobatics") premised, I will argue, not on a plummy fantasy of unmediated connection, nor a Habermasian "audience-oriented" intimacy that would train the subject to participate in rational-critical and market exchanges, but rather on a kind of subjective detachment produced by spectacle.

In his sustained connoisseurship of the intimate dimension of popular performance, Hartley surely was not alone, as the previous chapters have shown. But the stakes of his articulation of public intimacy, like the closely related terms of its conception—embodiment, vision, exteriorized detachment—were rather different from those informing, say, E. E. Cummings's celebration of the nonrelational thrill of being-in-public discussed in chapter 3.[5] In Hartley's case, these terms were clearly overdetermined by his homosexuality and its own fraught figuration within contemporary aesthetic and sexological discourse. In this sense, Hartley's attempt to think intimacy through itinerant public spectacles like the circus also resonates within the discourse of queer publicness, of homosexual intimacies in the public sphere.[6] At the risk of drawing too easy or anachronistic an analogy between Hartley's modernist thing for acrobats and contemporary queer politics, we might say that Hartley's acrobatic investments were attempts to imagine and legitimate, but not overly publicize, a fugitive mode of idealized relation. If not true intersubjectivity, this proximate grammar—constructed of figures both corporeal and linguistic—flickers between intimacy and publicity, social attachment and detachment, emotive personalism and spectacular disembodiment, surfacing both in Hartley's painting and in his writing in the form of what I call, after Hartley, the acrobat's "light figure." In what follows, I trace the graceful utility of these figures and their attendant grammar: as their conditions of possibility emerge in the "age of blood and iron" of Wilhelmine Berlin, as they mediate Hartley's tenuous relationship to New York Dada and the Stieglitz circle in the 1920s, and as they make their final, most eloquent performance in "Elephants and Rhinestones."

Feeling Outward

As Hartley saw it, the intimacy achieved by the truly light figure entailed a perceptual attunement to a larger plurality, the "hobnobbing with the universe" to which he was privy both on the streets of bohemian Paris and in that—for him—*flagrant* interior of Gertrude Stein's salon: "[Y]ou had much, in all human ways, out of an evening there. . . . [Y]ou had the quality of yourself and others, a kind of William James intimacy, which, as everyone knows, is style bringing the universe of ideas to your door in terms of your own sensations" (*AIA* 194–95).[7] Like James, Hartley insisted on the complex beauty of a world of difference composed of "innumerable unforetold particulars" but accessed ultimately through individual perceptual experience, the "stuff of which everything is made."[8] Hartley put it thus in his essay "Concerning Fairy Tales and Me":

> I am related to the world by the way I feel attached to the life of it as exemplified in the vividness of the moment. I am, by reason of my peculiar personal experience, enabled to extract the magic from the moment, discarding the material husk of it precisely as the squirrel does the shell of the nut.
> I am preoccupied with the business of transmutation—which is to say, the proper evalution of life as idea, of experience as delectable diversion. (*AIA* 8)

"Experience as delectable diversion." This logic seems simple enough: the more vivid the moment, the more bound to life one becomes; the more entrancing the spectacle, the stronger the attachment between the spectator and the heterogeneous splendor of outside life. And yet this moment of attunement is also figured as a separation of sorts, a discarding of the "material husk" of experience in the moment of "delectable diversion." As Hartley explains this tension in an essay on the "new kind of poetic diversion" in the work of Emily Dickinson, a kind of "sublime, impertinent playfulness" is achieved through a "celestial attachedness, or must we call it detachedness" (*AIA* 200). Here, Hartley offers us a freighted modernist category, "experience," that remains strangely unrecognizable. This kind of feeling outward, we might say, is Jamesian insofar as its vehicle is the perceiving individual, but decidedly un-Jamesian in its centrifugal movement away from the "private and the personal" and toward the "cosmic and the general," in its seeming departure from the true self whose geometric locus James once identified at "the innermost center of the circle."[9] For Hartley, as for Walter Benjamin and the Frankfurt School tradition more broadly, "experience" is a conceptual "hinge between consciousness and world, inside and outside, monadic subject and community," but there is no mourning here of the eclipse of genuine *Erfahrung* by enervated *Erlebnis*.[10] Nor is "diversion" a compensatory perceptual mode, as "distraction" is in Benjamin's and Siegfried Kracauer's formulations.[11] Conceptually speaking, diversion is delicious, rich with tasty antinomies Hartley toys with but refuses to resolve: the senses exist in a state of heightened receptivity and diversion simultaneously, and experience radiates away from the individual yet remains rooted in private delectation.

These erotic dynamics materialized early in Hartley's career in the streets of Wilhelmine Berlin, where the painter moved from Paris after befriending the German sculptor Arnold Rönnebeck. As Hartley explained in his autobiography, the spectacle of the Kaiser's parade renewed his "love for any kind of pageantry, all coming from early boyhood and . . . the coming of the circus to Lewiston"; in the "voluptuous tension" of prewar Berlin, Hartley "at last could have all [he] wanted of crowd parade pageantry public glamour and the like" (*SP* 87, 86, 90). Located within this unpunctuated chain of figures for publicness that joins cherished moments from Hartley's boyhood to the urban present of martial modernity, the Kaiser's parade and the "real Barnum circus" code and cross-reference each other. What Hartley conjures, as a result, is less a glib militarism that conflates war and play than a potent and portable fantasy of spectatorial release, of the joyous and intimate dynamic of "feeling outward" mobilized, in this instance, by the martial scene: "I could always know that I was quite like other people when I was with a lot of people. [The crowd] would take me out and make me feel outward and that has always been necessary—for it is a very bad thing to live inside so much—as no one has learned better than myself" (90). In this, Hartley's riff on the "man of the crowd," Charles Baudelaire's dandy fails to confirm his heroic individualism; Georg Simmel's "blasé" metropolitan man finds himself suddenly, erotically resensitized.[12] Most important, the sensual publicity occasioned by the Kaiser's parade satisfies the expatriate's need "to feel outward" in a way that manages to be both common (it reminds him that he "was quite like other people") and intimate (it makes him "feel at home") at once.[13] Thus, this scene is remarkable not because it reworks a familiar trope of modern sociality or, more locally, a common swerve in Hartley's career from inwardness to exteriority and publicity, but rather because it marks an instance in which these distinctions collapse: a moment of intimate pleasure that Hartley would repeatedly seek in public spaces—in music halls, at the Kaiser's parade, or near the trapeze.[14]

Hartley realized early on that this dynamic of "feeling outward" mobilized by public spectacle required a specific kind of body. In Berlin, the movement from the private to the cosmic was occasioned by the nation's thoroughly aestheticized military-political regime, embodied in the "Kaiser's special guard—all in white" and memorialized in Hartley's *The Warriors* (1913) (SP 90; see figure 11). Hartley was overcome by the "flair and perfection" of the guard and, by extension, of the thoroughly martial German nation, whose "spick and spanness" and "cleanliness" in "the order of life [Hartley] had never witnessed anywhere" (86). An homage to this order, *The Warriors* mirrors it with a perfectly balanced composition and, at the painting's edges, a symmetrical dispersal of the soldiers within an abstracted field. The celestial, ethereal placement of these bodies as they march toward the setting sun (and thus, as Hartley explains, toward their deaths) makes clear that these are bodies en route to becoming *Geist,* political myth: "A real ecstasy for war is the only modern religious ecstasy—The only means of displaying the old time martyrdom—one shall not forget their handsome smiling faces going by—waving hands, throwing kisses and shouting auf Wiedersehen."[15]

Seemingly celestial, these handsome bodies are not yet truly light figures; more pedantic than playful, they offer a hard lesson in the costs of a spectacular attachment, and one that energizes Hartley's formulation of public intimacy. Critics tend to agree that *The Warriors* marks Hartley's "first significant figurative effort" in an early career marked by a reluctance to treat the human form;[16] further, this figuration carried an especially intense private charge for Hartley, who had fallen for Germany's militarism, its liberated *Leibeskultur,* and its relatively tolerant atmosphere toward homosexuality as he fell for a specific soldier, Lieutenant von Freyburg (Rönnebeck's cousin), who would die in the Great War in 1914. Given these personal attachments and the powerful associations between the German military and homosexuality in the early decades of the twentieth century, *The Warriors* works as a thoroughly spectacular index of private feeling.[17] Further, this exteriorization of intimacy—anchored in the mystico-spiritualist theories then fueling German artistic culture—implies an untroubled correspondence between formal exterior and subjective interior, a "heavy figure" that resurfaces, in intensely gendered terms, in the aesthetic theories of Stieglitz circle critics.[18]

If Hartley increasingly turns, as I argue below, to the light figures that confound such easy trafficking between surface and depth, the War Motif series—begun in 1914, as a memorial to von Freyburg—lays the conceptual groundwork for these figures' emergence. These paintings, including *Portrait of a German Officer* (1914) (see figure 12) and *Painting No. 47, Berlin* (1914–15)

Figure 11. Marsden Hartley, *The Warriors,* 1913. Oil on canvas, 47 1/2 × 47 1/4 in. Private collection, Massachusetts. Courtesy Salander-O'Reilly Galleries, New York.

(see figure 13), mark a salient departure from the *The Warriors'* unchecked rhapsody of an ecstatic collectivity that depends upon public bodies poised in martial orchestration and political sublimation. Though Hartley would publicly disavow any personal symbolism in these paintings, his friend Rönnebeck decoded some of the imagery: von Freyburg's initials, his age at death (twenty-four), the Iron Cross he received for his acts in battle. These symbols are superimposed on the trappings of the German military such that the flat collages scan anthropomorphically, recalling the lost totality of von Freyburg's body through a quasi-cubist fragmentation (*SV* 152). The disfigurement and death that Hartley could romanticize, prior to von Freyburg's own, as a kind of martyrdom are, these paintings suggest, the cost of the spectacular body dangerously attached to a larger totality. For here, von Freyburg's body is literally all spectacle, dispersed into a field of military signs in a manner bespeaking not spiritual triumph but the painful absence of a body. But for Hartley, the recalcitrant exteriority of the painting is quite useful.

Two of Hartley's more astute critics, noting this strategic disembodiment, have emphasized the "elaborate veiling, layering, and masking of identity" undertaken in these images and suggested how Hartley "keep[s] desire at bay" here by withholding the physical body of his lover, how he diffuses homosexual desire "through the multiple masks of literary obfuscation, abstract style, encoding, and death" (*PGCT* 179; *SV* 161, 162). The implications of this technique can be drawn even more sharply: these paintings demonstrate Hartley's investment in surpassing the dichotomies of private and public, interiority and exteriority. As such, Hartley's lesson in the excesses of ecstatic intimacy in the War Motif series becomes a nascent theory of public intimacy: at once *all* sign and hushed, the paintings suggest how Hartley's attachment to corporeal glamour—of the Prussian guard, of Barnum and Bailey—was premised on detachment, on spectacle's ability to absent the self rather than present it.

"Vivacious Hobbyhorse"

In 1921, in the crossfire of the American avant-garde's reigning aesthetic and corporeal paradigms—the Stieglitz circle and Dada's New York avatar—Hartley published his first book of criticism, *Adventures in the Arts: Informal Chapters on Painters, Vaudeville, and Poets*. Over and against New York Dada's cerebral and detached treatment of the commodified, mass-produced body, Alfred Stieglitz promulgated what Marcia Brennan has recently dubbed "embodied formalism," a "general discursive tendency" swirling around those artists (Georgia O'Keeffe, Arthur Dove, John Marin, and, more peripherally, Charles Demuth and Hartley) whom Stieglitz promoted as part of his call for an organic American art, freed from Puritan repression and continental effeteness (*PGCT* 8). This tendency, Brennan argues, was rooted in a model of "aestheticized, integrated selfhood" in which abstract and symbolic forms were understood by painters and their critics alike as transparent, sublimated "analogues of the artists' own gendered presences," and "no divisions obtained between the subject's body, their spirit, and the world around them" (43, 3, 43).

Hartley's *Adventures* is literally framed by these discourses: it begins with an introduction by Waldo Frank, Stieglitz's friend and champion, ends with

Figure 12. Marsden Hartley, *Portrait of a German Officer,* 1914. Oil on canvas, 68¼ × 41⅜ in. The Metropolitan Museum of Art, Alfred Stieglitz Collection, 1949 (49.70.42). Image © The Metropolitan Museum of Art.

Figure 13. Marsden Hartley, *Painting No. 47, Berlin,* 1914–15. Oil on canvas, 39 × 31⁵/₈ in. Hirshhorn Museum and Sculpture Garden, Smithsonian Institution. Gift of Joseph H. Hirshhorn, 1972. Photograph by Lee Stalsworth.

Hartley's essay "The Importance of Being 'Dada,'" and is filled in between with a range of essays on painting, poetry, film, and performance, all penned in Hartley's quirky style—witty, epigrammatic, and relentlessly Emersonian in its elliptical manner. Frank's opening salvo presents the author as itinerant, various, and profoundly intimate; his essays are "chronicles not so much

[of] these actual worlds as his own pleasure of them. They are but mirrors, many-shaped and lighted, for his own delicate, incisive humor."[19] Yet they are also, by virtue of their critical publicity, a form of embodiment:

> When the creator turns critic, we are in the presence of a consummation: we have a complete experience: we have a sort of sacrament. For to the intrusion of the world he interposes his own body. In his art, the creator's body would be itself intrusion. The artist is too humble and too sane to break the ecstatic flow of vision with his personal form. The true artist despises the personal as an end. He makes fluid, and distills his personal form. He channels it beyond himself to a Unity which of course contains it. But Criticism is nothing which is not the sheer projection of a body. The artist turns Self into a universal Form: but the critic reduces Form to Self. Criticism is to the artist the intrusion, in a form irreducible to art, of the body of the world. What can he do but interpose his own?[20]

Notice here how Frank figures the act of criticism—the sheer projection of the body into the world—as a secularized transubstantiation, one that reverses the centrifugal movement of aesthetic production from private to cosmic, forcing Hartley-as-critic back into a personalism and, by extension, a body whose publicity Hartley found increasingly dangerous in the wake of the war's carnage. While this frame is in keeping with Frank's relentless stumping throughout the 1920s for a corporeal nativism in American art, it sits awkwardly around the variegated essays of *Adventures,* which bounce nervously between the competing charms of corporeality and intellection, personalism and detachment, intimacy and publicity.[21] As exercises in taste, then, these critical essays entail not just, as Frank explains, the "sheer projection of a body" but also, as Joseph Litvak puts it in a slightly different register, the queer projection of an excessive desire—a sophistication that seems suspiciously "*impure,* contaminated from the outset by a desiring, and thus disgusting, body" within a culture wherein gay men "have traditionally functioned as objects of such distinguished epistemological and rhetorical aggressions as urbanity and knowingness."[22] As an adventure in queer sophistication, Hartley's critical delectation stands not—as Frank would have it—in opposition to the "actual" world but as its very contested terrain; here, Hartley's indulgence in circus matters, like the mode of intimacy these spectacles occasion, is as excessive as it is expertly controlled.

The terms of these dialectics are established in "Whitman and Cézanne," for Hartley, the "two most notable innovators" in poetry and painting, alike in "esthetic intention" but divided by their "concepts of, and their attitudes toward[,] life": "For the one, life was . . . something to stay close to always, for the other, it was something to be afraid of almost to an abnormal degree; Walt Whitman and his door never closed, Paul Cézanne and his door seldom or never opened, indeed, were heavily padlocked against the intrusion of the imaginary outsider" (*AIA* 30, 32). Hartley nevertheless notes that Whitman's open-door policy fueled a corporeal extensiveness that was

> at one and the same time his virtue and his defect. For mystical reasons, it was imperative for him to include all things in himself. . . . That he could leave nothing out was, it may be said, his strongest esthetical defect, for it is by esthetical judgment that we choose and bring together those elements as we conceive it. . . . So that it is the tendency in Whitman to catalogue in detail the entire obvious universe that makes many of his pages a strain on the mind as well as on the senses, and the eye especially. (34)

With this critique of Whitmanesque publicity comes an important revision of the terms of spectacle: in imperial Berlin, Hartley's eye is insatiable, overcome by stimuli from the outside, ecstatic with the pleasure of an exteriorized self made intimate with the universe: "The coming face to face with so much life and art all at once—was all but blinding—but I have blue eyes and blue eyes can take in all things and not be disturbed by them—except to be extatically [*sic*] disturbed—which is their way of being passionate" (*SP* 90). Now, he seems suspicious of the moment of self-absenting that—in the Emersonian and Whitmanesque model—enlarges the appetite of a gluttonous "I." These "primitives" have "voiced most of all the imperative need of essential personalism, of direct expression out of direct experience, with an eye to nothing but quality and proportion" (*AIA* 36). Whitman's limitation, then, is not his personalism but the centrifugal movement of his senses. The excesses of the mystical eye, we might say, must be chastened by the kind of discrimination and taste found in Cézanne: "It is the mark of good taste to reject that which is unessential, and the 'tact of omission,' well exemplified in Cézanne, has been found excellently axiomatic" (34).

For the training of the newly tractable eye, and for an example of the controlled relations such sight, and such spectacles, occasion, Hartley turns to the popular performances of vaudeville and the circus in three thematically related essays: "The Twilight of the Acrobat," "Vaudeville," and "A Charming Equestrienne," all written between 1917 and 1920. Musing wistfully on the acrobat's "aesthetic" death as "Twilight" opens, Hartley pouts that in contemporary variety, "everything seems tuxedoed for drawing room purposes" and blames this loathsome state on "the so-called politeness of vaudeville," which has eliminated "our once revered acrobats. The circus notion has been replaced by the parlor entertainment notion" (*AIA* 156, 158).[23] The "variety that was once a joy is now a bore," and the "habitual patron can no longer endure the offerings of the present time with a degree of pleasure, much less with ease" (160). So Hartley promptly calls for "the re-creation of variety into something more conducive to light pleasure for the eye," heralding the "return of the acrobat in a more modern dress" (160). What Hartley has in mind,

> for instance, [is] a young and attractive girl bareback rider on a cantering white horse inscribing wondrous circles upon a stage exquisitely in harmony with herself and her white or black horse as the case may be; a rich cloth of gold backdrop carefully suffused with rose. There could be nothing handsomer, for example, than young and graceful trapezists swinging melodically in turquoise blue doublets against a fine peacock background or it might be a rich pale coral—all the artificial and spectacular ornament dispensed with. (159)

Wishing aloud, in vain, for a "Beardsley of the stage," a messianic set designer who might best frame his scopic pleasure, Hartley will go it alone, indulging in hypothetical fancy: the acrobats "need first of all large plain spaces upon which to perform, and enjoy their own remarkably devised patterns of body" (*AIA* 163, 162–63).[24] This enjoyment is both the performer's narcissistic self-enjoyment as spectacle (the equestrienne "exquisitely in harmony with herself") and, paradoxically, a spectatorial pleasure premised on "intimacy with the beauty" of the performer, which Hartley would intensify, in his example, by relocating the Brothers Rath acrobats to the coveted center of the bill (163). And it is this scene's paradoxical nature—the way the performers' theatricalized isolation heightens spectatorial intimacy—that pleases Hartley. The intimacy it imagines between the acrobat's body and the spectator's eye is mediated by beauty, made tractable by framing, orchestration, and discernment. In this way, when Hartley's fantasies of orchestration seem most excessive, they are, in fact, the most controlled, the most tasteful, and thus the most delightful.

Indeed, while Hartley decries the enervating ornamentation of higher vaudeville, his own set design nevertheless goes for baroque:

> I want a Metropolitan Opera for my project. An orchestra of that size for the larger concerted groups, numbers of stringed instruments for the wirewalkers and jugglers, a series of balanced woodwinds for others, and so on down the line, according to the quality of the performer. There should be a large stage for many elephants, ponies, dogs, tigers, seals. The stage should then be made more intimate for the solos, duets, trios, and quartets among the acrobats. I think a larger public should be made more aware of the beauty and skill of

these people, who spend their lives in perfecting grace and power of body, creating the always fascinating pattern and form, orchestration if you will, the orchestration of the muscles into a complete whole. (*AIA* 164)

Another fantasy of drilled figures, this dream recalls the Kaiser's parade, the drama of sublimated bodies whose exposure, in von Freyburg's case, promises politico-spiritual totality but ends in death and loss. Hartley himself draws the mnemonic links between this playful project of corporeal orchestration and a historical moment of prewar erotic plenitude in "A Charming Eques-trienne," when he dates his "happiest memories" of circus expression, of the "artists of bodily vigor, of muscular melody," to "the streets of Paris before the war, the incomparably lovely fêtes. Only the sun knows where these dear artists may be now" (176, 175, 176). (In fact, the language here anticipates his later description of *The Warriors* in his autobiography who, remember, "went out into the sun and didn't come back.")[25] Thus, Hartley's circus fan-tasy is both nostalgic, harking back to a prelapsarian, prewar intimacy, and strategic, remembering erotic fullness within the controlled domain of "light pleasure for the eye" (160).

More than just the fruit of Hartley's erotic investment in the acrobat's body, intimacy (again, of a decidedly tractable sort) provides the foundation of what he calls the "idea of acrobatics": the functionality of the acrobat both as a body viewed and as a mode of embodiment, a visible object of "light pleasure" and a figure of proximate relation. Consider, for example, Hartley's rendering in the "Vaudeville" essay of an especially striking "acrobatic novelty" in "The Legrohs" act: "This 'Legroh' knows how to make a superb pattern with his body, and the things he does with it are done with such ease and skill as to make you forget the actual physical effort and you are lost for the time being in the beauty of this muscular kaleidoscopic brilliancy. You feel it is like 'puzzle—find the man,' for a time" (*AIA* 171–72). Offering the performative version of the same "puzzle" of the War Motif series, the acrobat's skill is his ability to trace a pattern so spectacular that it absents the performer, whose humanity (find the man!) transforms into "lovely flower and animal forms" or, even more abstractly, into "ever changing ever shifting bits of colour" and pattern (172). This loss is doubled in the spectator, whose purely visual pleasure unburdens him of thought as "the tumbling blocks of the brain . . . fall into heaps": "You have no chance for the fatigue of problem [*sic*]. You are at rest as far as think-ing is concerned. It is something for the eye first and last" (173, 172).

The "idea of acrobatics," for Hartley, is oxymoronic, since this art jettisons ideation in both practitioner and spectator: It "is the art where the human mind is for once relieved of its stupidity. The acrobat is master of his body and he lets his brain go a-roving upon other matters, if he has one" (173). Issuing from the acrobat's mindlessness (a state surely anathema to Marcel Duchamp and Francis Picabia) is a silence that is itself useful for Hartley, suggestive of a Jamesian sociality: "He is expected to be silent. He would agree with William James, transposing 'music prevents thinking' into 'talking prevents silence.' In so many instances, it prevents conversation. That is why I like tea chit-chat. Words are never meant to mean anything then. They are simply given legs and wings, and they jump and fly. They land where they can, and fall flat if they must" (173). The logic is seemingly paradoxical—talking prevents silence *and* conversation—until we realize that Hartley is after a kind of speech situated precisely on the seam of sociality. The privileged quiescence of the acrobat hinges on a special, physical language that in becoming publicly embodied (like the words that, in tea talk, sprout appendages) is evacuated of heavy significance and deep interiority. Unlike the more familiar mode of modernist impersonality as, for example, T. S. Eliot defines it—wherein the poet detaches from the enervating immediacy of modern personation by finally embedding his language in the marrow of cultural tradition—Hartley depersonalizes in order to preserve less entangling interpersonal connections, to facilitate more mobile, more tractable attachments.[26] Hostile, like Eliot, to Romantic notions of interiority, Hartley idealizes a language whose lightness enables an intersubjective condition at once flighty and controlled.[27] Not saddled with ponderous meaning, this tacit speech allows the agile ego to absent itself by becoming entirely spectacular, relieved of semantic weightiness and, by extension, of the burden of corporeal transparency.

Given the logic of sexual transparency espoused by the Stieglitz circle, the terms of Paul Rosenfeld's review of *Adventures* fail to surprise.[28] Picking up on the book's campy ostentation, Rosenfeld notes how "Hartley has striven to make his writing a superior sort of talk, part of a seriously developed aesthetic of a spirit exquisitely civilized and urbane."[29] But he dismisses the "more simple, more slight, more fluffily iridescent" prose of *Adventures* as an attempt

> to transcend the arid empty space about him by playing with bits of bright silk, curious toys, heavy and fantastic flower-cups. Grace and charm and peacock-like magnificence hide and yet betray utter fatigue with never having really lived. Author and audience are in tacit conspiracy to fix their minds on some jolly and curious fragment of physical, unthinking life on "minstrels of muscular musical melody," on girls who play ivory and silver diamond-studded accordions, on the "brilliant excitation of the moment," that the immanence of death and corruption be forgotten.[30]

For Rosenfeld, Hartley's dandified idiom is all small talk: it fixates on the unthinking corporeality of its subjects with a compensatory intensity that would transcend an underlying experiential sterility (the price, no doubt, of a bad object choice) or, in still more cowardly fashion, ignore the heavy reality of the exterior, the "immanence of death and corruption." In this reading, then, Hartley's language hoists itself on its own petard: when it trains its attention on the physical, it is too light, its subject's seeming corporeality a mere pretext for unthinking detumescence.

Dismissing the book's talkiness as the flaw of a gabby queer whose language and pigment are alike unmanned by a "vagabond *libido,*" Rosenfeld's review misses the subtleties of Hartley's argument about language, especially as this communication is figured through the acrobat, who may be dumb but is never stupid.[31] As Hartley later frames it in "The Greatest Show on Earth," he "puts his mind into his muscles and into his eyes and he leaves purely cerebral concepts and words to their own natural futility."[32] Intellect and language have not been abandoned, as Rosenfeld would assert, but are no longer *purely* cerebral—rather, they are embodied in a fashion that produces their "exquisite speechlessness." As "bodies made intelligent as well as perfect," Hartley's acrobats model a synthesis of body and mind as well as the kind of spectatorship predicated on this synthesis (GSE 88):

> With the proper training of the eyes to register shape and movement with intelligence, there will be no time for those inward dramas involving the tragedies of mankind. It is eyes, I believe, that must do the work of the world, eyes that must satisfy all aesthetic needs. Eyes that truly see and, seeing, transmit to the mind those impressions that make for the sheer charm of existence, devoid of interpretation and confused commentary; eyes that really possess synthetically what they encounter; eyes that make emotional history out of casual opportunity; what a rarity they are, even among artists! (GSE 33)

These eyes are the acrobat's and, potentially, those of his spectators. And this passage is riddled with a series of paradoxes that surge from Hartley's attempt to articulate the sort of intimacy this figure enacts with his viewer. On the one hand, the circus spectacle produces a simple distraction; its sensory intensity provides a diversion from "inward dramas" and "the sense of life's disillusionments." In this sense, à la Rosenfeld, the acrobat is simply a figure of detachment and an occasion of the same in his viewer. But Hartley's fantasy is more ambitious: the acrobat's eyes are charged not just with "satisfying aesthetic needs" but also with the work of the material world. They are linked to the mind, but their semantic yield resists "interpretation and confused commentary." They are attached to their object (they "possess synthetically what they encounter") and subject (they "make emotional history out of casual opportunity"). As such, they come to embody a Dickinsonian attached detachment, the conceptual cynosure of "experience as diversion."

This experience, not surprisingly, is irresistible for Hartley, who concludes his essay with yet another circus fantasy, and one that he can enjoy not just as spectator but as participant: "If there really is to be a Heaven hereafter, then let me go straight by pelican air service to that division of it set apart for the circus and go pellmell for the rings and the bars, till I can join the splendid horde all turning and springing and flying through the properly-roped spaces and merge myself in the fine pattern which these superior artists make in what will no longer be 'The Greatest Show on Earth'" (GSE 88). In this passage, with its characteristic mix of abandon and orchestrated restraint (the space of ecstasy must always be "properly-roped"), Hartley enacts his version of Dada as he formulates it in "The Importance of Being 'Dada,'" the final essay in *Adventures*: "I ride my own hobby-horse away from the dangers of art which is with us a modern vice at present, into the wide expanse of magnanimous diversion from which I may extract all the joyousness I am capable of from the patterns I encounter" (*AIA* 251). This essay is not, as Brennan argues, a statement of "affiliation with the New York Dada movement" that inaugurates Hartley's growing disavowal of the personal (PGCT 169–70).[33] Nor is it, as Rosenfeld would have it, a rhapsody of the "brilliant excitation of the moment" that trades fancy for life itself. Rather, Hartley's understanding of Dada as a kind of capricious individualism is neither Duchampian nor Picabian but itself highly capricious, a jejune misreading of the movement.[34] Hartley is "a dada-ist because it is the nearest" he has come to "a scientific principle in existence," a principle of fanciful enjoyment that is nevertheless outward-bound: "I have a hobby-horse therefore—to ride away with, out into the world of intricate common experience; out into the arena with those who know what the element of life itself is, and that I have become an expression of the one issue in the mind worth the consideration of the artist, namely fluidic change" (*AIA* 251).

This joyride remains controlled insofar as the experience finds Hartley tastefully merged within a fine pattern.[35] Rocking through flux with an engineer's precision, Hartley's hobbyhorse nevertheless refuses to settle, or to settle down. Rather than substituting the sterile, opaque, or otherwise detached Dada corporeality for a vital, transparent one in the mold of the Stieglitz circle, Hartley's acrobat—flitting on the seam of public and private—allows him to think both at once. Neither, alone, would satisfy, the former forsaking the virility and vitality of the plastic body for the mind, the latter predicated on weighty and trouble-some semantic equations between art and essence, text and sex, publicity and intimacy. Attached to the "intricate world of common experience," the light figure mediates the self and "that to which I am not related" with a rhetoric of corporeal intimacy that, by virtue of its lightness, achieves a celestial detach-ment:

> You will find, therefore, that if you are aware of yourself, you will be your own perfect dada-ist, in that you are for the first time riding your own hobby-horse into infinity of sensation through experience, and that you are one more sat-isfactory vaudevillian among the multitudes of dancing legs and flying wits. You will learn that after all that the bugaboo called LIFE is a matter of the tightrope and that the stars will shine their frisky approval as you glide, if you glide sensibly, with an eye on the fun in the performance. (*AIA* 253)

Experience as diversion here remains resolutely childish, and this passage is not simply innocent, as Frank would have it, but strategically so. To bor-row from Litvak again, Hartley's hobbyhorse figures a kind of sophisticated naïveté, riding away not from the actual but from the monotonous actuality of "universal heterosexualization, whereby 'growing up' in fact means shut-ting down, tuning out, closing off various receptivities that make it possible to find the world *interesting*."[36] In "Elephants and Rhinestones," Hartley would struggle to disentangle the acrobat's vitality from his heterosexual deathliness. But for now, this walk on the high wire is predominantly a gay affair.

The "Codona Madness"

If it is not the properly "historical account" of the wonders of acrobatic life proposed in *Adventures,* "Elephants and Rhinestones" remains Hartley's last and most sustained foray into the vicissitudes of public intimacy and the fate of its enabling figures. "Elephants" is loosely organized through Hartley's ruminations—ranging in length from paragraph-long bursts to four-page rhapsodies—on individual performers, acts, lore, and trends in the circus, the institution that he has "loved . . . all [his] life, just as one loves one's dog, or pet canary, one's marmoset, or one's cockatoo" (C2, 1). Fragmented and fawning, "Elephants" is this circus fan's *Passagen-Werk* and generally as-sumes catalogue form: Hartley lists the individual name of a performer or event ("Barbette," "Spangles—A Continental Circus," "Grock," and so on) and follows it with his reminiscence, often driven by a wildly associative train that leads him across time and space and then (usually) back to the subject under consideration, which is always both the ostensible subject and Hartley himself. This freewheeling narrative, while personal, sentimental, and quite melancholy, deploys throughout an inherently intersubjective rhetorical mode. As it was for Henri de Toulouse-Lautrec, "one of the few great artists of modern times to whom the circus was an intimate language," the circus for Hartley is a matter of "you" and "I," and Hartley's linguistic gambit in "Elephants" is to talk in an intimate language that approximates the elusive speech of the acrobat, to fashion a proximate grammar of relation from the intimate world of the circus (C1, 57). Not surprisingly, then, Hartley's linguistic figures, like the privileged physiques of their corporeal analogue the acrobat, are rarely weighty. Rather, to poach the terms of Hartley's critique of certain acrobatic "egoists" like the Fratellinis and Con Colleano, this "type of work calls for a slight and agile figure . . . for light figures" (C2, 10). Such lightness, as a mode of gender (not, like Colleano, "too masculine"), as well as a condition both semantic (it is not saddled with ponderous meaning) and, by extension, subjective (it is an ego negated through spectacle), continues and extends the "tea chit-chat" he champions in *Adventures*.

But in "Elephants," Hartley seems torn between keeping his figures light and burdening them with significance. Indeed, in the middle of "Circus," we find, in isolation, three quotations from the British sexologist Henry Havelock Ellis, which appear under the phrase "Elephants and Rhinestones" on what looks like a provisional title page. These epigraphs, which effectively give the lie to Hartley's lightness, appear as follows:

> I never grow weary of the significance of little things. It is the little things that give its bitterness to life, the little things . . . that direct the current of activity, the little things that alone really reveal the intimate depths of personality.
> —Havelock Ellis

> Everything is serious and at the same time frivolous.

> There is the whole universe to dream over and one's life is spent in the perpetual doing of an infinite series of little things. It is a hard task, if one loses the sense of the significance of little things, the little loose variegated threads which are yet the stuff of which a picture of the universe is made. H.E. (C1, 72)

Taking the frivolous seriously and imbuing the superficial with interiority, Ellis's epigraphs reverse the work of the light figure, making too big a deal of little things. Thus, Hartley would seem to overburden his light figures, which now not only carry the referential heft of sexological discourse but are here

uniquely charged with "really reveal[ing] the intimate depths of personality." Hartley's ambivalence toward his light figures is, in fact, the structuring contradiction of the rhetoric of "Elephants," whose lightness conjures a
vital, intimate community of spectacular performers and "fan-atic" spectators, but is haunted throughout by loss, death, and the annihilation of the
acrobatic self. At the center of this world, and of this grammar, is the drama
of husband-and-wife duo Alfredo Codona and Lillian Leitzel, for Hartley
the lightest, most spectacular of aerialists: "I miss with a wide band of deep
mourning on my arm those two grand artists of the air . . . both of whom
came to such tragic ends, one by a fall while performing in Copenhagen, and
the other by his own hand after the tragic denouement described elsewhere"
(C2, 3). And as Hartley's language traces its florid designs though this world,
his circumlocutions keep circling back to the personal and public "tragedy
of the Codona madness," whose "holocaustic finalities" come to embody the
drama of public intimacy, the obscenity of the exposed self, and, perhaps,
the triumph of flesh-as-idea, a newly material imagination (C2, 7; C1, 8).
In "Elephants," Codona and Leitzel emerge at once as the ideal avatars of
public intimacy and as the corporeal index of this relational mode's acute
vulnerability; thus, the trauma of the "Codona madness" and the stakes of
its imaginative negotiation in "Elephants" are only meaningful if we keep
in sight the intense theoretical burden these light figures bear in Hartley's
imagination.

For Hartley, to convey properly the intimate language of the circus in
"Elephants" is to allow his reader to share his fantasy space, to undergo a
queer rite of initiation into a kind of intimacy.[37] His acrobatic "eye" depends
throughout "Elephants" on proximate, apostrophic address to his reader. And
so, while the manuscript abounds with a first-person voice actively engaged
in the act of imaginative vision-as-memory, it beckons a reader and enlists
a confidence:[38]

> [T]he circus is like a multicolored globe—into which you look and see the
> many wonders of the imagination's world like the humongous crystal ball il-
> luminated from under by a revolving prismatic plate in the geological dept.
> of the museum of natural history. . . . After all, between you and me, life itself
> is all right—isn't it—do we not live by what we know[,] the idea of life—and
> not what humans think it is—haven't the dynasties and millenniums proven
> that nothing can change the quality of the thing itself? Too much of elemental
> metaphysics possibly for a book like this. (C1, 67)

"Between you and me": these moments of lyric apostrophe proliferate in

"Elephants" as Hartley fashions a communion of vision with his addressee: "If you saw [the juggler Enrico] Rastelli once only, you would watch the dimness gather like a cloud" (C1, 18); "but you will know" ringmaster Fred Bradna "when you see him again" (C2, 6). The second-person pronoun, of course, posits an addressee, another subject whose invocation, as Emile Benveniste teaches us, establishes the "polarity of persons" as the "fundamental condition in language."[39] But in Hartley's case, the seemingly commonsensical point that intersubjectivity in language is inevitable and is, in fact, its enabling condition is at once reassuring and profoundly unsettling: reassuring, because it makes him "feel outward," an exteriority whose rhetorical manifestation is apostrophe, a turning-outward; unsettling, because such communication always threatens to become, semantically speaking, heavy. And as a result, the balanced "polarity of persons" is thrown out of whack by a voracious subjectivity, and the silent purity of corporeal language is sullied by the tedium of talk. If, as Maureen McLane puts it, "intimacy happens if apostrophe works," this success is always an ambivalent one for Hartley, and as a result, his reader's initiation is always incomplete.[40]

We can get a better grip on this ambivalence if we consider the means by which Hartley communicates to his initiate. The explosion of first-person plurals that accompanies Hartley's occasional rants on the distasteful commercial attempts to provide "ultra-variations" on conventional circus numbers provides a clue: "A terrible show awaited us who think of ourselves as strictly orthodox in circus matters . . . who like our circus 'neat'" and who "like to have our forms keep to form" (C1, 29). "We" are an imagined community of real, orthodox "circus fanatics" open to a language of intimacy that speaks to the eye with special eloquence: "for the circus is the greatest spectacle of joy that has ever been invented for the eye alone—the eye being the greatest medium of receptivity," and sight, "as Paul Valery says . . . the most intellectual of the senses" (C1, 3, 1). And "all you have to do at the circus as with everything else—open your eyes and keep them open. . . . [Y]ou are I am [sic] talking like a real circus fan" (C1, 60). So, in the following instance, Hartley will attempt to summon the "quality of the thing itself," of the materiality of the circus, through communicative vision and the intimacy that is its goal: "You must inhale the odors of warm straw of the all but hot fragrances of various animal life—and you will want to do like the charming clown did . . . mister clown wrapping his arms around Rosie's trunk saying to her with real emotion 'You are such a beautiful girl, Rosie'—Rosie seeming to soak up all this affection blinking her right eye as if downward to show some slight acknowledgment of her deep woman's feelings" (C1, 68). The circus is clearly a matter of physical presence, of a proximity that Hartley would intimate to his reader and that he tropes here in the pure, emotive communication of Rosie and "mister clown." "Animal affection," muses Hartley elsewhere, "is a very exceptional affair" (C1, 21–22). The sentiment might be simply laughable if it were not so sincere; indeed, it is not too much to say that Hartley wishes to love and be loved, know and be known, in the mode of relation of Rosie and her trainer:

> I love the elephants most of all but it is chiefly because they have some sort of sense of simple companionship—they like their keepers and their director and I suspect every elephant of knowing it is loved and by whom . . . you can hug an elephant—at least trunkwise, and feel fine after it. You can pat or even kiss a seal if you want to, and you have been changed, and all it is a kind of transferred affection we may develop among the more tractable animals, when it comes to the wild feline idea—you've got something else there, literally . . . (C1, 20–21)

Here again, intimacy is idealized insofar as it remains controlled, a simple companionship of transferred affection between proximate, knowing bodies. But delivering this sort of corporeal co-presence to "you," Hartley's reader, remains seemingly beyond the scope of his evocative language and its synaesthetic aporias, its desire to make the reader see the smells and touches of the circus. As in most publicly mediated intimacies, the "potential failure to stabilize closeness always haunts [the] persistent activity" of Hartley's attempt to posit a "we."[41] Entrance into this intimate community of "ecstatic spectators" is premised not on literal vision but on visionary talk, on the ability of Hartley's language to conjure successfully first an addressee and, beyond that, the vital presence of what he sees and has seen. And this will prove doubly problematic, both because the acrobat's language, like intimacy itself, would eschew speech and aspire to a condition of silence, and because the more Hartley talks about "this vivid human world of the circus," the more it looks like death (C2, 7).

If the success of Hartley's apostrophe is predicated on his ability to open the eye of his addressee and fill it—lovingly, erotically—with the vital matter of the circus, this communication eventually founders on the very nature of this matter, which proves mutable stuff indeed. The performers themselves appear before Hartley's mnemonic sight only to shimmer, wink, and then disappear: "Alas, what has become of all these little jewel boxes, and will there be found ring artists to keep the great tradition alive?" (C2, 4). These characters are so fascinating for Hartley, in part, because in bodying forth sublime pictures of corporeal plenitude, mastery, and beauty, they conjure precisely the opposite: "The public does not know however that very often acute suffering is involved because muscles can stand only so much anyhow, and the life of a circus performer is never any too long, that is, for performing purposes" (C2, 12).

Caught between a desire to talk intimately and the urge to keep silent, "Elephants" achieves an acute poignancy; as community is imagined only to be dissolved, presence is conjured only to be forestalled. Put another way, Hartley's catalogue of circus performers catches an oddly welcome case of *le mal d'archive*, Jacques Derrida's term for the inescapable loss that corrodes all attempts to archive originary moments of presence, singularity, or contingency.[42] This double bind—incarnated in the short, but intense, life of the circus performer—is most obvious when Hartley tries to breathe life into his Metropolitan Opera fantasy of nearly twenty years past by calling for "a grand opera de luxe program of those great artists in this field who are still living and enhance the present day values. There would alas not be a Barbette, there would not be a Grock, there could not be a Joe Jackson, but already I see the idea in outline" (C1, 52–53). Here, though, the vision Hartley would share with his readers cannot be materialized, fully fleshed out, because it is structured around absences: no Barbette, no Grock, no Joe Jackson. So, in one of the most remarkable moments in "Elephants," Hartley will transfer his hopes from the real world to the imagination. This attempt to reconcile his desire that the stuff of the circus be, like the elements of Joe Jackson's clownery, "dateless and deathless" (C1, 48), with his sense that the greatest artists "have dropped out from their accustomed spots in the pattern" (C2, 3), is a work of fantasy that dismantles its own assemblage as it builds it in the mind's eye: "Let anyone who has loved this style of show all his life—line up in his memory the high spots of his experience—and gather his galaxy of splendours for at least one de luxe performance at the Metropolitan Opera" (C1, 37). And headlining Hartley's "galaxy of splendours" are Codona and Leitzel, in a position that signals the centrality of their absence for Hartley and for "Elephants," whose rhetorical mode is now in lockstep with what McLane calls the "self-imploding logic of romantic apostrophe" that culminates (or collapses) in the elegiac: "Death pushes apostrophe to its limit; to apostrophize the dead is to trace the faultiness always threatening to rupture the fantasy of successful, reciprocal address. Such apostrophe gestures towards the dream of perfect interlocutionary communion even as it undoes it."[43]

In Hartley's case, the failure of apostrophe to posit a presence—for McLane, a "drama experienced most painfully and intimately within and by the self"—

inheres in the position of his most beloved acrobats, Codona and Leitzel, on the sticky seam of private and public.[44] Their specialty, as it were, is their ability to be intimate and spectacular at once, to encourage attachments in the spectators who enjoy them publicly but to conceal or absent themselves by virtue of their very publicity. In "Elephants," Hartley is drawn, obsessively, to the liminal, libidinal moments where the performers emerge into publicity, or—the equally attractive converse—when the public spectator goes backstage, inside the performer's dressing chambers. And the ur-moment of backstage pleasure is Hartley's introduction to Leitzel and Codona, a scene that is referred to once in the first draft and no less than five times in the second draft:

> Such . . . charm greeted us—Leitzel in her own little tent with oriental rugs on the floor and the maid dusting barrels of powder over her in all her chiffon and glitter. There was a boyish looking fellow standing always to one side, in a white duck marine officer uniform, smoking a large cigar. When I had finished with Leitzel for she was getting in the usual state typical of artists, I closed with her by saying "there is one other artist I want to meet and that is Codona"—"There he is" she said and he stepped up from the other side and we were introduced—and I greeted this bright alert person with "I want to write about you too"—"G—I'd drop dead if anyone wrote anything nice about me"—"well, I am planning to try at least" I said—"it may never be printed, but we must all wait and see." I was presented with a handsome sheaf of signed photos of both these artists—and they are both on my walls to this day—flying and leaping as was their daily custom. (C1, 96–97)

In this intimate moment, Hartley, backstage, talks with his most beloved artists, who are (as they should be, as they almost *always* are) proximate and yet admired at arm's length. They are clothed, we might say, in the auratic garments of the celebrity image. Leitzel, in a haze of makeup, is "all . . . chiffon and glitter" and talks of her Bohemian descent (though Hartley suspects she is American). Codona, whose public performances Hartley has seen "numbers of times," is unrecognizable, and he and Hartley exchange pleasantries befitting a nervous fan and his object of worship. This chastened intimacy (fan to star) is echoed in the affection between Codona and Leitzel, which, like the performers themselves, like the love between Rosie and Mr. Clown, is "very simple." Their relation is less an index of heteronormative desire than, as Hartley explains in Leitzel's elegy, the ungendered "love of sweet-heart for sweet-heart," or, in a coolly professional register, the "deep admiration of one supreme artist for another" (C1, 85). So too, presumably, Hartley's love for Codona, whose supreme beauty in performance "can only be verified by those," like Hartley, "who have been privileged to see this artist at work numbers of times" (C1, 86).

Strategically occluded in these imaginative revisions is the "ensuing drama" of this pair: after Leitzel died in a public fall from the rings in 1931, Codona married another acrobat, Vera Bruce, with whom he performed as "The Flying Codonas." Their tempestuous private relationship was a far cry from the spectacular, simple intimacy of Leitzel-Codona. It ended on 30 July 1937 when they met in a lawyer's office to discuss a property settlement in their divorce. There, Codona shot and killed his wife before turning the gun on himself. What Hartley will only refer to obliquely as the "Codona madness," then, marks the volatility of this seam between privacy and publicity; it indexes the disaster of a tractable intimacy thrown out of control by the obscenity of the exposed self. In Codona's case, this heaviness is especially devastating. As Hartley explains in "The Flying Man," his curious nonelegy for the acrobat, Codona is the paragon of an "art that pacifies and satisfies completely because for here for once the mouth is stopped—the intellect robbed of its powers, and the body is given full play to be its best and comforting self—and what is better than a perfect body—being itself, completely itself. The body is clean and the life inside and out of it is clean" (C1, 94).[45] Now, as Hartley explains in his 1937 poem "The Trapezist's Despair," Codona is "the over-sensuous trapezist" whose "acrobatic vanity" got too heavy. With the amnesia of self-absorption, he forgets that the honorific "butterflies upon the silk of his garments," a costume he first wore in memoriam to Leitzel, were made both to remember and to release—to make him light as this "little gauze playmate" who had "flown to the upper air."[46] This chilling contrast between figures light and heavy is illustrated in a magazine article (see figures 14 and 15) that Hartley tore out and placed in a file of miscellaneous research materials he was collecting for the "Elephants" project. At the bottom left of the page is a photo of Vera and Alfredo in the midst of "The Passing Leap," which the caption glosses as the "most spectacular display of the Codona's perfect coordination." To the right, another scene of public intimacy, captioned: "Last curtain went down on the Codonas lying side by side as they fell, Vera dying, Alfredo dead."

In "Elephants," however, Hartley is clearly displeased by this "dead end of love": "I miss . . . Lillian Leitzel and Alfredo Codona, both of whom came to such tragic ends, one by a fall while performing in Copenhagen, and the other by his own hand after the tragic denouement described elsewhere. The which [sic] was to snuff out a romance before their marriage, at which juncture I met them through the kindly offices of Dexter Fellowes in the tent

WORLD'S GREATEST AERIALIST KILLS HIMSELF AND WIFE

Codonas were trapeze partners

Alfredo Codona could do a triple somer-sault off the high trapeze into his brother Lala's hands, but it was more than that supreme stunt which made him the greatest aerialist in the world. Son of a Mexican circus acrobat, Co-dona began training as soon as he could stand, made his first public appearance at 4. He grew up to be the Nijinsky of the circus, displaying in his spectacular whirls and leaps a flowing grace as beau-tiful and moving as a seagull's flight or a Debussy tone picture. Like Nijinsky's, his life wound up in tragedy. In 1931, his beloved second wife, the famed woman aerialist Lillian Leitzel, was killed by a fall in Copenhagen. Two years later a fall in New York finished Codona's career, left him to the preying unhappiness which he ended by his own hand in Long Beach, Calif. on July 30.

The Great Codona (*left*) married his Australian-born trapeze partner Vera Brt (*right*) in 1932, the year after Lillian Leitzel's death. He was then 39, she :

Figure 14. "Public Intimacy," from an unidentified publication in Hartley's files on "El-ephants and Rhinestones," The Yale Collection of American Literature, Beinecke Rare Book and Manuscript Library, Yale University, New Haven, Connecticut.

in Brooklyn" (C2, 3). Swiftly, lightly, tragic denouement occasions a comic *détournement,* as Hartley rewrites Codona's death as a necessary erasure, one that facilitates his reunion with Leitzel. Thus, Hartley's grammar of intimacy restores a "celestial bond" of "ideal sweethearts" who had, presumably, been separated "forever by the indifferent spirit of death" (C1, 86). But what of Hartley's affection for Codona, and the sort of intimacy he figures? The an-swer lies, it would seem, in the way Hartley remembers him, bodying forth his object of worship through the alchemy of the imagination: "Codona [had an] almost mystic sense that permits, when the artist wishes to dislodge the body from the idea, and the idea becomes a thing for its own sake; plenty of performers have no doubt done the same thing . . . but they do not have that special magic which is vouchsafed to the pure artist, who strives as it were to fall into the arms of the true meaning of things themselves" (C2, 4).

Codona's "special magic" is a mystic sense that allows him to transcend

"The Passing Leap" was the most spectacular display of the Co-dona's perfect co-ordination. Swinging 60 ft. above the arena,

Vera would catapult from Lala's hands to Alfredo's trapeze ju as her husband was soaring over her into his brother's hand

Vera Bruce Codona continued performing after her husband's injury ended their partnership. Alfredo managed her new act, brooded bitterly over his lost career. On June 28, Mrs. Codona sued for divorce, charging extreme jealousy. On July 30, the pair met in a Long Beach lawyer's office to discuss a property settlement. There Codona whipped out a revolver, shot his wife, then turned the gun on himself. Last curtain went down on the Codonas lying side by side as they fell, Vera dying, Alfredo dead (*right*).

Figure 15. "The Dead End of Love." Detail, from an unidentified publication in Hartley's files on "Elephants and Rhinestones," The Yale Collection of American Literature, Beinecke Rare Book and Manuscript Library, Yale University, New Haven, Connecticut.

mere corporeality (to dislodge the body from the idea) and become a newly hybrid figure for the substantiality of fantasy, of flesh-as-idea. The language here effectively duplicates the terms of Hartley's essay "The Element of Absolutism in Leonardo's Drawings" (circa 1939). Like Hartley's Codona, Leonardo's "creatures are of the flesh, but the flesh does not dictate their existence in his vision, he sees them as ideas, as symbolic representations of the whole thing, as the absolutist consummation of one thing."[47] Codona is no longer a mere body. Only in this way does tragedy become the stuff of comedy, which is sustained not by death and loss but by an aesthetics of mystical intimacy that preoccupied Hartley in roughly the last decade of his life, as he turned firmly away from the excessive personalism of a Romantic imagination and toward a selfless art.[48] As Hartley explained in 1929, "I want to be life and not myself, and how is one all tinged with questioning and tinged with mystic longings and relations ever to get out of the dull bondage. . . . I don't want to be condemned to spectatorship. I want to be released by it."[49] With this release, Hartley revises the aesthetico-mystical imperative as he defined it in *Adventures*—that voracious intimacy of Whitman, whose desire to "include all things into himself" constituted his "strongest esthetical defect" (*AIA* 34).

Fueled by the mystic writings of George Santayana, Miguel de Unamuno, Lucretius, and others, Hartley finally understood self-annihilation—and the perceptual clarity that accompanies it—as a goal to be achieved through precisely this spectatorial ecstasy, in which the spectator/artist loses himself in his object of vision, in the sensuous quiddity of the thing. Thus, this self-annihilation must not be understood as a closeted silence, or as the violent repudiation of queer subjectivity, but as the latter's very enactment in the mode of the light figure's attached detachment.

Keeping in mind this formulation (subjective release via optical attachment), we might return briefly, and with fresh eyes, to Hartley's puzzling *Sustained Comedy* (see figure 16). In the familiar accounts of this work, Hartley's self-portrait has all the gravitas of self-inflicted martyrdom, the body's fleshly surface overwritten with a dense network of images connecting, indeed condemning, the figure to the death and loss of the painter's past.[50] This subjective weight—Whitmanesque in its attempt to include all things *onto* itself—is only compounded by acts of critical decoding, through which superficial symbolism reveals a rich but troubled emotional interior. Read through Codona's butterfly, and through fantastic retelling of the Codona madness in "Elephants," in which elegy gives way to intimacy, the painting may tell another story, now of identity's comic undoing rather than its tragic overdetermination.[51] In this story, the titular "comedy" is not bitterly ironic but an apt description of the intimacy that accompanies mystical release. This reading would underscore how the eye, always an erotic site in Hartley, is penetrated with arrows aflame in butterflies, which ascend and dematerialize with acrobatic buoyancy. Within the logic of such visionary optics, when Hartley seems most firmly physical he is, paradoxically, detached and disembodied, thus laying claim to a privilege historically denied to modernity's others. Released by spectatorship, though, Hartley's disembodiment is no solipsistic idealism and is less a relational modality for being entirely fantastic.

Irreducible to a sublimation or metaphysicalizing of desire, the sustained comedy of Hartley's light figures discloses a modern mode of intimacy that is immanent, antisubjectivist, and finally enabled by the affective circuitry of a mediated public sphere. In this sense, Hartley's light figures urge us not just to reconsider the nature of modernist detachment, to recover "all that is energizing and active about a depersonalizing tendency," but to do so with sensitivity to the ways that such liberating vectors "away from the psychological and from personal identity itself" emerge through changes in modern publicity and visuality.[52] The public sphere is, of course, a familiar space of inauthenticity in modernism, guilty, it seems, by association with a disrepu-

Figure 16. Marsden Hartley, *Sustained Comedy,* 1939. Oil on board, 28¹/₈ × 22 in. Carnegie Museum of Art, Pittsburgh; gift of Mervin Jules in memory of Hudson Walker.

table constellation of falsities—mass culture, mediation, the feminine, the masses, reproduction, and *Erlebnis,* to name just a few. Such commonplaces have been productively challenged in recent years, perhaps most forcefully by Miriam Hansen, who argues that the public sphere's value inheres not in its relative authenticity but in its pragmatic utility as a "sensory-reflexive horizon" for negotiating modernity's conflicting energies.[53] For me, Hansen's account is compelling for at least two reasons: 1) in understanding publicity as a terrain of experiential negotiation, she refuses to accept lapsarian accounts of the fate of an authentic public sphere in technologically mediated modernity; and 2) she complicates recent critiques of modernism's ideology of authenticity as suspiciously wed to a rejection of a certain logic of visibility. Drawing our attention to what we might call modernism's unseen—but no less potent—cultural erection, such critics notice the downright dubious trick whereby modernism shores up its authority by secreting authenticity to a private, interior, invisible space.[54] Here, modernism's strategic inwardness must dismiss a too-visible, too-superficial, and thus inauthentic public meaning. In fact, Bill Brown has described the seeming inevitability of modernist interiority as "the mark of a limit within modernism's effort to accept opacity, to satisfy itself with mere surfaces," and noted how the modernist "effort to accept things in their physical quiddity becomes an effort to penetrate them, to see through them, and to find . . . within an object . . . the subject."[55]

For my purposes, such trenchant appraisals of a dominant modernist gambit linking vision, authenticity, and privatized interiority serve to underscore the very quirkiness of Hartley's sentimental meditations on these matters. Normative modernism's "iconophobia" has, of course, also been productively considered by queer theory, perhaps most iconically by Eve Sedgwick, who understands modernism's characteristic aversion to realistic representation—its currents of antifigurality and abstraction—as a repudiation of sentimentality and of the desired, eroticized male body that is excessive feeling's occasion.[56] Sentimentality, Sedgwick argues, is less a theme or subject than a vicariously self-implicating "structure of relation, typically one involving the author- or audience-relations of spectacle."[57] Hartley's iconophobia, as a painterly technique, was intermittent at best; but his sentimental iconophilia, as a spectatorial mode, was unwavering. The conceptual trick of Hartley's light figures, then, is to show how a gushy optical investment is really an erotic divestiture. Take, for example, Hartley's visionary indulgence in the public spectacle of Codona's thingly figure—his "flesh-as-idea"—which effectively flips both Brown's and Sedgwick's formulations: rather than penetrating, his vision disperses; rather than implicating the spectator, it finds no subject, only a fleeting attachment that Hartley secures by losing himself. The dominant mode of modernist visuality, as the critical accounts I've discussed here all variously suggest, depends on a series of relatively stable and interlocking binaries (public/private, exteriority/interiority, visibility/invisibility, surface/depth) and privileges the second term in all of them. In Hartley's eyes, by contrast, these binaries are strategically surpassed through his paradoxical formulation of public intimacy and, beyond that, through modernity's "sensory-reflexive dimension," which is, after all, the light figure's affective terrain. In this sense, Hartley's light figures emerge alongside, but remain irreducible to, other privileged tropes—the "impression," "innervation," or the "flâneur"—for mediating modernism's felt relations between its "insides" and its "outsides" amidst a changing public sphere whose own mediated nature confounds a more traditional trafficking between them.[58] This would mean understanding the light figure as an attempt to think *through* what Kracauer once called the "motley externalities" of modern life, indeed, to revalue the surface as the site not of the experiential poverty of the modern but rather of its dynamic affective potential: here, for an erotic depersonalization that remains a relation—spectacular, to be sure, but also profoundly intimate.[59]

5

Tenderness

Love is the ability to see the similar in the dissimilar.
—Theodor Adorno, *Minima Moralia*

For Joseph Cornell, film was a technology of tenderness. Cinema provided a mode of intimate attention to the welter of experience whose exploratory optics the artist describes in his homage to the actress Hedy Lamarr, published in *View* magazine in the winter of 1941. Lamarr, Cornell gushes, is the "Enchanted Wanderer" whose "magnified visage" opens "realms of wonder, more absorbing than the artificial ones, and where we have already been invited by the gaze that she knew as a child."[1] *The gaze that she knew as a child.* The language of this and similar reveries has helped to cement Cornell's critical reputation as an uncomplicated romantic, a nostalgic modern haunted, in P. Adams Sitney's terms, by the "aesthetic mediation of experience."[2] This Cornell would idealize the "poetic and evocative language of the silent film" as a foregone realm of plenitude and presence; this Cornell would understand the "gaze that [Lamarr] knew as a child" as a visual modality lost to the modern, yet recuperated through nostalgic attempts to archive presence through mimetic technologies, to freeze or frame the ephemerality of the moment in one of his box-constructions.[3] This Cornell, the obsessive collector, has caught a bad case of archive fever, that same loss corroding Marsden Hartley's efforts to remember his favorite circus stars. I wish to suggest, however, that Cornell's cinematic achievement lies elsewhere—specifically, in its tender phenomenology of modern experience as eventful and enchanted, ethical and public.[4] His work is marked by an acute awareness of the way the unfolding of experience makes demands on one's attention, inviting care or indifference, but in either case calling for a kind of posture, a particular comportment toward this relentless happening. And it is film, for Cornell, that is charged with a special capacity for feeling outside the box, for responding to the sensual solicitations of public life, and for learning there how best to love the wondrous pulse of the human.

This chapter argues that the ethics of Cornell's cinematic wandering—the particular modes of responsiveness and attention it calls for and enacts— unfold through his cultivation of the eccentric feelings of mood and sensual mimesis, which I read as modes of tender adaptation to the incessant otherness of quotidian experience. Attention to Cornell's reckoning with experience, which is consistently misrecognized, will better equip us to understand his cinematic achievements, especially his overlooked collage trilogy: *Cotillion, The Midnight Party,* and *The Children's Party* (circa 1938–69).[5] A curious kind of cinematic vaudeville, these films bear uniquely on Cornell's formulation of experience and more broadly on modernism's various public intimacies, the eccentric feelings that deliver them, and the forms of performative virtuosity that occasion their formulation.[6] And here, Cornellian emotion is especially instructive since—like Cornellian eros—it has always been understood as an almost parodic extreme of bourgeois privacy, always centripetal in its movement, tracing melancholic arcs around loss but never, ever publicly oriented (see figure 17).[7]

Enchanted Attention

I mean my tender idiom to recall André Bazin's claim for cinema's "particular kind of tenderness," his sense of the ways film, "more than any other art, is particularly bound up with love."[8] Made in the context of his well-known essay on Italian neorealism, and specifically on Vittorio de Sica's "way of feeling," Bazin's remarks about cinema's particular mode of sentimentality are bound to his formulation of neorealist style as *itself* the sentiment of particularity. For Bazin, de Sica's radical phenomenological immanence lay in his "not betraying the essence of things, in allowing them first of all to exist for their own sakes, freely; it is in loving them in their singular individuality."[9] And in this sense, of course, neorealism's singular feeling for singularity epitomized the relationship between realist mimesis and love that, for Bazin, lay encoded within the inhuman ontology of the photographic image itself:

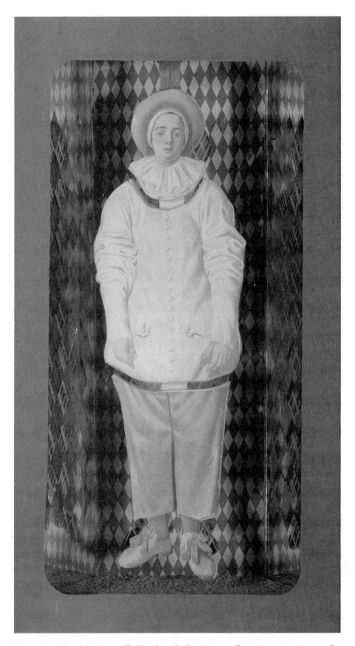

Figure 17. Joseph Cornell, "Melancholic Privacy." *A Dressing Room for Gilles,* 1939. Box construction; 15 × 8⁵/₈ × 5⁵/₈ in. (38.1 × 21.9 14.4 cm). Richard L. Feigen, New York.

> The aesthetic qualities of photography are to be sought in its power to lay bare the realities. It is not for me to separate off, in the complex fabric of the objective world, here a reflection on a damp sidewalk, there the gesture of a child. Only the impassive lens, stripping its object of all those ways of seeing it, those piled-up preconceptions, that spiritual dust and grime with which my eyes have covered it, is able to present it in all its virginal purity to my attention and consequently to my love.[10]

Thus do the Romantic terms of Bazin's realist mimesis declare themselves: to re-see the objective world through an impassive agent (the camera) is to be newly attentive to its complex fabric and thus to love it more. In this way, film's tenderness is an ethics.

The surrealists, Bazin noticed, were particularly impressed by the photograph's potency. For insofar as "the photograph as such and the object in itself share a common being" in a particular web of time and space, photography does the work of surrealism's Romantic imagination, *contributing* to the order of natural creation and thus erasing the distinction between the imaginary and the real, the object and the image (OP 15). The photograph, in Bazin's typically luminous phrase, is a "hallucination that is also a fact" (16). As first glance, Bazin's formulations read as a reprise of Walter Benjamin's claim for film's potential to unfold an "optical unconscious," its gnostic power to "bring to light entirely new structures of matter" through slow motion and the close-up (WA 117). But the material environment revealed by Benjamin's apparatus is less the site of virginal immanence than the proliferation of opaque and illegible detail that remains more mysteriously other. And it is "other," Benjamin clarifies, "above all in the sense that a space informed by human consciousness gives way to a space informed by the unconscious" (117). Cinematic technology assures humans of what Benjamin dubs a "vast and unsuspected field of action," exploding the "prison-world" of quotidian experience with "the dynamite of the split second, so that now we can set off calmly on journeys of adventure among its far-flung debris" (117).

Such is the messy terrain of Cornellian experience. In his expansive diaries, for example, Cornell notes his "exquisite pleasure" in the "feeling of textures revealed in close-up movie [*sic*]" (*TM* 141). And this pleasure in "heightened reading" is erotic and strategic: Cornell ruminates on the "possibilities of 'blowing up' separate parts of photo" and the "abstract and imaginative quality" of this newly found space (141, 142). Here lies an "unexpected treasure waiting to be revealed, discovered afresh" (142). One "enters 'another world' in these enlargements' grainy texture," and what's more, Cornell notes eagerly, access to this world "can be purposively cultivated" (142). Cornell shares Benjamin's conviction that the surrealist image produced by the optical unconscious is not the site of Bazinian mummification—of perfect, auratic semblance—but rather a space of play. Overcome by the excesses of experience enabled by cinema, Cornell will cultivate the tender, dispersed mood that he later calls "unfoldment."

Let me lay my experiential cards on the table. As my references to mimesis and mood indicate, I hope to materialize the ecstatic space-time of Cornellian experience—too easily dismissed as yet another form of spilled religion within romanticism—in relation to the thought of Benjamin and Martin Heidegger, whose meditations on the category of experience have received renewed critical attention.[11] Like Benjamin and Heidegger, Cornell understands modern experience as radically eventful, which is to say, excessive, futural, and contingent: never entirely self-present because it is imbued with the disjunctive historicity of occurrence; refusing totalizing or teleological closure and therefore open to infinite transformation. Experience is an inessential voyage. For my purposes, it is less important to decide whether the disjunctive unfolding of experience is or is not, for Cornell, the work of purposive spirit—to decide finally whether his account of modern experience is metaphysical or materialist (as for Benjamin, it is intermittently both)—than it is to underscore the potential of this eventfulness: the way the noncoincidence of experience produces enchantment, and thus intimate attachment to the material world, all while prompting a tender mode of cinematic production commensurate with such experience.[12]

At its most redemptive, what Cornell calls "unfoldment," or the "wonderful feeling of detachment," is, paradoxically, a reinvestment in the surprising alterity of experience (*TM* 95). In returning below to the potential of Cornell's buoyant moods for generosity and tenderness, I draw on Jane Bennett's provocative rethinking of enchantment: her sense that the mood of enchantment "might be deployed to produce ethical generosity."[13] "Enchantment, as a mood," requires what Bennett calls "a cultivated perception, a discerning and meticulous attentiveness to the singular specificity of things" (*EM* 37). Attuned to material singularity and the eventfulness of the modern, enchantment also entails a sensual awareness of pattern, ensemble, and repetition. This is what Benjamin might call enchantment's mimetic dimension, since for him mimesis is primarily *correlating behavior*: a mode of relating to the external world through the production—in ritual, in performance, and in the space for play opened by the optical unconscious—of "nonsensuous correspondences," noniconic, abstract, spiritual patterns of similitude and resemblance.[14] For Cornell, cinema's mimetic potential is rooted not in any allegiance to the phenomenological essence of things or experiences (surrealist wandering is, if nothing else, a consistently noncoincident mode of experience) but rather in its ability to cultivate stances of moody observation, attunement to patterns of similitude and affinity opened up by technological mediation itself. Hedy Lamarr's "tenderness," Cornell explains, "finds a counterpart in the summer night."[15] And Cornell's tenderness, we might say, is often just this work of finding counterparts.

Thus, for Cornell, cinema's capacity for love lies in its ability both to connect with a broad range of prerational, mimetic practices and to fashion an extensive atmosphere of surprise, joy, curiosity, and wonder. This is, perhaps, the only affective climate in which a mimetic subject can tenderly unfold, since moods, as we will see, are particularly given to cognitive and epistemological disorientation, to forms of agential receptivity. And producing similitude is a hallmark not only of the curious ordering of material in Cornell's box-constructions—which draw on formal and thematic association to link spatio-temporally discreet objects—but also of his editing strategies as a filmmaker, which model mimetic modes of observation and relation, as well as the disjunctive and recursive temporalities of experience that invite a kind of tender agency.

And both Cornell and Benjamin knew that children are the best mimics, modeling idealized modes of prerational behavior. In his personal copy of Jean Piaget's *Language and Thought of the Child,* Cornell underlines a passage that reads: "The fact remains that many expressions, which for us have a purely conceptual meaning, retain for many years in the child's mind a significance that is not only affective but also well-nigh magical."[16] For Benjamin, the child's creative reception of modernity's world of things is itself a model for the collective's revolutionary mimetic innervation of technology: "Just as a child who has learned to grasp stretches out his hand for the moon as it would for a ball, so humanity . . . sets its sights on currently utopian goals as on goals within reach" (WA 124). For humanity's relationship with cinema to become mimetic, humans must be irrational spielers, playing with and thus adapting to otherness of technological second nature; they must, Benjamin asserts, "have [their] organs in the new technology," which means perforce extending the human sensorium beyond the limits of the individual body, "unhing[ing] experience and agency," in Miriam Hansen's terms, "from anthropomorphic identity" (WA 125).[17]

Tender subjectivity is also the affective yield of Romantic mood, where agency unfolds into transpersonality, lingering before its objects. In Cornell's particular form of Romantic surrealism, moody disorientation abets a re-orientation of productive agency toward the material world—here wondrously other and worthy of attention and intimacy. Consider the following formulation, typical of Cornellian awe: "An abstract feeling of geography and voyaging I have thought about before of getting into objects, like the Compass Set with map. A reminder of the earliest school-book days when the world was divided up into irregular masses of bright colors, with vignettes of the pictorial world scattered, like toy picture-blocks" (*TM* 95). This abstract mode of feeling thus accompanies a re-attachment to things—a "getting into objects"—and returns both the act of making and the maker to a space of possibility, of color, prior to the regularity of form and the organization of the visual field, its stories at once scrambled and poised for joyful recombination.[18] Cornell's children, like Benjamin's, are materialists.

But the eventfulness of experience also provokes a crisis of production central to modernist aesthetics: How does one fashion art in a way that is responsive to the world's incessant alterity? How does one get into things without reducing them with the conceptual certainty of an imperious subjectivity?[19] Cornell's answer, I argue, will be cinematic tenderness. His collage trilogy, protagonized by children and other inhuman performers, enacts the reorganization of human experience that is his constant concern: in Benjamin's terms, this tender subject of Cornellian experience *has its organs* in the technology of the collage film, modeling the kind of mimetic adaptation—the forms of agency and affective orientation—toward second nature that might be ethically adequate to experience. We need to keep in mind here the relationship between cinematic tenderness as a mode of commensurability (mimetic correlation) with the eventfulness of experience and Mary Ann Doane's recent argument for cinema's privileged role as part of a larger "cultural imperative: the structuring of time and contingency in capitalist modernity."[20] Cinema, Doane contends, has been historically allied with the very idea of "the event and the unfolding of events as aleatory, stochastic, contingent," and this is all the more true of film in surrealist hands (*EC* 140–41). Early cinema, especially the "actuality" genre, thus mobilizes a dialectic of contingency, whereby the "specter of pure loss, the possibility of complete obliteration of the passing moment, the degradation of meaning" also "elicits a desire for its opposite— the possibility of structure," which film provides in both narrative and the atemporality of spectacle (140).

As we will see, Cornell's writing and filmmaking is marked by a similar movement between event and structure, chaos and order, and the corresponding division between those affects and moods accompanying eventfulness (wonder, enchantment, joy, surprise) and those issuing in what Doane calls "dead time," when nothing happens (boredom, depression, anxiety). Indeed, his collage technique depends on the insight that cinema can in fact *produce* eventfulness and that its accompanying moods and mimetic bearings toward the world can be cultivated. However, such a production is, finally, to be differentiated from the structuring of contingency, insofar as structure is understood as the taming of the eventful unfolding of experience, or an attempt "to bind the primary alterity of the material world."[21] Here, Cornell's 1945 letter to Marianne Moore is particularly eloquent. Returning to the thread of a letter to Moore the previous year in which he explained his paralysis in the face of the experience—that there "seems to be such a complexity, a sort of endless 'cross-indexing' of detail (intoxicatingly rich) in connection with what and how I feel that I never seem to come to the point of doing anything about it" (*TM* 104)—Cornell now explains:

> Regarding my own work I've precious little to show for all the time and labor that have gone into it for the past few years, and life, I am afraid, "does become strange to me from time to time." Elaborating upon this subject out of self-pity or self-justification gets me nowhere. Let me say simply that if the welter of material that I work with (matched too often by a like confusion of mind) seems too often like endless and hopeless chaos—there are times enough that I can see my way through this labyrinth and feel enough at home among its many "by-paths of romance" (to quote your apt phrase) to be grateful. When I think of the unspeakable things that have been visited upon so many countless thousands during this same period of time I don't have too many misgivings about not having "produced" more. (*TM* 123)

In this remarkable explanation, Cornell links a certain "productivity" to the catastrophic violence of World War II (between 1943 and 1944, Cornell himself worked for eight months at an Allied defense plant in Long Island City, assembling and testing radio controls). At the same time, he points to an alternate mode of production, one in which he accommodates himself to the labyrinthine prolixity of experience, finding there not despair but gratitude for the very interruption of productive agency.[22] The gift of Moore's poetic phrase, the inspired "by-paths of romance," is to bring into focus "so sharply and clearly and helpfully" the way Cornell feels "about certain aspects of [his] research" (TM 104–5). In this dimension of surrealist research lie the affective rudiments of cinematic tenderness, not in the capture of contingency (and the loss that inevitably attends it) but the concurrent unfolding of vagrant consciousness and its objects of experience: at once deliriously other and mimetically within reach. This is the way montage might unfold.

Adventures in Public Mood

Cornell was notoriously moody and mercurial by temperament, and his diaries are, among other things, chronicles of these sensational shifts in the color of waking or dreaming experience.[23] Exercises in experiential connoisseurship, the entries work to pinpoint the fluctuating texture of being in phrases like "a feeling of X," or in even more quintessential formulations of quintessence like "that element of X": "*morning after* with its 'back to life' freshness although that element of cloudiness—that flavor of drugged sleep of infinitely varying degrees—experienced with the good & bad so mixed as to never satisfactory elucidation or recording" (*TM* 81). Perhaps, Cornell seems to reason, this confusing mixture of moods will sort itself out if I abstract myself from the moment, if I just get sufficiently *systematic*, if I allow my moods the retrospective coherence of, say, a season, like so:

> *Summer 1943*
> General Outline
> Contrast of moods—quick shiftings tired feeling at first
> Panoramic or bird's eye view of workers coming to work—variety
> Emotional feeling evenings Sat. afternoons
> Nervous feeling in morning sense of pressure (101)

But as this experiment reveals, the price of descriptive abstraction—doubling the panoramic view it relates—is precision and particularity: "that element of X" gets swamped in the baggy adjective "emotional," which describes not a "variety" of activity or emotion but a redundancy of feeling common to evenings and Saturday afternoons alike. Birds' eyes, it seems, are overrated.

Similarly unsatisfying is Cornell's own weakness for the typification or statistical rationalization of feeling glimpsed in the referential vagueness of phrases like the "better than average feeling" (*TM* 120) or a "feeling of more than average naturalness" (124) or, even more bleakly, a "better than nothing feeling" (151). Indeed, language often fails Cornell's attempts to be adequate to the temporal eruptions of experience:

> August 15, 1944
> bike ride on way to Bayside West—a clear flash of working in the summer of 1937 (?) at Paramount art studio (Traphagen Period, Mrs. Yates) recollection of the "week-endy" feeling (miserable phrase to denote a feeling that has been recurrent as long as I can remember about New York City on my

own—it extends father back than a mere "relaxation" from business routine and has generally had a strong connotation (anticipatory pleasure) associated with departure for the country to new places—[a feeling of the past of New York City as I remember it vaguely from earliest years, with parents, etc. my grandmother (earliest memory 1910 Eden Musee wax-works) end of digression.] (111)

The misery of a phrase like "'week-endy' feeling" lies not in its adjectival inelegance but in its suggestion that the complex of recurrent feelings it denotes are the typical, compensatory feelings of bourgeois leisure built into the organization of time into laboring weeks and liberating weekends and not the impossible temporal conjunction approximated in this entry's wandering excess: flashing memories of New York's past *and* the futural, anticipatory pleasure of leave-taking from that same metropolis.

The diaries thus show Cornell to be routinely overcome by the liberation from "routine feeling," "endless[ly] marvelling at the way in which routine experience suddenly becomes magically imbued and transformed with a joy too elusive to catch in words" (118, 235). The bewildering profusion of moods upon which Cornell consistently remarks bears out the Heideggerian insight that one is always in some kind of a mood or another, since mood is not so much a subjective or psychic state as a particular mode of attunement, a way of disclosing one's situatedness (*Befindlichkeit*), that is, one's involved agency in the complex of Being-in-the-world.[24] Being in a mood is being-in-context: thus, whether Cornell finds himself unexpectedly coming and going in a "week-endy" feeling or hemmed in by the "pressure and 'claustrophobia' of the approaching daily routine" (104), he is always situated in the world, the mood simply disclosing that world differently, shaping its salience in a different key. As Heidegger notes, the "pallid lack of mood which dominates the 'grey everyday' through and through" is "not to be mistaken for a bad mood, [and] is far from nothing at all. Rather, it is in this that Dasein becomes satiated with itself. Being has become manifest as a burden."[25] The central question is not whether the mood of Cornellian enchantment that erupts within routinized feeling is or is not a compensatory affect within a ruthlessly rationalized modernity, but rather *how* enchantment attaches and to what *kinds* of attention to the material world it delivers him. And lest we worry that I've bent Cornell's musings too closely to the existential abyss, consider Cornell's darkly self-aware reply to Marianne Moore, in which he requests her recommendation for his (unsuccessful) Guggenheim Fellowship application: "Yes, Miss Moore, I think that I do 'know . . . what minute (infinitesimal) living can be'—but in spite of the compensation of moments of deep peace and beauty in the midst of this oftentimes cruel claustrophobia there are occasions enough when its whole illusory mesmeric nature is exposed for the nothingness it really is" (*TM* 122).

In these moments, Cornell experiences anxiety, for Heidegger, a signal mood in which the meaningful complex of involvements that constitute everyday being "collapses into itself," and "the world has the character of completely lacking significance."[26] Insofar as anxiety arises, Heidegger claims, not in the face of something *in* the world but from the asignifying character of the world itself, anxiety becomes the foundation of existential heroism: by disclosing the naked thrownness of being, by allowing the subject to discover itself at its most contingent and groundless, anxiety redeems subjective agency, "individualiz[ing]" Dasein and freeing it into its authentic potential.[27] And yet Cornell's most anxious moments prompt neither existential individuation nor authentic action but instead a lingering in the blurred, transpersonal agency of mood, in what we might call a tender publicness. Moods, as Charles Altieri has pointed out, are rather particular modes of feeling in which "the sense of subjectivity becomes diffuse, and sensation merges into something close to atmosphere, something that seems to pervade an entire scene or situation" (*PR* 2). Thus, insofar as moods produce a kind of floating, transpersonal subjectivity—in which sensation is at once acutely personal and a state of mind, to borrow Altieri's language, in which "any subject might enter"—they challenge the rationalist telos of emotions that would orient the agent toward pragmatic action and judgment (54). In other words, the Heideggerian account of moods points us to, even if its existential values finally overlook, "the most fundamental feature of anxiety—that the corollary of objectlessness may also involve at its core a condition of subjectlessness," a condition whose enigmatic and transpersonal dimension is experienced as wandering pleasure by a range of modernist artists, including Cornell, who "hover over not quite objects in roles that do not quite establish subjects" (58). The unsettled subject of a Cornellian mood thus experiences those free-floating and impersonal psychological intensities that attend a subjective "letting go" and remain irreducible to normative and cognitive closure.

In his diaries, Cornell's privileged term for this dispersed affective state is "unfoldment," which he defines as follows: "'unfoldment' perspective in its poetic aspects—this frequent experience of a kind of enchantment in which a wavering frame of mind (after dreary frustration) the incidents of a day (or portion) unfold with such beautiful graciousness—the most 'trivial,' 'commonplace,' but life flows too fast, as now, there never seems time to catch up"

(*TM* 249). However poetic, the relentless unfoldment of experience here is met with some anxiety, outpacing even Cornell's breathless prose. Elsewhere, though, Cornell revels in "unfoldment," this happy neologism naming "one of those visitations or moods just (hovering on deep depression) and exultation in endless unfoldment of city doings in many directions" (206). In this latter, more specific formulation, "unfoldment" is at once a condition of urban experience—that is, the doings of the city that endlessly unfold—and a particularly diffuse mood adequate to, indeed sympathetically miming, the eventfulness of the modern. Experience, as a result, becomes less threat than thrill—here the warmth of relational being rather than the cool sentimentality of E. E. Cummings's sublime thrill. Put simply, as the inexhaustible happenings of the modern city unfold, so too does Cornell's mood, but in a fashion that is at once pervasive and protective of experiential and material particularity, of what Cornell calls "minutiae," those singularities sacrificed in the abstract reckonings of a bird's-eye view. So, Cornell describes the mood of "unfoldment" as "*above all* the warm sense pervading the minutiae of things and people" (198); or, in another entry, as "sudden overemotionalism" of "the warm 'music'—joy of being in the crowds and city—a minutiae permeated with a warm humanity" (200). Picking up on the etymological connection between enchantment and sonority—song or music—Cornell describes unfoldment here as an attunement to what Heidegger calls the moody refrain of public being itself: "Publicness, as the kind of Being that belongs to the Anyone, not only has in general its own way of having a mood, but needs moods and 'makes' them for itself."[28] In Heidegger's account, moods mark our co-situatedness in an everyday context of interpretation and shared understanding: "From this standpoint, moods are not 'private' or 'personal,' but rather essentially public, part of the 'world' instead of something *in* the 'self,'" always "generated by a shared attunement to public 'forms of life' in our culture."[29] But in Cornell's case, such attunement is particularly ecstatic, marked by the suddenness of the self's unfolding beyond its private contours and into a delirious new context. As such, the capaciousness of Cornellian unfoldment is just plain unsuited to Bazinian realism: permeant and encompassing, tenderness unfolds as minutiae proliferates, as the world becomes messier and more other rather than tidily reduced to any phenomenological essence.

But for Cornell, sometimes letting go is hard to do. His ambivalence about unfoldment inheres in its very excessiveness, its proximity to sensual ecstasy, material chaos, and subjective vagrancy. Unfoldment's eroticism, then, is linked to an overlooked, centrifugal mode of Cornellian desire, uncontained, sudden, and outward-flowing rather than easily boxed. A mode of sensual intimacy within, rather than against, modernism's public sphere, unfoldment answers to a desire provoked by the incessant, irreducible difference of the public. Instead of controlling desire's excess through a recurring detachment from identification, as Hartley does, or repudiating entirely the unstable relationship between identification and desire, as Cummings does, unfoldment's desire is provoked by what Kelly Oliver describes as the "excess of the other in one's own identification": such desire is fueled "not by an identification that turns the other into the same, you into me," but rather by "an identification that turns the same into an other, that takes me beyond myself and towards you."[30] Enchanted by a world of difference, such desire says, "Because you are not me, I can move out of myself towards you," an unfoldment about which Cornell is often ambivalent.[31] So, while Cornell will occasionally insist on the chastity of this particular mood (as in Cornell's reference to a "Jesus Christ kind of unfoldment"), at other moments he upbraids himself for those accidents of intemperate pleasure-taking in ecstatic publicness (*TM* 124, 200). Thus "tempered . . . against former too emotional extremes," he compliments himself for his good public behavior, noting his ability to enjoy a "napoleon and hot drink at [the] Sagamore cafeteria (not overemotional as often the case here and on such occasion)" (231, 207). However pleasurable the public unfoldment of experience, its erotic pulse threatens this good Christian Scientist's standards of propriety, just as its chaotic profusion, with which he can never catch up and which paralyzes his productive capacities, is cause for recurring anxiety. "Hovering" on the other site of unfoldment, then, is deep depression, the threat of an "endless and hopeless" welter of material and mind described in his letter to Moore. And this mess can only confound an obsessive subject for whom everything, most of the time, is of interest.

Most of the time. Cornell finds himself most anxious at home, with his mother and invalid brother, Robert, where he is routinely prone to a dispiriting shift in mood that he calls, ominously, "reversal." In these moments, wonder and enchantment are supplanted by an affective complex of tension and dullness, by the "home claim of stagnation (frustration and stress and pressure)" or worse, and more rarely by an "indifferent kind of mood again just skirting going under" (TM 124, 195). Here, in his own conceptual reversal of the typical gendering of public and private space, Cornell characterizes his moody oscillation between the mental tensions of the domestic and the sentimental unfoldment of public experience with the laconic opposition "household antagonism vs. tenderness," one that clarifies what I have been suggesting above: tenderness, as Cornell understands it, is a mode of publicness (138). And yet the call to public tenderness—which would spell the "damnable torpor that seems diabolically hard to keep out" of the domestic and the mind—is suspect in its uncertain motivations and unpragmatic orientations, and Cornell will criticize his own "obsessive feeling to 'get away'" or note, with relief, the "absence of wanderlust *nervousness*" (195, 153, 137). This is the double bind of the subject of Cornellian experience: to be stuck inside, threatened with indifference to your immediate context, while public experience is relentlessly happening without you; and to find, when you submit to unfoldment, that your capacities for care and attention are overwhelmed by the erotic intensity and material prolixity that attends such lusty wandering.

Unfoldment means letting go or, better still, going with the excessive flow of experience and yielding to the abstract, public affectivity of mood. Against this mode, Cornell flirts with another style of being-in-public, that abstraction *from* experience and in the defense of heroic individuality effected in the arch gaze of the Baudelairean flâneur, himself a kind of proto-existentialist hero. It is the detached observation of the bird's-eye view, which finds its most remarkable illustration in the diary entry dated 2 July 1949, in which Cornell describes his balcony view of Manhattan humanity, streaming and proliferant:

> glass of weak iced tea and liverwurst sandwich on the balcony about 4 o'clock overlooking 42 and 3rd Ave. with its typical stream of motley N.Y. humanity this sunny afternoon—right against the window with a ledge where I could open the RILKE in unhurried leisure and enjoy it along with all the minutiae of commonplace spectacle that at times like this take on so much "festivity"—a real happiness here in the sun, although too nervous to do justice to the Rilke text . . .—the preoccupation with the crowds below formerly a morbid obsession in the infinity of faces and heterogeneity—in particular a black robed nun with a rope or chain conspicuous for lack of usual immaculateness and a real type of uniquely unusual encountered only in a city like N.Y. or the large metropolises—thoughts lifted about things in general although not completely (pressure) as usual a significant kind of happiness is difficult to get into this "cataloging" but there it was none the less—this "on-the-edgeness" of something apocalyptic, something really satisfying. (*TM* 158)

Why, this passage seems to ask, can't I just enjoy the public like I enjoy my Rilke? What keeps me from being inside and outside at once, rapt in the insular bliss of readerly solitude while consuming, at my leisure, the "commonplace spectacle" of the public? The sweet-toothed Cornell wants to have his cake (or sticky bun, or cinnamon roll) and eat it too, and as a result, he

remains anxiously split: his loyalty to Rilkean pleasure betrayed by the nervousness caused by the teeming spectacle below, his desire to derive happiness from the cataloging of the public stymied by the pressure put on such
taxonomy by the sheer "infinity of faces and heterogeneity." Thus, Cornell's
attempt to differentiate his present "preoccupation" with the public from his
past "morbid obsession" with organizing, ordering, or otherwise controlling the relentless flow of differentiated humanity is rather unconvincing.
He seems, in fact, possessed by the attempt, however morbid, to totalize.
He remains convinced that he is on the brink of the apocalyptic satisfaction
that would come from the completion of this public scene, a closure here
tantamount to Kantian sublimity—the satisfaction of the self whose imaginative impotence in the face of ungraspable totality or infinity is transcended
by its superior faculty of reason and its categorical power. In a Levinasian
register, we might read this apocalypse as a guise for a kind of "ontological
totalitarianism," an omen of the lurking violence of ontological thought that
threatens to subsume the claim of the Other under the rubric of the One
(Being), or that seeks to reduce multiplicity to a finite concept, graspable in
its totality.[32] In other words, Cornell is anxious in the face of an unreasonable field of Being that refuses imaginative coherence, that remains impure
and mysteriously other, and whose "conspicuous" singularity is embodied
in the "black robed nun," a "real type of uniquely unusual encountered only
in a city like N.Y." And as a result, Cornell's anxious attraction to apocalyptic
totality precludes his surrender to unfoldment. In his desire to "do justice"
to Rilke, he stops just short of asking the question implied by his nagging
self-consciousness in the face of alterity: What might it mean to do justice
to public experience, to the plurality of modes of being human?

Cornell's diary entries from the late 1950s hint at an answer in their repeated
suggestions that cinema is the privileged technology for sounding the contours of the human, a special medium of warmth, of wonder, of tenderness.
While Cornell notes his "continued strong feelings about [the] *gulf* between
work with boxes and feeling for life, people, etc. not expressed by former"—
that is, precisely the abyss disclosed by Cornell's balcony anxieties above—he
increasingly understands cinematic unfoldment as a kind of public feeling
with an ethical thrust incompatible with the privatizing impulse of the boxes
(*TM* 252). Reflecting on the public experience of the subway ride, he suggests
that cinema has tempered his physiognomic "obsessions," turning them into
more gentle "preoccupations," and thus shifting his feeling about humanity
toward tenderness: "Subway ride home "people" etc. too obsessive people on
subway—preoccupation with faces—anew in this different setting—different

new since film work, feeling about people" (231). We might better grasp this obscure passage in constellation with two other entries, the first of which, written two years earlier, reads: "love of humanity—no matter how much might be taken on film this urge might not be satisfying—there is always the thing that the camera cannot catch—still gratitude should be felt for the fine things done with film so far" (193). The second, written a nearly a year after the subway passage, finds Cornell in Bickford's restaurant, a familiar haunt, where he notes his "appreciation of early morning elusive magic—permeating routine experiences the passers by as in a theatre the cold light lending its aura—but it is something deeper—the human—" (250).

The first entry returns to the pull of totality felt by Cornell on the balcony over Third Avenue while resuscitating the idiom of gratitude with which Cornell described his surrender to the many "by-paths of romance" of labyrinthine materiality in his 1945 letter to Moore. Here, it is the nature of cinematic contingency itself that will always dash Cornell's hope that his love of humanity be total, which is to say, finished and complete. And yet Cornell now forsakes the apocalyptic longing for such a technological capture of humanity's total self-presence, finding himself, instead, *grateful* in the face of the failure of immanence. This failure amounts to the tender acknowledgment of the human in all its radical finitude (here indexed by the failure of the photographic index) and of alterity in all its infinite inaccessibility (here signaled by the heterogeneous openness of the field of humanity). The second passage, read in light of the first, suggests that this "something deeper—the human," is an abstraction whose warm calls for attention and care are only tenderly approached, never finally achieved. This is what it means to be preoccupied, rather than obsessed, with faces in an asymmetrical ethical field. Film teaches Cornell how loving means letting go, how tenderness entails an always-unfolding approximation of the different objects and subjects of one's experience.

Attractions, Extensions, Etc.

Cornell's late films bear out precisely this lesson, demonstrating how the engrossing affects of mood might in fact complement the extensive sensations of mimesis, its cognitive work, and its relationship to alterity. I want to substantiate this claim now by turning my attention to Cornell's collage trilogy—*Cotillion, The Midnight Party,* and *The Children's Party*—a project he began in the late 1930s and nearly finished in 1969 with the assistance of filmmaker Lawrence Jordan. A pedagogy of tenderness, these short films are comprised of a dazzling assemblage of found footage from Cornell's extensive collection—footage of children, vaudeville performance, and educational films—that Cornell playfully edited in various combinations. Keeping in mind the detached, voyeuristic gaze that seems to dominate many of his lyrical documentaries, the theatrical openness—indeed, the showy *exhibitionism*—of the collage trilogy is especially striking, and Cornell seems to comment wryly on the pleasures and risks of such pedagogical publicness in the very manner of the performances internal to the films: at once playful, touching, and thrilling. *Cotillion,* for example, features an elaborate children's party where young gamers bob for apples, dance in awkward imitations of adult couples, and toss streamers with abandon. Intercut into this revelry are bits of films featuring babies sleeping, eating, and sneezing, as well as footage of a host of variety acts: acrobats, performing seals, and knife throwers. These performances are, of course, for the children's amusement—Cornell repeatedly cuts between the variety footage and the children's gleeful applause—and also for the pleasure of the film's spectator, who is repeatedly encouraged by Cornell to adopt "the gaze he knew as a child," to yield to a pervasive sensation of tenderness that one experiences both internally and as a teasing invitation to public mood that floats beyond the subject. At the same time, the variety acts comment on the children's own theatricality, as well as that of the collage film itself, thus collapsing the difference between players and spectators, subjects and objects of vision: the children perform, the seal performs, the camera performs—all are mimetic spielers, everyone is a star.

Taking its content, in part, from variety performance and modeling its own form on the performative seriality of the variety format (one theatrical event following another in various combinations), the collage trilogy's avant-garde theatricality assumes the mode of address that Tom Gunning has famously linked to the "cinema of attractions": early, pre-narrative cinema's willingness "to rupture a self-enclosed fictional world for a chance to solicit the attention of the spectator," inciting "visual curiosity and supplying pleasure through an exciting spectacle—a unique event, whether fictional or documentary, that is of interest in itself."[33] Gunning is primarily invested in linking the anti-absorptive, anti-auratic exhibitionism of the cinema of attractions to the quasi-Brechtian sensibility of critical detachment fueling a certain strand of twentieth-century avant-gardism and pervading the film-theoretical climate in which his essay was written. But not all absorptions are bound to narrative, or auratic humanism, or the inculcation of bourgeois subjectivity, and it is one of the tricks of Cornell's trilogy to maximize the eventfulness of experience while soliciting a kind of attention—the exteriorizing and antisubjective affectivity of tenderness—more open to the transformative potential of unfoldment, more sensitive than shock experience to difference and the differential vicissitudes of experience. The resulting scene of perception thereby collapses the Romantic boundary between mind and world, between the subject and object of experience conventionally understood as the constitutive frame of Cornell's cinematic gaze. We can place Cornell's cinematic aesthetics of surprise and suddenness not within the category of the sublime, which aestheticizes fear, or shock, a last gambit to rejuvenate fatigued systems of representation and thought, but as a mode of wonder. In wonder, as Philip Fisher explains, there is "the address to delight, to the bold useful stroke, to pleasure in the unexpected and in the extension of [technical and aesthetic] means outside of the limits where they might be thought to come to an end."[34]

What's more, this ecstasy is erotically charged and points us toward the kind of subjective *disorganization* that Cornell, in a curious letter to Charles Henri Ford, explicitly describes as a function of his having made technology his organ: "It has not been easy to reply to the 'what am (I) doing with (my) self' part because of a too shifting condition—in & out of various fields, cinema, ballet, boxes, 14th. St. & old book store browsing, L-P, etc. etc. Possibly one of the most interesting is the achievement of getting my Loie Fuller (Pathé 1905) on to new fresh modern prints—& in MOTION, not stills" (*TM* 229). Cornell's shifty, discombulated emotional condition—nicely performed by the parenthetical intermittence of his syntax—is here a function of his *incorporation* of the various media of his interest, an excessive identification that produces a being-in-a-medium defined by the constant movement in and out of context, in and out of unfolding fields of attention and care. Here, these fields are joined in an eccentric catalogue containing media (cinema and boxes), physical place (14th. St.), and action (browsing). Tellingly, the list ends inconclusively with a repeated "et cetera," a linguistic term that gestures toward unspecified future persons and things, toward extras, leftovers. The unqualified future terms posited by these "et ceteras" are often the same ilk or type, but *need not be so;* "et cetera" can gesture toward untotalizable remainders, qualitative change, as Cornell's heterogeneous list suggests. In this list and its repeated, inconclusive "et ceteras" lies the same tender relationship to the alterity of experience enacted in the overlapping and noncoinciding fields of action of the collage trilogy. Like Cornell's work with Loïe Fuller above, the films articulate a decidedly modern temporal

condition: between the time of live, ephemeral performance and that putative stability of cinematic recording; between the temporal suspension of
the still and the reanimation—the "new fresh modern prints"—of unrolling
cinematic movement; between, in Charles Baudelaire's famous formulation,
the "transient, the fleeting, the contingent; it is one half of art, the other being
the eternal and the immovable."[35] In other words, the achievement of the
collage trilogy is to enact both Cornell's model of experience and a mode
of tender comportment toward it, an ethical mode of mimetic unfoldment
whose habitat is marked by similitude as well as the disjunctive temporalities of modernity itself.

The Children's Party underscores and extrapolates such nascent patterns
of similitude, opening (mimetically enough) with an opening of a window
onto a nocturnal expanse spangled with stars. Cornell cuts to a young boy
staring offscreen and inserts a found pedagogical intertitle proclaiming: "The
Ancients, wondering what the stars were, pictured their heroes in the sky
. . ." This is followed by a series of dissolves to drawings of constellations
like Orion and the Great Bear and their corresponding intertitles. The film
that follows is a reassemblage, a re-constellating, of much of the footage of
Cotillion—acrobats, apple-bobbing, knife-throwing, sleeping babies, dancing children, children mugging for the camera, the camera mugging for the
children, flashing its own precocious talent for seeing affinities across the
spatio-temporal gaps of its diverse footage. So, for example, Cornell plays
with associations between the proximate vision of stellar acrobats performing
outside at night at the state fair and—in the following shot—the opening of
an observatory to the mysteries of the night, an opening that is itself mimed
thematically in *The Midnight Party*'s interest in comets and lightning, erup-
tions of light and electricity in the darkness not unlike cinematic projection
itself. In fact, throughout the trilogy, Cornell's associative editing pattern
draws affinities and likenesses in a fashion that always implicates the mimetic
potential of film. So, for example, we might notice how the star map of the
Great Bear is echoed in the pattern of thrown knives that constellate the
knife thrower's unharmed assistant, which itself suggests the showy cutting
and constellating of Cornellian montage. Or the way the spinning ball on
which the seal balances itself rhymes with the spinning form of an acrobat
suspended by her nose, which—in its own suspended dynamism—is much
like the slow- and stop-motion techniques with which Cornell repeatedly
stalls his trilogy's action: the observatory door stops before it is halfway open;
the knife thrower dons a blindfold only to have his act halted; a baby's face
is frozen in the midst of a sneeze.

Moments like these testify less to Cornell's archive fever than to the expansive and extensive experiential potential of cinematic mimesis itself, to Cornell's exhilarated wandering within the "vast and unsuspected field of action" of his found footage (WA 117). For in the various constellations of the trilogy, the starry firmament *will be* revealed, the knife *will be* thrown, the baby *will* sneeze, but in a different temporal context and a different moody key. In this sense, the amusing and often anarchic structure of the trilogy enacts the formal principle of variety performance itself—"the pleasure of infinite diversity in infinite combinations."[36] On the one hand, the trilogy celebrates the ephemerality of variety performances (acrobats, children, seals, and knife-throwers, etc., etc.), and the filming of live performance confronts what Doane calls the "problematic question of the *representability* of the ephemeral, of the archivability of presence" (*EC* 25). In this reading, part of the frisson produced by the films would be "the disjunctiveness of a presence relieved, a presence haunted by historicity" that is the very "pathos of archival desire" (23). On the other hand, the pleasure of the found footage format, the means that technologically enable Cornell's dexterous variations, seems irreducible to such pathos, related as it is to the surrealist delight of the *trouvaille,* the wondrous encounter of material alterity and subjective necessity. Like the playful repetitions of the attractions in the trilogy's vast combinatory, the found footage format itself seems to push the film's labors away from the stabilization of these performances' origins, away from the archivability (or not) of presence, and toward the wonder of a present that is always noncoinciding, profuse with multiple and overlapping temporalities. In other words, through the form and content of the trilogy, Cornell does everything he can to up the ante on temporal disjunction, betting on a more interesting set of questions: How am I repeating? What modes of temporality and relationships to difference do such repetitions and variations enact?

We can bring into relief the specificity of the collage technique in the trilogy by reference to Cornell's first and best-known film, *Rose Hobart* (1936), his stunningly obsessive homage to one of his favorite screen divas achieved through a meticulous re-editing of Universal Pictures' 1931 jungle melodrama *East of Borneo.* Cornell's editing strategically removes anything that would cement the unity of classical Hollywood narration (dialogue, plot progression, continuity editing, and the like) while it foregrounds transitional spaces (windows, balconies, doorways, thresholds), deliberately mismatched shots, and disconnected gestures that remain enigmatic, hysterical, and emotionally evocative. Simultaneously, though, Cornell re-auraticizes Hobart's screen presence, subjecting it to his technical control, and thus to his spectatorial mastery:

he slows the picture's projection speed from twenty-four frames per second to eighteen, a standard speed of silent films; he projects the film through a blue filter; and he eliminates the film's original soundtrack, replacing it with the hypnotic repetition of two songs from Nestor Amaral's album *Holiday in Brazil*, which he scrounged from one of his favorite Manhattan junkshops. The film, then, is at once a subversive *détournement* of a banal Hollywood product and a compulsive work of fandom that models how cultist consumption recodes and reroutes publicly circulated star images for private delectation. Theatrically atmospheric, mood in *Rose Hobart* operates not to invite transpersonal unfoldment but rather as the stage for fetishistic fantasy, as a means of controlling the threat that is the stuff of which such compensatory dreams are made. And this is to say that, in its early incarnation, Cornell's collage technique—instead of mimetically constellating the eventfulness of experiential unfolding—circles compulsively around the loss of presence, troped here by *Rose Hobart*'s climactic natural disaster—the eclipse.

The collage trilogy, by contrast, enacts a manner of repetition that Cornell, in his diaries, describes as a way of presenting the "'impromptu,' 'surprise,' element of [experience] in the casual everyday aspect" (*TM* 107). This kind of repeating involves returning—in written notes, in a memory provoked by a place or an object, or on a bicycle—to a prior scene of experiential intensity, in this instance, the "mystery & elusiveness of the experiences of the summer of 1944," and unfolding again: "The original inspiration—bicycle rides through outlying suburbs—all of which was repeated a hundred times—the exact reason for this cannot yet explain—the manner in which, riding blind, a succession of paths and by-paths would open up releasing unsuspected and extravagant 'joy of discovery' amidst nearby surroundings" (107). Such repetition, in fact, becomes a broader philosophy of experience that Cornell dubs "extension":

"Extensions"

evocations of experiences at unexpected times and places with such a force, significant + "extension" or complement of the original inspiration + joy as to make of them something worthy of being developed + evaluated. an "extension" should be kept distinct from the sense of perspective + accumulation + and variation on bike rides to the same places . . . The experiences . . . being all of a piece + because of their intensity brought about by a kind of "relationship" to other times. (TM 109)

As a manner of "going over the same ground so often without the disillusionment of revisiting scenes with overpowering experiences of beauty," an extension, for Cornell, is both a theory of experience and a means of techno-mimetic adaptation to such extensivity. "Extensions" are what Cornell named the infinitely expanding folders of clippings, scribblings, and ephemera with which he constellated his encounters with the various objects of his interest so that "so many (sometimes undecipherable and meaningless) chaotic notes can become the basis of exercises in experience" (TM 108). An extension, we might say, is unfoldment as technique, as prosthesis. And as an exercise in experience, extensions operate less as "complement[s] of the original" than by a supplementary logic, and Cornell explains his "profuse and overflowing" diaries as written testimony to the actual satisfactions of extensions' secondariness (109): "It is the way *in which the thread* of these former experiences (so real but nebulous) became *valid* + in the midst of this new happiness something deep must underlie this—it is perhaps the key to this work (journal obsession)" (146). Rather than a pale imitation of the first, real experience, then, writing is an inscription that, like the optical unconscious, is riddled with "little 'coincidences,'" chances and second chances that "are so often the occasion [for] making these experiences live again in the present in a way pleasurable and significant in their unexpectedness + appropriateness" (146). Extensions are joyful modes of virtual experience.

In this sense, while Cornell may have been modernity's greatest magpie, he has no truck with experiential hoarding. In fact, we might profitably consider Cornell's charming insistence, above, that experience should not be "variation[s] on bike rides to the same places" as a rather striking claim about the nature of experience writ large. Experience becomes unmoored from static being, a Hegelian orientation toward the progressive unity of absolute spirit, or the return of the same, following the path of Friedrich Nietzsche's eternal return as read by Gilles Deleuze, in which "identity in the eternal return does not describe the nature of that which returns, but, on the contrary, the fact of returning for that which differs."[37] "Returning is being," for Deleuze, "but only the being of becoming."[38] Read in this spirit, the "something deep" that underlies Cornell's joy in finding the threads of his former experiences newly validated in other contexts is a reprise of his enigmatic formulation "something deeper—the human": a way of conceiving being as primarily multiplicitous rather than reducible to a totality either lost or yet to come. My point is simply that underlying Cornell's joyful repetition, in moments like this, is something like a Deleuzian ontology: a world of primary difference and excessive being in which identity is secondary, produced from a fundamental difference, and, in Deleuze's Cornellian terms, "multiplicity, becoming, and chance are adequate objects of joy by themselves . . . only joy returns."[39] In fact, I should point out that Cornell supplemented the trilogy with yet another joyous variety turn, a film, entitled *Vaudeville De Luxe,* that remained, appropriately, unfinished.

More enchantment then, more production of repetitions as joyful refrains, as soundings of the multiplicities of being-wonderful. Or so goes the chant of the varying repetitions of the collage trilogy and its celluloid extensions. In *Difference and Repetition,* Deleuze draws a relevant distinction between "bare repetition," where repeating subsumes particularity under a universal form or concept, and a more transformative mode of repeating, which displaces a particular-universal relation with one of "non-exchangeable and non-substitutable singularities" (*DR* 1–2). In this latter mode, which Bennett dubs "spiral repetition," singularities are "always undergoing mini-metamorphoses," simultaneously repeating and mutating, giving birth to "wondrous and unsettling—enchanting—new forms," and thus breaking from a conservative repetition bound to the reproduction of the same (*EM* 40). Isn't such swerving of radical singularity from a field of multiplicity precisely what Cornell sees in the impurity of the black-robed nun, that "real type of uniquely unusual" encountered in the streets of Manhattan? Such repetition works intensively: by pushing one's objects of interest to extremes, one transforms their meaning in unique contexts, producing what Deleuze calls "modal" differences of varying intensities and degrees (*DR* 39). In the collage films, such intensive iteration works in a number of ways. In *The Children's Party,* for example, motion is intensive, and Cornell cuts between different acrobats moving in one shot across the x-axis and, in another, suspended from a trapeze, throbbing to and from the viewer on the z-axis, now vibrating with erotic intensity. Cornell, like Georges Méliès, also plays repeatedly with the intensivity of size, of degrees of largeness and smallness: not only in the tendency of his montage to move back and forth between material, animal, human, and cosmic orders, but more specifically in a curious trick shot, repeated in various lengths and contexts in the trilogy, that features a tiny tightrope walker suspended on a string supported by a larger, marveling version of herself (see figure 18). Speed, too, is intensive, and Cornell experiments brilliantly with pace throughout the films, playing with slow- and stop-motion techniques, varying the editing speeds of the same acts, splicing inserts of varying frame lengths, many of which are simply so brief as to be unreadable, registering only as subconscious blips, but others, like the following intertitle from *The Midnight Party,* of sufficient duration to comment wittily on the collage's own play: "A speed maniac in a world of speedsters—a comet caught in the act."

Figure 18. "Size Matters." *The Children's Party,* dir. Joseph Cornell, c. 1938–1969.

Most enchanting about the collage trilogy as a whole is the intensive variety of its repetitions, the quirky delight Cornell both takes and produces in the permutations of its assemblages: the way, for example, that so many of the particular acts and performances of the trilogy recur with varying modal inflections, transformed by their iteration in new contexts and, correspondingly, new moods. For, as Sianne Ngai observes, "Modal differences could thus be described as moody differences—unqualified, temperamental, and constantly shifting."[40] In *Cotillion,* for example, the trained seal's balanced ball is constellated with a suspended spinning acrobat and the whirling wheel of the observatory door, and his balanced chair rhymes with a man balancing a wagonwheel on his nose and, in an inverted image of acrobats racing on motorbikes, with gravity-defying celluloid's own balancing act, its own impossible suspension. In *Vaudeville De Luxe,* though, this animated seal finds itself not only recontextualized between a brief montage of Disney's animation film "Mickey's Circus" and images of seals in the wild, diving into water, but also now playing the banjo as part of "Pickerts Seals and the Marvelous Alaskan Wonder." One can almost hear Cornell, behind the scenes of his vaudeville stage, shouting, "More seal! More sealness!" with an intensity that, like a child's insistent repetition of phrase, frees it into nonsense or renders it auratically other.

Other repetitions seem bent toward explicitly temporal transformations: loopings, reversals, and disruptions of causality or linear development. In *The Children's Party*, the Indian knife-throwing act, the most explicitly violent event, occurs in roughly the middle of the film: here, the blindfolded male thrower twice constellates his partner, covered in paper, with knives and twice she frees herself, even though, as an intertitle quips, "Two inches out of the way, and Chief Zat Zam would not need to apply for divorce." In *Cotillion*, however, this is the final act of the film, yet the act itself begins in its middle and ends, with the film itself, as the woman frees herself from the paper, and Zat Zam dons the blindfold to begin his act again. This temporal looping and reversibility is a leitmotif of the trilogy as a whole: in fact, the first shot of *The Children's Party* is the intertitle "THE END," printed in reverse, an intertitle that returns in *Vaudeville De Luxe* and *The Midnight Party* to mark neither the end nor the beginning of the film but the ends of events within the film's delirious middle. Zat Zam's act, like the recursive, reversible, and interrupted temporality enacted by the collage trilogy, is forever defying irreversible teleologies, always cheating death to begin again, anew. Such temporality is, to a certain extent, embedded in the materiality of the found footage format itself: "Since," as Paul Arthur observes, "in most cases the temporality of the film fragment is split between a present context and the shadow of prior production circumstances, the historical provenance of recycled images is never entirely canceled."[41] At the same time, found-footage is particularly displaced from a singular ground, radically unoriginal: "The reuse of historical images does not 'simulate' anything. Pieces of found footage are in essence tokens of a type, like identical playing cards from different decks . . . for which there could be an infinite number of valid copies."[42] In this way, the ontology of Cornell's found footage is at once riven by historicity but liberated from bourgeois historicism; as extensions they are "being all of a piece" only "because of their intensity brought about by a kind of 'relationship' to other times" (*TM* 109). This relationship thus achieves the meaningfulness of repetition that, for Benjamin, constitutes historicized experience (*Erfahrung*), even as its instability frees repeating from its allegiance to origin.

Notice here that, unlike much of the found-footage work that has dominated avant-garde cinematic practice over the last twenty years or so, Cornell is not interested in the ideological shock effect produced by exporting found footage out of one sociocultural context or narrative and placing it in a new, discrepant one. Rather, the temporality of the collages bears out something far more radical: not in being out of an original context, but of the experiential condition of groundlessness; of being constantly de- and re-contextualized, of always having one's context shifted, and consequently of finding one's ethical faculties for care and attention constantly readjusted by the moods that disclose one's situatedness. In this sense, the repetitions of the collages enact the interminability of context by iterability itself, written as it is into the structure of every material inscription. As Jacques Derrida argues in "Signature, Event, Context," "every sign can be cited, put between quotation marks; in so doing it can break with every given context, engendering an infinity of new contexts in a manner which is absolutely illimitable."[43] In their relentless iterability, the collage films thus can be said to perform the essential impurity of the Austinian performative, which, try as it might, can never minimize the risk of contextual instability, of a nonteleological consciousness that is not always present to itself and never fully in control of its agency and intention. The capacious field of eventful experience enacted by the films is opened by the contingency of the optical unconscious and by the "structural unconscious" of iterability itself, which, like Cornell's joyful extensions, "prohibits any saturation of context" by splitting and dissociating the "pure singularity" of the performance events that structure them, whose repetitions are always other (SEC 18, 17).[44]

My point here is that the very materiality of these collage films, wandering as they do in the impure et cetera of experience, the "nonpresent *remainder* of a differential mark cut off from its putative 'production' or origin," seems to strain against Cornell's metaphysical impulses: his Paracelsian belief in the absolute singularity of a divine signature whose abiding spirit authorizes the possibility of mimesis, of finding counterparts, of tenderness (SEC 10). This tension between enchanted materiality and divine purposiveness is best encapsulated by the moody montage of *The Midnight Party*.[45] Here, the principle of modal distinction is written into the title, which indicates that its moody difference from *The Children's Party* will be largely one of degree: in its largely nocturnal setting and foreboding atmosphere. In it, the collage constellates, along with the familiar images of acrobats, seals, and observatory doors, a rather curious sequence, if such it can be called: we see a documentary image of a man scrambling to repair a tree branch that has fallen on an electrical wire on the exterior of a house, then an image of the tree falling on the wire, followed by fantastical image of Thor swinging a cudgel from which surge bolts of lightning. We cut to a shot of a washerwoman in a dilapidated room with a window, and then to a cloudy night sky superimposed with a text whose flashing and fading concludes the film: "He shall transform the households / of drudgery into homes of ease / and happiness / He shall work unceasingly day and night / And yet his origin shall remain / shrouded in mystery."

The pronoun's referent is decidedly ambiguous, gesturing perhaps toward Thor and, beyond that, to an occluded divine origin. But the film's broader displacement of signature by the fundamental instability of context is repeated again in this sequence's scrambled temporal order: men attempt to repair the "accident," the tree falls, Thor strikes, the woman awaits liberation from her miserable interior. In other words, the sequence suggests, "electricity happens." Notice too how this scene replays the terms of Cornell's opposition, "household antagonism vs. tenderness," returning to the subject of domestic anxiety—the washerwoman—trapped inside and threatened with indifference while, outside, experience relentlessly unfolds. If the woman's future happiness—her capacity for tenderness as public unfoldment—is pried from Thor's control by the unstable context of collage, then might we read this "work" as a rather mundane labor, a mode of joyous production again at home in Moore's many "by-paths of romance," open to the essential impurity of experience? This would mean finding happiness precisely in the exposure to what, for Derrida's Austin, is the very infelicity of an untotalizable context, where an excess of irreducible semantic residue escapes meaning's single horizon. Cornell seems to pine for just such happiness when, on the back of a picture he sends to his friend Leila Hadley, he scrawls, cryptically:

help
unfoldment
from gestalt. (*TM* 43)

Unfoldment from gestalt: this is, finally, as good a way as any to describe Cornell's cinematic tenderness, which comes from the liberation of affect from teleological purpose. As an insight about the heterogeneous field of the human with which unfoldment always brings Cornell into ecstatic intimacy, this amounts to a plea for openness and receptivity, for the loving of human being in its very irreducibility to a graspable whole greater than the sum of its parts, remainders, etc. This love, predicated as it is on the dispersed subject of a mood, is simply incompatible with the aggressive emotional agency of modernism's more overtly sympathetic agencies, bent on the assimilation of alterity to the preexisting categories of human being and feeling. Perhaps it is just this eccentric kind of openness that Cornell signals in the categorical instability of the human in the collage films, protagonized as they are by untotalizable remainders, starring the not-quite-subjects of children and animals rather than interiorized and fully human individuals, and forsaking a progressive plotting of human development from origin to end for the stuff of real wonder: irruptive events, impure performances, and intensive, transformative repetition. Transformation, predicated on this eventfulness of experience, is written into the very material structure of Cornell's cinematic collages, which yield mimetically to technological second nature, and whose images are thus anything but falsely corporeal. And here we need only remember that Cornell's most insistent formal technique in the films is the arrest of his potential not-quite-subjects in a freeze frame: a caesura that bears witness to radical human finitude, indexed here and elsewhere in Cornell's work by the failure of photographic indexicality (see figure 19).

As the site of an immanent absolute, Cornell's modern experience is always unfolding—becoming at once more other and more replete with similitudes. And the most poignant of these, the one that best grounds our faculties for care, is the trace of our shared human finitude. In this sense, the wonder of

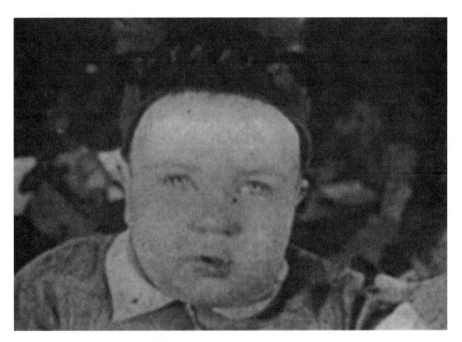

Figure 19. "Being Amazed." *The Children's Party,* dir. Joseph Cornell, c. 1938–69.

modern experience is its ability to keep us enchanted by its otherness, its refusal of closure, and thus, like the vast combinatory of Cornell's films, its openness to infinite transformation, continual unfoldment. For this we can be grateful: The tenderness of these variety films both enacts and invites attention to the enchanted materiality of modern being, to the marvel of a world in which our technical and emotional capacities for tenderness increase the more surprising that world becomes.

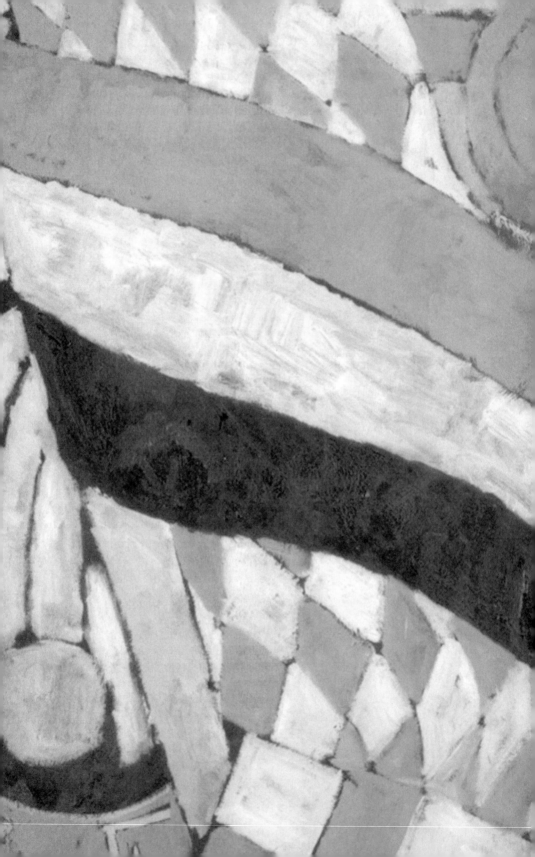

3
Comedy

6

Dead Pan

The human is the being that, bumping into things and only in this encounter, opens up to the non-thinglike. And inversely, the human is the one that, being open to the non-thinglike, is, for this reason, irreparably consigned to things.
—Giorgio Agamben, *The Coming Community*

Slapstick is, first and foremost . . . the dramatic expression of the tyranny of things.
—André Bazin, "Theater and Cinema, Part II"

We still underestimate the twistedness of Nathanael West's sense of humor, the radical strangeness of what he once called his "strange and unfunny jokes."[1] Recall the following bit of comic obscenity from *Miss Lonelyhearts* (1933). Near the beginning of this, West's second novella, the titular protagonist, who writes an advice column for a New York newspaper and considers this messianic work, has a dream in two acts: in the first he "found himself on the stage of a crowded theater. He was a magician who did tricks with doorknobs. At his command, they bled, flowered, spoke."[2] When the dream scene shifts, he finds himself on a drinking spree with his college chums. Wandering into the country, they decide to buy a lamb to kill and eat, "but on the condition that they sacrifice it to God before barbequeing it" (*ML* 68). They prepare an altar on a rock in the woods, which they adorn with flowers; they elect Miss Lonelyhearts "priest"; and they chant "Christ, Christ, Jesus Christ" until Lonelyhearts brings the knife down for the kill. At this point, religious ritual becomes a rather gruesome slapstick:

The blow was inaccurate and made a flesh wound. He raised the knife again and this time the lamb's violent struggles made him miss altogether. The knife broke on the altar. Steve and Jud pulled the animal's head back for him to saw at its throat, but only a small piece of blade remained in the handle and he was unable to cut through the matted wool.

Their hands were covered with slimy blood and the lamb slipped free. It crawled off into the underbrush.

As the bright sun outlined the altar rock with narrow shadows, the scene appeared to gather itself for some new violence. They bolted. . . . After some time had passed, Miss Lonelyhearts begged them to go back and put the lamb out of its misery. They refused to go. He went back alone and found it under a bush. He crushed its head with a stone and left the carcass to the flies that swarmed around the bloody altar flowers. (*ML* 68)

This, I submit, is slapstick in textual form, a scene whose grisly mechanics yield an emotional uncertainty in the reader that routinely accompanies Miss Lonelyhearts's "bumping into things." Indeed, insofar as West regularly refuses to provide the affective codes that might give his reader a clue about how to feel, his clowning presentation is a burlesque routine, capitalizing on what Gilbert Seldes described as the burlesque's great virtue: "its complete lack of sentimentality in the treatment of emotion and its treatment of appearance."[3] Is the scene funny because it is so unreal, or horrifying because its violent reality is so nakedly presented? We would laugh, presumably, if we only knew the lamb's misery was patently false, overdone; if we could fix West's facetiousness toward a scene that moves so precipitously from sacral terror to kitschy bungling. The lack of such certainties here marks West's radical departure from the theories of affective universality surrounding slapstick, which, as we'll see, assert not just that we laugh because we are similarly embodied beings but also because the status of physical suffering, and of material reality itself, is knowable and true. But in *Miss Lonelyhearts*, our laughter, like our sympathetic identification with either the subject or object of the violence, is foreclosed—stalled by the scene's suspended presentation as neither fully proximate, inviting sympathy and pity, nor sufficiently distant, allowing a consoling disidentification. This is the tyranny of materiality in Lonelyhearts's world: things are at once too near and too far, never fully appearing, but never really disappearing either.

As a privileged instance of West's antisentimental sense of humor—his deadpan affectivity—the lamb episode is also emblematic of the broader emotional landscape of the novel, everywhere destabilized by the epistemological and ontological uncertainty of a rationalized and differentiated socius.

In this world of uncertain feeling, what I call Miss Lonelyhearts's project of sympathetic publicity—his desire to feel the pain of his mass readership, "to love the whole world with an all-embracing love"—can only fail, indeed, *must* fail (*ML* 67). And critics generally understand Miss Lonelyhearts's failure as symptomatic of the novel's failed social world, figured here as the recurring modernist nightmare of the bad city: of enervating *Gesellshaft* and experiential decay, of the falsification of organic community and public discourse by mass media and their compensatory, and paradoxical, recuperation in the bathetic labors of "the Miss Lonelyhearts," the "priests of twentieth-century America" (62). Two of West's best recent critics have worked not only to explain but to somehow transform the sense of failure that pervades the novel. So, distinguishing *Miss Lonelyhearts* from the relentless blackness of West's other work, Jonathan Veitch locates the novel's affirmative force in West's "genuine empathy" for the power of the public's physical pain to "preserve the meaning of presence, immediacy, and wholeness" in the context of the novel's reified world.[4] Rita Barnard, on the other hand, locates the novel's radicality precisely in its negativity, showing how West adopts a subversive, proto-situationist critical practice that undermines and unworks the affirmative force of aesthetic creation itself.[5] And yet, as they scrutinize West's deadpan presentation of modernity's reified world for signs of how, precisely, to take it, neither critic quite takes West seriously enough: Veitch, because he underestimates both pain's distance from sentimental apprehension and West's quarrel with sympathy itself, a conflict he erases by collapsing West's attitude—his "genuine empathy" with public pain—and the sympathetic quest of the beleaguered protagonist West everywhere mocks; Barnard, because she restricts her analysis of the critical force of West's deadpan to his critique of art and not, beyond that, to the terms of modern publicness and community. Neither of these readings sees the novel's failures all the way through.

My gambit in what follows is to inhabit more fully the failures in the novel by taking West's antisentimental comedy as seriously as possible, a task as unsettling as the humor itself. How, I ask, might the success and critical potential of West's joking lie in the specific terms of Lonelyhearts's failure, which is, after all, a failure of public sentiment? How, more specifically, might West's comic treatment of this project—a dimension critics consistently overlook—entail a critical anatomy of certain emotional protocols of modernity, of the violence they entail and of the outmoded notions of public and communal belonging they sustain? And what would this critique of affect do to current critical notions of how modernism understands the role of emotion in negotiating modernity's mediated public sphere? To answer these questions, my argument begins with the simple observation that much of the slapstick comedy of the novel comes at the expense of Miss Lonelyhearts's project of sympathetic publicity. I further argue that the singularity of this humor be read against the negative foil of two broader comic discourses and the ideologies of affect that structure them: the antisentimental, elite *humour noir* of the surrealist avant-garde and the emotional protocols of vernacular slapstick comedy. In the first segment of the chapter, then, I show how the terms of West's appraisal of reified sentiment—which is also a critique of the humanist terms of the bourgeois public sphere—emerge over and against both vernacular and elite modernist comic discourses: the former echoing the universalizing affective logic of Enlightenment humanism that underwrites bourgeois publicity, the latter predicated on a superhuman transcendence of the material world. In the chapter's second section, I turn to *Miss Lonelyhearts* to show how the critical potential of West's deadpan allows us to rethink the politics of modernist antisentimentality, which for West is less a familiar attack on a feminized domestic or middle-class culture than a trenchant critique of the dangers of the Enlightenment heritage of the modern public sphere, whose reified horizon is dubiously structured by sympathetic relations and their demand for abstraction.[6]

Thus, I intend my reading of *Miss Lonelyhearts* to put some critical pressure on recent approaches to modernism's public sphere that have refused lapsarian accounts of its mass-mediated fate, to transform (again) our sense of its failure. Here, I have in mind Miriam Hansen's influential arguments that mass-mediated publicity need not be cause for Habermasian revulsion, so long as we understand modern publicness as an affective, experiential "horizon"—an expressive and sensory discursive landscape that anchors the seemingly groundless experience of modernity.[7] The cynical rejoinder issuing from West's novel is two-pronged: first, that the guarantors of the cultural "ground" (whether in the form of language or, more generally, sympathetic currents across public horizons) are always failing, producing either the violent explosions or the affective stallings I've begun to discuss; second, that when public horizons are affective, they are too often sentimental, and when they are sentimental, they are constitutively violent, structured by dubious Enlightenment ideologies of emotion and interiority that would either collapse experiential difference in sameness or—in the narcissistic work of black humor that is the cult of feeling's logical inversion—assert it defensively and aggressively. Thus, the laughter in *Miss Lonelyhearts,* emerging from ungrounded subjects, discloses a social world of confounding affective particularity that remains, mercifully, unfelt by its protagonist. In the final section of the essay, I argue that the radical potential of West's humor lies in its exposure of the limits of public and communal belonging conceived in conventionally humanist terms, where community would be secured by sympathy and the logic of identity that subtends identification.[8] Refusing a host of familiar modernist gambits for securing community, West opts for an active nihilism that dwells within experiential decay and signals, negatively, the contours of an ethical publicness on the other site of sentimentalism. His deadpan only succeeds when it fails completely.

Comedies of Human Nature

We can begin to get a better purchase on West's "private and unfunny jokes" by briefly considering them in relation both to the aristocratic black humor of the surrealist avant-garde and the vernacular tradition of slapstick comedy. The affective protocols of both traditions are referenced in the lamb sacrifice, an episode I consider representative of West's deadpan, and the dissenting work of West's humor becomes legible in their company. If West's flat presentation of this violent episode seems sick, inhuman, we should recall that for West, pathology and dehumanized comedy are necessarily bound. As West himself makes clear in the dust-jacket blurb for his first novel, *The Dream Life of Balso Snell* (1931), because "N. W. West . . . is vicious, mean, ugly, obscene and insane," he "can well be compared" with the French: "In his use of the violently dissociated, the dehumanized marvelous, the deliberately criminal and imbecilic, he is much like Guillaume Apollinaire, Jarry, Ribemont-Dessaignes, Raymond Roussel, and certain of the surrealists."[9] The "black humor" often linked to West's work was first coined and codified in André Breton's *Anthologie de l'humour noir.* Defining this brand of humor as "the mortal enemy of sentimentality" and identifying Jonathan Swift and the Marquis de Sade as black humor's first practitioners, Breton suggests that black humor is, in fact, Enlightenment sentimentality's dark shadow, a Romantic reaction formation against the "cult of feeling."[10] A response to the Romantic subject's dissatisfaction with the protocols of Enlightened feeling, his discovery that "the external world does not perfectly respond to his innermost nature," black humor promises a triumphant resolution of the Romantic soul and the material world through, paradoxically, "the concentration of the soul upon itself."[11] Turning to Freud's 1928 paper "Humor," Breton explains in the introduction to the *Anthologie* how the discrete charm of humor lies precisely in its ability to effect this internal resolution: "Obviously, what is fine about [humor] is the triumph of narcissism, the ego's virtuous assertion of its own invulnerability. It refuses to be hurt by the arrows of reality or to be compelled to suffer. It insists that it is impervious to the wounds dealt by the outside world, in fact, that these are merely occasions for affording it pleasure" (*ABH* xviii). In this fashion, the black humorist distances himself from the traumas and injustices of the objective world, turning them into sources of subversive *jouissance.* Explicitly aristocratic ("fine and elevating"), black humor is, in short, a Freudian version of Romantic irony, that faculty through which the artist, laughing, severs himself from the world of contingency.[12]

Now consider how this elevating, superhuman laughter itself comically falters in the lamb episode, in which the surrealist project of animistic re-enchantment—here figured as Lonelyhearts's dream of "doing tricks with doorknobs"—is itself a bad joke. Lonelyhearts fails to become a surrealist sorcerer à la Breton, capable of restoring aura to a ruthlessly rational world. Further, the botched sacrifice frustrates Lonelyhearts's spiritual transcendence of the material world, the very work of surrealist black humor. As the resolutely non-Romantic surrealist Georges Bataille argues, in sacrificing an animal the human would confirm its distance from the objective world by positing a "relation of subordination" between human subject and thingly object, effecting a "transcendence between the eater and the eaten."[13] "Insofar as he is spirit," Bataille continues, "it is man's misfortune to have the body of an animal and thus to be like a thing," and this tough luck is not just the grim lesson of the lamb episode but, in fact, the central comedy of *Miss Lonelyhearts,* whose protagonist's projects of symbolic uplift—his work of first feeling his readership's pain and then responding to it in a meaningful way—are thwarted at every turn, and who, despite his best efforts, finds this spiritual quest undone by a dead world.[14] In this sense, West's antisentimental deadpan here and elsewhere precludes the aristocratic violence of black humor understood as either a narcissistic buffering of the ego or a Romantic transcendence of material contingency.

If West thus finds the elevating certainty of black humor unsuited to the uncertain affective landscape of *Miss Lonelyhearts,* he seems equally dissatisfied with the emotional protocols of slapstick comedy. West's critics often remind us that the novelist described his theoretical experiment in *Miss Lonelyhearts* as an attempt to compose "a novel in the form of the comic strip," one befitting "a hasty people" and penned by a jokester who "is no longer a psychologist" and now "only [has] time to explode."[15] And while these critics have discussed the significance of West's "comic strip" novel for his broader investigation of mass culture's role in mediating the historical experience of the Great Depression, they have overlooked the novel's relation to the broader vernacular tradition in which the comic strip emerged—specifically the modern, urban comedy of American vaudeville beloved by West, and slapstick, its most representative comic form.[16] West's desire to embed his novel's comic violence in a putatively "American" structure of feeling is thus crucial for understanding *Miss Lonelyhearts,* not because it juxtaposes—with a familiar modernist appeal to the recalcitrance of locality—an authentic and unsentimental project of social criticism against the feminized affective protocols of a European tradition, but because American vernacular comedy itself depended on specific sentimental protocols to negotiate an urban public sphere that seemed dangerously differentiated, or better, variously local.[17] In this sense, vernacular comedy's cultural work anticipates *Miss Lonelyhearts's* project of sentimental publicity: both must negotiate an increasingly heterogeneous public sphere characterized by a vexing oscillation between the local and the universal, the particular and the typical.

Thus, unlike the disembedding laugh of the black humorist, the "low" vernacular laughter surging from vaudeville houses frequented by West was staunchly embedded in the urban world of early-twentieth-century modernity. Surging from and finding ample comic fodder in an increasingly heterogeneous society, vaudeville comedy carried on—albeit in domesticated form—a specific response to urban modernity and the explosive industrialization of amusement in the late nineteenth century that both contemporary commentators and later historians would call the "New Humor."[18] Fast-paced, efficient, and mechanical, the "New Humor's" most obvious cultural manifestations were the rapid-fire joking (the "machined monologue") of the vaudeville stage and the formal regularity of the comic strip.[19] Functionally, the new humor voiced the discontent of the immigrant urban masses with the ability of American institutions to fulfill their promises, and its economy and pace mirrored the hurried tempo of urban life, the "hasty people" of West's imagined readership. Central to vaudeville's domestication was its ability to negotiate pervasive middle-class anxieties about the New Humor and the increasingly heterogeneous society it indexed. In its desire for a mass audience, refined vaudeville thus inherited the hurried pacing, flippancy, and mechanical character of the New Humor and strategically negotiated the ethnic complexity it figured through two comic discourses—two modes, if you will, of comic abstraction: vaudeville's notorious racial comedy, with its crude systems of ethnic stereotyping, and the universalizing discourse of emotional mechanics surrounding slapstick.[20] Put another way, vaudeville comedy oscillated between its joke-work's social embeddedness (its sensory immediacy and social topicality) and its disembeddedness (its affective universality). This comedy's mass appeal depended upon its negotiation of the particularity (ethnic and otherwise) of urban experience, yet its desire for a mass audience pushed it to elaborate reductive typologies, to embrace putatively universal themes, and to cultivate broadly resonant affects through an elaborate pseudoscience of emotional mechanics that would, presumably, reify a universal emotional current coursing through the audience.

Consider the terms of vaudeville comedy's contemporary theorists, in every way emblematic of this universalizing discourse, and of slapstick's privileged role in it. In a 1913 *McClure's* article entitled "The Mechanics of Emotion," George M. Cohan and George J. Nathan declare: "Emotionally we are essentially the same."[21] Just as "in physiology there are certain familiar phenomena known technically as reflex actions," certain "movements which were originally voluntary, conscious acts, but which, by constant repetition, have become reflex," so "there are emotional reflexes" that can be triggered by "mechanical preparation," by the shrewd writer's "tools of emotion."[22] Remarkably, though, after reducing human affectivity to pure mechanism and convention, Nathan and Cohan turn habit into essence: certain jokes will always work because certain jokes *have* always worked, and they have done so because they testify to a transhistorical emotional gestalt. "Down at the core of what have become merely mechanical stratagems for the arousing of theatrical emotion, constant, immutable human nature declares itself"; further, they hypothesize, perhaps "the permanence, through the ages, of the same type of humor is best illustrated by the circus clown."[23] Similarly, in his 1911 *Writing for Vaudeville,* Brett Page avers that the "fact that we all laugh—in varying degrees—at the antics of the circus clown, should be sufficient evidence of the permanence of certain forms of humor to admit of a belief in the basic truth that certain actions do at all times find a humorous response in all hearts."[24] As the references to the circus clown suggest, it was the "supposed infliction of pain" in slapstick comedy that seemed a particularly acute index of universal structures of affect.[25] Here, man experiences the inevitable physicality of his existence; he is exasperated by natural laws, harassed by gravity, and confronted with what Frank Capra once called the "mute intransigence of inanimate objects."[26] As a result, as the burlesque clowns Lew Weber and Joe Fields declared in their 1913 article "Adventures in Human Nature," "Human nature—as we have analyzed it, with results that will be told you by the cashier at our bank—will laugh louder and oftener at these spectacles . . . than at anything else one might name. Human nature here, as before, insists that the object of the attacks—the other man—be not really hurt."[27]

With such plummy fantasies in mind, we can return to the nightmare of Lonelyhearts's botched lamb sacrifice, which clearly fails to offer the familiar comforts of slapstick violence: because the material status of pain and suffering is so uncertain, Lonelyhearts's "bumping into things" offers no bromides about the basic physicality or immutability of human nature or of the spiritual privileges of the non-thinglike. Instead, the scene blurs the very distinctions— between humans and things, real and false pain, subjective certainty and material contingency—that the affective protocols of both slapstick and black humor must stabilize. In the case of black humor, bumping into things distinguishes a triumphant, antisentimental subject, distanced from the real traumas of the objective world; in the case of slapstick, the encounter with objects confirms the universality of human nature that, in sentimental fashion, feels itself everywhere. By contrast, West's antisentimental deadpan, his defamiliarized slapstick, speaks less to humanity's universal physicality than to a more historically localized awareness of the tyranny of things. As Bill Brown reminds us, the 1920s—the heyday of American cinematic slapstick—was also the decade when things "emerge as the object of profound theoretical engagement" in the work of Martin Heidegger, Georg Lukács, Siegfried Kracauer, and Walter Benjamin.[28] Indeed, interwar writings on American film stressed its ability to index the "new physicality, the exterior surface or 'outer skin' of things," an expressive potential especially reassuring in a modernity wherein, as Georg Simmel saw it, objects, "by their independent, impersonal mobility . . . complete the final stage of their separation from people."[29] In this way, for West, slapstick's comedy of bodies and objects at once too close and too far from each other indexes not the fundamental constancy of "human nature" but the specific social world of Fordist mass culture, of regimes of rationalization and mechanization that would do increasing violence to the categories of the human and the natural in the period of late modernism.[30] So, rather than reifying the fundamental constancy of human nature, West's slapstick traces the human's reified emotional contours in a fashion that recalls the historical-materialist terms of Kracauer's reading of Charlie Chaplin, slapstick's most famous clown: the "human being that Chaplin embodies or, rather, lets go of, is a *hole*. . . . He has no will; in the place of the drive toward self-preservation or the hunger for power there is nothing inside him but a void which is as blank as the snow fields of Alaska."[31]

In *Miss Lonelyhearts,* this inhuman violence, and its historical connection to a certain kind of antisentimental comedy, finds a face in Miss Lonelyhearts's editor, Shrike: "Although his gestures were elaborate, his face was blank. He practiced a trick used much by moving-picture comedians—the dead pan. No matter how fantastic or excited his speech, he never changed his expression. Under the shining white globe of his brow, his features huddled together in a dead, gray triangle" (*ML* 64). West's pun ("the dead pan") neatly demarcates the conditions of expressivity both in and of the novel: it links Shrike's alienated gestures to the movie's mediated public sphere and to the kind of reified slapstick that everywhere permeates the book's social world, while it simultaneously tropes the zero degree of comic affect that is the hallmark of West's own antisentimentalism. Given the critical tendency to understand Shrike as the real monster in West's novel, this association between Shrike's "trick" and West's own deadpan affectivity is crucial for my reading: it suggests that we understand Shrike's frozen physiognomy not only as the result of reification's violence to the human but also as a kind of critical antisentimentalism that both precipitates and follows this failure to secure so-called human nature. One would be tempted to associate Shrike's defensive trick with the black humor of the surrealist except that, as we will see, Shrike is also the character most resolutely critical of Lonelyhearts's spiritual quest, and indeed of any and every transcendent logic of the sort that animates the black humorist's refined sensibility. In what follows, then, I read West's comic critical practice as an extrapolation of the dialectical logic of Shrike's face, arguing that West urges not nostalgia for a lost human interiority but the inhabiting of an alienated essence, a nesting within the decay of experience that no character models better than Shrike. Sounding precisely this dessicated terrain, West's own strategic deadpan is likewise harnessed to the task of inhabiting—not transcending—a resolutely contingent social world where "human nature" has lost conceptual coherence. In this world, the affective current that would, in the case of vaudeville comedy, reify human nature is insistently confounded, short-circuited by a public world of difference and particularity beyond sentimental apprehension. And on this urban scene, Shrike's gesture unworks: its trick figures the strategic stalling of feeling's machinery that defines West's critique of Lonelyhearts's sympathetic work; and as such, its interruptive, historicizing gesturality models an alternative form of publicness and community irreducible to humanist notions of interiority and identity.

Doing Tricks with Doorknobs

Miss Lonelyhearts can be understood as West's attempt to re-situate, within the reified socius of urban modernity, a philosophical conundrum debated in *The Dream Life of Balso Snell,* itself, Veitch explains, a "manifesto of sorts for a materialist aesthetics."[32] As Balso begins his rank journey through the anus of the Trojan Horse, his "guide" recalls "the eternal wrangle between the advocates of the Singular and those of the Plural. As [William] James puts it, 'Does reality exist distributively or collectively—in the shape of *eaches, everys, anys, eithers* or only in the shape of an *all* or *whole?*' If reality is singular then there are no feet in nature, if plural, a great many."[33] Miss Lonelyhearts's job as one of the "priests of 20th-century America"—a vocation West considered an ironic response to James's *The Varieties of Religious Experience*—is to narrate, love, and resuscitate the social whole: to use his advice column to confer meaning on the senseless and contingent material world that palpitates just behind his readers' letters. Or, as Lonelyhearts himself explains in one of his more pathetic fantasies, in his column he "would ask Broken-hearted, Sick-of-it-all, Desperate, Disillusioned-with-tubercular-husband" to come to a little park near his office and "water the soil with their tears" (*ML* 63). In this park, one of the text's more insistent emblems of the "dead pan," Lonelyhearts would perform his own miracle, transubstantiating his readers' particularized suffering into natural beauty; but this attempt to realize a vital social monad leaves a residue of heterogeneity, which West codes as podiatric: "Flowers would then spring up, flowers that smelled of feet. 'Ah, humanity . . .' But he was heavy with shadow and the joke went into a dying fall. He tried to break its fall by laughing at himself" (63).[34] There are feet in nature, after all, and Lonelyhearts's joke about an aphoristically generalizable suffering (Melville's "Ah, humanity") is doubly funny: first because, as Lonelyhearts knows, it rings so hollow; second, because West mimics this empty moment of failed sympathy with a heavy-handed metaphor of maternal fullness that itself forces Lonelyhearts into a false identification with the pain of his largely female audience. Thus, the "shadow of lamp-post," which "pierces him like a spear," leaves him "heavy with shadow" and sends his joke into freefall.

Lonelyhearts's quest to love the whole world wholly is thus comically confounded by both the uncertain ontological status of reified matter itself and by the affective particularities of the social (the eaches and everys of feeling). While we might be tempted to see in this love something like

Cornellian "unfoldment" (which he, like West, occasionally associates with the messianic), Lonelyhearts is never a gentle agent, and his loving everywhere lacks the tenderness that marks Joseph Cornell's encounters with the incessant otherness of the social world. Given his thorough cynicism about the possibility and desirability of such totalizing feeling, West's gambit is to maximize the particularity of the social as it suggests itself in the letters of Lonelyhearts's readers, epistles that bear witness to suffering of such a freakish degree that Lonelyhearts's sentimental project can *only* fail. This is to say that the deck is clearly stacked against our hero, whose readership testifies to an unbelievable range of physical pain that tends to be localized, as our priest's "piercing" makes clear, in the female body (a convenient location given the historical gender exclusions to universal ideals of Enlightenment humanism). He receives letters from "Sick-of-it-all," a pregnant housewife with seven children, whose "kidneys hurt so much" she wants to kill herself, but whose husband—who has promised no more children—will not allow her to abort the child; from a teenage boy whose thirteen-year-old sister, deaf and dumb, was raped and impregnated by a stranger on the roof of her house; from "Broad Shoulders," a woman who can't bring herself to leave her husband, a deadbeat sadist who sleeps with weapons under his bed for killing her; and, most memorably, from "Desperate," a little girl born with "a big hole in the middle of [her] face that scares people even [herself]" (*ML* 60). Desperate's de-facement signals the obscene paradoxes of *Miss Lonelyhearts*'s world, since here the presence of extreme particularity is granted through physiognomic absence, the social whole at once signaled and obscured by a facial hole. Taking a cue from W. H. Auden, we might call West's project of heightening social particularity through such grotesquerie the "logic of the cripple," since as Auden explains, "a cripple is unfortunate and his misfortune is both singular and incurable. . . . Each one makes the impression of a unique case. Further, the nature of the misfortune, a physical deformity, makes the victim repellent to the senses of the typical and the normal, and there is nothing the cripple or others can do to change his condition."[35]

For West, the unknowability of the cripple is an epistemological consequence of mass publicity. Thus, while each letter-writer's pain in *Miss Lonelyhearts* is "singular" and material in its extreme physicality (a singularity that gives the lie to Lonelyhearts's visions of totality), these pains are only legible through the mass-mediation of the newspaper and through the specific conventions of the advice column to which the sufferers submit. Through this convention—itself a formal microcosm of the amply theorized communicative ideal of the public sphere, which subjects access through processes of self-abstraction and disembodiment—the signatories assume names like "Desperate" and "Broad Shoulders," abandon their marked particularity and effectively name their typicality. In this sense, the letters' ontological ambiguity—are they material manifestations of singular ills or codified abstractions of universal suffering?—means that, much like vaudeville comedy and the New Humor, they oscillate between social embeddedness and disembeddedness, pulled, like Lonelyhearts himself, between negotiating affective particularity and embracing putative universals. In the letters themselves, as critics have long noted, such universals take the form of those pervasive "sentimental clichés of American culture—home, marriage, and true love"—that structure their authors' attempts to render the particularity of their suffering.[36] In this sense, Lonelyhearts notes, the letters suffer the fate of mass-production even before their publication in the paper: they are "all of them alike, stamped from the dough of suffering with a heart-shaped cookie knife" (*ML* 59).[37]

And this commodification of suffering has serious implications for the business of comic affect in the book, since as the novel begins, Miss Lonelyhearts realizes that "the letters were no longer funny," that "he could not go on finding the same joke funny thirty times a day for months on end" (*ML* 59). Later, the Latin-themed restaurant to which he takes Shrike's wife, whom he is attempting to seduce, indicts the same, and altogether unfunny, "business of dreams": "He had learned not to laugh at the advertisements offering to teach writing, cartooning, engineering, to add inches to the biceps and develop the bust. He should therefore realize that the people who came to El Gaucho . . . were the same people as those who wrote to Miss Lonelyhearts for help" (83). In both cases, it remains altogether uncertain whether laughter is impossible because the suffering signalled by the letters (and the larger business of mass desire) has been brought too proximate—that is, made real in a way it was not before, when the letters *were* funny—or because it is so frustratingly immaterial.[38] Unable to make the double move of distinction from/identification with suffering that is at the heart of slapstick, Lonelyhearts can't laugh at the letters because he can neither fully distance himself from their writers ("I'm glad I don't suffer as you do") nor adequately sympathize with them ("I suffer like you").[39]

This tremulous condition, as I have been arguing, defines West's deadpan slapstick, and it needs to be stressed that while West takes this condition seriously, he is not himself beyond laughter. In fact, he finds ample comic fodder in Lonelyhearts's bumbling attempt to negotiate this shaky material world and repeatedly mocks his messianic sententiousness. In this project, West finds an unlikely ally in the commodified materiality of the "El Gaucho" stamp, as, for example, when Lonelyhearts removes an "ivory Christ" from its cross and nails it to the wall with "large spikes. But the desired effect had not been obtained. Instead of writhing, the Christ remained calmly decorative" (*ML* 67). Transcendent suffering is comically undercut by kitsch, which here attains a quiet inertia. For this reader, West is at his funniest when Lonelyhearts's Christ complex fuels a mania for ordering a particularized material and social world, a penchant for purification that, in West's hands, is repeatedly coded as not just futile but sadistic and ultimately psychotic. After his slapdash bludgeoning of the lamb, Miss Lonelyhearts

> found himself developing an almost insane sensitiveness to order. Everything had to form a pattern: the shoes under the bed, the ties in the holder, the pencils on the table. . . . For a little while, he seemed to hold his own but one day he found himself with his back to the wall. On that day all the inanimate things over which he had tried to obtain control took the field against him. . . . The collar buttons disappeared under the bed, the point of the pencil broke, the handle of the razor fell off, the window shade refused to stay down. He fought back, but with too much violence, and was decisively defeated by the spring of the alarm clock.
>
> He fled to the street, but there chaos was multiple. Broken groups of people hurried past, forming neither stars nor squares. The lamp-posts were badly spaced and the flagging was of different sizes. (*ML* 70)

Lonelyhearts's battle against inanimate things here is pure slapstick, and West's attention to the tragedy of the object here underscores the lurking menace of Lonely's pathological sensitivity to order, which moves unhesitatingly and threateningly in this scene from material disorder to the "multiple" chaos of the social world.[40] As Miss Lonelyhearts explains in a later chapter, while the "physical world has a tropism for disorder, entropy," man "has a tropism for order" (*ML* 93). West signals the implications of these warring tendencies in the much-discussed dream in which Lonelyhearts finds himself in a pawnshop window surrounded by "the paraphernalia of suffering": fur coats, watches, fishing tackle, diamond rings, and the like. In yet another example of the novel's characteristic confusion of suffering subjects and unfeeling objects, the gift knife in the window is "tortured," and a "battered horn grunted with pain" (93). Throwing himself into the scene of materialized sorrow, Lonelyhearts engages in a project of symbolic purification, forming first "a phallus of old watches and rubber boots, then a heart of umbrellas and trout flies, after these a circle, triangle, square, swastika. But nothing proved definitive and he began to make a giant cross" (93). Attempting to separate the Christ from the business once and for all, Lonelyhearts can only substitute one form of fetishism (of the commodity) for another (of religion), and the swift progression of totalizing abstractions from phallic patriarchy to fascism to Lonelyhearts's own Christ complex underlines the totalizing impulse driving his quest for universal social feeling.

Lonelyhearts is much more comfortable with abstractions than material particularities, and this becomes laughably obvious in the slapstick confrontations with the body of his readership, which he tends to understand as obscene materializations of his letters, physical manifestations of suffering that remain maddeningly unknowable. So, for example, when Lonelyhearts meets Fay Doyle, who has written for advice about the state of her unhappy marriage to "a cripple," he is overcome by her corporeal thingliness: when he takes her arm, "it felt like a thigh" (*ML* 89); when he watches her thighs, these "massive hams" become "like two enormous grindstones" (89); when he sleeps with her, she is a leviathan—"she made sea sounds; something flapped like a sail; there was the creak of ropes; then he heard the wave-against-a-wharf-smack of rubber on flesh" (90); and when, postcoitus, she tells the "long, long, story" of her suffering, the "life out of which she spoke was even heavier than her body. It was as if a gigantic, living Miss Lonelyhearts letter in the shape of a paper weight had been placed on his brain" (90–91). The joke here, as Lonelyhearts is quite literally em-bed-ed by Fay ("dragged . . . to the bed" in the chapter's final line), is not that Lonely's transcendence is thwarted by Fay's earthy materiality but that the material status of her pain remains confused, and Miss Lonelyhearts can only respond to her story by saying, rather lamely, "'You're still pretty' . . . without knowing why, except that he was frightened" (92).

This fearful confrontation with social particularity tends to end violently, erupting either in Lonelyhearts's resentful antagonism toward a differentiated society that refuses order or in the physical world's very denial of symbolic ordering, a refusal that repeatedly takes the form of slapstick. In one instance, after enjoying a drunken fantasy in which he imagines himself the masterful player of a universal music, a dream of geometry's formal purity that anticipates his junky abstractions in the pawnshop ("Square replacing oblong and being replaced by circle. Every child, everywhere; in the whole world there was not one child who was not gravely, sweetly dancing"), Lonelyhearts accidentally collides with another man in the bar. Lonelyhearts's apology is met with "a punch in the mouth" and "a lump on the back of his head" (ML 76).

West adds: "He must have fallen. The hurdle was higher than he thought" (76). Lonelyhearts then leaves the bar with an equally wasted comrade and proceeds to the little park where he finds an elderly homosexual man seated on the toilet of the public restroom. Here, it seems, is a fine candidate for Lonelyhearts's fellow-feeling: a sexual "deviant," cruising, presumably, to consummate his particularity. They drag him to a nearby restaurant where, in the scientific guise of "Havelock Ellis" and "Kraft-Ebbing," they demand to know "the bastard's life story," whether he is "a pervert," and when he first discovered "his homosexualistic tendencies" (77–78). Lonelyhearts, mechanically "loading his voice with sympathy," insists that the "old fag" tell his sad tale, and when the man refuses, Lonelyhearts wrenches his arm. By Lonelyhearts's logic, this physical violence is synechdochic; in forcing this man to confess, to let his particular tale be abstracted into a universal narrative of suffering, he is "twisting the arm of all the sick and miserable, broken and betrayed, inarticulate and impotent." The old man starts screaming, and "somebody hit[s] Miss Lonelyhearts from behind with a chair" (78). The chapter ends. Again, West's clinical anatomy of masculine violence reveals a specific reaction on Lonelyhearts's part to the fluctuating ontology of matter, presumably confused by his proximity (as advice columnist) to the reifying operations of mass culture: his anger toward the old man reminds him of the time he had accidentally stepped on a frog, whose "spilled guts" first "filled him with pity, but when *its suffering had become real to his senses,* his pity had turned to rage and he had beaten it frantically until it was dead" (77–78, my emphasis).

Moments like this, when genuine emotion seems to surface, are so enraging because they are so rare, and they remind Lonelyhearts of the pervasive affective estrangement, the unreality of laughter and tears, that pervade his world. And yet the possibility of such sensory attunement to the material world Lonelyhearts can only preach halfheartedly: "Every man, no matter how poor or humble, can teach himself to use his senses. See the cloud-flecked sky, the foam-decked sea. . . . Smell the sweet pine and heady privet. . . . Feel of velvet and of satin . . ." (*ML* 87). This suggestion is laughable because it is so obviously betrayed by West's own insistent presentation of characters as alienated from their affects, which are mechanical, stylized, and stagey: like Shrike, Miss Lonelyhearts's friends are "machines for making jokes" (75); Mary Shrike "talks in headlines" and with "something clearly mechanical in her pantomime" (81, 83); and Lonelyhearts, especially when he is on the make, experiences his feelings theatrically, simultaneously performing them and critiquing the show. Overly rationalized and functionalized, sexual relations and love itself have grown mechanical; so, when he asks Mary for sex, "there was too much method in his caresses and they both remained cold" (85); when he argues with his girlfriend Betty, he accompanies his shouts with "gestures that were too appropriate, like those of an old-fashioned actor" (72). Betty's seeming sincerity—as maddeningly real as frog guts—proves especially problematic for Lonelyhearts, who cannot abstract her feeling to a type: "She was laughing at him. On the defense, he examined her laugh for 'bitterness,' 'sour-grapes,' 'a-broken-heart,' 'the devil-may-care.' But to his confusion, he found nothing at which to laugh back. Her smile had opened naturally, not like an umbrella, and while he watched her laugh folded and became a smile again, a smile that was neither 'wry,' 'ironical,' nor 'mysterious'" (71).

By this rather Bergsonian logic, laughter is provoked in the presence of inauthenticity and mechanism; when Lonelyhearts dissects Betty's laugh and finds a "smile" that opens "naturally," his emotive performance founders and turns violent, and Betty, not surprisingly, becomes a "kitten whose soft helplessness makes one ache to hurt it" (*ML* 72).[41] This moment is, of course, emblematic of the violence attending the dialectic of Enlightenment: "Once the objective order of nature has been dismissed as prejudice and myth, nature is no more than a mass of material," returning in repressed form in either animate kitsch or, here, in the category of the feminine itself, with which Miss Lonelyhearts does battle.[42] Reduced to its biological function (Betty's pregnancy) and vexing naturalness (her laugh), or associated with distorted returns to the state of nature (think of Betty and Miss Lonelyhearts's "Field Trip" to the country), the female body in *Miss Lonelyhearts* remains the recurring site of repression and masculine dominance. Interestingly, in this instance, Lonelyhearts remains convinced that Betty's "reality" only manages to stabilize its nature and authenticity because it is partial: "Her world was not *the* world and could never include the readers of his column" (71). Whereas Lonelyhearts's efforts are stymied by their social scope, their pretense toward affective totality, and result in comic disorder, Betty's "sureness was based on the power to limit experience arbitrarily. Moreover," West adds ironically, "his confusion was significant, while her order was not" (71).

Lonelyhearts is, of course, deluded and more than a little disturbed. Because he refuses "to limit experience arbitrarily," his sentimental project becomes first hysteria and finally psychosis, in which, ironically, his quest for "all-embracing love" ends in his own experience of grotesque particularization, his total estrangement from the social world. If, as I have been arguing, the normal dynamic of slapstick is one in which the experience of false, and thereby comic, violence brings the subject to an awareness both of certain affective universals and of a stable material world, West's slapstick operates when the subject, who can neither feel the world's pain nor ascertain the status of the material world, explodes in comic-strip violence or feels his feeling stall out. This slapstick, which finds its most convincing illustration in the novel's final scene, is clearly funny for West, especially if we consider the careful symmetry with which he blocks Lonelyhearts's desire to work his sympathetic magic on the world of doorknobs. First, Lonely's consistent repression of his own thingliness in his efforts to achieve an unsullied spirituality (as, for example, in the sacrifice of the lamb) returns in the form of his increasing inanimation in the novel. He finds his struggle to "bring his great understanding heart into action again" momentarily successful when he holds the hand of long-suffering cripple Peter Doyle and busies himself "with the triumphant thing that his humility had become" (*ML* 84, 113). In West's hands, this "thing" becomes hilariously and progressively literal: Lonelyhearts "felt like an empty bottle, shiny and sterile"; then, Lonelyhearts "felt like an empty bottle that is being slowly filled with warm, dirty water"; until, finally, he becomes a rock that "did not feel. The rock was a solidification of his feeling, his conscience, his sense of reality" (113, 116, 123).

Lonelyhearts's transformation from subject to thing is mirrored and inverted in his religious experience, in which the dead world of things turns monstrously vital. This animation, in West's world, can only take the form of a psychotic break, the consummation of his previously confessed flirtation with "hysteria, a snake whose scales are tiny mirrors in which the dead world takes on the semblance of life" (*ML* 67). Thus, in the final chapter, the Christ on his wall becomes

> a bright fly, spinning with quick grace on a background of blood velvet sprinkled with tiny nerve stars.
> Everything else in the room was dead—chairs, table, pencils, clothes, books. He thought of this black world of things as a fish. And he was right, for it suddenly rose to the bright bait on the wall. It rose with a splash of music and he saw its shining silver belly.
> Christ is life and light. (*ML* 125)

West offers no surrealist romance of the hysteric's disconnection from the defiles of the reality principle, no Romantic resolution of subject and object through black humor, just a "black world of things" that sets up the novel's final bit of slapstick violence as Doyle—now fully aware he has been cuckolded—rings the doorbell of Lonelyhearts's apartment carrying "something wrapped in a newspaper." Lonelyhearts, ready to "embrace the cripple" and make him "whole again," rushes down the stairs to execute his final miracle. In their struggle, Doyle "tried to get rid of the package. He pulled his hand out. The gun inside the package exploded and Miss Lonelyhearts fell, dragging the cripple with him. They both rolled part of the way down the stairs" (126). West's joke here about the failure of Lonelyhearts's transcendent sympathy is especially funny—but dubiously grounded—if we notice that his last flop is incomplete (they roll only "part of the way" down the stairs), that his ontological status is uncertain (is Lonelyhearts dead?), and that he has been shot not by a person but by *some thing* wrapped, appropriately enough, in a newspaper.

Unfeeling Modernist Gestures

As I have suggested above, it is in precisely these moments of emotional uncertainty, interruption, or incompletion where West frustrates sympathy's violence toward the affective complexity of the social. So, too, the novel's irresolute conclusion reveals Lonelyhearts's Christ complex to be the stuff of bad faith, ultimately foundering on the totalizing formal logic of abstraction that underpins both the Enlightenment's cult of feeling and the machinations of a mass-cultural public sphere.[43] In this final section, then, I want to argue that West's antisentimental humor—and beyond that, his deadpan modernism—is most radical when it rejects the notion that affect does the emotional work of self-preservation, generating laughter instead from the self's undoing and ungrounding, when subjects become things whose thingliness is not purged, as Henri Bergson would have it, in the laugh. For West's deadpan entails nothing less than an embrace of the experiential poverty of the modern, a form of active nihilism that—because it pursues the violence of reification to its inhuman limit—necessarily dismantles the Enlightenment logics of communal and public belonging that depend, in *Miss Lonelyhearts,* on inoperative notions of sympathy and identity. As I suggested earlier, the violent nonagent of this undoing is Shrike, whom West draws aggressively and strategically outside the human type. (A shrike, after all, is a hooked-beaked bird of prey that kills its victims by first impaling them upon thorns before eating them.) In closing, then, I want to suggest how Shrike's work, like his deadpan visage, demarcates the potential for an noninstrumental—indeed, ethical—publicness that emerges only by accommodating, not sentimentalizing, the spectacular emptiness of the modern public sphere. Further, to see this possibility in West's presentational mode not only complicates critical understandings of the politics of modernist sentimentalism but also suggests how modernist texts that seem to be marked by a reactionary nostalgia for an eclipsed public world may, in fact, be more involved in a more rigorous examination of both the devastation and promise of modernity's spectacular nature.

To recover this potential means understanding the alienated gesture of Shrike's face as a fully modern one, which is to say resolutely non-nostalgic and non-recuperative. Here I have in mind Giorgio Agamben's account of modernity as a "generalized catastrophe of the sphere of gestures," one that signals a broad lack in the bourgeois symbolic: a loss of humanity's naturalness, a loss of easy—and divinely assured—movement between outside and inside, and a loss of the very legibility of social meaning.[44] This condition of modernity as gestural loss is, of course, enacted in the bodily tics, jerks, or otherwise alienated movements that make up the very spasmodic field of West's modernity and diagnosed in the novel by a nameless friend of Miss Lonelyhearts's: "The trouble with him, the trouble with all of us, is that we have no outer life, only an inner one, and that by necessity" (ML 75). And yet as we've seen, while Miss Lonelyhearts's outer life is surely troubled, he doesn't have much of an inner one either, and this, as I've shown above, is all a laughing matter. Lonelyhearts's sympathetic labors thus amount to a recuperative modernism, a quaint, comical effort "to trace the magic circle in which humanity tried for the last time to evoke what was slipping through its fingers forever" (ME 54).

Suspicious of such nostalgic returns, West's understanding of the modern's gestic potential lies in his dialectical understanding of Shrike's deadpan as, to poach Agamben's terms, "a figure of annihilated human existence" and "at the same time, its self-transcendence not toward a beyond but in 'the intimacy of living here and now,' in a profane mystery whose sole object is existence itself."[45] Shrike's facial "trick," modeled on the gestures of moving-picture comedians, epitomizes the nature of human nature in West's novel—a human physis so besieged that it has mimetically incorporated the alienated image sphere of mass culture for its very existence.[46] Put another way, if recuperative modernism's ploys for reestablishing authenticity are enabled by a "symptomatic" relationship to mass visuality, Shrike's face figures West's dissenting modernism, one that enjoys its symptom.[47] To incorporate estrangement as a survival strategy, one Miss Lonelyhearts himself everywhere refuses, is to see the failure of the novel's public world all the way through and to see, on the other side of this failure, a different mode of public belonging. For Agamben, this mode—community without identity—must come from humanity's in-habitation *within* the spectacular public sphere of its fundamental alienation from linguistic being. What Agamben calls spectacle's "positive possibility" thus lies in the way it "disarticulates and empties . . . traditions and beliefs, ideologies and religions, identities and communities," enabling the possibility of a community with "neither presuppositions nor a state" (*ME* 85).[48] Such a claim for the radical potential of spectacular emptiness allows us to understand Shrike less as a figure of Nietzschean overcoming than of the immanent life of a thingified world. He is, we might say, an Enlightenment monster, systemati-cally skewering—in perhaps his most memorable tirade—all of Lonelyhearts's transcendent schemes, each one an already-played-out modernist gambit, a too-tired gesture of return: Betty's plan of "escape to the soil" ("too dull and laborious"); primitivism ("the South Seas are played out and there's little use in imitating Gauguin"); aesthetic hedonism ("You fornicate under pictures by Matisse and Picasso" until "after much good fun, you realize that soon you must die"); and, of course, religion (*ML* 95–97). Shrike's dirty work, then, is to disarticulate and empty, to return all of Lonelyhearts's transcendent ends to means, to visualize the communicative estrangement that lies frozen at the icy heart of the novella, and that motivates Lonelyhearts's abortive, comic quest to feel the pain of his readership, that expropriated phantom public on the other side of his newspaper's mass-mediated language.

It is in his shrewd mockery of Lonelyhearts's instrumentalization of feel-ing—his efforts "to bring his great understanding heart into action again"—that Shrike's disarticulate deadpan becomes a rich, critical gesture: stalling while staging the violence of an Enlightenment ideology of affect that would secure community through sympathy or through the logic of identity that subtends identification. In this sense, the ethical thrust of Shrike's deadpan, and West's own, lies in their shared noninstrumentality: in them, "nothing is being produced or acted, but rather something is being endured and sup-ported" (*ME* 57). Put another way, Shrike's job is *only* to laugh at Lonelyhearts, to inculcate an internal monologue of mockery that both disarms and dis-mantles the self, interrupting his comic attempt to put the universalism of the bourgeois public sphere to work in a world where human nature has been so radically transformed. Indeed, Shrike's comic vocation is described as a structural necessity: Lonelyhearts knows that he will never be fired because he made "too perfect of a butt for Shrike's jokes" (*ML* 79). These wisecracks are not only mass-produced (as "a button machine makes buttons") but ex-changed between Lonelyhearts and Shrike with mechanical efficiency: "It was Miss Lonelyhearts' turn to laugh. He put his face close to Shrike's and laughed as hard as he could" (75, 82). Together, Shrike and Lonelyhearts comprise two movements in a steely rite that West refers to in *Dream Life* as a specific "ritual of feeling": one that "burlesques the mystery of feeling at its source" and "laugh[s] at the laugh."[49]

This structure of redoubled laughter in *Miss Lonelyhearts* must first be understood as a response to the purgative utility of laughter in the familiar Bergsonian formulation, in which the human first sees and disidentifies with "that side of himself which reveals his likeness to a thing," and then laughs "as a social gesture that singles out and represses a special kind of absent-mindedness in men and in events."[50] Shrike's laugh, insofar as it undercuts Lonelyhearts's own, proves that society will have no such revenge, that its risible repressions and laughing purgations are doomed to fail. More radically, though, to burlesque the mystery of feeling at its source is also to laugh at feeling's ground—that is, the subject traditionally conceived and extrapolated through the metaphysical operation whereby subjectivity is asserted through the circular claim that emotion requires subjects. West is not Jacques Derrida, to be sure, but the antihumanist ritual of feeling in *Miss Lonelyhearts,* through which comic affects issue from ungrounded subjects, does echo the poststructuralist insight that emotion is always second-order, requiring *the death* of the subject.[51]

Even as it refuses the instrumental violence of emotion that it everywhere connects to the technologies of abstraction underlying Enlightenment sentimentality, bourgeois publicity, and mass culture, West's deadpan does indeed work, on a metacritical level, to estrange the politics of modernist antisentimentality. For West's antisentimental humor is, finally, irreducible to a reactionary turn against "everything modernism would exclude"—a feminized, domestic, middle-class culture, or more broadly, the sphere of everydayness, politics, and historicity itself.[52] West's point is not to entirely foreclose modernity's public sphere as an affective horizon but to underscore its epistemological and ontological instability as well as its complicity with certain modes of sympathetic violence—here, both in the universalizing logic of Enlightenment sentimentality and in the particularized mode of transcendent self-preservation that is its black double. Such modernist antisentimentality, then, is less an effort to separate the sophisticated emotional iciness of the modern from the domain of morality, politics, and community that sentimental discourse has historically encoded in America than an attempt to sever sympathy from the affective repertoire through which one experiences the reified public sphere of modernity, and thus to square comic antisentimentalism with alternative, and perhaps more ethical, modes of public experience.

And here, the peculiar conjunction of dark humor and radical deperson-alization that marks West's novella joins a broader critical sensibility within late modernism: one that turns to comedy to register both the breakdown of public feeling conceived in the terms of humanist universalism and the concomitant circulation of inhuman affective intensities irreducible to type or quality. Consider, in this regard, the affinities between the critical force of West's alienated gestures and those in the work of Wyndham Lewis, who, along with Djuna Barnes, is one of modernism's greatest comic antihuman-ists. Critics have long observed how Lewis's formulation of comedy, which locates "the root of the Comic [. . .] in the sensations resulting from the obser-vations of a *thing* behaving like a person," is a direct riposte to the humanist terms of Bergsonian laughter (*CWB* 158). Lewis's comedy—formalized, as we have seen in chapter 1, in his grotesque aesthetic of externality—not only entails a productive analysis of Romantic sympathy's imperious nature and its complicity with industrial rationality (a critique rather like West's own) but also thinks modernity's reified public sphere dialectically, which is to say that the grotesque grimace of the Lewisian type anticipates the frozen look of Shrike's deadpan. Like West, then, Lewis will eschew a nostalgic distinction between a premodern publicness of primitive sensation and the mediated affectivity of mass culture. In Lewis's case, however, this critical inhabitation of spectacular emptiness comes at the price of his violent shaping of the social order as modernism's self-styled internal "Enemy," whereas West resolutely refuses such aggressive ends, gesturing instead to the limits of community traditionally conceived. In fact, in the next chapter I show how the erup-tions of dark comedy in Barnes's *Nightwood* mark a similar limit of modern community through the depersonalized passions of its animal remainders. These passional intensities disclose what West's slapstick everywhere gestures toward and what his fumbling protagonist can only face with horror: a public without qualities, an inhuman community.

In West, as in Lewis and Barnes, such alternatives become visible only by fully inhabiting the decay of modern experience and the transformation of human nature that attends it. In this sense, one should not say of West's dead-pan, as critics have of modernist antisentimentality more broadly, that his beef with sentiment belies a deeper sympathy with it, or that modernism's ironists are its greatest sentimentalists, or that the more inauthentic West reveals the public sphere to be in *Miss Lonelyhearts,* the more he betrays a nostalgia for a halcyon publicness.[53] However tasty their ironies may be, such claims blunt the critical edges of West's comic antihumanism. They also recuperate a host of sentimental categories attending the human—authenticity, identity, interiority—whose operation West has so carefully stalled. West's modernism calls for no heroic outwarding of inwardness, as per the Romantic model of expressivity; no Habermasian faith in the disembodied abstraction though which humanity feels itself in public; and no surrealist bid to confirm, via laughter, an embattled inside against a reified exterior. Emerging across the cool surfaces of his fiction, West's deadpan remains unsettling and doggedly, mercifully inhuman: rejecting both authenticity's ground and the lure of transcendence, it is embedded, as it were, in an abyss. If this abyss of negation marks the failure of Lonelyhearts's quest to feel the world's pain—to locate a community founded on identity and cemented by sympathy—it may also gesture toward the less coercive imperatives of a community yet to come. Read through the logic that the proximity to the poison may well be the cure, West's deadpan modernism may just have potential yet.

7

The Passion to Be a Person

Within *Nightwood*'s surreal bestiary, Jenny Petherbridge is an especially odd creature, always making a scene. Much like Nathanael West's pathetic Miss Lonelyhearts, Jenny seems an exemplary modernist failure and the occasion for some of Djuna Barnes's most bravura bits of comic characterization. She is a bundle of quirks and instincts but adds up to nothing like a person. Quivering and uncertain, her "beaked head" rocking within "the broken arc of two instincts, recoil and advance," Jenny's body is all wrong. In fact, Barnes quips, "Only severed could any part of her have been called 'right,'" because she is, at heart, not one.[1] Rather, Jenny is primarily *secondary* in her emotional life, which means that her love objects, her possessions, and her words become hers only by first being somebody else's: "As, from the solid archives of usage, she had stolen or appropriated the dignity of speech, so she appropriated the most passionate love that she knew, Nora's for Robin. She was a 'squatter' by instinct" (*N* 68).

As such, Jenny is all bourgeois characteristicness but absent the interior vitality of modernist character—her personality, instead, the public product of her aggressive appropriations. Because "her emotional reactions were without distinction," she overcompensates with gesture, with "florid *commedia dell' arte* ejaculations" during her bouts of lovemaking, or with the practiced fit-throwing of the drama queen (*N* 68). As Dr. O'Connor notes of one of Jenny's more extravagant performances, this one occasioned by Robin's erotic interest in a young girl, "by weeping she appeared like a single personality who, by multiplying her tears, brought herself into the position of one who is seen twenty times in twenty mirrors—still only one, but many times distressed" (75). Jenny's tantrum is a travesty of sorrow whose goal is to produce the appearance of personality, as if the magnificent narcissism of this expressive outburst might validate the singularity of her inner life, and this "in spite of the incapacity of her heart" (75). Barnes asks us to understand this incapacity in its strongest sense, as the lack of room, the very absence of a feeling interior. Jenny is all outside. Nothing is within her, nothing is properly hers. In her theatrical publicness, in her secondariness, in her middle-class avidity, Jenny "defiled the meaning of personality in her passion to be a person; somewhere about her was the tension of the accident that made the beast the human endeavor" (67).

The passion to be a person: Barnes insists that Jenny is never a person in any recognizable sense, that she is, in fact, a figure for the suspension of human personhood as such. Passion can do that to a person. As a feeling term, passion is decidedly ambiguous. Etymologically, passion connotes subjective passivity, the visitation or seizure of the suffering soul by demons of affect; but passion has also come to mean a kind of zealous intentionality or a willful teleology. Observing this tension in passion, whose "very force makes it seem compulsive," Rei Terada has recently argued that passion thus "drives intentional subjectivity to its self-undoing in senseless vigor—an undoing that does not have to be figured as decadent excess, but can be conceived as an interior limit of volition. Passion, therefore, characterizes the nonsubjectivity within the very concept of the subject."[2] Jenny's passion to be a person marks a similar limit within *Nightwood:* her eccentric feeling points to a broader crisis of expressivity in the novel's social world, whose inhabitants repeatedly fail to be persons, properly speaking, and whose emotions signal, more than anything else, the rampant failure of passion to secure human personality.

Then what kind of a being is Jenny, passionate in spite of an inhuman incapacity for feeling? What do we make of this odd bird, hovering at the limit between animal and human striving, in a zone of indistinction enacted by the descriptive vagaries of Barnes's style? We laugh at her, of course. Barnes's famous wit is never so piercing as when it skewers those noble lineaments of the human species: passion, language, and laughter itself. Not *inside* Jenny, but "somewhere about her," is the very contingency that separates man and animal—Charles Darwin's historical "accident" here embodied in the stalled animation of her instinctual and hungry gestures, recoiling and advancing at once, moving away from and toward the human condition, encroaching on the dignity of speech. We might say that Jenny is funny the way poker-playing dogs are funny: she is a bad copy, a poor imitation of a human being, and in this way typical of *Nightwood*'s eccentric denizens. Take Dr. Matthew Dante O'Connor, whose hands "he always carried like a dog who is walking on his hind legs"—an odd simile that at once asserts and blurs the limit between man and animal, robbing O'Connor of those privileged appendages of the human through his resemblance to an animal figure that is itself dissembling, faking a human gait (*N* 32).

Defiling the meaning of personality, Jenny's comic gestures, like the protocols of her emotional life, epitomize how laughter in *Nightwood* is yoked to the novel's regime of depersonalization. If her animal expressivity or O'Connor's canine posture get laughs, these are only more local instances of the pervasive animality of laughter in *Nightwood,* an affect that everywhere contraindicates the human. In this sense, I argue that the inhuman vantage of Barnes's comedy, its position of ironic exteriority on the human condition, is implicated in the larger question of the animal in *Nightwood* and of the emotional impropriety and expressive incapacities of nonhuman others. Laughter, of course, has long been seen a quality of properly human being, as a discrete capacity that separates the apperception of human experience from the unreflective immediacy of animals and thingly nature. And, relatedly, the question of animal has not only been central to the story of modernity (as mankind's progressive severing of its primordial link to nature) but also bound to the tradition of Western metaphysics that attempts to define and delimit what is proper to human being. Set in modernity's twilight, Barnes's novel is rich with creatures—animal-human hybrids—whose laughter sounds the very instability of the boundary between self-reflection and involuntariness, thought and the simplicity of sensation, distinction and impropriety, alienated nature and the ecstasy that characterizes, in Judith Butler's recent formulation, "the inevitable sociality of embodied life" (*UG* 22). Laughter marks, in fact, the failure of the human as a restrictive type of life and discloses, instead, a social environment of pervasive eccentricity, of local creatures of habitat, beyond the human norms of public recognition.[3] In this particular social world of laughter, suffering, and passional excess, publicness becomes an arena of impropriety and depersonalization. Here, publicly exposed, Barnes's characters learn how it feels to be incapacitated: to share the radical exteriority and finitude of animal being.

Impersonal Optics

How do we approach *Nightwood*'s deformations of human personality or make sense of this nocturne's bewildering affects? Under what conditions, or through what optic, does its peculiar world become visible, its creatures recognizable? Who proclaims familiarity with its estranged and estranging landscape, and what does it mean to be intimate with *Nightwood,* to claim it as one's own? These questions, asked anew in the various phases of *Nightwood*'s canonization since the early 1980s, have dogged the novel since its initial publication. I want to begin to answer them by considering two commentaries on *Nightwood* written by two of Barnes's intimates: T. S. Eliot's well-known 1937 introduction to the novel, and Marsden Hartley's unpublished review of the book. These two essays establish the broader aesthetic and political field of implication in which the novel's surfeit of animal expressivity—its production of inhuman affects—might be read. Addressing the question of *how one reads* one of the twentieth century's most difficult novels, these essays also allow us to inquire about the public horizon of legibility within which its social environment—and its emotional climate—becomes of interest. It is the pressure of this horizon that shapes *Nightwood*'s affects and prompts its rethinking of publicness itself.

Eliot's preface has become a kind of critical whipping-boy for recent treatments of the novel, which decry the poet's condescension, his New Critical sangfroid, and his implicit denial that *Nightwood* could offer a local meditation on gender or sexuality. As an anachronistic primer for a waning high-modernist aesthetic, Eliot's introduction is a study in how to make wholes from parts, a business in which many of the novel's characters are themselves embroiled, though less successfully and, I will argue, rather more comically than Eliot. The novel's plot, of course, is rather lean and sounds like the beginning of a randy joke: Felix Volkbein, a faux aristocrat of Jewish descent, meets an unlicensed, Irish-Catholic gynecologist, Dr. Matthew O'Connor, whom we later find out is a homosexual. O'Connor introduces Felix to a mysterious young American woman named Robin Vote, whom Felix marries and who bears the "Baron" a child through which he can prolong his fabricated noble lineage. Wandering Robin, "La Somnambule," soon leaves Felix and their son, Guido (who is, alas, an enfeebled imbecile), for a woman named Nora Flood, whom she meets at the Denkman circus and with whom she lives happily for a short time. Eventually, Robin abandons Nora as well, moving to America with another woman, Jenny Petherbridge. The imbroglio of desire, suffering, and loss into which Robin involves Felix, Nora, and Jenny is narrated in various contexts over the course of the novel, but mostly in the nocturnal audiences Felix and Nora have with O'Connor, whose filigreed and convoluted monologues constitute the bulk of the novel. This formal difficulty and figural density, Eliot concedes, frustrates the hermeneutic work of even the most prodigious talent: "For it took me, with this book, some time to come to an appreciation of its meaning as a whole" (*N* xi). For Eliot, this involves reconsidering his hunch that the novel's opening was "slow and dragging," its final chapter "superfluous," and its overall balance disturbed by his initial sense of the novel's inconsistent characterization—that O'Connor is singularly vital, "alone in a gallery of dummies" (*N* xii–xiv).

This vitality is doubly problematic for Eliot, since it marks both a formal dilemma and a disturbing attraction to "personality" as such that he must, in keeping with his own aesthetic doctrines, disavow. Lest we lose faith in Possum's totalizing potency, or fail "to see all that [he] has come to perceive in the course of a developing intimacy" with the novel, Eliot does manage to make it whole, and he does so without having to scrap his initial sense of the centrality of the self-named "Dr. Matthew-Mighty-grain-of-salt-Dante-O'Connor," the novel's sometimes transvestite and inveterate liar (*N* xi). The good doctor must be seen, Eliot explains, as a "constituent of the whole pattern," a character whose "egotism and swagger" are balanced by a "desperate disinterestedness and deep humility" (xiii). Similarly, O'Connor's torrential monologues should be understood not as instances of verbal onanism "dictated by an indifference to other human beings, but on the contrary by a hypersensitive awareness of them" (xiii). As a figure of sympathy, to whom the novel's cast of *misérables* comes (as O'Connor puts it) "to learn of degradation and the night," the doctor needs these "other real, if less conscious, people in order to realize his own reality" (xiv).

To share Eliot's regard, the reader is asked to see O'Connor as emphatically *not* a personality in the Eliotic, which is to say disparaging, sense. We should recall that Eliot's slippery and often inconsistent defense of impersonality in art was primarily an attack on the hegemony of the Romantic "I" and its dangerous political extrapolation in the unstable "we" of Victorian liberalism.[4] In this political model, individualism was bereft of a common ground for negotiating competing political claims that could only be guaranteed, in Eliot's mind, by an ever more stringent orthodoxy. Eliot's appraisal of the proper relationship between personality and sociality in *Nightwood* is in lockstep with these aesthetic and political commitments. Notice, then, how O'Connor's paradoxical combination of "disinterestedness" and "hypersensitive awareness" of the social world of the novel approximates the "finely perfected medium" of the artist in "Tradition and the Individual Talent," who achieves his personal greatness through a preternatural attunement to the organic whole of tradition that resounds through him, impersonally, and thus per-son-ates him.[5] Personality, for Eliot, only becomes a problem when it is out of place, hypertrophic, or in an otherwise disproportionate relation to the sociopolitical "pattern."

To see O'Connor "alone in a gallery of dummies" is thus to judge him as Eliot would the linguistic "morbidity" and ethical degeneracy of A. G. Swinburne or D. H. Lawrence: imprisoned in an artificial and self-enclosed linguistic realm, a dissociated space of language sundered from sense, of affect so in excess of worldly facts that "human feelings" simply "do not exist."[6] The crime of Swinburne's poetry, for example, is the way, in his verse, "the object has ceased to exist. . . . [T]he meaning is merely the hallucination of meaning, because language, uprooted, has adopted itself to an independent life of atmospheric nourishment" (*SE* 327). Such language is all atmosphere, radically anti-mimetic, and thus fundamentally asocial, producing a "singular life of its own" that "does not depend upon some other world which it simulates" (327). *Nightwood,* of course, received a similar censure. In a 1937 *New Masses* review, a horrified Phillip Rahv recoiled from the novel's foreclosure of "the objectively real. Of no avail its brilliant phrasing and metaphysical wit, for its people are ghosts . . . and its world no longer the solid globe we know, but the shifting sands of decadence at its most absolute."[7] The problem with Barnes's aestheticism is not, Rahv assures us, its "unseemly" subject matter but that it fails to approach "the homoerotic . . . operating within the real world" with "an eye to its social relations and exchanges."[8] Concerned, like Rahv, about language's decadent potential for narcissistic nonrelation, Eliot insists that the work of O'Connor's excessive speech is not "to engross conversation, quench reciprocity, and blanket less voluble people" but to bring the novel's characters into "significant relationship" (*N* xiii, xii). And this happens through a sort of universalizing echolalia: "Most of the time he is talking to drown the still small wailing and whining of humanity, to make more supportable its shame and less ignoble its misery" (xiv). By talking compulsively, O'Connor knits the novel's characters into a human horizon of recognition, converting the puniness of personal suffering and bodily vulnerability into the nobility of something greater than the self.

For Eliot, only this broader humanity, this universalized and thus ennobled pain, is interesting. What begins as a formal lesson—that "it is the whole pattern that [the characters] form, rather than any individual constituent, that is the focus of interest"—becomes an interpretive one, according to which the novel is decidedly "not a psychopathic study" (*N* xv). The "miseries that people suffer through their particular abnormalities of temperament are visible on the surface: the deeper design is that of the human misery and bondage which is universal" (xv). Eliot thus here repeats his dismissal of the perverse singularities of feeling in "Tradition," where he insists:

> It is not in his personal emotions, the emotions provoked by particular events in his life, that the poet is in any way remarkable or interesting. . . . One error, in fact, of eccentricity in poetry is to seek for new human emotions to express; and in this search for novelty in the wrong place it discovers the perverse. The business of the poet is not to find new emotions, but to use the ordinary ones, and in working them up into poetry, to express feelings which are not in actual emotions at all. (*SE* 21)

Particularities of feeling are so many eccentric perversions from the ordinary, swerving from the matrix of poetic and social "concentration" (*SE* 21). For this reason, Eliot must subsume *Nightwood*'s wayward parts into a formal whole, "particular abnormalities of temperament" into affective universality. In so doing, he concludes his preface with an act of sympathy with *Nightwood*'s habitués befitting his celebrated doctor and reminiscent of Miss Lonelyhearts himself: "To regard this group of people as a horrid sideshow of freaks is not only to miss the point, but to confirm our wills and harden our hearts in an inveterate sin of pride" (*N* xvi). For Eliot, to read the novel this way, to feel this way about *Nightwood,* would risk making the same mistake on the interpretive level—of prideful feeling that precipitates indifference and asociality—that Eliot only narrowly avoided attributing to O'Connor himself.

There are other ways to read, and be familiar with, *Nightwood.* For heuristic purposes, consider Hartley's review of the novel, one invested in the very particularity of which Eliot would divest himself. Referring to the latter's "slightly patronizing preface," Hartley admits to being amused by the book's advance praise: "That the book comes out with all the stamps of approval for public purposes that it could have, is one of those funny things that can happen to a book."[9] This is funny, presumably, because the novel does nothing, in either its form or content, to appeal to a wide audience. Anticipating recent queer readings of the book, which hold that there "is no 'mainstream' in this novel—or, rather, its social misfits and undesirables have *become* the mainstream," Hartley notes simply that *Nightwood* "reads out of a prevailing key."[10] Hartley's strategy, then, is to declare himself on intimate terms with both its author (as one of "the multitude . . . who know Djuna and are innately fond of her") and keyed into its subject: "It will mean nothing to the author that I write of the book here . . . but it is easy to say at least, that the book being alive with such material as it has, and a lot of us know the material most definitely, this is in the main, it seems more in the nature of familiar conversation to be talking of it, since it has come into our street and it is we who live on that street."[11]

Speaking of *Nightwood,* as Hartley does, in the first-person plural also appeals to a kind of impersonality: here by invoking the local knowledge and particular tastes of a community decidedly not "in the main" but rather of the Left Bank bohemian circles shared by Hartley and Barnes in the 1920s. On this street, Hartley explains, unfolded Barnes's tempestuous relationship with American sculptor Thelma Wood, the autobiographical referent of the doomed affair between Nora and Robin in the novel ("there is Robin and Nora, and again to say, a lot of us were there in that midst when this history was being made").[12] This street, then, also runs through a specifically homosexual demimonde with which Hartley is familiar and whose inhabitants he figures as at once animal and resolutely external:

> The life of the mollusc and the parasite are never interesting in human form, save as specimens to be put under glass, and without determining to do this exactly, Djuna Barnes has put some of them under glass after she has learned all about the outside of them, and she sees that, after all, under glass, they have legs and tails, and carnivorous antennae, and they have violent though invisible octopus like tentacles which they wrap around their victims, and the only obvious outer sign of this, is an engaging smile.[13]

On one level, Hartley's bizarre figuration of *Nightwood*'s queer types spoofs the medical-sexological discourse of the day, which routinely associated homosexuality with animality, atavism, and degeneration, traits by which Hartley later identifies himself as he describes the novel's contagious affect: "I feel all squirmy when I think of *Nightwood,* but I suppose that is silly, but it sort of gums up the eyes with death mucus, and you sort of feel your hands or at least fingers becoming webbed and that you will soon be swimming away instead of walking, as you once so readily did . . ."[14] On another, Hartley's overworked metaphors parody the baroque style of *Nightwood* itself, acknowledging the book's relentless emphasis on externality, style, and surface. After Barnes has learned all she can of the *outside* of her characters, she puts them under a microscope for a better look, one that is (Hartley realizes) but another, now microscopically detailed, view of the exterior—of the "particular abnormalities of temperament . . . visible on the surface" that Eliot would forgo for the "deeper design" (*N* xv).

Most intriguing is what makes *Nightwood* of interest for Hartley: its biological deviation from "the human form" and its production, in him, of an indefinite, creatural affect, the "squirmy" feeling of animalization, a becoming-fishy. Like Eliot's, Hartley's profession of intimacy with *Nightwood*'s material leads him to consider the fate of human personality in the novel, as well as the conditions under which persons become interesting and the modes of feeling generated by this interest. Let me be clear. Both Eliot and Hartley understand the visible—*Nightwood*'s surface—as a figure for discursive inscription, the public horizon of legibility that inscribes and reifies "personality" as sexual identity. In Eliot's terms, the visible surface produces identity, or the "particular abnormalities of temperament," as "psychopathic" registrations. Impersonality militates against the production of these social identities (whose fixing in conventional narrative and poetic forms Eliot elsewhere decries as the work of rhetoric: the Prufrockian "eyes that fix you in a formulated phrase")[15] and draws on universal structures of feeling to do so. The problem with Eliot, then, is not that he is unaware of the social production of sexual identity but that he underestimates the difficulty with which such persons might become recognized as human and trivializes subhuman emotions as perverse novelties. He can only see an opaque locality of feeling as narcissism or pride and not the "particular abnormalit[y] of temperament" of a publicly unrecognizable mode of human life. Only properly human feeling, of which these characters have no share, is of interest.

Hartley sees things a bit differently. While he notes the coercive potential of regimes of public visualization, producing scientific objects of knowledge ("specimens to be put under glass"), he also understands the potential of the visual as a site of identity's undoing, as I've argued in greater detail in chapter 4. Further, Hartley ascribes such potential to the figure of the animal and its position of exteriority on human being. Through Barnes's auratic optic of estrangement, Hartley suggests, the more one looks at *Nightwood*'s strange creatures, the greater the distance from which they look back. They become of interest in their animality—their break with human form—which invites attention to their habitat and produces animalized affects that beggar description. In stressing the particularity of *Nightwood*'s affective landscape, its difference from the world of Eliot (who, Hartley notes, "had the strength to call it a valuable book, the which he certainly himself could never have written"), the painter describes part of the novel's *punctum* as a particular kind of laughter at a certain "kind of life": "What is between the covers of *Nightwood* is certainly something to stir the quills of the fretful porpentine [*sic*], and these quills will stick in everybody's flesh, tear it a little, and send trickles of blood down the clothing, for it is meant to sting and to burn, and in a strange way to laugh at the colossal stupidity of believing in anything, of taking at least that kind of life seriously for a minute."[16]

Here, winking and nudging about the prickly stuff that goes on "between the covers" of *Nightwood* and the laughter it provokes, Hartley turns to irony to distance his mode of familiarity from Eliot's, which finally swaps intimacy for sympathy. Hartley's joking manner is a performance of intimacy, constructing a community of insiders and outsiders, those who live on *Nightwood*'s street and those who don't. And his fretful porpentine is a fellow intimate: the animal metaphor strains to name the irresolute sensation produced by reading *Nightwood*—a mixture of embodied vulnerability to arousal, pain, and nihilistic laughter—and in so doing itself enacts a temperamental abnormality, a locality of feeling that pulses with intensity, if not subjectivity. In *Hamlet,* remember, the porpentine's affect is a hypothetical response to the indescribable horrors of hell, inaccessible to human "ears of flesh and blood" but intimated to the prince by his father's ghost.[17] In *Nightwood*, Hartley suggests, the actual hell of inhuman marginality—of "that kind of life" beyond the horizon of human legibility—is made bearable by comedy and its own violence, rending the discursive fabric that decides on life. Eliot, Hartley suggests, just doesn't get the joke, which is, after all, about the destruction and desacralization of human experience (its Jenny-fication), and is best faced by O'Connor: "Dr. O'Connor, he of the most priceless sense of humour to whom nothing was sacred, for little or nothing had turned sacred toward him[;] he was completely out of the scale of romancing because he had plowed through the whole of it before the rest of the characters got going, and was therefore able to shock them into sensibility of the actual thing while they were still yet in the kindergarten of their experience."[18]

To exist in the "kindergarten of experience," we might say, is to forget the lesson of Jenny, that dealer in "second-hand and therefore incalculable emotions" (*N* 68). Such blissful infancy lives in denial of the primary secondariness of emotions and forgets what Butler describes as the "fundamental sociality of embodied life," the way the body is "given over from the start to a world of others . . . formed within the crucible of social life" (*UG* 22). In this sense, the shock of growing up comes from owning up to the paradoxical impropriety of being an embodied person, to the way "to be in a body is to be given over to others even as a body is, emphatically, 'one's own'" (20). This is, in Hannah Arendt's terms, the desacralized political space of modern public life itself.[19] In this ethical field, one's emotions always exist in a space of fundamental *incalculability,* impervious to a utilitarian calculus or a mathematical reduction to the stuff of bourgeois privacy. This lesson—being deprived of privacy—is one that *Nightwood*'s characters will learn primarily through laughter, or fail to learn because they fail to laugh and thus to be brought into what Hartley calls the "sensibility of the actual thing" by O'Connor's aptly "priceless" sense of humor. In this light, we might read O'Connor's odd declaration "I'm damned, and carefully public!" not as an uncharacteristic bit of discretion (a shameless cruiser, he's all too happy to make a scene) but as a claim for publicness as necessarily a site of radical exposure and care, both for himself and for others (*N* 163). He is, to spin the language of Eliot's preface, "knotted together" with others, "as people are in real life, by what we may call chance or destiny rather than by deliberate choice of each other's company" (xv). And it is this particular vulnerability and immediacy of his embodied life that always already enmeshes him in "significant relationship."

What Hartley seems to identify is O'Connor's comic awareness of the discursive inscription of his form of life—the way, in Butler's terms, his desire is ec-statically constituted by those external and preexisting "norms of recognition that produce and sustain our viability as a human" (*UG* 19). As O'Connor himself puts it, he and his intimates make "the unpardonable error of not being able to exist" (*N* 93). Barnes, as we will see, herself often deploys the language of ecstasy, of being beside oneself, as when Nora unexpectedly happens upon O'Connor in bed, dressed in a woman's nightgown, his face made-up: "He dresses *to lie beside himself,* who is so constructed that love, for him, can be only something special" (80, my emphasis). In his priceless sense of humor—in his laughter—lies a faculty of survival, a conative faculty in the Spinozan sense. O'Connor's humor allows him to persist in his own being even as his desiring body inevitably positions him in a world that fails to recognize this being and feeling as human and psychopathologizes his specialness. His laughter—like that of *Nightwood*'s other personal and emotional misfits—is necessarily inhuman, failing to reproduce humanly recognizable emotions. Such is the dilemma of eccentric feeling and, more broadly, the crisis of animal expressivity that pervades *Nightwood*. Throbbing with passional intensity, *Nightwood*'s laughter points, as do Jennys, molluscs, and fretful porpentines, to the irreducible multiplicity of animal life in which beings can be finally human only with a certain violence. Barnes's wish for her characters, we might say, is a public of perpetual ecstasy.

Animal Expressions

In the Western philosophical tradition, laughter is the discrete property of the human being. Aristotle himself says so in *On the Parts of the Animals:* "No animal laughs save Man."[20] A sign of the human capacity for reflection on phenomenal experience, laughter, like language, marks the human's unique ability, in Martin Heidegger's terms, to appropriate the things of its environment *as such,* that is, as conceptual entities.[21] This means that while animals are unable to laugh, humans can laugh at animals, and in fact, animals are often most funny in their failed imitations of human beings—in, for example, satire's typical inversions of human-animal relations, which only retrace the ontological divide between these forms of life. Henri Bergson makes a similar argument in *Le Rire* ("Laughter") (1900), perhaps modernism's most influential treatise on comedy. The comic, Bergson asserts, "does not exist outside the pale of what is strictly *human.* . . . You may laugh at an animal, but only because you have detected in it some human attitude or expression."[22] Like other silly things, animals are laughable by virtue of their location within a mimetic system in which nonhuman animals and other inanimate beings only further reify the human in their very imitative failings. So, Bergson continues, although "several have defined man as 'an animal which laughs,'" they "might equally well have defined him as an animal which is laughed at; for if any other animal, or some lifeless object, produces the same effect, it is always because of some resemblance to man, of the stamp he gives it or the use he puts it to" (L 62–63). In this theory of laughter, animals go the way of other machines, reduced to thingly encrustations on the "inner suppleness of life," glitches in the élan vital (89). Humans, then, are funny animals when they are mechanical, inelastic, overly habitual, automatic, iterative, or otherwise "absentminded" in their gestures—when they are Jenny-funny.

However successfully Bergson's vitalistic ontology has been recuperated by Deleuzian poststructuralism to theorize political becoming—and beyond that, a rhizomatic socius freed of mimetic truth-modeling—his theory of laughter is strikingly normative.[23] As a "sort of *social gesture,*" laughter, Bergson insists, "pursues a utilitarian aim of general improvement" by "soften[ing] down whatever the surface of the social body may retain of mechanical inelasticity" (L 73, emphasis in original). Primarily purgative, laughter recognizes and eliminates automatisms that would frustrate the salutary social dynamic of "reciprocal adaptation." By this, Bergson means the mutual recognition and co-development of social organisms, or the "increasingly delicate adjustment of wills which fit more and more perfectly into one other" (72). As a result, Bergson continues, "society will therefore be suspicious of all *inelasticity* of character, of mind and even of body, because it is the sign of a slumbering activity, as well as an activity with separatist tendencies, that inclines to swerve from the common centre round which society gravitates: in short, because it is the sign of an eccentricity" (73, emphasis in original). Outside of this vital, common "sphere of emotion and struggle" lies slumbering eccentricity: the nonharmonizable, a "certain rigidity of body, mind, and character that society would still like to get rid of in order to obtain from its members the greatest possible degree of elasticity and sociability" (73–74). Laughter is thus not just socially *useful* but also has "something esthetic about it," since "the comic comes into being just when society and the individual . . . begin to regard themselves as works of art" (73). Putting humans, things, and animals in their proper place, laughter regulates a vital, and therefore beautiful, social order. It is wedded to a mimetic social regime that reproduces itself by curbing the waywardness of its uglier, because more static, elements, reigning in its asocial sleepwalkers and other creatures of habit.

In a Bergsonian formulation of *Nightwood*'s comic elements, Elizabeth Pochoda has observed that some of the most amusing passages in the novel are those "descriptive of style,"[24] those in which a character's excessive stylization produces laughter. But the reverse is also true: laughter, by this logic, provokes a heightened awareness of style and its cognates (surface, externality, convention, and falsity) in the book, both for *Nightwood*'s characters and its readers. In this reversal inhere the terms of Barnes's comic technique and her dissent from the purgative function of Bergsonian laughter. Thus, Barnes carefully delineates Felix, Nora, Jenny, and Matthew by their ability or inability to laugh and, thus, to be made aware of the pervasive secondariness of their emotional lives. To be capable of laughter is not to be vitally human but rather to be an improper person, to realize the trace of animality within the self that belies its singularity.

This close relation between laughter and inauthenticity helps explain why Felix is so nonplussed by his laughter, for him as intractable as Robin's wandering. Consider his paroxysm at Count Altamonte's:

> Felix . . . on the phrase "time crawling" broke into uncontrollable laughter, and though this occurrence troubled him the rest of his life he was never able to explain it to himself. . . . He began waving his hands, saying, "Oh, please! please!" and suddenly he had a notion that he was doing something that wasn't laughing at all, but something much worse, though he kept saying to himself, "I am laughing, really laughing, nothing else whatsoever!" (*N* 18–19)

While Felix neither understands his laughter nor really even recognizes it as such, Barnes means to connect it to the joke he tells the doctor a few pages later: "I like the prince who was reading a book when the executioner touched him on the shoulder telling him that it was time, and he, arising, laid a paper-cutter between the pages to keep his place and closed the book" (*N* 21). In both instances, the joke is on Felix, who is truly spooked by "time crawling" because he believes, like the proud prince, that there will be more time—that he will ensure the futurity of his debased noble heritage, a masculine line that will be twice sterilized, first by his son Guido's idiocy and later by the obstinate nonreproductivity of Robin's eccentric movement, the very slumbering separatism of Bergson's animalized social world. The ludicrousness of such a belief is noted immediately by the doctor, who quips of the "Baron": "Ah, that is not a man living in his moment, it is a man living in his miracle" (21). To live in a miracle, perhaps, is to live a teleological fantasy that reproduces the (false) past into the future without loss or, even more miraculously, masters the alterity of time—what Felix elsewhere calls "the secret of time"—through divine intercession (121). Such miracles would waylay human finitude, or deny the sheer contingency of animal existence.

Nora is similarly disconnected from a laughter that would, like Felix's, betray the uniqueness of her desire for Robin, or protect her from the devastation of that desire's falsification. Barnes's narrator explains how

> one missed in her a sense of humor. Her smile was quick and definite, but disengaged. She chuckled now and again at a joke, but it was the amused grim chuckle of a person who looks up to discover that they have coincided with the needs of nature in a bird.
> Cynicism, laughter, the second husk into which the shucked man crawls, she seemed to know little or nothing about. (*N* 53)

One suspects that Nora knows so little of laughter because it entails a certain relation to animal secondariness ("the second husk" of an already "shucked" self) that her arrogance and self-absorption cannot countenance. Her Puritan heritage convinces her of her own uniqueness ("By temperament Nora was an early Christian; she believed the word. There is a gap in 'world pain' through which the singular falls continually and forever") so that only in a disengaged fashion can she experience the chuckle that mocks the singularity of her need, throwing her desires into an unsettling coincidence with those "of nature in a bird" (*N* 51, 53). For Nora, "singularity" connotes the particularity of one's passions—the exclusivity that separates human feeling from the commonplace of animal need. Of course, the bird that destroys Nora's illusory sense of her desire's singularity is Robin, whose work of deprivation comes into view in a famous passage in which Nora looks into the garden outside her apartment's window to find her lover in the arms of another woman:

> Unable to turn her eyes away, incapable of speech, experiencing a sensation of evil, complete and dismembering, Nora fell to her knees, so that her eyes were not withdrawn by her volition, but dropped from their orbit by the falling of her body. Her chin on the sill she knelt, thinking, "Now they will not hold together," feeling that if she turned away from what Robin was doing, the design would break and melt back into Robin alone. She closed her eyes, and at that moment she knew an awful happiness. Robin, like something dormant, was protected, moved out of death's way by the successive arms of women; but as she closed her eyes, Nora said "Ah!" with the intolerable automatism of the last "Ah!" in a body struck at the moment of its final breath. (N 64)

That this passage is meant to mark, with wicked irony, the betrayal of Nora's singular passion is signaled in the way Barnes's remarkable description of Nora's falling body echoes her early account of Nora's fantastic singularity, falling through the "gap in 'world pain'" like "a body falling in observable space, deprived of the privacy of disappearance" (N 51). In this scene of privation's reversal, Nora is robbed of the authenticity of her desire and as she falls can only gaze upon its too-public betrayal in an intensely theatrical frame. This is a scene of what we might call comic passion. And Nora's body is comic in a specifically Bergsonian sense, which is to say, all animal: "incapable of speech," bereft of volition, heavy with the materiality of habit, marred by an intolerable automatism. More pointedly, this scene, bearing all the hallmarks of extreme emotion, is a joke about the passions classically understood. As Philip Fisher claims, in moments of passional intensity, the world of mutuality and reciprocity is suspended, and the claims of others disappear as the self asserts the pressing singularity of its emotional life over and against all others. For Fisher, it is the sudden, involuntary *"publication of feeling within the passions"*—the "tears and sobs of grief, the shouts of rage, the blush of embarrassment, and perhaps most of all the bright 'Ah!' of wonder"—that breaks with the emotional protocols of modern inwardness.[25] This, because modern privacy inheres in a zone of intimacy severed from the public world, a separation that allows us to conceive of the stuff of our inner life as so much emotional property to be shared with or carefully distributed to others as a result of "acts of choice."[26] If, in Fisher's account, the theatrical publicizing of passion makes the claims of others vanish, in Barnes's formulation the reverse is true: the publicity of Nora's passion disintegrates its singularity, returning it to a social field in which the claims of others forcibly appear.

The comedy of Nora's falling body is sustained by two untenable fantasies of emotional propriety: first, that her desire for Robin is still unique, that this other couple cannot "hold together"; second, that the future movement of Robin's nomadic desire as it carries her through "successive arms of women" might somehow protect her lover, and perhaps her love. With yet another turn of the ironic screw, the woman who poaches the privacy of Nora's desire is (who else?) Jenny Petherbridge, for whom, as O'Connor has it, "only someone's love is her love" (*N* 98). Perhaps more self-absorbed in her nonself than Nora, Jenny is likewise unable to laugh: "She had no sense of humour or peace or rest, and her own quivering uncertainty made even the objects which she pointed out to [her] company . . . recede into a distance of uncertainty, so that it was almost impossible for the onlooker to see them at all" (66). This uncertainty carries over into her aggressive attempt to lay claim to Robin, for the more violently she asserts her possession of her, the more tremulous her grasp becomes. Like an animal, Jenny is bad with property.

The extent of Barnes's commitment to the secondariness of emotional life in this novel is suggested by her willingness to laugh at Robin in the very scene that would introduce her to us as a real primitive. Aptly enough, this scene is preceded by a slapstick conversation between O'Connor and Felix marked by the doctor's characteristic philosophical confusion between universality and particularity: first, Matthew opines confidently about the difference between "the Jew and the Irish" ("Jews meddle and we lie, that's the difference, the fine difference"); then, he explains that such differences are ultimately unimportant ("No man needs curing of his individual sickness; his universal malady is what he should look to"). This claim is then abruptly overturned by a series of aphorisms that, in rather unaphoristic fashion, insist upon the incommensurability of the passions: "I also know this. . . . One cup poured into another makes different waters; tears shed by one eye would blind if wept in another's eye. The breast we strike in joy is not the breast we strike in pain; any man's smile would be consternation on another's mouth. Rear up, eternal river, here comes grief!" (*N* 31–32).

The doctor's increasingly absurd pontificating about the peculiarity of taste ("All cities have a particular and special beverage suited to them") is interrupted when he is called to a hotel to awaken Robin from a faint. With Felix in tow, O'Connor arrives to find Robin lying, "heavy and dishevelled," on a bed framed by a "confusion of potted plants, exotic palms and cut flowers" (*N* 34). This intensely voyeuristic scene, whose thematic burden is to introduce Robin's difference as "the born somnambule," a "woman who is beast turning human," is doubly undercut by laughter: first, the bit of physical comedy Barnes indulges in as the doctor exclaims, "Where the hell is the water pitcher!" before, "with amiable heartiness," flinging a handful of water against Robin's face (37, 35); then, as Robin blinkingly awakens from "the pose of her annihilation," the more winking acknowledgment that, as Joseph Boone has it, this is not "a portrait of Robin in her primordial 'essence'" but "a *staging* of the primitive, one whose artifice is underlined by the junglelike room's resemblance to Rousseau's paintings of 'framed nature'" (35).[27] The slapstick culminates as the doctor, taking advantage of Felix's "double confusion," snatches a few drops of Robin's perfume, powders his chin, applies some rouge to his lips "in order to have it seem that their sudden embellishment was a visitation of nature," and, "still thinking himself unobserved," sneaks a hundred-franc note of Robin's into his pocket (35–36).

The laughter this scene produces, like the dialogue between "stage Irishman and stage Jew" that introduces it, results from Barnes's refusal—within a spectacular scene—to access or stabilize particularities of temperament: here, either Robin's primitive otherness, whose essence is questioned by theater, or O'Connor's sexuality, whose naturalness is confused by performance.[28] As such, it finds an analogue in the comic opening sequence of "Watchman, What of the Night?," in which Nora pays a late-night visit to O'Connor's apartment and finds him in bed, dressed in a "woman's flannel nightgown":

> The doctor's head . . . was framed in the golden semi-circle of a wig with long pendant curls that touched his shoulders, and falling back against the pillow, turned up the shadowy interior of their cylinders. He was heavily rouged and his lashes painted. . . . Nora said, as quickly as she could recover herself: "Doctor, I have come to ask you to tell me everything you know about the night." As she spoke, she wondered why she was so dismayed to have come upon the doctor at the hour when he had evacuated custom and gone back into his dress. (*N* 79, 80–81)

The comedy of this scene itself inverts the dynamics of Robin's bedroom, issuing not from the failure of particularity but from O'Connor's inability to consummate the universal. Put simply, O'Connor is too queer to be universal, yet Nora understands this gown—falsely—as "the natural raiment of extremity": "What nation, what religion, what ghost, what dream, has not worn it—infants, angels, priests, the dead; why should not the doctor, in the grave dilemma of his alchemy, wear his dress?" (*N* 80). But Barnes's playful claim that O'Connor, donning the gown, "had evacuated custom and gone back into his dress" suggests not, as Nora believes (as do some critics), that "the doctor, in putting on his gown, begins to approach undifferentiated anonymity" but that his quest for passional universality is undone by the particularity of his sexual habits.[29] But neither is Barnes willing to equate this particularity with "nature," since "behind one covering ('custom') lies another ('dress')."[30] Rather, we can understand O'Connor's comedy as directly connected to "the grave dilemma of his alchemy." If alchemy names an impossible change of nature, then O'Connor's ability to realize his difference is foreclosed by his fundamental impropriety, because there is no being himself, only ecstasy: "He dresses to lie beside himself, who is so constructed that love, for him, can be only something special" (*N* 80).

The comic apogee of O'Connor's dilemma comes in "Go Down, Matthew," when he tells Nora of his spectacular confrontation with the genital equipment of his special love. The scene works to materialize the joke of the chapter's title, which plays on the African spiritual to link Matthew's abjection to his penchant for fellatio. Kneeling in the corner of a church dimly illuminated by votives, a spot where he has come to "be alone like an animal, and yet think," O'Connor pulls out his penis—which he has named "Tiny O'Toole"—asks, "What is this thing, Lord?," and begs to know "what is permanent of me, me or him?" (*N* 131–32). This is also an odd form of slapstick. But O'Connor's "thing," in all its flaccid materiality, is tyrannical here not because of its reified unreality, as in *Miss Lonelyhearts,* but because it is an irreducible instrument of O'Connor's desiring body. To invoke one of O'Connor's own aphorisms, "even the greatest generality has a little particular"; here, said particularity assumes the limp form of Tiny O'Toole and figures a queer alienation rooted in the knowledge that "to be innocent . . . would be to be utterly unknown, particularly to oneself" (89, 138). Matthew's transcendent suffering is compromised both by the recalcitrance of his fleshy longing and by the highly stagy—indeed, melodramatic—mise-en-scène: "Crying and striking [his] left hand against the *prie-dieu,*" and with Tiny in his right, "lying in a swoon," O'Connor finds his singular scene of sorrow comically relativized, brought low by his contingent spot in the world:

> And there I was in the empty, almost empty church, all the people's troubles flickering in little lights all over the place. And I said, "This would be a fine world, Lord, if you could get everybody out of it." And there I was, holding Tiny, bending over and crying, asking the question until I forgot and went on crying, and I put Tiny away then, like a ruined bird, and went out of the place and walked looking at the stars that were twinkling, and I said, "Have I been simple like an animal, God, or have I been thinking?" (*N* 132)

Matthew's moment of going down, dick in hand "like a ruined bird," is especially funny for having been set up in Barnes's earlier description of the doctor at Mass, "bathing in the holy water stoup as if he were its single and beholden bird, pushing aside weary French maids and local tradespeople with the impatience of a soul in physical distress" (N 29).

Would animal simplicity shield Matthew from his suffering, which reflection only exacerbates? Or is thought a necessary tool for attenuating the misery of embodied life? O'Connor suggests the latter in recounting the advice of one Father Lucas, which was "to be simple as the beasts in the field; just being miserable isn't enough—you have got to know how," a phrase that suggests the incompatibility of O'Connor's particular sorrow and the suffering protocols of his world (N 131). To be simple like an animal is to acknowledge the reality of a desiring body whose social illegitimacy torments O'Connor in spite of his usually studied suffering. Perhaps, then, it comes as no surprise that his lachrymose outburst is figured as at once earthbound and estranging: "And I began to cry: the tears went like rain goes down on the world without touching the face of Heaven. Suddenly I realized that it was the first time in my life my tears were strange to me because they just went straight forward out of my eyes" (N 132). In this way, the chapel scene offers a hilarious retroactive gloss on O'Connor's Shrikean claim to Nora earlier in the novel that "there is no pure sorrow" because it is "bedfellow to lungs, lights, bones, guts, and gall! There are only confusions" (22). O'Connor's passional singularity is undercut by the mortality he shares with animal life, which always enmeshes him in a world of social and ethical relations.

We should also notice the inclusion of "lights" here, an archaic synonym for lungs that would be otherwise redundant in this list of bodily matter except for its more particular use to refer to an animal slaughtered for food. Linking the purity of sorrow to a sacrificial economy, this passage sets up one of O'Connor's most curious anecdotes about "how the tragedy of the beast can be two legs more awful than a man's," a parable of animal suffering I take to be central to Barnes's argument about the primary sociality of embodied life and its attendant ethical imperatives (N 22). In it, O'Connor describes being once caught during the war in a bombing raid in a small town and forced to huddle in a cellar in the company of an Irishman, an old Breton woman, and her cow. As the bombs fall outside and the cow "was softly dropping her dung" inside, O'Connor, thankful that he "had [the animal] head on," exclaims:

> "Can't the morning come now, so I can see what my face is mixed up with?" At
> that a flash of lightning went by and I saw the cow turning her head straight

back so her horns made two moons against her shoulders, the tears soused all over her great black eyes.

I began talking to her. . . . I put my hand on the poor bitch of a cow and her hide was running water under my hand, like water tumbling from Lahore, jerking against my hand as if she wanted to go, standing still in one spot; and I thought, there are directions and speeds that no one has calculated, for believe it or not that cow had gone somewhere very fast that we didn't know of, and yet was still standing there. (N 22–23)

What does O'Connor see in the teary eyes of the animal, addressed by its gaze, exposed to its face, and thus faced with the mortal vulnerability that is also his own and with which he is always mixed up? The emotional extremity of this scene hinges on the very passivity of its protagonists' exposure to each other, their vulnerable and terrified cohabitation at the limit of human feeling. It is, I would suggest, freighted with what Jacques Derrida has recently called "the *passion of the animal, my* passion *of* the animal, my passion of the animal other," which follows from the experience of "seeing oneself seen naked under a gaze that is vacant to the extent of being bottomless . . . uninterpretable, unreadable, undecidable, abyssal and secret."[31] By arguing that the radical passivity of the animal other inheres in Jeremy Bentham's question—Can it suffer?—Derrida scraps the humanist question of whether the animal possesses whatever *capacity* or *quality* that marks the properly human (reason, speech, language, laughter, and so on). Instead, for Derrida it is the vulnerability of this animal incapacity that is the "most radical means of thinking the finitude that we share with animals" and that grounds his ethical thought (AT 396). This ethics is based in the response to alterity—to an otherness both outside *and* inside the self—that is always animal. On both sides of this abyss between so-called man and so-called animal, Derrida provocatively suggests, lies "the infinite distance of the animal, of this little innocent member, so foreign and yet so close in its incalculable estrangement" (404). And isn't it this "incalculable estrangement" of animal being—which separates us from ourselves and other animals but also binds us to them as similarly finite beings—that O'Connor glimpses in the cow's terrified gaze, pointing to those "directions and speeds that no one has calculated"? This ethical structure is not built on a humanist abyss between the human and nonhuman animal but requires a rethinking of the nature of the abyss itself, whose other side is not "the Animal" in general but rather the "heterogeneous multiplicity of the living" (AT 399). We have, Derrida suggests, to "envisage the existence of 'living creatures' whose plurality cannot be assembled within the single figure of animality that is simply opposed to humanity" (415).

What Derrida proposes, then, is another way for us to think singularity—and more specifically, to approach the failure of expressive singularity by *Nightwood*'s animals. Such singularity is not the lie of emotional propriety believed by someone like Nora, nor the passionate singularity that—in Fisher's account—lifts the self out of a framework of social reciprocity. Rather, it is the "unsubstitutable singularity" of an "irreplaceable living being"—one structured by the trace of shared finitude and thus embedded, from the start, in a contract of infinite responsibility (AT 378–79). It is this combination of animal singularity and animal compassion that Derrida implies when he says that the animal, like the I, is a "general singular" or "an indeterminate generality in the singular" (417). This structure of compassion binds the denizens of *Nightwood*'s social world, whose shared and passionate impropriety exists to protest what Derrida suggests is truly bestial: the attribution of propriety to being, the attribution "to the essence of the living, to the animal in general . . . this aptitude to being itself" (417). Against such imperatives to self-identity, O'Connor and *Nightwood*'s others will choose techniques of self-distance. They opt, as will Felix's beloved circus performers, to dazzle their estrangement.

Derrida means his reformulation of the figure of the animal-human abyss to challenge the threat of an immanent "biologistic continuum" that always implies political decisions about what constitutes properly human life (AT 398). Instead, he locates the passion of the animal outside of the melancholy temporality of redemption, original sin, and moral propriety. He thus encourages us to be skeptical of the sort of modernist biopolitics of comedy that is evident in Bergson's vitalism. For Bergson's organicist formulation of laughter depends on a moral imperative that connects the conditions of social, expressive, and aesthetic vitality and thus places him in an intellectual tradition of what we might call evolutionary expressivity that stretches from Darwin to Max Nordau and beyond. "When we speak of expressive beauty" in a face, Bergson claims, "when we say that a face possesses expression," we mean a soulful mobility of facial expression, a "certain indecision in which are obscurely portrayed all possible shades of the mind it possesses" (L 76). Expressive elasticity intimates, but can never encapsulate, the vitality of human mental life. A comic face, by contrast, "is one that promises nothing more than it gives. It is a unique and permanent grimace. One would say the person's whole moral life has crystallized into this particular cast of features"

(76). The frozen grimace marks a life—and character—congealed into habit, stiffened into automatism, and absent the reflective propriety of human being. Instead, this face is mired in the body's habitual matters; it bespeaks "a certain *fundamental absentmindedness,* as though the soul had allowed itself to be fascinated and hypnotized by the materiality of a simple action" (77). Such mental and moral inelasticity, Bergson clarifies, is the condition of "every variety of insanity"; such rigidity of character is evident in eccentric asociality, those "cases of the gravest inadaptability to social life, which are the sources of misery and at times the causes of crime" (72).

In short, eccentric expressivity is, for Bergson, the expressivity of animal life, whose fixity, and slumbering habits, are comic but also potentially criminal. In his suspicions about asocial habits congealed in animal expressions, he departs from Darwin's own confidence about the telos of animal expressivity in *The Expression of the Emotions in Man and Animals* (1872). While Darwin argued for the universality of types of expression across races and species to prove the descent of various species from a common ancestor, he also used the evolution of the moral sense to distinguish higher and lower animals by degree, if not kind. Animals and humans share "the social instinct" of sympathy, a feeling that is "much strengthened by habit."[32] But morality, which needs a temporal horizon within which one compares and judges past and future actions, depends upon the reflective powers of intellection. While nonhuman animals are sympathetic, they are beyond good and evil; nevertheless, evolutionary habits, over time, produce the conditions for a moral social body: "The social instincts—the prime principle of man's moral constitution—with the aid of active intellectual powers and the effects of habit, naturally lead to the golden rule."[33]

Instead, Bergson's association of animal expressivity with insanity, crime, and the betrayal of reciprocal adaptation approaches the reactionary biologism of Max Nordau. In the section of *Degeneration* entitled "Ego-Mania," Nordau offers a bilious appraisal of aestheticism and decadence in the arts, a screed whose racism and homophobia are notorious and themselves played for laughs today by modernist scholars. Less familiar is Nordau's particular concern with the eccentric and anti-mimetic force of animal feeling. Art, Nordau explains, stems from emotion in the organism. While the primary aim of art is psychophysiological discharge, the satisfaction of the organism's need "to transform its emotions into movement," the secondary aim, which he shares with "every other animal living in society," is action upon others: "Man has, in consequence of his racial instinct, the aspiration to impart his own emotions to those of his own species. This strong desire to know himself in emotional communion with the species is sympathy, that organic base of the social edifice."[34] Because art is a "manifestation of an individuality" with a social aim, aesthetic emotions and the organic desires they make manifest can be tested by the principles of law and morality, and artists whose emotions are judged "pernicious" to the vitality of the social organism can be criminalized and pathologized (*D* 325). In the highest works of art, in which beauty is synonymous with morality, the aesthetic is the "manifestation of vital force and health," since "the emotion from which the divining work of art springs is the birth throe of the quick and vigorous organism pregnant with the future" (335, 334). Thus, the degenerate morbidity of aesthetes and decadents is primarily a failure of emotional propriety: denied sympathetic communion with the species, their affect is animal, devoid of life and social futurity.

I bring Bergson's vitalistic account of laughter into the discursive ambit of Darwin and Nordau advisedly. At times, Bergson's romance of the soulful promise of the expressive human face seems a return to the transcendental physiognomy of Sir Charles Bell that Darwin's naturalist narrative of expressivity was meant to supplant.[35] And of course, for Bergson, it is fixity proper that is asocial and criminal, not homosexuality per se, as it is for Nordau. More important for my purposes is the location of animal or inhuman affects in these evolutionary accounts of social reproduction and the role of laughter in disclosing the social demands placed on expressivity. The threat of Bergson's comic face is an animalized socius, which is to say, one whose habits swerve from the reciprocal adaptation of the vital center and can only be purged through laughter. Further, this purgation creates the specifically political character of social life. In a putative condition of sheer immediacy with the material world, animals merely live, but society, Bergson insists, "is not satisfied with simply living. It insists on living well" (*L* 72). His terms are Aristotelian. Reciprocal adaptation produces the good life—political life—from mere life, and it does so by ridding itself of comic automatisms, of creatures of habit like *Nightwood*'s infamous trapeze artist, Frau Mann, whose body is shaped by corporeal automatism of her trade: "something of the bar was in her wrist," the bulge of her crotch "was as solid, specialized, and polished as oak" (*N* 12, 13). What, Bergson teaches us to ask, is the comedy of Frau Mann's frozen visage? What sort of person does it reflect? "In her face was the tense expression of an organism surviving in an alien element. . . . The stuff of the tights was no longer a covering, it was herself; the span of the tightly stitched crotch was so much her own flesh that she was as unsexed as a doll. The needle that made the one the property of the child made the other the property of no man" (13).

Frau Mann is a Bergsonian eccentric, a comic body with separatist tendencies. As Felix clarifies, it "was with the utmost difficulty that he could imagine her 'mixed up' with anyone, her coquetries were muscular and localized" (*N* 12). As such, Frau Mann's person—corporeal, exteriorized, and socially and politically improper—is a fitting metonym of *Nightwood*'s inelastic expressive field and, thus, the overly localized sociability of its public world, protagonized as it is by automatons, mimics, frauds, and a somnambulist, a "beast turning human." Here, to borrow the language of the novel's opening pages, the human "is shaken down from his hold on heaven with the laughter of a man who forgoes his angels that he may recapture the beast" (2). An animalized affect, laughter signals *Nightwood*'s radically differentiated public; it marks an eccentric rupture with the vital currents of social life. In these terms, we might say that *Nightwood*'s laughter is the mode of expressivity proper to a disqualified public, to people like Frau Mann, for whom merely living is work enough.

Impossible People

Frau Mann, remember, is introduced as a specific kind of person, not just comic but one of those "impossible people" invited to dine at the home of Count Altamonte, an aristocratic Italian passing through Berlin and amused by the low company of such "living statues." As a category, "impossible people" extends not only to Mann, Felix, and O'Connor, whom Felix first meets at Altamonte's party, but also to the faux aristocracy of actresses and circus performers who fascinate Felix, those "gaudy cheap cuts from the beast life, immensely capable of that great disquiet called entertainment" (N 13, 11). These unsettling beasts exert on Felix a dynamic of fascination that Barnes's narrator describes as follows: "The emotional spiral of the circus, taking its flight from the immense disqualification of the public, rebounding from its illimitable hope, produced in Felix longing and disquiet. The circus was a loved thing that he could never touch, therefore never know" (12).

Sentences like these confirm that one can only underread *Nightwood*. How should we construe this circuitous syntax and the circus affect it describes? At first glance, circus feeling names a structure of longing produced by distinguishing skilled virtuosos from their disqualified spectators, creating a reciprocal alienation. And yet the capable performers are also impossible, bestial, and thus *disqualified* people like Felix, an alienated Jew. In this sense, the qualified, rather than separating from ("taking flight" as flying away from) the disqualified public in this emotional spiral, imitate their disqualification ("taking flight from" as borrowing its restless movement). Barnes's syntax is impossible. In its very ambiguity about who is qualified, and about what capacities or properties place one inside or outside this sphere of quality and qualification, this emotional spiral enacts the freighted political work of constructing a people and the disquiet of its remainders. Its oscillation suggests what Giorgio Agamben describes as an inherent ambiguity in the function of the concept of people in Western politics—always split between political life (*bios*) and mere animal life (*zo*), between the People as an integral and inclusive body politic without remainder and, on the other hand, "the *people* as a subset and as fragmentary multiplicity of needy and excluded bodies," an "exclusive concept known to afford no hope."[36] The exclusionary violence with which the human species becomes a body politic is, as Agamben has recently explained, abetted by "fundamental metaphysico-political operation" of humanism's "anthropological machine," offering incessant decisions on the boundary of human and animal life.[37]

For Felix, the company of circus virtuosos seems to suspend momentarily such violent cuts between the qualified and the unqualified, human and animal: in their "sham salons . . . he aped his heart. Here he had neither to be capable nor alien. He became for a little while a part of their splendid and reeking falsification" (*N* 11). In this theater of the inauthentic and the inessential, Felix can be improper to the core, aping his heart. By doing so, he earns a reprieve from the demands of a people constructed by attributes, property, and representable conditions of belonging. Impossible people, on the other hand, take titles "merely to dazzle boys about town, to make their public life (and it was all they had) mysterious and perplexing." And so Felix "clung to his title to dazzle his own estrangement. It brought them together" (11). In this formulation lie the terms of Barnes's rethinking of publicness as itself a site of impropriety and depersonalization: a public without qualities, a being together in ecstasy.

To gauge Barnes's revision of the concept of publicness in *Nightwood*, we should return briefly to the sensational dynamics of modernity's public world described in her early journalism. No site better epitomizes this kind of sensationalism than Coney Island, whose faded glory Barnes chronicles in four separate pieces between 1913 and 1917.[38] Taken as a whole, these articles condense Barnes's ideas about modern variety and her early position on the alienated social world it implicates. About many of the pleasure-seekers Barnes notes "a characteristic hurry, a ferocity, a hustling determination to be amused at any cost, even if it is painful. They will weep that they might laugh" (*NY* 277). But this laughter is fleeting, "the kind glad feeling" of the park realized only for a moment, and then "it's time to go home" (35). And this business of amusement is ritualistic, its product a narcotic: "A few hundred people per day bring sedate, weekend dregs of ambition here merely to dose them with cheerful chemicals in chiffon" (148). Consistent with her sense of fashion's deathly nature, Barnes is exhausted by the relentless novelty of the park: "What's the use of going into details about the things that are new about Coney, anyway? Everyone knows that each season brings its surprises" (148). In this account of sensational publicness, comedy is pursued masochistically; following a pervasive boredom and suffering, the public's laughter confirms a still-human capacity for feeling, for being amused, and thus reifies an empty circuit of amusement.

However, like Siegfried Kracauer, Barnes remains aware that Coney's distractions remain authentic insofar as they expose, while compensating for, an experiential lack.[39] In a particularly inhuman example of the destroyed experience to which Coney Island ministers, Barnes describes a child literally formed by modern attractions:

> The noise increases. A throng of children hoots at the man calling out his wares. A thin little girl like an old woman steps up onto the sidewalk, both dirty hands on her hips, her short, broken blond hair stretched back in two braids. She begins to cackle, copying the crowd; "Get your picture—nice pictures of baby and mamma"; and then in a more insolent voice than before, "A picture of your wife, right this way." There is something incomplete in her great, horrifying completeness; she seems to be an outcome of past cries, curses, shouts, laughter, music, dancing, hubbub, and merry insolence. She is a little girl who has collected herself from the gutter and molded herself into this saucy, angular body from the refuse of great noises—that are, alas, never grand noises, but the hue and cry of a thousand middlemen making a nickel. A handful of confetti and popcorn, a splash of soda water and beer, dust of a dime and a boot.
>
> She has taken her shoes off that she may feel her connection with the world. When she walks in the gay, crowded street, she has entered her home; when she sits upon the curb, she has found the lap of her mother. (*NY* 280)

This passage condenses a host of familiar modernist anxieties about a mimetic-sympathetic public sphere whose inauthenticity is, at best, the dialectical diagnosis of modern malaise, sad but true. Carrying within herself an archive of the sensational affects of consumer desire, the girl's lack tells the truth about a modern loss of authentic experience (*Erfahrung*). But her incompleteness has another critical edge: a product of publicness, rather than conjugal bourgeois intimacy, the girl's inhuman being is primarily social and in a certain way critical of bourgeois sociality. The compulsive mimicry of group behavior, as in chapter 1, is again troped by the photograph, but here the camera's reproductive powers are abetted by its normative content: more pictures of mommies and babies, more shots of husbands and wives. The modern *flâneuse,* formed of the disjecta membra of this public, is thus a kind of satirist: saucy and sharp in body, she copies the crowd while mocking its social reproductions. In public she is incomplete, but also at home.

Nightwood's disqualified public brings home this logic, as Barnes's early ambivalence about the inauthenticity of public life gives way to a comic project that everywhere links the dynamics of being in public to the energies of depersonalization. This is most evident in the relationship Barnes establishes between public visibility and the unworking or incoherence of identity, as in Nora's comic fall into publicity, "deprived of the privacy of disappearance" and faced with the primordial sociality of her self; or in O'Connor's encounter with the animal that he also is; or in Frau Mann's costume that made her "the property of no man." Instead, for Barnes, public visibility becomes a technology of ecstasy, of owning up to the self as improper, bereft of qualities that perpetually vanish—like Robin—in the incalculable distance of the night.

This allows us to make sense of Barnes's quirky use of linguistic formulations that, a first blush, scan as declarations of solitude or narcissism but end up as testimonies to states of being-beside-oneself, of the dazzled estrangement of public life. Of the party as Altamonte's, Felix asks of Mann, "Does one enjoy oneself?," and she replies, "Oh, absolutely" (*N* 14). In a similar avowal of the pleasures of self-distance, O'Connor explains to Nora: "I tuck myself in at night, well content because I am my own charlatan" (96). Of Nora's nocturnal tracking of Robin, the narrator explains how she "would go out into the night that she might be 'beside herself'" (59). Such primary estrangement, these locutions suggest, is a condition of linguistic being, of the impersonal force of language and discursivity, which operates by its own dynamic of expropriation, speaking its users. The gambit of Barnes's impossible people, it seems, is to inhabit fully this aspect of language; they proceed, like O'Connor, by "speaking of being destroyed" (130). Public speech like this is voiced in the performing circus body of "Nikka the nigger," another impossible person literally overwritten with a host of cultural inscriptions about black masculinity: "[T]attooed from head to heel with all the *ameublement* of depravity! Garlanded with rosebuds and hackwork of the devil—was he a sight to see!" (16). Spoken of as an animal by culture, Nikka will remain improper; when asked by O'Connor "why all this barbarity," he "answered he loved beauty and would have it about him" (17). It is as if, in the intense visibility of his public life ("Was he a sight to see!"), his identity, rather than coercively determined, is disqualified by the inhuman aspect of language itself. It is this ex-appropriating force of language that Derrida has named *l'animot,* a neologism for the trace of animality within language and, further, for a mode of being improper: namely, the "irreducible living multiplicity of mortals," a singularity that "is neither a species nor a gender nor an individual" (AT 409).[40] With characteristic wit, Barnes herself connects public impropriety and animality in O'Connor's lament for "all poor creatures putting on [the] dog," an apt description of the fate of personality in the novel (*N* 99). In this slangy expression for excessive style—which has its likely origins in the use of pets as accoutrements of wealth—animality becomes theater, the public display not of conspicuous property but rather the passionate impropriety of beasts. Barnes herself was once poised for such public effrontery, suggesting that *Night Beast* would make a perfect title for the book, "except for that debased meaning now placed on that nice word beast."[41]

Robin, "La Somnambule," is the novel's extreme version of the twinning of publicness and depersonalization. She is the most public, the most animal, the least a person in any recognizable sense. At one point, she is likened by O'Connor to a spectacle of paralysis at Coney Island, a man "who had to lie on his back in a box . . . and suspended over him where he could never take his eyes off, a sky-blue mounted mirror, for he wanted to enjoy his own 'difference'" (*N* 146). O'Connor intends this bizarre analogy as a comment on Robin's vanity, on the way "she herself is the only 'position,'" but there is, of course, nothing static about Robin's personality or its public itinerary. She is, rather, an ecstatic figure whose animal becoming sets in motion the novel's broader repudiation of the humanist attribution of essential property to being. In her eye, Felix sees "the long unqualified range in the iris of wild beasts who have not tamed the focus down to meet the human eye," and yet he will attempt, in vain, to calculate her being as, alternatively, an experiential fullness, or a fantasy of bourgeois coupledom, or a mode of racial authenticity: "Sometimes one meets a woman who is beast turning human. Such a person's every movement will reduce to an image of forgotten experience; a mirage of an eternal wedding cast on the racial memory" (37).

Most striking about Robin is how her animality, and thus her emotional incalculability, inverts the discursive relationship between somnambulism and the operation of modernism's mimetic-sympathetic public sphere. Like its cognate psychic disorders, hysteria and hypnosis, somnambulism emerged in late-nineteenth- and early-twentieth-century social psychology as a figure for the riot of lower, "animal" faculties (brute sensation, motoricity, automatism, instinct, the unconscious) and for the contagious imitation of social behavior brought about by public being and its pressures on the sovereignty of the emotionally self-contained individual. In Gabriel Tarde's influential formulation, remember, the somnambulist, because of his or her imitative behavior, is the paradigmatic figure of modernity's social person: *"Society is imitation and imitation is a kind of somnambulism."*[42] These formulations, as I've explained earlier in the book, were largely indebted to the residual romanticism of crowd psychology and specifically Romantic notions of sympathy as a universal, vitalistic force in nature that date back at least to Franz Anton Mesmer's theories of animal magnetism. As Akira Lippit notes, while animals "have always been accorded the faculties of transmitting affect," in the late nineteenth and early twentieth centuries, they became crucial figures in the "articulation of new forms of communication, transmission, and exchange" in a range of disciplinary approaches to the question of how ideas and affects are transmitted "from one body to another, one forum to another, one consciousness to another."[43] Within this tradition, those deemed most susceptible to affective transmission were socially improper, unreasonable, or otherwise animal bodies: women, racial others, children, the criminal, and the insane. Barnes's break from this legacy is obvious in the way her novel's impossible people are those *least* susceptible to the reproduction of human feeling. And this people's expressive incapacity is primarily signaled through the animality of laughter, a consistently minoritarian affect that marks their being deprived of the legibility and recognition of a public world.

In *Nightwood*, this incapacity defines the impossible political subjectivity of its eccentric creatures, whose tortured expressivity is most evident in Robin's fit of animal passion in the novel's concluding episode. In this notorious scene, Nora and Robin reencounter each other in a decaying chapel where Robin has taken to sleeping. Robin, startled by Nora's appearance, goes down before Nora's terrified dog, "grinning and whimpering," striking him against his side until Robin "began to bark also, crawling after him—barking in a fit of laughter, obscene and touching" (*N* 170). The strange ritual ends as both give up and lie down, Robin with her face "turned and weeping," the dog with "his eyes bloodshot, his head flat along her knees" (170). So rich with pathos, so absent "human" subjects, the encounter undoes passion's intentionality, returning it to its original passivity and its social field. Robin, Nora, the dog: three creatures huddled together, three beings infinitely estranged, mutually inexplicable.

At once "obscene and touching," this outburst of laughter, which Eliot initially found "superfluous," seems entirely appropriate to *Nightwood*'s mode of "hilarious sorrow," especially since the novel's expressive landscape everywhere fails to confirm what is proper to human personality.[44] Robin's fit marks the subjective condition of O'Connor's failed aphorisms, exploding the logic of a proper human nature with an affect that eludes type. Her laugh-cry-bark is a way of "speaking of being destroyed," voicing the radical singularity of *l'animot*. In this sense, Robin's passionate dehumanization is a fitting variant of the dynamic of depersonalization that attends the political operation of eccentric feeling in modernism's public sphere. In fact, we might say that *Nightwood*'s production of animal affect best captures the paradoxical imagination of eccentric feeling as typical and atypical, discursively produced and yet experientially singular. While Barnes is aware of the violent social logic of the proper that distinguishes the mereness of animal life from political subjectivity and social viability, she also recuperates, in Robin's animal cry, the long-standing philosophical interest in the pre- or antidiscursive force of animal expression, which extends from Burke, Rousseau, and Hegel, through Lyotard and Derrida.[45] For it is, finally, the *incalculability* of animal affect that most interests Barnes—its noninstrumentality, its social embeddedness, its ecstatic insistence on self-difference and thus its irreducibility to being qualified.

Nightwood's alliance with animal being, and animal affect, follows from its comic repudiation of emotional propriety and the sort of immanent community implied by Bergson's comic theory, or the more obviously horrific forms of collectivity of the late modernist period. In the previous chapter, I proposed that Nathanael West's antisentimentalism be considered an implicit critique of such coercive communitarian models and a gesture toward more ethical forms of publicness based neither on sympathy nor identity. *Nightwood*'s animalized comedy bespeaks a social world that West's fumbling protagonist could face only with horror: a public without qualities, an ecstatic community.[46] The novel's impossible people are a feeling multitude, an assemblage of passional intensities swerving from the molar, a pack. The Deleuzian language is apt, and perhaps inevitable here, since Gilles Deleuze and Félix Guattari's animal is surely eccentric in the sense that I've used the term in this book: a swerving intensity in modernism's mimetic-sympathetic public sphere. When Deleuze and Guattari turn to the animal to think molecular social alliances "with irreducible dynamisms . . . and implying other forms of expression," they insist that processes of "becoming-animal" are emphatically non-mimetic: they "will not involve imitating a dog" for they proceed "neither by resemblance nor analogy."[47] Instead, becoming-animal entails an unnatural engagement with animal *capacities*—that is, with the powers and affective intensities of animal bodies, actual or socially imagined, with "an affectability that is no longer that of subjects."[48] *Nightwood's* people are asked to possess their privation, to engage in a relation to their own animal incapacity: their expressive failings, their deprivations of public and political existence, their incalculable alterity, their creatural finitude.

Heidegger has famously described the animal's incapacity as its "poverty in world"—its manner of having a world in the manner of not-having it. The essence of animality, for Heidegger, is its radical "captivation," the way it "in principle does not possess the possibility of attending either to the being that it itself is or to beings other than itself."[49] So, for example, the moth, burned by the flame that seduces it, is a Heideggerian symbol of an animal openness to a world it cannot possess.[50] And it is one Barnes employs to describe the dazed wanderings of Robin and her relational opacity to the social world of her nocturnal encounters: "By her agitation she seemed a part of the function to the persons she stumbled against, as a moth by his very entanglement with the heat that shall be his extinction is associated with flame as a component part of its function. It was this characteristic that saved her from being asked too sharply 'where' she was going" (*N* 60). In Robin's experiential poverty, in her intense closeness to a world in which she functions as a nonperson, she achieves a strange kind of salvation. Her passional incapacity to be a person testifies to the very multiplicity of suffering life. In public, abandoned to the night, she may go her own, unknowable, way.

Epilogue:
Charlie Chaplin and the
Revenge of the Eccentric

For the modernist avant-garde, Charlie Chaplin was the quintessentially modern person. He was also modernity's greatest eccentric. In the first half of the twentieth century, no figure was more centrally ensconced in the emotional circuits of mass publicness—its mimetic-sympathetic social world, its intimate capacity, and its comedic affects—than Chaplin, the one-time British music-hall performer who came to stand for the potential of Hollywood cinema as a global, sentimental vernacular. That modernity's universal person could also be its most unaccountable outsider; or that the prototype of modern personality might be located in Chaplin's very inimitability; or that the world's greatest celebrity, its most instantly recognizable public figure, would also serve as a vital conduit of intimate feeling on a global scale—such seeming paradoxes are not unique to Chaplin's public persona but, as I have suggested through the book, constitute a fundamental fantasy of modernism's self-understanding, fueling the operation of its eccentric feelings. If, as Walter Benjamin suggests, Chaplin is a potent allegory of the mediated human being, then the Chaplinesque names this being's *manner*, its affective comportment, and its emotional potential.

Under the characterological umbrella of the Chaplinesque, moderns hastened to grasp the lineaments of human personality and the timbre of emotional life as they were transformed by capitalist modernity. Because the stakes of this process of discernment were so high, its tone, ludic and hyperbolic, was often modulated by utopian and even apocalyptic strains.[1] In its jerky and technologically mediated movements, Chaplin's Tramp promised, as it modeled, a kind of being best suited to modernity's public world: dis-

tracted and forgetful, dislocated and improvisational, aimless and instantaneous, at home in modernity's mechanical world of things. Leftist German
intellectuals like Benjamin and Siegfried Kracauer would go even further.
Chaplin's anarchic personality exploded bourgeois models of personality;
its "negative expressionism" set him drifting from the demands of bourgeois sociality—moral propriety, consistency of character, domestication.[2]
If Benjamin's Chaplin is a cyborg, with his organs in the new technology,
Kracauer's is a man without content, an antisocial *unmensch*: "Other people
have an ego consciousness and exist in human relationships; he has lost the
ego; thus he is unable to take part in what is usually known as life. He is a
hole into which everything falls; what is otherwise connected bursts into
fragments as soon as it comes in contact with him."[3]

Chaplin's mutability in the modern imagination mirrors modernism's own
dissatisfaction with humanist notions of personality and character, abetting its
efforts to fashion alternative forms of personhood and publicness. This changeability was also central to Chaplin's Tramp persona, as Thomas Burke, a friend
of Chaplin's, remarked in 1932: "At no stage can one make a firm sketch and
say 'This is Charles Chaplin'; for by the time it has done the model has moved.
One can only say, 'This is Charles Chaplin, wasn't it?'"[4] Chaplin's biographer
explains this evanescent, protean quality as a function of Chaplin's training on
the relentlessly competitive music-hall stage, where the performer had precious
little time to leave a mark on his audience. But as I have argued in chapter 1,
this is also a reified stage that trades on—even as it belies—performances of
the self's expressive singularity. This is to say that Chaplin's allegory of the mediated human being is also always a story of the modern person's relationship
to temporality and historicity. This is a story, more specifically, of capitalist
modernity's rationalization of time, its structuring of the instant that is the
work of cinema and that is everywhere synonymous with the potential—and
threat—of Chaplin's eccentric personality.

Chaplinesque feeling is eccentric feeling: the emotional complex that constellates around the supposed outsides of instrumental reason—unstructured
contingency, singularity, unrepeatability, nonsense, and noninstrumentality—
and the forms of public being they energize. But, as Mary Ann Doane has argued, the lure of contingency is "saturated with ambivalence" (EC 11). "Time,"
Doane explains, "becomes heterogeneous and unpredictable and harbors the
possibility of perpetual newness, difference, the marks of modernity itself.
Accident and chance become productive. Nevertheless, these same attributes
are also potentially threatening. Their danger resides in their alliance with
meaninglessness, even nonsense" (11). Because Charlie's social being is in-

stantaneous being, contingent being, it is riven with a similar ambivalence. "Charlie," explains Gilles Deleuze, is "caught in the instant, moving from one instant to the next, each requiring his full powers of improvisation."[5] Deleuze reads Charlie here in the shadow of André Bazin, for whom Chaplin's gags depended on the "basic principle of never going beyond the actual moment."[6] In Chaplin's signature gesture, his backward kick, he proclaims "his supreme detachment from [the] biographical and social world"; it is "a perfect expression of his constant determination not to be attached to the past, not to drag anything behind him" (CC 149, 150). This kick is a modernist event, a rupture with normativity that is haunted by mechanism. The price Charlie pays for his anti-mimetic eccentricity—his "nonadherence to the formal sequence of events"—is what Bazin calls the "mechanization of movement," Chaplin's original sin:

> The activity of a social being, such as you or I, is planned with foresight and as it develops, its direction is checked by constant reference to the reality that it is concerned to shape. It adheres throughout to the evolution of an event of which it is becoming part. Charlie's activity on the contrary is composed of a succession of separate instants sufficient to each of which is the evil thereof. . . . The capital sin of Charlie, and he does not hesitate to make us laugh about it at his own expense, is to project into time a mode of being that is suited to one instant, and that is what is meant by "repetition." (CC 150–51)

This formulation is especially curious because it suggests that Chaplin's antisociality, his being-in-an-instant, in fact refuses *real* change, the co-evolution of "social being" and reality. In Chaplin's refusal of the past, and in his dwelling in the instant, he repeats. In repeating, he "has been imprudent enough, one way or another, to presume that the future will resemble the past, or to join naively in the game as played by society and to have faith in its elaborate machinery for building the future . . . its moral, religious, social and political machinery" (CC 152). Chaplin's comedy inheres in the ambivalence of contingency: his instant is always a repetition; his momentary life, rather than a rejection of the social order, bespeaks an absurd faith in its mimetic operation. When we laugh at Chaplin, Bazin suggests, we laugh at his conversion of the moment into an abstraction, a homogeneous temporal, moral, and social continuity projected seamlessly into the future.

Writing some twenty years before Bazin, Wyndham Lewis offered a related appraisal of Chaplin as a being-in-time in a short chapter of *Time and Western Man* devoted to "The Secret of the Success of Charles Chaplin." For Lewis, Chaplin's small personality holds the key to an emotional pathology of modern publicness: "For the pathos of the Public is of a sentimental and also a naïvely selfish order. It is its own pathos and triumphs that it wishes to hear about. It seldom rises to an understanding of other forms of pathos than that of the kind represented by Chaplin, and the indirect reference to 'greatness' in a more general sense, conveyed by mere physical size, repels it" (*TWM* 64). Chaplin, for Lewis, is a faux-revolutionary *mannerism,* an adjective or adverb, a *rhetoric* of emotional public appeal characterized by the "pathos of the small" (64). Such pathos skillfully packages revolutionary sentiment and child-style for "crowd-consumption" (64). In this sense, in the childish prose repetitions of Gertrude Stein and Anita Loos, Lewis discerns "all the craft of the Charlie Chaplin appeal, all those little, dissimulated threads run cunningly to the great, big, silly heart of the innocent public," which is, of course, "maternal" (57). The "naïvely selfish order" of Chaplinesque pathos cements the narcissism of democratic mass publics, aided in Lewis's paranoid narrative by the self-feeling of the Bergsonian "time-mind," which is the "time of the true-romantic" (64). And romantic temporality, for Lewis, just *is* the discontinuous capitalist temporality of fashion and advertisement, "which is fundamentally sensation [. . .] the glorification of the life-of-the-moment, with no reference beyond itself and no absolute or universal value; only so much value as is conveyed by the famous proverb: *Time is money*" (8, 11). Fueling this hermetic circuit of public sensation, Chaplinesque feeling amounts to a "perfidious flattery of the multitude," a sham "plainmanism" that marks, for Lewis, yet another vulgarization of the revolutionary "will-to-change" (60, 119). The phenomenon of Chaplin, the "great revolutionary propagandist," only further convinces Lewis that modernity's public world is incapable of authentic change; its fashionable revolts follow, and further reify, the rhythms of capitalist industry (64).

Sergei Eisenstein, who finally befriended Chaplin, his longtime hero, during his brief stint in Hollywood in 1930, found himself again preoccupied with the Chaplinesque near the end of his life as he struggled to complete the second part of *Ivan the Terrible.* In his essay "Charlie the Kid" (1945), Eisenstein locates "the unique and inimitable conceptions of what is called the Chaplinesque humor" in Chaplin's brand of "evolutionary escapism," his strategic "regress into infantilism."[7] Returning to the terms of his Disney essay, Eisenstein insists that Chaplin's infantilism is specifically American, allowing for an "intellectual and emotional exit" from America's ruthlessly rationalized social system, its "intellectual conveyor-belt system," and its "businesslike formality" (CK 112, 120). In putting humor to use as, paradoxically, an escape from use, Chaplin's humor reflects what Eisenstein sees as

America's dominant philosophical paradigm—pragmatism—which asks, above all, that humor be "*useful and applicable*" (113). Like joke books that instruct Americans how to use humor to hone the efficiency of their personality, to make it maximally effective within an environment, Chaplin's humor is both a cure for and a symptom of rationalization: at once "evidence of 'Americanism,' reaction to which gives birth to a particular kind of comic treatment: that of escape from this kind of 'Americanism'" (114). Chaplin's method performs a similar function for his spectators, "offering an infantile pattern for imitation, psychologically infecting the spectator" with a "leap into infantilism . . . as a means of psychological escape from the limits of the regulated, ordained and calculated world about him" (119).

The leap is no less appealing for being an ideological lure, "merely a palliative" (CK 120). Eisenstein's manifest theoretical burden in this essay is to use the Chaplinesque "cry of longing for that most perfect form of escape" to distinguish the shortcomings of American capitalism from the evident perfections of the Soviet state. "In the Soviet Union," Eisenstein continues, "we do not flee from reality into fairy-tales; we make fairy tales real" (120, 121). And yet the more Eisenstein insists that he has no sympathy with concepts like "infantilism" and "flight from reality," and the more rigidly he constructs a developmental narrative that positions the Soviets as "inevitably 'grown-ups,'" "people with a 'conscious purpose,'" the more he betrays his profound attraction to Chaplin's eyes, his wish "to see the images of things spontaneously and suddenly—outside their moral-ethical significance, outside valuation, and outside judgment and condemnation—to see them as a child sees them through a burst of laughter" (125, 124). I have argued earlier for the implications of Eisenstein's investment in affect freed from purpose and morality for our understanding both of his mimetic politics and his queerness. In "Charlie the Kid," Eisenstein's fascination with Chaplinesque humor—the burst of laughter that is a cry for escape "from interdiction on children's unrestricted desires"—reflects a similar longing. The outside of rationalization is also an outside of heteronormative and totalitarian social models (134). "Marriage," Eisenstein notes, "is the end of childish, infantile existence—the last little boy dies and an adult emerges!" (130). On the other hand, a grown-up man who "has retained unrestrained infantile traits in their fullest" is "a shameless aggressor, a conquerer, an Attila," an Ivan, Adenoid Hynkel (136). Sympathy eventually becomes identification with Chaplin's queer social position, with him who "will inevitably be unable to adapt himself to life, will always be placed in a ridiculous situation, will be funny and provoke laughter" (134). Eisenstein describes this situation in a variety of ways: it is the position of

Chaplin's favorite animal, the wolf, "obliged to live with the pack. But always to be alone . . . [a]lways at war with his own pack"; it is the position of Charlie in the final scene of *The Pilgrim* (1923), "one foot on the territory of the Sheriff, the law, shackled feet; the other foot on the territory of freedom from law, responsibility, court and police" (128, 135).

And it is also the position of satire, in which the Chaplin of *The Great Dictator* (1940) grows up, joining the great "age-long struggle of Satire with Darkness" while preserving the cruel "ruthlessness of the child's approach to phenomena" (CK 138). Anent the violent eccentricity of the satirist, its odd position both inside and outside the social world, Lewis and Eisenstein might have found some rare common ground with each other, and with Chaplin, at war with his pack in the 1940s. Lewis, remember, describes his own laughter as "chaplinesque in its violence," which is to say, in its exaggerated mimesis of the social, the way it "made a drama of mock-violence of every social relationship" (*CWB* 101). Chaplin's public image, and his public persona, had changed drastically in the 1930s and 1940s when, as Deleuze has put it, Chaplin's last films "both discover sound and put Charlie to death."[8] In *Monsieur Verdoux,* this book's last meditation on the relationship between laughter and depersonalization, comic violence operates in a specifically Lewisian fashion, as a mimetic excess of the social. In this film, the Tramp, modernity's most public person, is killed by satire, polished smooth and supplanted by an inhuman character—both a dandy and a serial killer of women. In so doing, the film's black humor at once enacts the violent defacement of Chaplin's own public image, perhaps modernity's most salable cynosure of human feeling, and provides the defensive cover for Chaplin's poetic performance of eccentric feeling, here under the sign of political exile.

When *Monsieur Verdoux,* "A Comedy of Murders," premiered in 1947, Chaplin's popularity was at its nadir, and the comedian was poised to make a killing. Chaplin's reputation had been savaged in the press in 1943 and 1944 following Joan Barry's much publicized paternity suit against the comedian, which resulted in two sensational public trials under Mann Act violations. Though blood tests confirmed that Chaplin was not the father of Barry's child, the jury in the second trial concluded differently and ordered Chaplin to pay child support. In the courtroom, and in the press, Chaplin was painted as a serial womanizer, an immoral alien, a "gray-headed old buzzard, little runt of a Svengali, [a] debaucher and a lecherous hound who lies like cheap Cockney cad," in the words of Barry's lawyer.[9] This surely hyperbolic example enacts the associative chain of otherness that accrued around Chaplin in the 1940s, when his sexual deviance blurred with his progressive political opinions, and both solidified his status as America's most famous internal other.

While Chaplin's form of socially critical filmmaking had long been celebrated by the Left in America and abroad—and would often be explicitly championed in the Soviet Union—the comedian's star image in the 1930s became increasingly wedded to those progressive political commitments expressed in his most celebrated satires, *Modern Times* (1936) and *The Great Dictator.* A consistent supporter of President Franklin D. Roosevelt and the New Deal, and a fervent anti-fascist, Chaplin was actively involved in Popular Front activities in Hollywood, attending meetings of the Anti-Nazi League and the Committee to Defend America by Aiding the Allies. In the wake of the Nazi invasion of Russia in 1941 and the United States' entry into the war, Chaplin became a featured speaker in at least a half dozen fund-raising rallies in 1942 for the Russian War Relief—speeches in which he embraced the Soviet allies as "comrades" and called for the opening of a second front. In the late 1940s, Chaplin's staunchly pro-Russian stance during the war—like his personal friendships with Hollywood's community of exiled leftists like Hanns Eisler, Lion Feuchtwanger, Salka Viertel, and Bertolt Brecht—was a sign of pro-communist dissidence, downright immoral in America's reigning postwar climate of liberal consensus and virulent anti-Stalinism. In this freighted political atmosphere of rising Cold War paranoia, sexual intimacies and private friendships were not just the stuff of public sensation but inescapably political, tainted by the recriminations of immorality, criminality, and ethnic alterity that stain the mantle of American bourgeois citizenship. Though he could never prove Chaplin a member of the Communist Party, J. Edgar Hoover, who had first become interested in Chaplin's subversive activities in the 1920s, began exhaustively documenting Chaplin's "subversive" activity in the 1940s and eventually amassed an FBI file on the comedian totaling nearly 1,900 pages. Hoover's paranoid construction of Chaplin as dangerous radical, abetted by the yellow press, conservative patriotic groups like the American Legion and the Catholic War Veterans, and Attorney General James McGranery, would—in 1952—result in Chaplin being denied a reentry permit into the United States by the Immigration and Naturalization Service following his trip overseas to promote *Limelight* (1952). By the time *Monsieur Verdoux* opened in 1947, the cruel political machinery that would, just five years later, result in Chaplin's decision to renounce his residence in the country that had been his home for forty years had been set in motion. Before leaving America for good, Chaplin was already on the path of exile.

Monsieur Verdoux should be understood as Chaplin's own self-instrumentalization: the efficient putting to work, and death, of a body so often positioned, in the modern imagination, as the outside of instrumental reason and proper social being. Based on an "idea" by Orson Welles, the film is a loose fictionalization of the life of the infamous murderer Henri Desiré Landru, a middle-class Frenchman and darling of the surrealists who swindled and killed ten women between 1915 and 1919 before being guillotined in 1921. Still set in France, Chaplin's film takes place in the context of the Great Depression and the onset of World War II. The film opens elegiacally with a shot of a tombstone, which reads "Henri Verdoux, 1880–1937." As the camera tracks across the cemetery, we hear the sound of a disembodied, sophisticated voice:

> Good evening. As you see, my real name is Henri Verdoux, and for thirty years I was an honest bank clerk until the depression of 1930, in which year I found myself unemployed. It was then that I became occupied in liquidating members of the opposite sex. This I did as a strictly business enterprise, to support a home and family. But let me assure you that the career of a Bluebeard is by no means profitable. Only a person with undaunted optimism would embark on such an adventure. Unfortunately, I did. What follows is history.

This cool opening suggests what the remainder of the film will bear out: that Verdoux's murderous line of work—wooing, marrying, and killing women— is overdetermined by the violent fluctuations and temporal rhythms of the capitalist economy and, in fact, goaded by an untenable fantasy of bourgeois domesticity. Verdoux, a monster of middle-class optimism, builds his personality on the future's market, but the lie of this futurity is underscored by the retrospective finality of the voiceover. The person of "undaunted optimism" is already dead, his future always a past.

This is also, of course, a joke about the demise of the Chaplinesque body, with which we are introduced in a series of displacements: first, as a frictionless, cultivated voice, speaking in 1937, from beyond the grave; second, as a picture produced by the Couvais family as they discuss their daughter's mysterious disappearance; and then, finally, in the flesh at Verdoux's villa in the south of France, where the killer tends to his rose bushes as the smoky remains of what can only be Thelma Couvais billow from a chimney in the background. From sound without a body (the inversion of Chaplin's silent screen persona), to the frozen contingency of the photograph, to monstrous animation—the defacement of the Tramp is theatrical and played for laughs. As the entirely unlikable Couvais family gathers around the photo of Thelma's new husband, Verdoux, Thelma's boorish brother notes: "Funny-looking bird, isn't he?" We cut to the photo of Verdoux, a torso shot. Attired in cufflinks, cravat, and beret, his left arm held across his midsection and supporting his right arm, the forefinger of his right hand poised delicately on his right cheek, Verdoux camps in the hysterical bosom of the bourgeois family. Thelma's father, holding the photo, notes, "Must be a pretty good salesman to sell anything with a face like that." Verdoux's dandification is central to the Tramp's execution, which the film accomplishes with nearly perfect symmetry, with mechanical efficiency. As Bazin noted long ago, "There is no feature of the former character that is not turned inside out like the fingers of a glove. No ridiculous cutaway, no bowler, no outsize boots, no bamboo cane, rather a dapper suit, a broad grey silk tie, a soft felt hat, a gold-handled cane."[10] If Charlie "is essentially a socially unadapted person; Verdoux is superadapted."[11] The most obvious sign of such domestication is Verdoux's marriage to a frail invalid, which Bazin reads suggestively as the mark of Charlie's adoption of bourgeois morality and interiority: "Love alone can prompt his desire [. . .] not only to adapt himself to society but one might even say to accept a moral way of living and a psychological individualism."[12] And yet this adaptation fails, or better yet, succeeds too well: it yields not morality but amorality, not stable interiority but a pathological blurring between the individual and the social, the public and the private.

Central to *Verdoux*'s modernism is its self-conscious reworking of the tropes of aestheticism and decadence, and specifically its knowing exaggeration of the aporias of the dandy's expressivism. Often overlooked in readings of *Verdoux* is the fact that Chaplin's serial killer is modeled not just on Landru but also on the English aesthete, art critic, painter, forger, and poisoner Thomas Griffith Wainewright, lionized in Oscar Wilde's famous essay "Pen, Pencil, and Poison: A Study in Green" (1889). Of Wainewright's virtuosic person, Wilde wrote: "But then it is only the Philistine who seeks to estimate a personality by the vulgar test of production. This young dandy sought to be somebody, rather than to do something. He recognized that Life itself is an art, and has its modes of style no less than the arts that seek to express it."[13] Wainewright's killings, Wilde continues, "gave a strong personality to his style," proving how one "can fancy an intense personality being created out of sin."[14] Using Wainewright's style to deny the "essential incongruity between crime and culture," Wilde's essay in many ways epitomizes aestheticism's role as a "counterdiscourse" of nineteenth-century bourgeois masculinity, one whose modernity "lay paradoxically in a proclamation of the exhaustion of the modern, a refusal of complacent bourgeois ideals of reason, progress, and industrious masculinity through a defiant celebration of the deviant."[15]

And yet the dandy's "heroism"—his repudiation of the rationalized sphere of work and nationalistic striving for the feminine space of consumption, style, and the cultivation of the self as an aesthetic object—depends upon the incessant production and consumption of novelty and difference. The dandy's private sphere of distinction is always the public temporal horizon of the market. If Chaplin's Verdoux is, as one contemporary reviewer suggests, a model of the "completely integrated bourgeois citizen," then Verdoux's status as both deviant dandy and paradigmatic businessman underscores the way the aesthete's heroic eccentricity—like the Chaplinesque, a supposed outside of bourgeois instrumentality—is, in fact, always on capitalist time.[16]

The temporality of Verdoux's private life—his serial intimacies and killings—is determined by the rhythms of the public world, ravaged as it is by economic depression and the onset of war. His murders, and his amorous techniques more generally, are a series of managerial responses to his uncertain financial health and the temporal vicissitudes of the marketplace. He marries and murders serially, we are led to believe, to sustain his "real" home with Mona, his invalid wife, and Peter, his cherubic son. For example, a call from his stockbroker informs him that if he doesn't come up with 50,000 francs by the morning he'll be wiped out, and so he resumes his identity as "Mr. Varnay" and hops on a train to see his wife Lydia, whom he kills after convincing her to withdraw all her money from the bank. But even when he is in the reassuring bosom of his first, true home, entertaining guests, he is at work, perfecting his criminal style by plying his pharmacist neighbor for information about undetectable poisons, "a humane method of doing away with dumb animals." The film's black humor thus comes, in large part, from Verdoux's increasingly intractable and multiplying domestic entanglements, his desperate crisscrossing of the French countryside as he attempts to manage his portfolio and, when necessary, "liquidate" his assets. "In this monoxide world of speed and confusion," he must "always be on the go every minute." For there is always a train to catch, and so his wooing must be rushed. His sonorous bromides about love and tenderness are punctuated by furtive glances at his wristwatch or the omnipresent clocks on the mantels of his multiple hearths. This is another way of saying that Verdoux's amorous being, like his domestic life, is about technique. "To be successful," Verdoux quips, "one has to be well-organized."

This is perhaps most evident in his seduction strategy for the unusually resistant Madame Grosnay. Verdoux goes to a local florist where he asks that Grosnay be sent three dozen roses and a corsage of orchids and that the order be repeated "twice a week for the next two weeks." Returning to the shop a week later, Verdoux asks how many orders Grosnay has received so far. "Two, Monsieur, one every three days." "So there's still a week to go?" Verdoux asks. "Very well," he continues, "we must keep up the good work and hope for the best." The violence of Verdoux's amorous style is remarked upon by Madame Grosnay, who explains to a female friend that the card accompanying the flowers is "always the same thing. Just two words: 'Please. Please.' I've never known such aggressiveness." Verdoux puts even roses to work, using the accoutrements of romance to mark and manage time. This passion is a relentless formalism, his entreaty a travesty of bourgeois manners that converts mercy into aggression, ruth into ruthlessness, as the film itself turns sentiment into satiric violence.

In the cold rhythms of Verdoux's intimate language—"Please. Please"—lies the fate of the film's public world, since Verdoux's time quite simply *is* social time, which is the deathly time of business and the state. This is clarified in the film's most compressed montage sequence, collapsing five years of world history into two minutes of screen time and a parable of economic determinism. The sequence intercuts banner headlines of Parisian newspapers ("Stocks Fall, Panic Ensues"; "Banks Fail, Riot Ensues") with exemplary shots of social devastation (anguish on the trading floor, suicides of the newly broke, bank riots) and personalized images of a distraught Verdoux, frantically pleading for more time on the phone as his bank threatens to foreclose on his mortgage: "Listen, give me ten minutes. Just ten minutes!" He begs for his domestic life: "You can't do that! My wife and child!" Granted a moment's reprieve, he calls his stockbroker and tells him to sell everything he has at once. "Are you crazy?" his broker responds. "You were wiped out hours ago!" The relationship between the public world and Verdoux's private and psychic life in this sequence is a local example of the mechanical causal logic enacted by the headlines: there are only actions and reactions in the monoxide world. Killed by the market before he knows it, Verdoux is thus a living anachronism, a zombie, a dead man walking. After a close-up on his stunned face, registering the news of his own death, he is inserted back into the hasty course of history, which, as the remaining montage clarifies, is heading toward its own, holocaustic finality. The newspapers keep rolling off the presses like the bills Verdoux counts with such professional alacrity in one of the film's recurring sight gags. The headline "Crisis in Europe" introduces another rapid montage: now, of Europe's gathering crowds, of Hitler and Mussolini speaking, of assembling martial masses. The sequence ends by returning to the diegetic world of the film with a close-up of a man holding a copy of *Le Figaro* where his face should be. The headline reads: "Nazis Bomb Spanish Loyalists. Thousands of Civilians Killed. War Imminent in Europe." The man lowers the paper. It is Verdoux, and he is now, evidently, an old man; bereft of his jaunty gait, he hobbles down the boulevard. His civilized exterior has crossed fully into decadence. The sequence—temporally efficient, and itself ruthless—confirms that Verdoux's businesslike killing is the same pathology as the mass murder of war, and that his violence, like the swift institutional cruelty of the state that puts him to death, is but the satiric extrapolation of the fundamental law of social relationships: "Business is business." And this violence, Verdoux explains near the close of the film, is *historical*—"That's the history of many a big business. Wars, conflict. It's all business. One murder makes a villain, millions a hero. Numbers sanctify."

The character most at home in the film's chancy world of "fear and uncertainty" is not, finally, Verdoux but his unkillable wife, Annabella Bonheur. In the repeatedly botched attempts by the vagrant seaman Captaine Bonheur (aka Verdoux) on Annabella's life, the film satirizes (while enjoying) aestheticism's own misogyny, its evident disdain for the female as natural, sentimental, corporeal, and vulgar. "Woman," Baudelaire remarked infamously, "is *natural,* that is to say, abominable. Also she is vulgar, that is to say, the contrary of the dandy." Verdoux claims to love women, but not *admire* them, because "they are of the earth, realistic, dominated by physical facts." This is especially true of the sublimely vulgar Annabella, a one-time showgirl who has found her fortune by winning the lottery. What she lacks in taste and discernment, which is a great deal, she makes up for in dumb luck. She is so lucky, a friend exclaims, that "if she fell on a banana peel with her neck out of joint, the fall would straighten it." This line is especially apt as it connects Annabella's luck to the corporeal unruliness and tyrannical thingliness of slapstick performance. Bazin has observed that what remains of slapstick—and beyond that, what remains of contingency—survives in the scenes with Annabella. But what kind of a survival is this? Annabella herself remarks to an incredulous Verdoux after one of her narrow escapes from murder, "Nothing affects me. I'm lucky." Slapstick's materiality depends upon *a body being affected,* upon the human's sudden awareness of the indomitable intransigence of nature and thus of its own temporal being, its changeability. Annabella's luck, rather, borders on the transcendent: it is hermetic, oblivious to exteriority rather than its very pathway. Liberating contingency blurs with the violent arbitrariness of the market, which grants Annabella the same salvation as the erstwhile war refugee whose life Verdoux had earlier spared. Verdoux reencounters the girl, transformed, at the end of the montage sequence that has been the death of him. "You know the story, from rags to riches," the girl explains. "After I saw you, my luck changed; I met a munitions manufacturer." "Ah," Verdoux replies, "that is the business I should have been in." What is abominable in Annabella Bonheur (the death of slapstick) is what is monstrous in this girl (the travesty of the rags-to-riches story, which is of course Chaplin's own): the fate of luck, reduced to a mirage of antebellum happiness. Chaplin, like Verdoux, like Captaine Bonheur, can never really go home again.

From slapstick idiosyncrasy to satiric asynchronicity. The death of eccentric feeling, within the film, follows from the satiric killing of the Tramp's temporal being, the swallowing of undomesticated contingency by the steely flows of capitalist time. But, as I have suggested throughout the book, modernism is equipped to contest the typicality of feeling through the poetic positing of alternative, noninstrumental models of publicness. In the case of Verdoux, this is evident in the film's enactment of temporal anachronism, its explicit production of disjunctive time. When the film debuted in 1947, capitalism—which had manifestly failed to deliver on its promises in the 1930s—had found its time again and its triumphant abode in America's postwar liberal consensus. The temporal setting of Verdoux in the years leading up to the depression and World War II is thus not a retrospective sealing of America's nationalistic time as destiny but a satiric mimesis of the social that returns to the past to plead for its recognition in the present, a repetition ("Please. Please.") that hopes to disrupt history's seeming inevitability. This disjunctive time (what Benjamin might call the *Jetztzeit*, or "now-time") brings the past and the present into forceful—and previously unrecognizable—constellation, opening the images of *Verdoux*'s past, perhaps, to a different future. This eventful turning of history into historicity is performed in the ambiguous temporality enacted by Verdoux's initial voiceover: "What follows is history."

In fact, this aggressive enactment of *Verdoux*'s radical untimeliness in the America of 1947 was built into the changes to the film's marketing strategy. The picture's failed initial run in New York in April was presaged in the infamous press conference at the Gotham Hotel that followed its premiere on April 11. Chaplin began the questioning by thanking the press for attending: "I am not going to waste your time. I should say—proceed with the butchery." And it was a bloodbath: Was Chaplin a communist "sympathizer" and could he "define his present political beliefs"? Was he "a personal friend" of Hanns Eisler, and did he think the composer a communist? Why had he never become an American citizen? Had he "no patriotic feelings about this country or any other country"? Did he intend to create sympathy for

Verdoux, and does he "attach any significance to the release of a depression picture *at this time*"? Chaplin's responses—that he sympathized with Russia during the war, that he had no "political persuasions whatsoever," that he was not nationalistic but rather considered himself a "citizen of the world," that Verdoux was a tragic symptom of the "cancerous conditions" of the nation in times of the catastrophe, and that these catastrophes are systemic—fell on largely unsympathetic ears.[17] And so Chaplin responded with his own violence, aggressively marketing the national release of the film with the publicity slogan "Chaplin Changes! Can You?," a formulation that insists on the temporal incommensurability of the film and its public (see figure 20). What's more, he timed the film's national release date in Washington, D.C., for 26 September, the day following Chaplin's scheduled testimony before the House Un-American Activities Committee, and sent the following statement to the press:

> It is no ironical coincidence that my comedy also opened in the nation's capital less than 24 hours after representative [*sic*] J. Parnell Thomas begins his probe into asserted communistic activities. . . . I have no better harbinger than my comedy *Monsieur Verdoux*. Also, if I am summoned to make personal appearances in the daytime in the House of Representatives Building I might just as well make a few such appearances in the evenings with my picture at the Capital Theater.[18]

Capitalizing on idiosyncrasy, Chaplin enacts his eccentric political sentiments by, paradoxically, insisting on the coincidence of his public persona and his personal politics, which here merge vertiginously. Doubling Verdoux's own work of imitative excess, Chaplin's vehement insistence on his proximity to a reified and ruthlessly instrumental social world effects a critical estrangement. This putting to death of the Tramp is also the eccentric's revenge: a form of mimetic critique, of passion cooled by form. In a biting telegram to Thomas, inflected with Verdoux's own sensibility, Chaplin clarifies that in his mimesis of national politics, as in humor, timing is everything: "In order that you may be completely up-to-date on my thinking, I suggest you view carefully my latest production, *Monsieur Verdoux*. It is against war and the futile slaughter of our youth. I trust you will not find its humane message distasteful."[19] Chaplin's timing is uncanny. For the more stridently he claims, effectively, "my cinematic body is me," and the more he insists on his punctuality, his very timeliness, the noisier his voice of dissent. The more vehemently he yokes together his public and private person in one unified identity, the more he enacts his temporal

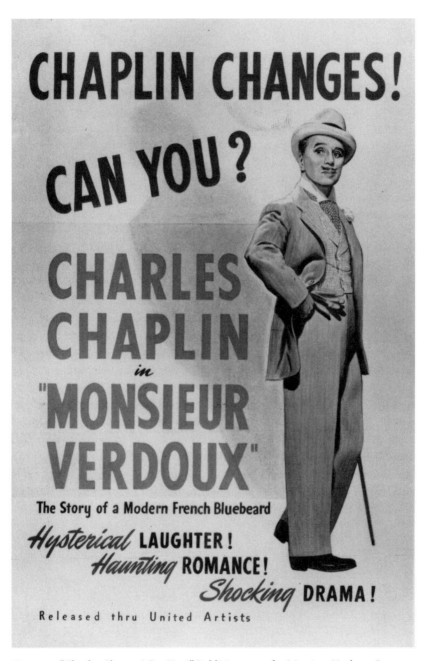

Figure 20. "Chaplin Changes! Can You?" Publicity poster for *Monsieur Verdoux*. Courtesy of the Roy Export Company.

displacement from prevailing current of patriotic sentiment. It is hardly a coincidence that Chaplin performs his political disidentification with America's emerging Cold War consensus in a film about a character who himself experiences the blurring between total publicity and homelessness. For just as Verdoux builds his private life on public time and finds himself uncannily doubled, so too does Chaplin's aggressive performance of public timing find the comedian nowhere at home. In its satiric poetics of displacement, *Verdoux* is, finally, a work of exilic feeling, imbued with an affective complex of political alienation, critical melancholy, and the mournful deprivation of privacy by public life. It is *Monsieur Verdoux,* and not *A King in New York* (1957), that is Chaplin's first and best film of exile. Verdoux's oft-remarked but undefined "funniness," like his ill-tuned voice, is that of the foreigner, the internal alien. Chaplin was, remember, a fellow traveler in the diasporic community of leftist Jewish émigrés in Hollywood in the 1940s. One of them, Theodor Adorno, whose contemporary *Dialectic of Enlightenment* thesis *Verdoux* in so many ways doubles, saw in Chaplin's mimetic personality not the stable features of the clown but a virtuosic kind of featurelessness, the "pure possibility" of the juggler: "Incessant and spontaneous change in Chaplin: this is the utopia of an existence that would be free of the burden of being-one's-self. His lady killer was schizophrenic."[20] The laughter provoked by Chaplin's strategic depersonalization in *Monsieur Verdoux* is modern insofar as it shares what we might call the ambiguity of modernist ecstasy, where the self's incessant untimeliness always courts both madness and liberation. It is, Adorno adds, in this laughter's "proximity to cruelty" that it "finds its legitimation and its element of the salvational."[21] The case of *Verdoux* suggests that the affects of modern privation need time to find their publics, and that this publicness, whatever its potential, best not be confused with the illusion of a first or final home.

Notes

Introduction: Eccentric Feeling

1. "Publicness," "publicity," and "the public sphere" are all imperfect translations of Jürgen Habermas's (and Immanuel Kant's, before him) German term *Öffentlichkeit*. On the vicissitudes of this term, see Miriam Hansen's foreword to Oskar Negt and Alexander Kluge, *Public Sphere and Experience: Toward an Analysis of the Bourgeois and Proletarian Public Sphere,* trans. Peter Labanyi et al. (Minneapolis: University of Minnesota Press, 1993).

2. Walter Benjamin, "The Work of Art in the Age of Its Technological Reproducibility: The Second Version," in *Walter Benjamin: Selected Writings, Vol. 3, 1935–1938,* ed. Michael W. Jennings, Howard Eiland, and Gary Smith, trans. Rodney Livingstone et al. (Cambridge, Mass.: Harvard University Press, 2002), 117.

3. See especially Miriam Hansen's rich comments on the concept of innervation in "Benjamin and Cinema: Not a One-Way Street," *Critical Inquiry* 25.2 (Winter 1999): 306–43.

4. Walter Benjamin, "The Formula in which the Dialectical Structure of Film Finds Expression," in *Walter Benjamin: Selected Writings, Vol. 3, 1935–1938,* 94–95.

5. Judith Butler, *Undoing Gender* (New York: Routledge, 2004).

6. See Janet Lyon, *Manifestoes: Provocations of the Modern* (Ithaca: Cornell University Press, 1999); and Mark Morrison, *The Public Face of Modernism: Little Magazines, Audiences, and Reception, 1905–1920* (Madison: University of Wisconsin Press, 2001).

7. See Jürgen Habermas, *The Structural Transformation of the Public Sphere: An Inquiry into a Category of Bourgeois Society,* trans. Thomas Burger (Cambridge: MIT Press, 1989).

8. See, most recently, Aaron Jaffe, *Modernism and the Culture of Celebrity* (Cam-

bridge: Cambridge University Press, 2005). See also Lawrence S. Rainey, *Institutions of Modernism: Literary Elites and Public Culture* (New Haven: Yale University Press, 1998); Stephen Watt and Kevin J. H. Dettmar, *Marketing Modernisms: Self-Promotion, Canonization, Rereading* (Ann Arbor: University of Michigan Press, 1996); Thomas Strychacz, *Modernism, Mass Culture, and Professionalism* (Cambridge: Cambridge University Press, 1993); and Jennifer Wicke, *Advertising Fictions: Literature, Advertisement, and Social Reading* (New York: Columbia University Press, 1988).

9. Arjun Appadurai, *Modernity at Large: Cultural Dimensions of Globalization* (Minneapolis: University of Minnesota Press, 1996), 10. See also Laura U. Marks, *Touch: Sensuous Theory and Multisensory Media* (Minneapolis: University of Minnesota Press, 2002); Ben Singer, *Melodrama and Modernity: Early Sensational Cinema and Its Contexts* (New York: Columbia University Press, 2001); Miriam Hansen, "The Mass Production of the Senses: Classical Cinema as Vernacular Modernism," *Modernism/Modernity* 6.2 (April 1999): 59–77; Michael Taussig, *Mimesis and Alterity: A Particular History of the Senses* (New York: Routledge, 1993); and Negt and Kluge, *Public Sphere and Experience.*

10. I am referring, of course, to Andreas Huyssen's classic *After the Great Divide: Modernism, Mass Culture, Postmodernism* (Bloomington: Indiana University Press, 1986). For a recent approach to modernism and the popular through a Bordieuian lens, see Barry Faulk, *Music Hall and Modernity: The Late-Victorian Discovery of Popular Culture* (Athens: Ohio University Press, 2004).

11. T. S. Eliot, "Marie Lloyd," in *Selected Essays,* ed. Frank Kermode (London: Faber and Faber, 1932), 456, 458.

12. F. T. Marinetti, "The Variety Theater," in *Let's Murder the Moonshine: Selected Writings,* ed. and trans. R. W. Flint (Los Angeles: Sun and Moon Classics, 1991), 128.

13. Miriam Hansen, *Babel and Babylon: Spectatorship in American Silent Film* (Cambridge, Mass.: Harvard University Press, 1991), 93, 70 (emphasis in original).

14. Ernst Bloch, *Heritage of Our Times,* trans. Neville Plaice and Stephen Plaice (Berkeley: University of California Press, 1991), 62.

15. Barry Faulk, "Modernism and the Popular: Eliot's Music Halls," *Modernism/Modernity* 8.4 (November 2001): 604.

16. Ibid., 609.

17. Mary Ann Doane, *The Emergence of Cinematic Time: Modernity, Contingency, the Archive* (Cambridge, Mass.: Harvard University Press, 2002), 208.

18. Max Horkheimer and Theodor W. Adorno, *Dialectic of Enlightenment: Philosophical Fragments,* trans. Edmund Jephcott (Stanford: Stanford University Press, 2002), 114.

19. Michael M. Davis, *The Exploitation of Pleasure: A Study of Commercial Recreations in New York City* (New York: Russell Sage, 1911), 32–33.

20. Wyndham Lewis, *Time and Western Man,* ed. Paul Edwards (Santa Rosa, Calif.: Black Sparrow Press, 1993), 394.

21. On the performative effects of naming in the constitution of political entities, see Slavoj Žižek, *The Sublime Object of Ideology* (London: Verso, 1989), and Ernesto

Laclau, *On Populist Reason* (London: Verso, 2005). Both accounts attempt to radicalize Saul Kripke's anti-descriptivist approach to naming as a primal baptism in *Naming and Necessity* (Cambridge: Cambridge University Press, 1980).

22. Hannah Arendt, "What Is Freedom?," in *Between Past and Future: Eight Exercises in Political Thought* (New York: Penguin, 1978), 154.

23. Hannah Arendt, *The Human Condition* (Chicago: University of Chicago Press, 1958), 50.

24. It is this risky, futural dimension of Arendt's description of public discourse that animates Michael Warner's recent definition of a public as "poetic world making": "Public discourse says not only 'Let a public exist' but 'Let it have this character, speak this way, see the world in this way.'" Throughout this book, I am indebted to Warner's attention to the poetic and performative nature of publicness in *Publics and Counterpublics* (New York: Zone Books, 2002), 114.

25. Bonnie Honig, "Towards an Agonistic Feminism: Hannah Arendt and the Politics of Identity," in *Feminist Interpretations of Hannah Arendt,* ed. Bonnie Honig (University Park: Pennsylvania University Press, 1995), 159.

26. Fredric Jameson, *The Political Unconscious: Narrative as a Socially Symbolic Act* (Ithaca: Cornell University Press, 1981), 230, 221.

27. Ibid., 236.

28. Fredric Jameson, *Postmodernism: Or, the Cultural Logic of Late Capitalism* (Durham: Duke University Press, 1991), 15.

29. Ibid., 16, 15.

30. Michel Foucault, *The History of Sexuality: Volume 1,* trans. Robert Hurley (New York: Vintage Books, 1990).

31. See Lauren Berlant, "The Subject of True Feeling: Pain, Privacy, and Politics," in *Cultural Studies and Political Theory,* ed. Jodi Dean (Ithaca: Cornell University Press, 2000); and Ann Cvetkovich, *Mixed Feelings: Feminism, Mass Culture, and Victorian Sensationalism* (New Brunswick: Rutgers University Press, 1992).

32. Lawrence Grossberg, *we gotta get out of this place: Popular Conservatism and Postmodern Culture* (New York: Routledge, 1992), 86; Brian Massumi, *Parables for the Virtual: Movement, Affect, Sensation* (Durham: Duke University Press, 2002), 28.

33. Eliot, "Tradition and the Individual Talent," in *Selected Essays,* 22; Ezra Pound, "Vortex: Pound," *Blast 1,* ed. Wyndham Lewis (Santa Rosa, Calif.: Black Sparrow Press, 1982). For an account of modernism's discomfort with unstructured affect and for an eloquent case study in the modern's preoccupation with emotion as the meeting ground of affect and ethical judgment, see Ed Comentale's "Hulme's Feelings," in *T. E. Hulme and the Question of Modernism,* ed. Edward P. Comentale and Andrzej Gasiorek (Hampshire: Ashgate Press, 2006).

34. Sara Danius, *The Senses of Modernism: Technology, Perception, and Aesthetics* (Ithaca: Cornell University Press, 2002); Karen Jacobs, *The Eye's Mind: Literary Modernism and Visual Culture* (Ithaca: Cornell University Press, 2001).

35. Charles Altieri, *The Particulars of Rapture: An Aesthetics of the Affects* (Ithaca: Cornell University Press, 2004), 30.

36. Mark Seltzer, *Serial Killers: Death and Life in America's Wound Culture* (New York: Routledge, 1998); Warner, *Publics and Counterpublics;* Lauren Berlant and Michael Warner, "Sex in Public," in *Intimacy,* ed. Lauren Berlant (Chicago: University of Chicago Press, 2000), 311–30; Michael Trask, *Cruising Modernism: Class and Sexuality in American Literature and Social Thought* (Ithaca: Cornell University Press, 2004).

Chapter 1: Tough Crowds

1. Caroline Caffin, *Vaudeville* (New York: Mitchell Kennerly, 1914), 135–36.

2. Adam Smith, *The Theory of Moral Sentiments,* ed. D. D. Raphael and A. L. Macfie (Indianapolis: Liberty Fund, 1984), 9.

3. David Hume, *Treatise of Human Nature, in Essays: Moral, Political, and Literary,* ed. Eugene F. Miller (Indianapolis: Liberty Classics, 1985), 316, 202–3.

4. Ibid., 317 (my emphasis).

5. Fredric Jameson, *Postmodernism: Or, the Cultural Logic of Late Capitalism* (Durham: Duke University Press, 1991), 15.

6. "Typage," itself developed from the Soviet fascination with variety theater, was coined by the Soviet avant-garde to describe an external, stylized, and easily recognizable form of characterization that challenged bourgeois notions of individualism and psychological interiority. In this chapter, I use "typage" more generally to refer to a strategic response to modern typicality in the Anglo-American context.

7. J. Arthur Bleackley, *The Art of Mimicry* (New York: Samuel French, 1911), 104.

8. Teresa Brennan, *The Transmission of Affect* (Ithaca: Cornell University Press, 2004), 3, 1.

9. Jürgen Habermas, *The Structural Transformation of the Public Sphere: An Inquiry into a Category of Bourgeois Society* (Cambridge: MIT Press, 1989), 49.

10. My discussion of mimetic-sympathetic publicness and my reading of Lewis are indebted to Tyrus Miller's treatment of the phenomenon of "generalized mimetism" in late modernism. See Miller, *Late Modernism: Politics, Fiction, and the Arts between the World Wars* (Berkeley: University of California Press, 1999), 42–43. However, unlike Miller, for whom mimetism names the general de-realization of the social world that is "one of the essential historical characteristics" of late modernism's emergent society of the spectacle (57), I am interested in the more specific relationship between mimesis and the affective dynamics of modernist publicness—the sympathetic charging of public scenes with abstract emotional currents and the role of such affect in the making and unmaking of public worlds.

11. Sigmund Freud, *Group Psychology and the Analysis of the Ego,* trans. and ed. James Strachey (New York: W. W. Norton, 1959), 27.

12. Rae Beth Gordon, *Why the French Love Jerry Lewis: From Cabaret to Early Cinema* (Stanford: Stanford University Press, 2001), 25.

13. Ibid., 10. Sergei Eisenstein, "Expressive Movement" (1923), in *Meyerhold, Eisenstein, and Biomechanics: Actor Training in Revolutionary Russia,* ed. Alma Law and Mel Gordon (Jefferson, N.C.: McFarland, 1996), 187.

14. Miriam Hansen, "Benjamin and Cinema: Not a One-Way Street," *Critical Inquiry* 25.2 (Winter 1999): 313. Note the similarities between the Benjaminian formulation of innervation and William McDougall's own attempt to explain the "primitive sympathetic response" of crowd behavior through "the principle of the vicarious usage of nervous energy" in *The Group Mind*. McDougall qtd. in Brennan, *Transmission of Affect,* 56.

15. Gabriel Tarde, *The Laws of Imitation,* trans. Elsie Clews Parsons (Gloucester: Peter Smith, 1962), 76, 87 (emphasis in original).

16. Ibid., xiv.

17. Michael M. Davis qtd. in Ruth Leys, "Mead's Voices: Imitation as Foundation, or, The Struggle Against Mimesis," *Critical Inquiry* 19 (Winter 1993): 277–307, 280.

18. Ibid., 297. Gilles Deleuze and Félix Guattari have recuperated Tarde as the founder of a "microsociology" that locates the social on molecular levels of differential and differentiating repetition rather than on identity and dialectical opposition. See Deleuze, *Difference and Repetition* (New York: Columbia University Press, 1994), 25–26, 308.

19. Roger Caillois, "Mimicry and Legendary Psychasthenia," trans. John Shipley, *October* 31 (Winter 1984): 30 (emphasis in original).

20. Ibid.

21. In Mark Seltzer's view, the serial killer marks the pathological exaggeration of this type of person. See *Serial Killers: Death and Life in America's Wound Culture* (New York: Routledge, 1998), 34.

22. See Herbert Marcuse, "The Affirmative Character of Culture," in *Negations: Essays in Critical Theory,* trans. Jeremy J. Shapiro (Boston: Beacon Press, 1968), 116.

23. See Caffin, *Vaudeville,* 3. See also Henry Jenkins, *What Made Pistachio Nuts? Early Sound Comedy and the Vaudeville Aesthetic* (New York: Columbia University Press, 1992), 63.

24. M. Alison Kibler, *Rank Ladies: Gender and Cultural Hierarchy in American Vaudeville* (Chapel Hill: University of North Carolina Press, 1999), 9–10.

25. T. S. Eliot, "Marie Lloyd," in *Selected Essays,* ed. Frank Kermode (London: Faber and Faber, 1932), 456.

26. This point should be understood as part of Caffin's humanism. As Caffin explains in the "Versatile Mimics" chapter, imitation is a matter of degrees of manipulation of the original, ranging from "straight portrait" (a "more or less exact imitation of the subject with only such emphasis placed on the individual peculiarities as shall help us to recognize the individual") to "caricature" ("in which the peculiarities are exaggerated and minor details eliminated and only the salient features selected") to a deformed "burlesque" ("in which only the peculiarities are shown, the rest being grotesque additions"). Caffin's hostility to grotesque distortion culminates in her chapter on acrobats, where she contrasts the "beauty and rhythmic poise of the well developed body in motion" to "the tricks of the contortionists, who bend and twist and tie themselves into every conceivable knot," enforcing "the grotesqueness of which [the body] is capable when thus distorted." "Can anybody," Caffin asks, "enjoy

both forms of entertainment? For my part, I confess the contortionist is not for me." See Caffin, *Vaudeville,* 136, 184.

27. Paradoxically, Caffin's acoustical metaphors of sympathetic vitality here—chords and strings—sound the eighteenth-century mechanistic idiom used by David Hume and others to describe the physiology of the performer's passions. This idiom, as Joseph Roach points out, was influenced by the pervasive scientific opinion "that all sensation is caused by acoustical vibrations in the nerves," and this "acoustical model provided all mental operations—memory, imagination, association—with a new, revised, mechanical basis." See Roach, *The Player's Passion: Studies in the Science of Acting* (Ann Arbor: University of Michigan Press, 1993), 104.

28. Freud called this sort of corporeal mimicry—based on the subject's ability to put itself in the place of the other via a sensory archive—"ideational mimetics" and located it at the root of the comic. See *Jokes and Their Relation to the Unconscious* (New York: W. W. Norton, 1960), 192–94.

29. Tarde, *Laws of Imitation,* xiv.

30. In a suggestive reading of *Vaudeville,* Susan Glenn equates the figurative language Caffin uses to describe the mimic's receptivity with the party line of *Camera Work,* which critiques the view that photography was a mere mechanical copy of nature by championing the photograph as a creative, artistic, and human rendering of its object. This reading overlooks the fact that Caffin ultimately notes "the failure of the imitator to do creative work" (*Vaudeville,* 149) but also obscures her ambivalence about the mimetic receptivity of the audience. See Glenn, "'Give an Imitation of Me': Vaudeville Mimics and the Play of the Self," *American Quarterly* 50.1 (1998): 47–76. On *Camera Work*'s relationship to international modernism more broadly, see Michael North's *Camera Works: Photography and the Twentieth-Century Word* (Oxford: Oxford University Press, 2005).

31. Bleackley, *Art of Mimicry,* 15, 16, 35, 16, 17, 44, 91, 44.

32. Caffin explains the difference between the actor and the imitator thus: "For one thing, [the mimic's] presentation of the instantaneous picture is different from the gradual building up and unfolding of a sustained character." The actor's "gestures and the character of them, the tones of his voice, his movements and carriage, are moulded from within. The imitator, however, begins at the other end. With him it is the gesture first and the character of it, and from that back to what prompted it" (*Vaudeville,* 147, 148).

33. See Max Beerbohm's 1896 "farewell" to London literary society, "Diminuendo," in *Aesthetes and Decadents of the 1890s,* ed. Karl Beckson (Chicago: Academy Chicago Publishers, 1981), 69.

34. Wyndham Lewis, *The Complete Wild Body,* ed. Bernard Lafourcade (Santa Rosa, Calif.: Black Sparrow Press, 1982), 158.

35. Julien Benda qtd. in Wyndham Lewis, *The Art of Being Ruled,* ed. Reed Way Dasenbrock (Santa Rosa, Calif.: Black Sparrow Press, 1989), 232 (emphasis in original).

36. This is Lewis's own self-description in *Blasting and Bombardiering*, qtd. in Hal Foster, "Prosthetic Gods," *Modernism/Modernity* 4.2 (April 1997): 20. Foster draws out the fascistic implications in such a statement, as does Jessica Burstein's "Waspish Segments: Lewis, Prosthesis, Fascism," *Modernism/Modernity* 4.2 (April 1997): 139–64.

37. Wyndham Lewis, *Rude Assignment: An Intellectual Autobiography*, ed. Toby Foshay (Santa Rosa, Calif.: Black Sparrow Press, 1984), 125, 121.

38. Paul Edwards makes a similar point in his recent study of Lewis's work, *Wyndham Lewis: Painter and Writer* (New Haven: Yale University Press, 2001), 15, 17.

39. See Peter Nicholls's useful description of Lewisian mimesis in *Modernisms: A Literary Guide* (Berkeley: University of California Press, 1995), 270 (my emphasis).

40. Ibid., 272 (Lewis's emphasis).

41. Lewis's later essay "The Dithyrambic Spectator" (1931) similarly suggests how the terms of identification ("ecstasy," "union," "fusion," etc.) of his early fiction have been co-opted and corrupted by the amateurization and collectivization of artistic production: "With religion, magic, or primitive 'mystery' . . . there is always a tendency to 'fusion' and ecstasy. . . . The full, blind collective ecstasy is not far off when this translation of *spectators* into *amateurs* has been effected." See Wyndham Lewis, *The Diabolical Principle and the Dithyrambic Spectator* (New York: Haskell House, 1971), 237–38.

42. Miller, *Late Modernism*, 75.

43. Wyndham Lewis, "Paleface: Or, Love? What Ho! Smelling Strangeness," *The Enemy*, no. 2 (September 1927): 49.

44. Wyndham Lewis, *Tarr: The 1918 Version* (Santa Rosa, Calif.: Black Sparrow Press, 1990), 299–300.

45. Wyndham Lewis, *Satire and Fiction* (London: Arthur Press, 1930), 47–48.

46. For other reactions to this pressure put on modernist aesthetics by the increasing mediation of perception by technology, see Sara Danius, *The Senses of Modernism: Technology, Perception, and Aesthetics* (Ithaca: Cornell University Press, 2002).

47. See Lewis's experimental, incomplete fiction, "The Crowd Master," first published in *Blast 2: War Number* (1915), qtd. in Paul Peppis, "'Surrounded by a Multitude of Other Blasts': Vorticism and the Great War," *Modernism/Modernity* 4.2 (April 1997): 50.

48. Selzer, *Serial Killers*, 19.

49. D. H. Lawrence, *Complete Poems*, ed. Vivian de Sola Pinto and F. Warren Roberts (New York: Penguin, 1977), 445.

50. See Eduardo Cadava, *Words of Light: Theses on the Photography of History* (Princeton: Princeton University Press, 1997), especially 106–15.

51. On modernism's encounter with mass visuality and its post-photographic reconstruction of authenticity, see Nancy Armstrong, *Fiction in the Age of Photography: The Legacy of British Realism* (Cambridge, Mass.: Harvard University Press, 1999).

52. On the constitution of the political—and of populism—as the rhetorical and

discursive "production of emptiness" and for a superb account of affect's role in cementing populist identities, see Ernesto Laclau, *On Populist Reason* (London: Verso, 2005).

53. Ibid., 57.

54. Foster, "Prosthetic Gods," 23.

Chapter 2: Eccentric Types

1. From the Eccentrist manifesto by Grigory Kozintsev et al., "A. B.! Parade of the Eccentric," in *The Film Factory: Russian and Soviet Cinema in Documents 1896–1939*, ed. and trans. Richard Taylor (London: Routledge, 1988), 59.

2. See Grigory Kozintsev et al., "Salvation in the Trousers of the Eccentric," in ibid., 58.

3. Yuri Tsivian, "Between the Old and the New: Soviet Film Culture in 1918–1924," *Griffithiana* 55/56 (1996): 15–63; Miriam Hansen, "The Mass Production of the Senses: Classical Cinema as Vernacular Modernism," *Modernism/Modernity* 6.2 (April 1999): 59–77; Sergei Yutkevich and Sergei Eisenstein, "The Eighth Art. On Expressionism, America, and, of Course, Chaplin," in *S. M. Eisenstein: Selected Works, Vol. I, Writings, 1922–34*, ed. Richard Taylor (London: British Film Institute, 1988), 29–32.

4. Kozintsev et al., "A. B.! Parade of the Eccentric," in *Film Factory*, 59.

5. Sergei Eisenstein, "The Montage of Attractions," in *The Eisenstein Reader*, ed. Richard Taylor (London: British Film Institute, 1998), 30.

6. Ibid.

7. In "Birth and Life of FEKS" (1928), Viktor Shklovsky describes Eccentrism's appeal in Formalist terms: "Eccentrism is based on the selection of memorable moments and on a new, non-automatic connection between them. Eccentrism is a struggle with the monotony of life, a rejection of the traditional conception and presentation." See also Vladimir Nedobrovo's comments in "The Eccentrism of FEKS" (1928): "The FEKS work on the alienation of the object. Alienation—the extraction of the object from its automatic state—is achieved in art by various methods. Shklovsky has demonstrated these methods in his *Theory of Prose*, which those who are neither mean nor lazy may buy and read." Both essays appear in *Futurism/Formalism/FEKS: "Eccentrism" and Soviet Cinema, 1918–36*, ed. Ian Christie and John Gillett (London: British Film Institute, 1978), 16, 19.

8. Mary Ann Doane, *The Emergence of Cinematic Time: Modernity, Contingency, the Archive* (Cambridge, Mass.: Harvard University Press, 2002), 11.

9. Ibid., 11.

10. Walter Benjamin, "Negative Expressionism," qtd. in Esther Leslie, *Hollywood Flatlands: Animation, Critical Theory, and the Avant-Garde* (London: Verso, 2002), 16.

11. Miriam Hansen, "Benjamin and Cinema: Not a One-Way Street," *Critical Inquiry* 25.2 (Winter 1999): 306–43.

12. Walter Benjamin, "The Formula in which the Dialectical Structure of Film Finds Expression," in *Walter Benjamin: Selected Writings, Vol. 3, 1935–1938,* ed. Michael W. Jennings, Howard Eiland, and Gary Smith, trans. Rodney Livingstone et al. (Cambridge, Mass.: Harvard University Press, 2002), 94.

13. Alma Law and Mel Gordon, eds., *Meyerhold, Eisenstein, and Biomechanics: Actor Training in Revolutionary Russia* (Jefferson, N.C.: McFarland, 1996), 164.

14. Joseph Roach, *The Player's Passion: Studies in the Science of Acting* (Ann Arbor: University of Michigan Press, 1993), 168.

15. Alma H. Law and Mel Gordon, "Eisenstein's Early Work in Expressive Behavior: The Montage of Movement," *Millennium Film Journal* 3 (Winter–Spring 1979): 30–38, 26.

16. Sergei Eisenstein and Sergei Tretyakov, "Expressive Movement," and Eisenstein, "Lecture on Biomechanics," are both reproduced in Law and Gordon, *Meyerhold, Eisenstein, and Biomechanics.*

17. Eisenstein, "The Montage of Film Attractions," in *Eisenstein Reader,* 47, 48.

18. Theodor Lipps, "Empathy and Aesthetic Pleasure," trans. Karl Aschenbrenner, in *Aesthetic Theories: Studies in the Philosophy of Art,* ed. Karl Aschenbrenner and Arnold Isenberg (Englewood Cliffs: Prentice-Hall, 1965). Empathy (*Einfuhlung*) for Lipps is something like an involuntary neuro-physiological response to physical form, 409.

19. Jay Leyda, *Kino: A History of Russian and Soviet Film* (New York: Macmillan, 1960), 183.

20. Ivor Montagu, head of the London Film Society, qtd. in ibid., 183.

21. Eisenstein, "The Problem of the Materialist Approach to Form," in *Eisenstein Reader,* 53.

22. Viktor Shklovsky, "Symposium on Soviet Documentary: S. Tretyakov, V. Shklovsky, E. Shub, and O. Brit," qtd. in Tyrus Miller's insightful discussion of the relationship between modernism and documentary, "Documentary/Modernism: Convergence and Complementarity in the 1930s," *Modernism/Modernity* 9.2 (2002): 228.

23. Sergei Eisenstein, "Through Theatre to Cinema," in *Film Form: Essays in Film Theory,* ed. and trans. Jay Leyda (San Diego: Harcourt Brace, 1949), 16.

24. Georg Lukács, *Realism in Our Time: Literature and the Class Struggle,* trans. John Mander and Necke Mander (New York: Harper and Row, 1964), 43 (emphasis in original).

25. Roland Barthes, "The Third Meaning," in *Image/Music/Text,* trans. Stephen Heath (New York: Hill and Wang, 1977), 56.

26. Robert Ray, "Roland Barthes: Fetishism as Research Strategy," in *The Avant-Garde Finds Andy Hardy* (Cambridge, Mass.: Harvard University Press, 1995), 106.

27. Bill Nichols, "Eisenstein's *Strike* and the Genealogy of Documentary," in *Blurred Boundaries: Questions of Meaning in Contemporary Culture* (Bloomington: Indiana University Press, 1994), 111.

28. For a thorough discussion of the debt *Strike*'s visual stereotypes—the husky

workers in caps and simple shirt and pants; the obese, cigar-smoking capitalists; the officious office manager in a white suit and straw hat—owe not just to the commedia but also the laconic formal repertoire of Civil War posters, avant-garde photomontage, and agit-prop puppet theater, see Roberta Reeder, "Agit-Prop Art: Posters, Puppets, and Propaganda in Eisenstein's *Strike*," *Russian Literature Triquarterly* 22 (1989): 255–78.

29. David Bordwell, "Eisenstein's Epistemological Shift," *Screen* 15.4 (Winter 1974–75): 29–58. Bordwell's early formulation of this shift is elaborated in his *The Cinema of Eisenstein* (London: Harvard University Press, 1993), 195, 190, 191.

30. Shklovsky, "Strike," trans. Chris Pike and Joe Andrew, in *Futurism/Formalism/FEKS*, 35.

31. On the *raccourci*, see Eisenstein's "Notes on Biomechanics" and "What Is a Raccourci and What Is a Pose?" in Law and Gordon, *Meyerhold, Eisenstein, and Biomechanics*, 164, 165.

32. On the parallels between the status of the grotesque in political theory and the grotesque in aesthetic theory, see William Solomon, *Literature, Amusement, and Technology in the Great Depression* (Cambridge: Cambridge University Press, 2002).

33. Peter Stallybrass, "Marx and Heterogeneity: Thinking the Lumpenproletariat," *Representations* 31 (Summer 1990): 88.

34. Ibid., 88, 70. See also Georges Bataille, "The Psychological Structure of Fascism," in *Visions of Excess: Selected Writings, 1927–1939*, ed. Allan Stoekl, trans. Allan Stoekl, Carl R. Lovitt, and Donald M. Leslie Jr. (Minneapolis: University of Minnesota Press, 1985).

35. See Yuri Tsivian's insightful commentary on the *Strike* DVD.

36. I mean this as a corrective to Nichols's reading of the spies as furtive passers, figures of the closet, falling short of the "homoerotic exuberance" of *Strike*'s vital workers, who embody the "potential for being-in-action that hierarchy or hegemony strives to control." For Nichols, the workers' futural subjectivity accompanies the film's enactment of a radical temporality on the model of Benjamin's *Jetztzeit*. See Nichols, "Eisenstein's *Strike*," 112–13.

37. Michael Taussig, *Defacement: Public Secrecy and the Labor of the Negative* (Stanford: Stanford University Press, 1999), 233.

38. Ibid., 233–34. For Max Horkheimer and Theodor W. Adorno's remarks on the organization of mimesis, see the chapter "Elements of Anti-Semitism" in *Dialectic of Enlightenment: Philosophical Fragments*, trans. Edmund Jephcott (Stanford: Stanford University Press, 2002).

39. Taussig, *Defacement*, 233–34.

40. These contemporary reviews are translated and cited by Anne Nesbet in her provocative recent study *Savage Junctures: Sergei Eisenstein and the Shape of Thinking* (London: I. B. Tauris, 2004), 21–22.

41. See Lev Kuleshov, "Our First Experiences," trans. Ronald Levaco, in *Futurism/*

Formalism/FEKS, 46. See also his remarks on *Strike* translated and cited in Nesbet, *Savage Junctures,* 25.

42. See Greg M. Smith, *Film Structure and the Emotion System* (Cambridge: Cambridge University Press, 2003), 114. For another cognitivist approach, here to the "Manichean moral structure" of *Strike*'s typage, see Murray Smith, *Engaging Characters: Fiction, Emotion, and the Cinema* (Oxford: Clarendon Press, 1995), 198.

43. Sergei Eisenstein, "Imitation as Mastery," in *Eisenstein Rediscovered,* ed. Ian Christie and Richard Taylor (London: Routledge, 1993), 67–68.

44. Ibid., 69.

45. Mikhail Yampolsky, "The Essential Bone Structure: Mimesis in Eisenstein," in *Eisenstein Rediscovered,* 187–88.

46. Eisenstein, "Film Form: New Problems," in *Film Form,* 44.

47. Wilhelm Worringer, *Abstraction and Empathy: A Contribution to the Psychology of Style,* trans. Michael Bullock (Chicago: Elephant Paperbacks, 1997), 12, 17. See also Rachael Moore, *Savage Theory: Cinema as Modern Magic* (Durham: Duke University Press, 200).

48. Eisenstein, "Montage 1937," in *S. M. Eisenstein: Selected Works, Vol. II, Towards a Theory of Montage,* ed. Michael Glenny and Richard Taylor, trans. Michael Glenny (London: British Film Institute, 1991), 27, 29, 30.

49. Eisenstein, "Dickens, Griffith, and the Film Today," in *Film Form,* 243–44.

50. Eisenstein, "Montage 1938," in *Towards a Theory of Montage,* 298. Much of this essay was translated earlier by Jay Leyda and published in Eisenstein's *The Film Sense* (New York: Harcourt Brace, 1942) as "Word and Image."

51. Bordwell, *Cinema of Eisenstein,* 176.

52. Sergei Eisenstein, *Nonindifferent Nature,* trans. Herbert Marshall (Cambridge: Cambridge University Press, 1987), 86.

53. Sergei Eisenstein, *Eisenstein on Disney,* ed. Jay Leyda, trans. Alan Upchurch (Calcutta: Seagull Books, 1986), 46, 42.

54. Eisenstein's understanding of the potentiality of matter is indebted to Frederick Engels's *The Dialectics of Nature,* trans. and ed. J. B. S. Haldane (New York: International Publishers, 1940). For a discussion of Eisenstein's Disney essay in the context of such evolutionary dialectics, see Leslie, *Hollywood Flatlands,* 16.

55. Sergei Eisenstein qtd. in Thomas Waugh, "A Fag-Spotter's Guide to Eisenstein," *Body Politic* 35 (July/August 1977): 16.

56. Fredric Jameson, *A Singular Modernity: Essay on the Ontology of the Present* (London: Verso, 2002), 136.

57. Ecstasy's non-dominating, sympathetic likening is not dissimilar from the sensual potential of the mimetic faculty, as Walter Benjamin describes it. I discuss Benjaminian mimesis in more detail in chapter 5.

58. Georg Simmel, "The Sociology of Sociability," in *Simmel on Culture: Selected Writings,* ed. David Frisby and Mike Featherstone (London: Sage, 1997), 120, 121. My thinking about the compatibility of Simmel's "play-form of association" and queer

sociality is indebted to Leo Bersani's "Sociability and Cruising," *Umbr(a)* (2002): 9–23.

59. Simmel, "Sociology of Sociability," 122.

Chapter 3: Kumraderie

1. As Bill Brown explains, Johnson "became one of Barnum's and America's most celebrated freaks, photographed by [Matthew] Brady and [Charles] Eisenmann, appearing in several dime museums in the 1890s, and still appearing at Coney Island well after the turn of the century." See *The Material Unconscious: American Amusement, Stephen Crane, and the Economies of Play* (Cambridge, Mass.: Harvard University Press, 1996), 217.

2. R. P. Blackmur, "Notes on E. E. Cummings' Language," originally published in *Hound & Horn* 4 (1931): 163–92, reprinted in *Critical Essays on E. E. Cummings,* ed. Guy Rotella (Boston: G. K. Hall, 1984), 111–12.

3. Suzanne Clark, *Sentimental Modernism: Women Writers and the Revolution of the Word* (Bloomington: Indiana University Press, 1991), 9.

4. Susan Buck-Morss, "Aesthetics and Anaesthetics: Walter Benjamin's Artwork Essay Reconsidered," *New Formations* 62 (Fall 1992): 125.

5. Ibid.

6. In 1952, the same year he voted for the Eisenhower–Nixon Republic ticket, Cummings remarked in a letter to his sister, "Have yet to encounter anybody in any manner connected with Harvard who isn't primevally pink." Qtd. in Richard S. Kennedy, *Dreams in the Mirror: A Biography of E. E. Cummings* (Toronto: George J. Mcleod, 1980), 443.

7. Frank Lentricchia, *Modernist Quartet* (Cambridge: Cambridge University Press, 1994), 3.

8. Ibid., 8, xi.

9. Qtd. in *Pound/Cummings: The Correspondence of Ezra Pound and E. E. Cummings,* ed. Barry Ahearn (Ann Arbor: University of Michigan Press, 1996), 2. Here, and throughout, when I quote Cummings I retain his eccentric style of punctuation.

10. Ibid., 7.

11. See Cummings's 1945 paean to Pound, "Re Ezra Pound: II," and its defense of Pound's putatively unpatriotic acts: "Every artist's strictly illimitable country is himself. An artist who plays that country false has committed suicide; and even a good lawyer cannot kill the dead." In *E. E. Cummings: A Miscellany Revised,* ed. George J. Firmage (New York: October House, 1965), 313.

12. To be sure, neither James's nor Pound's notions of the individual were consistently in keeping with a liberal ideology, and they were both shrewd critics of many of the excesses of liberalism. On the complex relationship between Jamesian pragmatism and a liberal self built on the model of private property, see Cary Wolfe's chapter

on pragmatism in his *Critical Environments: Postmodern Theory and the Pragmatics of the "Outside"* (Minneapolis: University of Minnesota Press, 1998), as well as his discussion of James in *The Limits of American Literary Ideology in Pound and Emerson* (Cambridge: Cambridge University Press, 1993). For Pound's relationship to the antinomies of liberal thought, see Michael North's classic study *The Political Aesthetic of Yeats, Eliot, and Pound* (New York: Cambridge University Press, 1991).

13. *Selected Letters of E. E. Cummings*, ed. F. W. Dupee and George Stade (London: André Deutsch, 1972), 51. This Cummings, the Cold Warrior, would be canonized as America's reigning poet of freedom in the 1950s for the same reason—staunch anti-collectivism—that he today is ensconced in literary-critical oblivion.

14. Lentricchia, *Modernist Quartet*, 6 (my emphasis).

15. Ibid., 5.

16. Wolfe, *Limits*, 30.

17. Ibid., 67.

18. See John Dos Passos's contemporary review of the novel, "Off the Shoals," in *Dial* 73 (1922): 100.

19. Ibid., 98.

20. Ibid.

21. Ibid. I am thinking here most obviously of Pound's 1921 translator's postscript to Remy de Gourmont's *The Natural Philosophy of Love* (New York: Boni and Liveright, 1922) and his absurd speculations there about the relationship between semen and production, specifically his wish to "[drive] any new idea into the great passive vulva of London, a sensation analogous to the male feeling in copulation" (207). On modernism's burlesque style in the 1920s, see Michael North's chapter "Across the Great Divide," in his *Reading 1922: A Return to the Scene of the Modern* (Oxford: Oxford University Press, 1999).

22. Qtd. in Cummings's unpublished notes in Milton Cohen's *Poet and Painter: The Aesthetics of E. E. Cummings's Early Work* (Detroit: Wayne State University Press, 1987), 70.

23. James here is quoted in Carrie Tirado Brammen's provocative discussion of Jamesian pluralism in *The Uses of Variety: Modern Americanism and the Quest for National Distinctiveness* (Cambridge, Mass.: Harvard University Press, 2000), 35.

24. William James, *A Pluralistic Universe* (1910), in *Writings 1902–1910*, ed. Bruce Kuklick (New York: Library of America, 1987), 749.

25. Ibid., 778.

26. James qtd. in Brammen, *Uses of Variety*, 35.

27. James, *Pluralistic Universe*, 776.

28. Cummings connects burlesk's vitality to that of Lachaise (as well as John Marin and Stravinsky) in his 1925 *Vanity Fair* article, "You Aren't Mad, Am I?," collected in *A Miscellany Revised*, 129–30. See Hartley's 1937 "Thinking of Gaston Lachaise" in *On Art, by Marsden Hartley*, ed. Gail R. Scott (New York: Horizon Press, 1982), 285.

29. On modernism's feminization of the masses, mass culture, and consumption

more generally, see Andreas Huyssen, *After the Great Divide: Modernism, Mass Culture, Postmodernism* (Bloomington: Indiana University Press, 1986), and Rita Felski, *The Gender of Modernity* (Cambridge, Mass.: Harvard University Press, 1995).

30. This last was part of Cummings's later description of Lachaise for an exhibition of the sculptor's work at the Weyhe Gallery in New York City in the mid-1950s (*A Miscellany Revised,* 24).

31. Janet Lyon, "Josephine Baker's Hothouse," in *Modernism, Inc.: Body, Memory, Capital,* ed. Jani Scandura and Michael Thurston (New York: New York University Press, 2001), 33, 41.

32. Hans Ulrich Gumbrecht qtd. in ibid., 41.

33. Anthony Vidler, *Warped Space: Art, Architecture, and Anxiety in Modern Culture* (Cambridge: MIT Press, 2001), 3.

34. Immanuel Kant, *Critique of Judgment,* trans. Werner S. Pluhar (Indianapolis: Hackett, 1987), 136.

35. Ibid., 180. For a fascinating account of the potential of a politics based on disgust rather than desire, see Sianne Ngai, *Ugly Feelings* (Cambridge, Mass.: Harvard University Press, 2005), 332–54.

36. See North, *Reading 1922,* 151.

37. For a useful overview of Cummings's Freudianism, see Milton A. Cohen, "Cummings and Freud," *American Literature* 55.4 (December 1983): 591–610.

38. Vidler, *Warped Space,* viii.

39. For a more extensive discussion of the circumstances leading to Cummings's imprisonment, see Charles Norman's account in his biography, *E. E. Cummings: The Magic Maker* (New York: Macmillan, 1958), and Richard S. Kennedy's foreword to the "Typescript Edition" of Cummings's *The Enormous Room* (New York: Liveright, 1978), 45.

40. Johanna Bourke, *Dismembering the Male: Men's Bodies, Britain, and the Great War* (Chicago: University of Chicago Press, 1996), 31.

41. Ibid., 31; Jessica Burstein, "Waspish Segments: Lewis, Prosthesis, Fascism," *Modernism/Modernity* 4.2 (April 1997): 141.

42. Brammen, *Uses of Variety,* 43. For affinities between James's anti-idealism and that of the Frankfurt School, see Ross Posnock, *The Trial of Curiosity: Henry James, William James, and the Challenge of Modernity* (New York: Oxford University Press, 1991).

43. James, letter to Mrs. Henry Whitman, 7 June 1899, qtd. in Brammen, *Uses of Variety,* 44.

44. Cummings made these connections between physical and psychic motion often. Consider his attempt to articulate a cinematic idiom of seeing-all-around: "As to language which employs this idiom. The 'language', as it seems to me, is concentric. It suggests Professor F's Repetition Compulsion. I should think that, as the camera went around the track . . . background occurences(flat;(flat-upright,bulging-fallingtoward,hollowing-falling away from)would give very much the same sensa-

tion as a good rollercoaster, or a lively Unconscious" (punctuation and spacing in original). See Cummings's letter to James Watson Jr., with whom he was developing film projects, qtd. in Lisa Cartwright's "U.S. Modernism and the Emergence of 'The Right Wing of Film Art': The Films of James Sibley Watson, Jr. and Melville Webber," in *Lovers of Cinema: The First American Film Avant-Garde, 1919–1945,* ed. Jan-Christopher Horak (Madison: University of Wisconsin Press, 1995), 174.

45. I refer here to Michel Foucault's well-known conception of the heterotopia as, among other things, a fundamentally contradictory site capable of juxtaposing "in a single, real place several spaces, several sites that are themselves incompatible." See Foucault, "Of Other Spaces," *Diacritics* 16 (Spring 1986): 22–27.

46. Vidler, Warped Space, 53.

47. Sigmund Freud, *Beyond the Pleasure Principle,* in *The Freud Reader,* ed. Peter Gay (New York: W. W. Norton, 1989), 616.

48. Diana Fuss, *Identification Papers* (New York: Routledge, 1995), 43.

49. On this ambivalence, see Fuss, *Identification Papers.* For an interesting discussion of Freud's claims that homosexuals are particularly sociable subjects, see Leo Bersani, "Sociability and Cruising," *Umbr(a)* (2002): 9–23.

50. Sarah Cole, "Modernism, Male Intimacy, and the Great War," *ELH* 68 (2001): 475.

51. Foucault calls this a "heterotopia of compensation," whose role "is to create a space that is other, another real space, as perfect, as meticulous, as well arranged as ours is messy, ill constructed, and jumbled." See Foucault, "Of Other Spaces," 27, 26.

52. Giorgio Agamben, *Infancy and History: The Destruction of Experience,* trans. Liz Heron (London: Verso, 1993), 53.

53. Georg Simmel, "The Stranger," in *The Sociology of Georg Simmel,* trans. and ed. Kurt H. Wolff (Glencoe, Ill.: Free Press, 1950), 402.

54. Georg Simmel, "The Aesthetic Significance of the Face," in *George Simmel, 1858–1918,* ed. Kurt H. Wolff (Columbus: Ohio State University Press, 1959), 276–81.

55. Ngai, *Ugly Feelings,* 334.

56. This visualization is at once an imperialist appropriation of the other as an object of knowledge (which depends upon stereotype and caricature) and the staging of a difference that exists, like all the Delectable Mountains, outside of knowledge. In this way, oddly, Cummings's commitment to radical individualism, which is consistently primitivist, nonetheless mitigates his racism.

57. Herbert Marcuse, *Eros and Civilization: A Philosophical Inquiry into Freud* (Boston: Beacon Press, 1955), 169.

58. E. E. Cummings, *Him* (New York: Liveright, 1927).

59. See Edmund Wilson's chapter "E. E. Cummings' *Him,*" in his *Shores of Light: A Literary Chronicle of the Twenties and Thirties* (New York: Farrar, Strauss and Young, 1952), 283. For the critical response, see Norman, *Magic Maker,* 170–71.

60. See Cohen, *Poet and Painter;* Eric Bentley, *Notes from the Modern Repertoire,*

282 · NOTES TO PAGES 131–35

Series Two (Denver: University of Denver Press, 1952); and Dickran Tashjian's chapter "E. E. Cummings and Dada Formalism," in his *Skyscraper Primitives: Dada and the American Avant-Garde, 1910–1925* (Middletown, Conn.: Wesleyan University Press, 1975).

61. Jean Genet, "The Funambulists" (translation of "Les Saltimbanques"), trans. Bernard Frechtman, *Evergreen Review* 32 (April–May 1964): 46.

62. On Anglophone modernism's sense of writing as a corporeal extension, see Tim Armstrong's chapter "Prosthetic Modernism" in his *Modernism, Technology, and the Body: A Cultural Study* (Cambridge: Cambridge University Press, 1998), 90.

63. Wilson, *Shores of Light*, 284.

64. Jacques Derrida, "The Double Session," in *Dissemination*, trans. Barbara Johnson (Chicago: University of Chicago Press, 1981), 245.

65. Cummings qtd. in Norman, *Magic Maker*, 168.

Chapter 4: Light Figures

1. Marsden Hartley qtd. in Townsend Ludington, *Marsden Hartley: The Biography of an American Artist* (Ithaca: Cornell University Press, 1998), 4.

2. See Hartley's essay "A Charming Equestrienne" in his *Adventures in the Arts: Informal Chapters on Painters, Vaudeville, and Poets* (New York: Hacker Art Books, 1972), 176, 179, 181.

3. See Hartley's circus manuscripts, "Circus" and "Elephants and Rhinestones," in the Yale Collection of American Literature (hereafter abbreviated as YCAL), Beinecke Rare Book and Manuscript Library, Yale University, New Haven, Connecticut. The first is a longer 104-page manuscript written in Hartley's spidery hand; the latter— likely a revision—is a typescript copy of roughly the first tenth of the earlier version. Taking Hartley's suggestion, I refer to the two manuscripts together as "Elephants and Rhinestones" (or simply as "Elephants").

4. See Paul Peppis, "Rewriting Sex: Mina Loy, Marie Stopes, and Sexology," *Modernism/Modernity* 9.4 (November 2002): 575. See also Jessica Burstein, "A Few Words about Dubuque: Modernism, Sentimentalism, and the Blasé," *American Literary History* 14.2 (2002): 227–54.

5. On the various stakes of the fantasy of subjective transparency and its concomitant disavowal of embodiment in modernism, see Karen Jacobs, *The Eye's Mind: Literary Modernism and Visual Culture* (Ithaca: Cornell University Press, 2001).

6. For a discussion of the past, present, and future of such intimacies in the public sphere, see Lauren Berlant and Michael Warner, "Sex in Public," in *Intimacy*, ed. Lauren Berlant (Chicago: University of Chicago Press, 2000), 311–30.

7. For Hartley's remarks on the pleasures of Parisian sociality, see Hartley to Norma Berger, 31 July 1912, qtd. in Ludington, *Marsden Hartley*, 74. That Hartley should credit Gertrude Stein's salon for a similar "kind of William James intimacy" is no surprise; Stein, of course, studied under James while a psychology student at Harvard and in

fact loaned Hartley her copy of James's *The Varieties of Religious Experience,* which Hartley would claim as a major influence on his work.

8. James qtd., respectively, in Cary Wolfe, *The Limits of American Literary Ideology in Pound and Emerson* (Cambridge: Cambridge University Press, 1993), 30, and Patricia McDonnell, "El Dorado: Marsden Hartley in Imperial Berlin," in *Dictated by Life: Marsden Hartley's German Paintings and Robert Indiana's Elegies,* ed. Patricia McDonnell (Minneapolis: Fredric R. Weisman Art Museum, 1995), 21.

9. I refer here to James's claim in *The Varieties of Religious Experience* that "so long as we deal with the cosmic and the general, we deal only with the symbols of reality, but as soon as we deal with private and personal phenomena as such, we deal with realities in the completest sense of the term," qtd. in McDonnell, "El Dorado," 22; and his definition of self-possession in *The Principles of Psychology,* qtd. in Wolfe, *Limits,* 78. Susan Elizabeth Ryan has also observed the self-absenting that pervades Hartley's work, noting how Hartley repeatedly "seems drawn to this idea of a centrifugal self-referentiality that leaves the self, itself, out." Again, Hartley's own comments are illustrative in this regard. As he puts it in a letter to Rebecca Strand in 1929, "My main trouble . . . is a passionate desire to eliminate myself. I don't want to be the object of self-interest that one is supposed to be." See Susan Elizabeth Ryan, introduction to *Somehow a Past: The Autobiography of Marsden Hartley,* ed. Susan Elizabeth Ryan (Cambridge, Mass.: MIT Press, 1997), 28, 32.

10. See Juan Suárez, *Bike Boys, Drag Queens, and Superstars: Avant-Garde, Mass Culture, and Gay Identities in the 1960s Underground Cinema* (Bloomington: Indiana University Press, 1996), 20. For a rigorous discussion of this category's centrality to modernity, see Krzysztof Ziarek, *The Historicity of Experience: Modernity, the Avant-Garde, and the Event* (Evanston, Ill.: Northwestern University Press, 2001), and, more recently, Martin Jay, *Songs of Experience: Modern American and European Variations on a Universal Theme* (Berkeley: University of California Press, 2005).

11. Walter Benjamin, "The Work of Art in the Age of Mechanical Reproduction," in *Illuminations,* ed. Hannah Arendt, trans. Harry Zohn (New York: Schocken Books, 1969); Siegfried Kracauer, "The Cult of Distraction," *New German Critique* 40 (Winter 1987), reprinted in *The Mass Ornament: Weimar Essays,* trans. and ed. Thomas Y. Levin (Cambridge, Mass.: Harvard University Press, 1995).

12. Charles Baudelaire, "The Painter of Modern Life," in *Charles Baudelaire: Selected Writings on Art and Literature,* trans. P. E. Charvet (London: Penguin, 1992), 390–435; Georg Simmel, "The Metropolis and Mental Life," in *Simmel on Culture: Selected Writings,* ed. David Frisby and Mike Featherstone (London: Sage, 1997), 174–86.

13. For a critique of the ideological stakes of this desire to feel common and to identify across class in the spectacular spaces of public performance, see T. J. Clark's chapter "A Bar at the Folies-Bergère" in his *The Painting of Modern Life: Paris in the Art of Manet and His Followers* (New York: Knopf, 1985).

14. Jonathan Weinberg, one of Hartley's most astute critics, characterizes the

conflation of the martial and the ludic here as a retroactive dodge: "As if worried by the militarism and eroticism of this description, Hartley attributed his attraction to pageantry to his early love of the circus." This underestimates how, for Hartley, the martial and ludic orders were interchangeable to the extent that they informed a more systematic, theoretical investigation of spectacle—and, by extension, of public embodiment and public intimacy—that spanned Hartley's entire career. See Weinberg, *Speaking for Vice: Homosexuality in the Art of Charles Demuth, Marsden Hartley, and the First American Avant-Garde* (New Haven: Yale University Press, 1993), 147.

15. Hartley to Stieglitz, 2 September 1914, YCAL, qtd. in Weinberg, *Speaking for Vice*, 154.

16. See Weinberg, *Speaking for Vice*, 145.

17. On the connections between the German military and homosexuality, see Modris Ecksteins, *Rites of Spring: The Great War and the Birth of the Modern Age* (New York: Doubleday, 1989), esp. 80–90; and McDonnell, "El Dorado." For Hartley, McDonnell explains, the German military uniform functioned as a "coded gesture" that enabled Hartley both to reveal and conceal his desire.

18. See August Macke's manifesto of the Blaue Reiter group, "Masks": "Man expresses his life in forms. Each form of art is an expression of his inner life. The exterior form of art is its interior." Quoted in Ludington, *Marsden Hartley*, 84. On the gendered aesthetic discourse of the Stieglitz circle, see Marcia Brennan, *Painting Gender, Constructing Theory: The Alfred Stieglitz Circle and American Formalist Aesthetics* (Cambridge, Mass.: MIT Press, 2001).

19. Waldo Frank, introduction to Hartley, *Adventures in the Arts*, xvi.

20. Ibid., xiii–xiv.

21. See, for example, Waldo Frank's study *The Re-discovery of America* (1929), in which he notes that the "sense of aesthetic form is an unconscious adumbration of our sense of unity with our own body." Qtd. in Brennan, *Painting Gender*, 9.

22. Joseph Litvak, *Strange Gourmets: Sophistication, Theory, and the Novel* (Durham: Duke University Press, 1998), 6, 4 (emphasis in original).

23. Hartley's suspicion is, of course, correct and shrewdly identifies a particular stage in the transformation of vaudeville "from a marginalized sphere of popular entertainment, largely associated with vice and masculinity, to a consolidated network of commercial leisure," one that catered to the female consumer with "refined," "respectable," indeed "wholesome" acts—opera singers, famous actors from the legitimate stage, Shakespearean dramas, and the like. See M. Alison Kibler, *Rank Ladies: Gender and Cultural Hierarchy in American Vaudeville* (Chapel Hill: University of North Carolina Press, 1999), 5, 152.

24. Hartley wants to frame the acrobat's body rather than jettison it. Thus, Hartley's notion of masculine ornamentation departs from aestheticism insofar as it rejects the imperative to transcend the materiality of the body, a corporeality associated with "feminine" nature. On the centrality of this mandate to the aestheticist project, see

Rita Felski's chapter "Making Masculinity: The Feminization of Writing" in her *The Gender of Modernity* (Cambridge, Mass.: Harvard University Press, 1995).

25. The language of facing or entering the sun recurs often enough and in such highly cathected contexts that it becomes a queer nexus in Hartley's work. Consider that, in addition to the instances of solar encounter already cited, Hartley described the dense imagery of his Amerika Series' all-male *Indian Fantasy* (1914) as the enactment of his racialized dream of "going Indian and traveling 'to the West [to] face the sun forever.'" Hartley qtd. in Wanda Corn, "Marsden Hartley's Native Amerika," in *Marsden Hartley,* ed. Elizabeth Mankin Kornhauser (New Haven: Wadsworth Atheneum Museum of Art and Yale University Press, 2003), 71.

26. T. S. Eliot, "Tradition and the Individual Talent," in *Selected Essays,* ed. Frank Kermode (London: Faber and Faber, 1932).

27. See Peter Nicholls, "Apes and Familiars: Modernism, Mimesis, and the Work of Wyndham Lewis," *Textual Practice* 6.3 (Winter 1992): 421–38.

28. Such critics read Hartley's work as artificial and hermetic, lacking in the ejaculatory intensity of John Marin, the womanly fecundity of Georgia O'Keeffe, or the earthly naturalness of Arthur Dove. In *Port of New York,* Paul Rosenfeld characterizes Hartley's problem thus: "On the materials of the exterior cosmos he establishes a little sealed world declarative of his own inward human order." Qtd. in Brennan, *Painting Gender,* 166.

29. Paul Rosenfeld, "Paint and Circuses," YCAL, 2.

30. Ibid., 2, 3.

31. "Vagabond *libido*" is Rosenfeld's phrase and emphasis in "Paint and Circuses," YCAL, 5.

32. Marsden Hartley, "The Greatest Show on Earth," *Vanity Fair* 22.6 (August 1924): 88.

33. Brennan's formulation reduces the complexity of Hartley's negotiation of these competing avant-gardes: first, it assumes that Hartley was more prudish about acknowledging his sexual preferences than he was, as his enjoyment of the acrobat in *Adventures in the Arts* suggests; second, it follows a broader critical tendency to ignore Hartley's abiding and erotic preoccupation with public spectacle; finally, it suggests that Hartley understood Dada as Duchamp or Picabia did, which he did not.

34. See, for example, his implicit definition of Dada in another *Adventures in the Arts* essay, "The Appeal of Photography": Stieglitz, Hartley notes, "will not care to be called Dada, but it is nevertheless true. He has ridden his own vivacious hobbyhorse with as much liberty, and one may even say license, as is possible for one intelligent human being" (111).

35. Richard Sheppard draws a useful distinction between the French Dadaists Duchamp and Picabia, who viewed nature as "inherently patternless" and "proclaim[ed] the Dada state of mind *against* a background of absurdity and chaos," and Zurich Dada and the non-Marxist Berlin Dadaists, who, by contrast, "were prepared to affirm or at least countenance the coexistence in Nature of chaos and elusive pattern,

dynamism and fluid structure." Hartley's embrace of flux and his desire to be merged into pattern aligns him clearly with the latter. See Sheppard's chapter "Radical Cheek: Or, Dada Reconsidered" in his *Modernism-Dada-Postmodernism* (Evanston, Ill.: Northwestern University Press, 2000), 193.

36. Litvak, *Strange Gourmets*, 79.

37. On the centrality of scenes of "queer initiation" for gay men, see Michael Moon, *A Small Boy and Others: Imitation and Initiation from Henry James to Andy Warhol* (Durham: Duke University Press, 1988).

38. In this sense, "Elephants and Rhinestones" returns to Hartley's interest in the autobiographical mode as a means of exploring the connection between vision and memory. On this mode, see Ryan, introduction to *Somehow a Past*, 2.

39. See Emile Benveniste's chapter "Subjectivity in Language" in his *Problems in General Linguistics*, trans. Mary Elizabeth Meek (Coral Gables, Fla.: University of Miami Press, 1971), 225.

40. See Maureen McLane, "'Why Should I Not Speak to You?': The Rhetoric of Intimacy," in *Intimacy*, ed. Lauren Berlant (Chicago: University of Chicago Press, 2000), 436. My formulation of Hartley's intimacy as a "grammar" is indebted to McLane.

41. See Lauren Berlant, "Intimacy: A Special Issue," in *Intimacy*, 2.

42. Jacques Derrida, *Archive Fever: A Freudian Impression*, trans. Eric Prenowitz (Chicago: University of Chicago Press, 1996).

43. McLane, "'Why Should I Not Speak to You?'" 436, 439.

44. Ibid., 439. McLane's essay reformulates the dark logic of Paul de Man's well-known deconstructive essay "Autobiography as De-facement," which laid bare how any system of cognition built on language cannot but forestall presence, a fact that is especially unsettling in the genre of autobiography, which presumes to "reveal reliable self-knowledge." Paul de Man, "Autobiography as De-facement," in *The Rhetoric of Romanticism* (New York: Columbia University Press, 1984), 80.

45. Even if we suppose that Hartley wrote "The Flying Man" before Codona's death in 1937, which is unlikely, his choice neither to include the details of this death in "Elephants and Rhinestones" nor to elegize Codona as he does Leitzel is a striking disavowal of the denouement of the Codona madness.

46. *The Collected Poems of Marsden Hartley, 1904–1943*, ed. Gail R. Scott (Santa Rosa, Calif.: Black Sparrow Press, 1987), 170; Hartley, "Circus," YCAL, 91.

47. See *On Art, by Marsden Hartley*, ed. Gail R. Scott (New York: Horizon Press, 1982), 291.

48. See especially his attack on surrealism's solipsism in the essay "Max Ernst" (1928) in *On Art*, 133–34.

49. Hartley to Adelaide Kuntz, 22 September 1929, qtd. in Scott's introduction to *On Art*, 41.

50. Critics have read the painting as a strongly emblematic work of mourning

and a conflation of death and homosexual desire not unlike the War Motif series: the flaming arrows allude to St. Sebastian and beyond that to a gay subculture; the pierced heart, like the ship, recalls Hart Crane, the gay poet whose suicide by drowning Hartley had commemorated in his earlier work *Eight Bells Folly: Memorial for Hart Crane* (1933); "the rose on his shoulder and the Christ figure recall the various paintings associated with the Mason family," a Nova Scotian fishing family whom Hartley befriended and with whom he lived during the summers of 1935 and 1936, and whose sons Alty and Donny, beloved by Hartley, were drowned at sea in July of 1936; the "form of the painting, with a single figure placed in the center against a dark background, over which the various symbols are collaged, is a reprise of the war motif series" (Weinberg, *Speaking for Vice*, 188).

51. As an example of the latter reading, I have in mind Bruce Robertson's recent claim that this "self-portrait knits together Hartley's identity at a point when it might have been dangerously frayed." See his essay "Marsden Hartley and Self-Portraiture" in *Marsden Hartley*, ed. Kornhauser, 155.

52. Fredric Jameson, *A Singular Modernity: Essay on the Ontology of the Present* (New York: Verso, 2002), 132, 135.

53. See Miriam Hansen, "America, Paris, the Alps: Kracauer (and Benjamin) on Cinema and Modernity," in *Cinema and the Invention of Modern Life*, ed. Leo Charney and Vanessa R. Schwartz (Berkeley: University of California Press, 1995), 374.

54. See Karen Jacobs's formulation of modernism's "interior gaze" as an attempt to "wed the visionary with the empirical" by "represent[ing] the idea of visual truth as a quality irreducible to visual surfaces, and thus requiring an expert, artistic gaze capable of perceiving and bringing to visibility an inner truth." See Jacobs, *Eye's Mind*, 27. Consider also Nancy Armstrong's similar claim that modernism located "whatever it considered authentic in nature or culture within an invisible domain on the other side of the surfaces one ordinarily sees." Nancy Armstrong, *Fiction in the Age of Photography: The Legacy of British Realism* (Cambridge, Mass.: Harvard University Press, 1999), 11.

55. Bill Brown, *A Sense of Things: The Object Matter of American Literature* (Chicago: University of Chicago Press, 2003), 12.

56. Eve Kosofsky Sedgwick, *Epistemology of the Closet* (Berkeley: University of California Press, 1990), 161.

57. Ibid., 143, 150.

58. On the mediatory role of the impression in modernist literature, see Jesse Matz, *Literary Impressionism and Modernist Aesthetics* (New York: Cambridge University Press, 2001). On the *flâneur*'s interiorization of modernity's exterior, see Walter Benjamin, *Charles Baudelaire: A Lyric Poet in the Era of High Capitalism,* trans. Harry Zohn (New York: Verso, 1983); as well as Tom Gunning's "The Exterior as *Intérieur*: Benjamin's Optical Detective," *boundary 2* 30.1 (2003): 105–30.

59. Kracauer, "Cult of Distraction," 327.

Chapter 5: Tenderness

1. Joseph Cornell, "'Enchanted Wanderer': Excerpt from a Journey Album for Hedy Lamarr," in *The Shadow and Its Shadow: Surrealist Writings on Cinema,* ed. and trans. Paul Hammond (San Francisco: City Lights Books, 2000), 206.

2. P. Adams Sitney, "The Cinematic Gaze of Joseph Cornell," in *Joseph Cornell,* ed. Kynaston McShine (New York: Museum of Modern Art, 1980), 69. The language of nostalgia and loss also dominates the discussion of Cornell's cinematic investments in Jodi Hauptman's recent *Stargazing in the Cinema* (New Haven: Yale University Press, 1999).

3. Cornell, "'Enchanted Wanderer,'" 206.

4. There are few substantive treatments of Cornell's filmmaking. See Sitney, "Cinematic Gaze," as well as his brief discussions of Cornell as a forefather of the "lyrical film" in *Visionary Film: The American Avant-Garde, 1943–1978* (New York: Oxford University Press, 1973); on Cornell's cinematic working method's, see Thomas Lawson, "Silently, by Means of a Flashing Light," *October* 15 (1980): 49–60. Hauptman's *Stargazing* focuses on Cornell's non-filmic homages to female movie stars and discusses only *Rose Hobart* in depth. The only detailed treatment of Cornell's filmmaking as a whole, and one that argues for the centrality of the collage trilogy to his cinema, is Marjorie Keller's *The Untutored Eye: Childhood in the Films of Cocteau, Cornell, and Brakhage* (London: Fairleigh Dickinson University Press, 1986). *Rose Hobart* is the only Cornell film mentioned in Paul Arthur's excellent history of American avant-garde film, *A Line of Sight: American Avant-Garde Film since 1965* (Minneapolis: University of Minnesota Press, 2005), though its inaugural role in the found-footage genre is noted, as well as its impact on post-1960s styles of avant-garde portraiture.

5. The centrality of this trilogy—and of Cornell's experimental filmmaking in general—in the history of American avant-garde cinema has again been brought to light with the commercial release in 2007 of many of Cornell's previously unavailable films in two ambitious DVD and DVD-ROM projects: The Voyager Foundation's *The Magic Worlds of Joseph Cornell* and Anthology Film Archive's monumental *Unseen Cinema: Early American Avant-Garde Film, 1893–1941,* a seven-disc collection that constitutes nothing short of a reinvention of the history of the American avant-garde, one according pride of place to Cornell's trilogy.

6. It deserves mention that Cornell was familiar with the poetry of Cummings and was especially taken by Hartley. Cornell described Hartley's *Adventures in the Arts* as "a beautiful and highly sensitive book of appreciations . . . to which I owe an eternal debt of gratitude" and called the event of reading the book "a transcendent experience." *Joseph Cornell's Theater of the Mind: Selected Diaries, Letters, and Files,* ed. Mary Ann Caws (New York: Thames and Hudson, 1993), 63, 145.

7. For more familiar readings of Cornell's desire as premised on containment, repression, and control, see Mary Ann Caws, "Looking in a Box: Or, Eros Contained,"

in *Joseph Cornell's Theater of the Mind*; Hauptmann, *Stargazing*; and Keller, *Untutored Eye*.

8. André Bazin, "De Sica: Metteur en Scène," in *What Is Cinema? Volume 2*, ed. and trans. Hugh Gray (Berkeley: University of California Press, 1971), 72.

9. Ibid., 69.

10. André Bazin, "The Ontology of the Photographic Image," in *What Is Cinema? Volume 1*, ed. and trans. Hugh Gray (Berkeley: University of California Press, 1967), 15.

11. See Krzysztof Ziarek, *The Historicity of Experience: Modernity, the Avant-Garde, and the Event* (Evanston, Ill.: Northwestern University Press, 2001); Miriam Hansen, "Benjamin and Cinema: Not a One-Way Street," *Critical Inquiry* 25.2 (Winter 1999): 306–43; Howard Caygill, *Walter Benjamin: The Colour of Experience* (London: Routledge, 1998); Giorgio Agamben, *Infancy and History: The Destruction of Experience*, trans. Liz Heron (London: Verso, 1993); and, most recently, Martin Jay's chapter "Lamenting the Crisis of Experience: Benjamin and Adorno," in his *Songs of Experience: Modern American and European Variations on a Universal Theme* (Berkeley: University of California Press, 2005), 312–60.

12. I am indebted here and throughout this chapter to Ziarek's formulation of the "event-structure of experience," an experience that unfolds like the "propriative event" (*Ereignis*) in Martin Heidegger's phenomenological formulation, never a self-identical "temporal punctuality or an instant of presence, but instead, a dynamic and open-ended field of forces, whose historicity prevents experience from closing into representational constructs, physic spaces, or lived instants." As a result, event-structured experience, in sharing "radical de-essentialization of happening" itself, is "always open to the future and transformation." Ziarek, *Historicity of Experience*, 14, 4.

13. Jane Bennett, *The Enchantment of Modern Life: Attachments, Crossings, Ethics* (Princeton: Princeton University Press, 2001), 3.

14. Benjamin's "Doctrine of the Similar" (1933), 697; see also the revision of the same, "On the Mimetic Faculty" (1933), as well as "On Astrology" (1932) and "The Lamp," in *Walter Benjamin: Selected Writings, Vol. 2: 1927–1934*, ed. Michael W. Jennings, Howard Eiland, and Gary Smith, trans. Rodney Livingstone et al. (Cambridge, Mass.: Belknap Press, 1999), 694–98, 720–72, 684–85, 691–93, respectively. See the "Second Version" of the Artwork essay, which, as Hansen has argued, is centrally concerned with the mimetic potential of cinema, a dimension that all but drops out of the essay's later, more familiar and more Brechtian version. See Hansen, "Benjamin and Cinema" and "Benjamin, Cinema, and Experience: 'The Blue Flower in the Land of Technology,'" *New German Critique* 40 (Winter 1987): 179–224.

15. Cornell, "'Enchanted Wanderer,'" 207.

16. Cornell, qtd. in Keller, *Untutored Eye*, 106. While Keller reads the collage trilogy's structure as an attempt to "mimic the mental organization of the child," she is primarily interested in how childhood becomes a "veil" through which Cornell reveals his repressed sexuality (139, 111).

17. Hansen, "Benjamin and Cinema," 323.

18. On color as a trope for a transformative model of experiential potential, see Benjamin's early fragments "Aphorisms on Imagination and Color" (1914–15) and "A Child's View of Color" in *Selected Writings, Vol. 1: 1913–1926*, ed. Marcus Bullock and Michael W. Jennings (Cambridge, Mass.: Belknap Press, 1996). See also Caygill's argument for the centrality of color to Benjamin's post-Kantian concept of experience in *Colour of Experience.*

19. For a superb account of this crisis of production, see Douglas Mao, *Solid Objects: Modernism and the Test of Production* (Princeton: Princeton University Press, 2002). For a compelling reading of the materialist politics of things in Cornell's work, see Juan Suárez's "Joseph Cornell and the Secret Life of Things" in his *Pop Modernism: Noise and the Reinvention of the Everyday* (Urbana: University of Illinois Press, 2007).

20. Mary Anne Doane, *The Emergence of Cinematic Time: Modernity, Contingency, the Archive* (Cambridge, Mass.: Harvard University Press, 2002), 3–4.

21. Suárez, "Joseph Cornell," 183.

22. On Cornell's wartime labors, see Deborah Solomon's biography, *Utopia Parkway: The Life and Work of Joseph Cornell* (Boston: MFA Publications, 1997), 148.

23. On Cornell's moody and magical temperament, see Mary Ann Caws, "Joseph Cornell as Seen by Others," in *Joseph Cornell's Theater of the Mind*. See also Solomon, *Utopia Parkway.*

24. For two recent attempts to think through the kind of agency involved in a mood, see Charles Altieri, *The Particulars of Rapture: An Aesthetics of the Affects* (Ithaca: Cornell University Press, 2004); and Sianne Ngai's *Ugly Feelings* (Cambridge, Mass.: Harvard University Press, 2005).

25. Martin Heidegger, *Being and Time,* trans. John Macquarrie and Edward Robinson (New York: Harper and Row, 1963), 395, 173. See also Charles Guignon, "Moods in Heidegger's Being and Time," in *What Is an Emotion? Classic Readings in Philosophical Psychology,* ed. Cheshire Calhoun and Robert C. Solomon (New York: Oxford University Press, 1984), 180–90.

26. Heidegger, *Being and Time,* 231.

27. Ibid., 232 (emphasis in original).

28. Heidegger, qtd. in Guignon, "Moods," 187.

29. Guignon, "Moods," 187–89.

30. Kelly Oliver, *Family Values: Subjects between Nature and Culture* (London: Routledge, 1997), 95.

31. Ibid., 95.

32. Emmanuel Levinas, "Difficult Freedom," in *The Levinas Reader,* ed. Sean Hand (Oxford: Blackwell, 1989), 257. For more on Levinas's critique of ontology (specifically of a Heideggerian kind), see also his *Totality and Infinity: An Essay on Exteriority,* trans. Alphonso Lingis (Pittsburgh: Duquesne University Press, 1969).

33. Tom Gunning, "The Cinema of Attractions," in *Early Cinema: Space, Frame, Narrative,* ed. Thomas Elsaesser (London: British Film Institute, 1990), 57, 58.

34. Philip Fisher, *Wonder, the Rainbow, and the Aesthetics of Rare Experiences* (Cambridge, Mass.: Harvard University Press, 1998), 6.

35. Charles Baudelaire, "The Painter of Modern Life," in *Charles Baudelaire: Selected Writings on Art and Literature,* trans. P. E. Charvet (London: Penguin Books, 1992), 403.

36. Henry Jenkins, *What Made Pistachio Nuts? Early Sound Comedy and the Vaudeville Aesthetic* (New York: Columbia University Press, 1992), 63.

37. Gilles Deleuze, *Nietzsche and Philosophy,* trans. Hugh Tomlinson (London: Athlone Press, 1983), 48.

38. Gilles Deleuze, *Difference and Repetition,* trans. Paul Patton (New York: Columbia University Press, 1994), 41.

39. Deleuze, *Nietzsche and Philosophy,* 190.

40. Ngai, *Ugly Feelings,* 250.

41. Arthur, *Line of Sight,* 140.

42. Ibid., 141.

43. Jacques Derrida, "Signature, Event, Context," in *Limited Inc* (Evanston, Ill.: Northwestern University Press, 1993), 12.

44. Derrida emphasizes that "*iter,* again, probably comes from *itara,* 'other' in Sanskrit, and everything that follows can be read as the working out the logic that ties repetition to alterity," a logic that aligns his project with the Deleuze of *Difference and Repetition.* Derrida, "Signature, Event, Context," 7.

45. Here, I borrow Bennett's useful formulation of "enchanted materialism" to designate the capacity for wonder immanent in the material world, conceived apart from a divine telos: "A world capable of enchanting need not be designed, or predisposed towards human happiness, or expressive of intrinsic purpose or meaning." Bennett, *Enchantment,* 11.

Chapter 6: Dead Pan

1. See Nathanael West's letter of 5 April 1939 to F. Scott Fitzgerald: "Somehow or other, I seem to have slipped in between all the 'schools.' My books meet no needs except my own, their circulation is practically private and I'm lucky to be published. And yet I only have a desire to remedy all that *before* sitting down to write, once begun I do it my way. I forget the broad sweep, the big canvas, the shot-gun adjectives, the important people, the significant ideas, the lessons to be taught, the epic Thomas Wolfe, the realistic James Farrell—and go on making what one critic called 'private and unfunny jokes.'" Qtd. in Jay Martin, *Nathanael West: The Art of His Life* (New York: Farrar, Straus and Giroux, 1970), 334.

2. Nathanael West, *Miss Lonelyhearts,* in *Nathanael West: Novels and Other Writings,* ed. Sacvan Bercovitch (New York: Library of America, 1997), 68.

3. See Gilbert Seldes's chapter "Burlesque, Circus, Clowns, and Acrobats" in his *The Seven Lively Arts* (New York: A. S. Barnes, 1962), 251.

4. Jonathan Veitch, *American Superrealism: Nathanael West and the Politics of Representation in the 1930s* (Madison: University of Wisconsin Press, 1997), 76.

5. I second Barnard's sense that, for the West of *Miss Lonelyhearts,* the only "possibility left open for a writer was not the creation but the critique of culture," here specifically a critique of the novel's affirmative force—its purchase on *Bildung,* or its Lukácsian function as a redemptive social totality. But I want to extend the scope of this critique to include West's unworking of the terms of modern community and publicness. See Rita Barnard, *The Great Depression and the Culture of Abundance: Kenneth Fearing, Nathanael West, and Mass Culture in the 1930s* (Cambridge: Cambridge University Press, 1995), 210.

6. On the often reactionary politics of modernist antisentimentalism, see Suzanne Clark's *Sentimental Modernism: Women Writers and the Revolution of the Word* (Bloomington: Indiana University Press, 1991). Glenn Hendler describes the sympathetic structure of the bourgeois public sphere thus: "Just as the experience of sympathy depended upon a fantasy that differences could be effaced by defining human identity affectively, publicity depended upon a fictional erasure of status attributes." See *Public Sentiments: Structures of Feeling in Nineteenth-Century American Literature* (Chapel Hill: University of North Carolina Press, 2001), 19.

7. Miriam Hansen, "Fallen Women, Rising Stars, New Horizons: Shanghai Silent Film as Vernacular Modernism," *Film Quarterly* 54.1 (2000): 10. See also Hansen's "Mass Production of the Senses: Classical Cinema as Vernacular Modernism," *Modernism/Modernity* 6.2 (April 1999): 59–77.

8. My argument is indebted to James English's observation that the "problematic within and upon which joke-work takes place" is always that of community itself—its production or failure, its inclusions and exclusions, its ideologies of affect. See English's *Comic Transactions: Literature, Humor, and the Politics of Community in Twentieth-Century Britain* (Ithaca: Cornell University Press, 1994), 19.

9. See West's "Through the Hole in the Mundane Millstone" in *Nathanael West,* ed. Bercovitch, 397.

10. André Breton, "Lightning Rod," in his *Anthology of Black Humor,* trans. Mark Polizzotti (San Francisco: City Lights Books, 1997), xix.

11. Thus, Romantic self-reflection, for Breton, allows both for a heightened receptivity to the material world, or what Breton calls, referencing Hegel's notion of "objective humor," a "penetration" or "[captivation] by the object in its real form," and for subjective detachment—a repudiation of the contingency of the external (*Anthology of Black Humor,* xvi). Of course, Breton's attempt—in the anthology and elsewhere—to theorize black humor as the triumphant resolution of the Romantic subject and the material world failed to impress his critics, who found his reorientation toward the object merely another occasion for narcissistic lyricism and oneiric wankery. Here, Henri Lefebvre's attack is most representative: surrealist poetry produced only "an illusory fusing of subject with object in transcendental metabolism. Their purely verbal metamorphosis, anamorphosis or anaphorization of the relationship between

'subjects' (people) and things (the realm of everyday life) overloaded meaning—and changed nothing." Henri Lefebvre, *The Production of Space,* trans. Donald Nicholson Smith (Oxford: Blackwell, 1991), 19.

12. See Giorgio Agamben's formulation of Romantic irony in *The Man without Content,* trans. Georgia Albert (Stanford: Stanford University Press, 1999), 55. Surrealist black humor also reprises the Baudelairian laughter that stems from "the feeling of joy at [man's] own superiority and the joy of man's superiority over nature." Charles Baudelaire, "Of the Essence of Laughter, and Generally of the Comic in the Plastic Arts," in *Charles Baudelaire: Selected Writings on Art and Literature,* trans. P. E. Charvet (London: Penguin, 1992), 161.

13. Georges Bataille, *Theory of Religion,* trans. Robert Hurley (New York: Zone Books, 1992), 17–18.

14. Ibid., 40.

15. Nathanael West, "Some Notes on *Miss L,*" in *Nathanael West,* ed. Bercovitch, 401.

16. While Miss Lonelyhearts's particular relationship to slapstick is overlooked and undertheorized, West's broader fascination with burlesque, vaudeville, and the tradition of slapstick comedy has long been noted by his critics. Jay Martin, West's biographer, speculates that a healthy portion of West's adolescent leisure time was spent exploring New York's many burlesque theaters and vaudeville houses; he read Bernard Sobel's *Burleycue* (1931), one of the first cultural histories of burlesque, as he started work on *Miss Lonelyhearts;* he got to know personally many of the old burlesque and vaudeville comics who had moved to Hollywood to find work in the 1930s; his brother-in-law and close friend, S. J. Perelman, co-wrote the script for the Marx Brothers film *Monkey Business* (1931); and his work is replete with knockabout slapstick routines and burlesque characters, perhaps most famously the broken-down vaude Harry Greener in *The Day of the Locust* (1939).

17. Here I have in mind the terms of West's "Some Notes on Violence," his response to Hugh Sykes Davies's sniffy denunciation of the lamb episode as an "almost pathological" depiction of emotion: "If an 'emotional description' in the European sense is given an act of violence, the American should say, 'What's all the excitement about,' or, 'By God, that's a mighty fine piece of writing, that's art.'" West, "Some Notes on Violence," in *Nathanael West,* ed. Bercovitch, 399.

18. On vaudeville comedy's challenge to the "refined" comedy of the nineteenth century, see Henry Jenkins, *What Made Pistachio Nuts? Early Sound Comedy and the Vaudeville Aesthetic* (New York: Columbia University Press, 1992), 28.

19. See Albert McLean Jr., *American Vaudeville as Ritual* (Lexington: University of Kentucky Press, 1965), 119. See also Brett Page, *Writing for Vaudeville* (Springfield, Ill.: Home Correspondence School, 1913), 74–79. Further connecting the affective dynamics of West's comic-strip novel and the tradition of vaudeville laughter is Jenkins's observation that the burgeoning popularity of the comic strip in the early twentieth century was itself the most obvious instance of "the large-scale commodi-

fiction of the joke" that shaped the New Humor. Jenkins, *What Made Pistachio Nuts?*, 38.

20. On vaudeville's coarse system of ethnic stereotyping and its debt to the American minstrel tradition, see Robert Snyder's *The Voice of the City: Vaudeville and Popular Culture in New York* (New York: Oxford University Press, 1989), 110. On the politics of minstrelsy, see especially Eric Lott, *Love and Theft: Blackface Minstrelsy and the American Working Class* (New York: Oxford University Press, 1995); and Michael Rogin, *Blackface, White Noise: Jewish Immigrants in the Hollywood Melting Pot* (Berkeley: University of California Press, 1998).

21. George M. Cohan and George J. Nathan, "The Mechanics of Emotion," *McClure's*, November 1913, 70.

22. Ibid., 70–71.

23. Ibid., 74, 70–71.

24. Page, *Writing for Vaudeville*, 101–2. Interestingly, Page first countenances the particularity of humor before assuring the future gag scribbler of the transcendent appeal of certain themes: "'Each eye,' the Italians say, 'forms its own beauty,' so every nation, every section, and each individual forms its own humor to suit its own peculiar risibilities. Still, there are certain well-defined kinds of stories and classes of points in which we Americans find a certain delight" (71). See also Page's warnings against overly localized themes in vaudeville monologues (81).

25. Ibid., 100.

26. Frank Capra qtd. in Alan Dale, *Comedy Is a Man in Trouble: Slapstick in American Movies* (Minneapolis: University of Minnesota Press, 2000), 10.

27. Lew Weber and Joe Fields qtd. in Page, *Writing for Vaudeville*, 103. In the early twentieth century, such claims for the slapstick clown's universal laughter—of the circus clown as the very principle of affective universality—would find their seeming realization in the class-transcendent global sensation of Charlie Chaplin, which itself helped bolster another potent modern myth about cinema's own hieroglyphic universality.

28. Bill Brown, "The Secret Life of Things (Virginia Woolf and the Matter of Modernism)," *Modernism/Modernity* 6.2 (April 1999): 3.

29. Hansen, "Mass Production," 71; Simmel qtd. in Brown, "Secret Life," 12.

30. In this sense, West's novel seems to confirm a governing assumption of Tyrus Miller's revision of modernist periodization—namely, that the transcendent negation of a traumatic socius became more difficult during "late modernism." And yet West's joking eschews what Miller identifies as the self-defensive, self-confirming laughter that pervades late modernism and marks "the minimal 'spatial' difference between conscious life and the pure extensivity of dead nature: a difference that preserves the subject, however diminished, in situations of adversity." Tyrus Miller, *Late Modernism: Politics, Fiction, and the Arts between the World Wars* (Berkeley: University of California Press, 1999), 51.

31. This is Miriam Hansen's translation of Siegfried Kracauer's (writing under the

pseudonym "Raca") "Chaplin (on *The Gold Rush*)," *Frankfurter Zeitung,* 6 November 1926, in her "America, Paris, the Alps: Kracauer (and Benjamin) on Cinema and Modernity," in *Cinema and the Invention of Modern Life,* ed. Leo Charney and Vanessa R. Schwartz (Berkeley: University of California Press, 1995), 373. Kracauer saw in the comic antics of circus clowns the anarchic remainder of capitalist modernity, belying dreams of total rationalization: "One has to hand this to the Americans: with slapstick films they have created a form that offers a counterweight to their reality. If in that reality they subject the world to an often unbearable discipline, the film in turn dismantles this self-imposed order quite forcefully." See "Artistisches und Amerikanisches," *Frankfurter Zeitung,* 29 January 1926, qtd. in Hansen, "America," 373.

32. Veitch, *American Superrealism,* 35.

33. Nathanael West, *The Dream Life of Balso Snell,* in *Nathanael West,* ed. Bercovitch, 9.

34. See Georges Bataille's "The Big Toe" in *Visions of Excess: Selected Writings, 1927–39,* ed. Allan Stoekl, trans. Allan Stoekl, Carl R. Lovitt, and Donald M. Leslie Jr. (Minneapolis: University of Minnesota Press, 1985). See Veitch, *American Superrealism,* for more on the connections between *Balso's* critique of Western idealism and Bataille's materialism.

35. W. H. Auden, "Interlude: West's Disease," in Jay Martin, comp., *Nathanael West: A Collection of Critical Essays* (Englewood Cliffs: Prentice-Hall, 1971), 121.

36. Veitch, *American Superrealism,* 74.

37. Notice that West anticipates Ann Douglas's well-known argument that sentimental discourse lays the ideological groundwork for the emotional rhetoric of consumerism that dominates twentieth-century mass culture. See Douglas, *The Feminization of American Culture* (New York: Farrar, Straus, Giroux, 1998).

38. On West's sincerity regarding such "materialization[s] of wishing," see Barnard, *Great Depression,* 166, 173.

39. As comic Bert Williams puts it, slapstick's joke depends not just on really knowing that the pain is false but upon a secondary identification with the comedic victim ("I feel like you") that proceeds from an initial distinction ("I'm glad I don't feel like you"): "This is human nature. If you will observe your own conduct whenever you see a friend falling down the street, you will find that nine times out of ten your first impulse is to laugh and your second is to run and help get him up." Williams qtd. in Dale, *Comedy,* 12.

40. I suspect West's description of his hero's resounding defeat at the hands of a clock may have been inspired by the famous scene in Chaplin's *The Pawnshop* (1916) in which the Tramp thoroughly disembowels an alarm clock that an unsuspecting customer has brought to him for cash.

41. Recall Henri Bergson's argument in *Le Rire* (1900) that comic automatism in humans signals an "*absentmindedness* on the part of life," a collision of the habitual and the variable indicative of a dangerous unsociability—a mechanical breach in the

élan vital. See Bergson's "Laughter" in *Comedy,* ed. Wylie Sypher (Baltimore: Johns Hopkins University Press, 1980), 117.

42. Max Horkheimer and Theodor W. Adorno, *Dialectic of Enlightenment: Philosophical Fragments*, trans. Edmund Jephcott (Stanford: Stanford University Press, 2002), 78.

43. Here I have in mind the way the critical dynamics of Westian slapstick recall Horkheimer and Adorno's reading of Sade and Nietzsche as "dark writers of the bourgeoisie," whose work exaggerates, and monstrously inverts, the structural logic of the Age of Reason. In *Miss Lonelyhearts,* West seconds Horkheimer and Adorno's antihumanist critique of the ideology of emotion: namely, that the cult of feeling emerges to ameliorate emotion's actual eclipse in the logic of self-preservation that structures the economic system, but that "the elevation of feelings to an ideology does not abolish the contempt in which they are really held." See Horkheimer and Adorno, "Excursus II: Juliette, Or Enlightenment and Morality," in *Dialectic of Enlightenment,* 92, 72.

44. Giorgio Agamben, "Notes on Gesture," in *Means without End: Notes on Politics,* trans. Vincenzo Binetti and Cesare Casarino (Minneapolis: University of Minnesota Press, 2000), 51.

45. Giorgio Agamben, "Kommerell, or On Gesture," in *Potentialities: Collected Essays in Philosophy,* trans. Daniel Heller-Roazen (Stanford: Stanford University Press, 1999), 84.

46. Here I have in mind Walter Benjamin's concept of "innervation" as an experiential shuttle between the technologized embodiments of mass culture (Shrike's moving-picture comedians) and personal and collective affect. For better or worse, Shrike's deadpan is the result of a human physiognomy that, in Benjamin's terms, has made technology its organ. On mimetic innervation, see Benjamin's second version of "The Work of Art in the Age of Its Technological Reproducibility" in Walter Benjamin: Selected Writings, Vol. 3, 1935–1938, ed. Michael W. Jennings, Howard Eiland, and Gary Smith, trans. Rodney Livingstone et al. (Cambridge, Mass.: Harvard University Press, 2002), and Miriam Hansen's "Benjamin and Cinema: Not a One-Way Street," *Critical Inquiry* 25.2 (Winter 1999): 306–43.

47. On modernism's "symptomatic" relationship with mass visuality, see Nancy Armstrong, *Fiction in the Age of Photography: The Legacy of British Realism* (Cambridge, Mass.: Harvard University Press, 1999).

48. Agamben's dialectical logic proceeds as follows: insofar as the reign of spectacle represents "the extreme form of the expropriation of the Common," exacerbating the "estrangement of the communicative essence of human beings," it allows, in a dynamic reversal, "for human beings to experience their own linguistic essence." Agamben, *Means without End,* 82, 84, 85.

49. West, *Dream Life of Balso Snell,* 25.

50. Bergson, "Laughter," 117.

51. On this circular logic of this metaphysical operation, and for a superb post-

structuralist account of affect, see Rei Terada, *Feeling in Theory: Emotion after the "Death of the Subject"* (Cambridge, Mass.: Harvard University Press, 2001).

52. Clark, *Sentimental Modernism*, 9.

53. See Clark's account of modernist antisentimentalism's bad faith, as well as Eve Kosofsky Sedgwick's influential formulation of the discourse of sentimentalism as a vicariously self-implicating structure of relation that operates by the logic "It takes a sentimentalist to know a sentimentalist." See Sedgwick's *Epistemology of the Closet* (Berkeley: University of California Press, 1990), 156. For a trenchant reassessment of modernist anti-sentimentality that bends it toward the ethical, see Jessica Burstein, "A Few Words about Dubuque: Modernism, Sentimentalism, and the Blasé," *American Literary History* 14.2 (2002): 227–54.

Chapter 7: The Passion to Be a Person

1. Djuna Barnes, *Nightwood* (1936; New York: New Directions, 1961), 65.

2. Rei Terada, *Feeling in Theory: Emotion after the "Death of the Subject"* (Cambridge, Mass.: Harvard University Press, 2001), 5.

3. For an attentive reading of *Nightwood*'s laughter as a form of defensive self-preservation and marker of the death throes of modernism's formal gambits, see Tyrus Miller, "Beyond Rescue: Djuna Barnes," in *Late Modernism: Politics, Fiction, and the Arts between the World Wars (Berkeley: University of California Press, 1999).*

4. I borrow this nifty formulation from Charles Altieri's talk "Impersonality and the Limitations of Personality," part of the Approaching Impersonality panel at MSA 7: The Modernist Studies Association Conference, Chicago, Illinois, 3–5 November 2005.

5. T. S. Eliot, "Tradition and the Individual Talent," in *Selected Essays,* ed. Frank Kermode (London: Faber and Faber, 1932), 18. The classic account of Eliotic impersonality is Maud Ellman's *The Poetics of Impersonality: T. S. Eliot and Ezra Pound* (Brighton, Eng.: Harvester Press, 1987). For a provocative rethinking of this doctrine's relationship to erotic and textual perversion, see Colleen Lamos, *Deviant Modernism: Sexual and Textual Errancy in T. S. Eliot, James Joyce, and Marcel Proust* (Cambridge: Cambridge University Press, 1998).

6. Eliot, "Swinburne as Poet," in *Selected Essays,* ed. Kermode, 327.

7. Philip Rahv, "The Taste of Nothing," *New Masses* 23.7 (May 1937): 32.

8. Ibid., 33.

9. See Marsden Hartley's unpublished review of *Nightwood* in his papers in YCAL.

10. Joseph Boone, "Queer Sites in Modernism: Harlem/The Left Bank/Greenwich Village in the 1920s and 1930s," in *Libidinal Currents: Sexuality and the Shaping of Modernism* (Chicago: University of Chicago Press, 1996), 235; Hartley, review of *Nightwood*, YCAL.

11. Hartley, review of *Nightwood,* YCAL.

12. Ibid.

13. Ibid.

14. Ibid.

15. T. S. Eliot, "The Love Song of J. Alfred Prufrock," in *T. S. Eliot: Selected Poems* (New York: Harcourt, 1936), 13.

16. Hartley, review of *Nightwood*, YCAL.

17. *Hamlet*, Pelican edition, ed. Willard Farnham (New York: Penguin, 1970), 1.5.15–22:

> I could a tale unfold whose lightest word
> Would harrow up thy soul, freeze thy young blood,
> Make thy two eyes like stars start from their spheres,
> Thy knotted and combined locks to part,
> And each particular hair to stand on end
> Like quills upon the fretful porpentine.
> But this eternal blazon must not be
> To ears of flesh and blood.

18. Hartley, review of *Nightwood*, YCAL.

19. See Hannah Arendt's formulation of the publicness as "the Common" in *The Human Condition* (Chicago: University of Chicago Press, 1958), 50–58.

20. Aristotle, *De Partibus Animalum*, qtd. in Simon Critchley, "Is Humor Human?," in *Becoming Human: New Perspectives on the Inhuman Condition*, ed. Paul Sheehan (Westport, Conn.: Praeger, 2003), 42.

21. Martin Heidegger, *The Fundamental Concepts of Metaphysics: World, Finitude, Solitude*, trans. William McNeill and Nicholas Walker (Bloomington: Indiana University Press, 1995).

22. Henri Bergson, "Laughter," in *Comedy*, ed. Wylie Sypher (Baltimore: Johns Hopkins University Press, 1980), 62 (emphasis in original).

23. See especially Brian Massumi, *Parables for the Virtual: Movement, Affect, Sensation* (Durham: Duke University Press, 2002); and Michael Hardt, *Gilles Deleuze: An Apprenticeship in Philosophy* (Minneapolis: University of Minnesota Press, 1993).

24. Elizabeth Pochoda, "Style's Hoax: A Reading of Djuna Barnes's *Nightwood*," *Twentieth-Century Literature* 22.2 (May 1976): 183.

25. Philip Fisher, *The Vehement Passions* (Princeton: Princeton University Press, 2002), 57 (emphasis in original).

26. Ibid., 57.

27. Boone, *Libidinal Currents*, 249.

28. I borrow this suggestive characterization of Felix and O'Connor's dialogue from Laura Marcus's "Laughing at Leviticus: *Nightwood* as Women's Circus Epic," in *Silence and Power: Djuna Barnes, a Reevaluation*, ed. Mary Lynn Broe (Carbondale: Southern Illinois University Press, 1991), 236.

29. Erin Carlston, *Thinking Fascism: Sapphic Modernism and Fascist Modernity* (Stanford: Stanford University Press, 1998), 66.

30. See Boone, Libidinal Currents, 249.

31. Jacques Derrida, "The Animal That Therefore I Am (More to Follow)," trans. David Willis, *Critical Inquiry* 28 (Winter 2002): 381 (emphasis in original).

NOTES TO PAGES 240–47 · 299

32. Charles Darwin, *The Expression of the Emotions in Man and Animals* (London: John Murray, 1872), 82.

33. Ibid., 106.

34. Max Nordau, *Degeneration,* trans. George L. Mosse (Lincoln: University of Nebraska Press, 1993), 324–25. For a reading of *Nightwood*'s "bestiality" in the context of the sexological "science" and its idiom of degeneration, see Dana Seitler's "Down on All Fours: Atavistic Perversions and the Science of Desire from Frank Norris to Djuna Barnes," *American Literature* 73.3 (September 2001): 525–62.

35. For a helpful discussion of Darwin's departure from Bell's conviction that grimaces and smiles were forms of a natural language of transcendental origin, see Lucy Hartley, "Universal Expressions: Darwin and the Naturalization of Emotion," in *Physiognomy and the Meaning of Expression in Nineteenth-Century Culture* (Cambridge: Cambridge University Press, 2001).

36. Giorgio Agamben, "What Is a People?" in *Means without End: Notes on Politics,* trans. Vincenzo Binetti and Cesare Casarino (Minneapolis: University of Minnesota Press, 2000), 31.

37. See Giorgio Agamben's searching meditation on this machine's historical and philosophical operation in *The Open: Man and Animal,* trans. Kevin Attell (Stanford: Stanford University Press), 21, 29.

38. In what follows, I treat as a unitary meditation what are, it should be noted, four discrete pieces of writing: "The People and the Sea: How they Get Together" (1913), "The Tingling, Tangling Tango as 'Tis Tripped at Coney Isle" (1913), "If Noise Were Forbidden at Coney Island, a Lot of People Would Lose Their Jobs" (1914), and "Surcease in Hurry and Whirl—On the Restless Surf at Coney" (1917). All are included in Djuna Barnes, *New York,* ed. Alice Barry (London: Virago Press, 1990).

39. I have in mind here Siegfried Kracauer's well-known remarks on how the discontinuous, fragmented variety format of the opulent Berlin picture palaces contributed to a "cult of distraction." Predicated on the celebration of sensuous surfaces (what Kracauer calls "pure externality"), such distraction revealed and compensated for an experiential hole in modern man. See Kracauer, "The Cult of Distraction," in *The Mass Ornament: Weimar Essays,* trans. and ed. Thomas Y. Levin (Cambridge, Mass.: Harvard University Press, 1995), 326.

40. For earlier discussion of the relationship between "ex-appropriation," the logic of the trace, and Derridean ethics, see Jean-Luc Nancy, "'Eating Well,' or the Calculation of the Subject: An Interview with Jacques Derrida," in *Who Comes After the Subject?,* ed. Eduardo Cadava, Peter Connor, and Jean-Luc Nancy (London: Routledge, 1991), esp. 105–11.

41. Letter from Djuna Barnes to Emily Coleman, qtd. in Bonnie Kime Scott, "Barnes Being 'Beast Familiar': Representation on the Margins of Modernism," *Review of Contemporary Fiction* 13 (Fall 193): 41.

42. Gabriel Tarde, *The Laws of Imitation,* trans. Elsie Clews Parsons (Gloucester: Peter Smith, 1962), 87.

43. Akira Mizuta Lippit, *Electric Animal: Toward a Rhetoric of Wildlife* (Minneapolis: University of Minnesota Press, 2000), 121, 2.

44. Barnes uses the phrase "hilarious sorrow" to describe O'Connor's language in a letter to Emily Coleman. See Phillip Herring, *Djuna: The Life and Work of Djuna Barnes* (New York: Penguin Books, 1995), 213.

45. Lippit offers a useful overview of this tradition in *Electric Animal*, 42–54.

46. On the place of ecstasy in a theory of community without "individuality, in the precise sense of the term" or "pure collective totality," see Jean-Luc Nancy, *The Inoperative Community*, trans. Peter Connor (Minneapolis: University of Minnesota Press, 1991), 6.

47. Gilles Deleuze and Félix Guattari, *A Thousand Plateaus: Capitalism and Schizophrenia*, trans. Brian Massumi (Minneapolis: University of Minnesota Press, 1987), 237, 258.

48. Ibid., 258. On becoming-animal as an engagement with animal capacity, see Paul Patton, *Deleuze and the Political* (London: Routledge, 2000).

49. Heidegger, *Fundamental Concepts of Metaphysics*, 248. For powerful critiques of the essential difference Heidegger draws between the animal's poverty in world and the human's status as "world-forming," see Jacques Derrida's *Of Spirit: Heidegger and the Question*, trans. Geoff Bennington and Rachel Bowlby (Chicago: University of Chicago Press, 1989), and, more recently, Cary Wolfe's "In the Shadow of Wittgenstein's Lion: Language, Ethics, and the Question of the Animal" in *Zoontologies: The Question of the Animal*, ed. Cary Wolfe (Minneapolis: University of Minnesota Press, 2003). See also Agamben's return to the question of the poverty of the animal for an ethical project in which the human "appropriates his own concealedness, his own animality, which neither remains hidden nor is made an object of mastery, but is thought as such, as pure abandonment" (*The Open*, 80).

50. Heidegger, Agamben argues, intends the moth as a reference to mystical knowledge, a problematic allusion since the mystical knowledge depends upon the experience of non-knowledge as such, while the moth is blind to its captivation by the flame (*The Open*, 60). For a compelling reading of *Nightwood*'s final scene as a mode of mystical speech, see Miller, *Late Modernism*.

Epilogue: Charlie Chaplin and the Revenge of the Eccentric

1. On the postwar Parisian avant-garde's reception of "Charlot" as a figure of modern, cinematic beauty, see Louis Dulluc, "Beauty in the Cinema" (1917), and Louis Aragon, "On Decor" (1918), in Richard Abel, ed., *French Film Theory and Criticism: Volume 1: 1907–1939* (Princeton: Princeton University Press, 1988), 137–39, 167–68. See also Sabine Hake, "Chaplin's Reception in Weimar Germany," *New German Critique* 51 (Autumn 1990): 87–111. On Chaplin's role in a modernism's comic and corporeal poetics, see Susan McCabe, "Delight in Dislocation: The Cinematic Modernism of Stein, Chaplin, and Man Ray," *Modernism/Modernity* 8.3 (September 2001): 429–52.

2. Walter Benjamin, "Negative Expressionism," qtd. in Esther Leslie, *Hollywood Flatlands: Animation, Critical Theory, and the Avant-Garde* (London: Verso, 2002), 16.

3. Siegfried Kracauer's review of *The Gold Rush* (1926) qtd. in Hake, "Chaplin's Reception," 93.

4. Thomas Burke, quoted in Alan Dale, *Comedy Is a Man in Trouble: Slapstick in American Movies* (Minneapolis: University of Minnesota Press, 2000), 37.

5. Gilles Deleuze, *Cinema 1: The Movement Image,* trans. Hugh Tomlinson and Barbara Habberjam (Minneapolis: University of Minnesota Press, 2003), 169.

6. André Bazin, "Charlie Chaplin," in *What Is Cinema? Volume 1,* ed. and trans. Hugh Gray (Berkeley: University of California Press, 1967), 149.

7. Sergei Eisenstein, "Charlie the Kid," in *Film Essays, with a Lecture,* ed. and trans. Jay Leyda (London: Dennis Dobson, 1968), 108–39.

8. Deleuze, *Cinema 1,* 171.

9. The remarks of the prosecuting attorney in the case, Joseph Scott, are reproduced in D. William Davis, "A Tale of Two Movies: Charlie Chaplin, United Artists, and the Red Scare," *Cinema Journal* 27.1 (Fall 1987): 48.

10. André Bazin, "The Myth of Monsieur Verdoux," in *What Is Cinema? Volume 2,* ed. and trans. Hugh Gray (Berkeley: University of California Press, 1971), 106.

11. Ibid., 106.

12. Ibid., 115.

13. Oscar Wilde, "Pen, Pencil, and Poison: A Study in Green," in *Intentions* (New York: Albert and Charles Boni, 1930), 65.

14. Ibid., 89.

15. Ibid., 90; Rita Felski, *The Gender of Modernity* (Cambridge, Mass.: Harvard University Press, 1995), 95.

16. See Arnaud D'Usseau's "Chaplin's *Monsieur Verdoux*" in the Communist journal *Mainstream* 1 (Summer 1947): 309.

17. George Wallach's recording of "Charlie Chaplin's *Monsieur Verdoux* Press Conference" has been recently reprinted in *Charlie Chaplin Interviews,* ed. Kevin J. Hayes (Jackson: University Press of Mississippi, 2005), 103–18.

18. Chaplin qtd. in Davis, "Tale of Two Movies," 53. For a detailed account of this press campaign, see also Charles Maland, *Chaplin and American Culture: The Evolution of a Star Image* (Princeton: Princeton University Press, 1989).

19. Chaplin qtd. in Davis, "Tale of Two Movies," 61.

20. Theodor Adorno, "Chaplin Times Two," trans. John MacKay, *Yale Journal of Criticism* 9.1 (1996): 59.

21. Ibid., 59–60.

Index

acting: biomechanical theories of, 69, 71–76, 83–85; Eccentrism and, 68; experiential schools of, 74; Meyerhold's theories of, 49; vs. mimetic performance, 49; montage and, 74; Soviets and, 67–71; Stanislavky's theories of, 49. *See also* performance; popular performance

Adorno, Theodor, 11–12, 24, 86, 163, 296n43

aestheticism, 21, 50, 66, 240–41, 259–60, 262, 284n24

aesthetics: corporeal nature of, 105; T. S. Eliot, 222–25; of homogeneity, 108–16; idealist, 132; modernist image, 107–8; modernist in Lukács, 76–78; mystical, 158–62; organic sociality, 230–31, 239–42; of satire, 64–66; socialist realism, 76–81; of Stieglitz circle, 139–42, 146–47; of urge to abstraction and, 90

affect: aestheticism and, 21; affective state of unfoldment, 173–78; alienation from, 210–16; animal, 227–29, 247; autonomy of, 94; behaviorism and, 72; of collectivity, 123; comic, 207; compensatory, 172; contagious, 226; deadpan, 204; depersonalization and, 18, 25; desubjectivized, 97; Disney cartoons and, 93; emotion and, 20, 73; Enlightenment ideology of, 215; hostility to reason and instrumentality, 21–23; inhuman, 27, 222; innerva-

tion and, 3–4, 38–39, 45; instinctual, 73; mediated, 97; of modern privation, 266; negative, 121–23; nondiscursive, 95; nonidentitarian, 98; noninstrumental, 71, 98; nonpurposive, 93, 97, 189, 255; plasmatic, 93; postmodern intensity and, 18–19; prediscursive, 20; premodern, 87; pseudomechanics of, 41–42; structured vs. unstructured, 20–21, 69; ungendered, 70; universality and, 27, 196, 202–3, 224–25; unstructured, 94; visual transmission of. *See also* emotion; feeling

Agamben, Giorgio, 123, 214–15, 243, 281n52, 296n46, 300n46, 300n50

Altieri, Charles, 21–22, 94, 173, 290n24, 297n4

Americanization, 67–71, 72, 93, 254–55

animal: animal attraction, 153; animality in language, 246; in Barnes, 219–49; becoming, 248–49; captivation of, 249; desiring body of, 236–37; ethics of animality, 238–42; expressivity, 230–42, 246–49; homosexuality and, 226–29; vs. human, 93, 239–42; laughter and, 28, 220–21, 230–31, 248–49; mimesis and, 85; modernist impersonality and, 27, 226–29; publicness and, 246–47; question of, 221; sacrifice of, 200; secondariness, 232; somnabulism of, 247; suffering, 237–42; thingliness of, 200;

transmission of affect and, 247; within self, 231

antisentimentality. *See* sentimentality

Apollinaire, Guillaume, 199

Appadurai, Arjun, 7

Arendt, Hannah, 14–16, 28, 298n19

Aristotle, 27, 230

Armstrong, Nancy, 287n54, 296n47

Arthur, Paul, 187

Auden, W. H., 206

Baker, Josephine, 16, 112, 114–16, 122, 123, 125, 130

Barnard, Rita, 197

Barnes, Djuna: aestheticism of, 224; animal expressivity and, 28, 230–42, 246–49; biopolitics and, 242–43; characterization in, 219–21, 226; comic technique of, 231–42; depersonalization in public and, 243–49; failure of public feeling and, 27–28; Marsden Hartley and, 225–26; impersonality and, 27–28; journalism of, 243–45; laughter in, 219–21, 230–38; *Nightwood,* 27, 214–49

Barnum, P. T., 11

Barthes, Roland, 78

Bataille, Georges, 84, 200

Baudelaire, Charles, 27, 136, 176, 181, 262, 293n12

Bazin, André, 164, 166, 253, 259

Beckett, Samuel, 77

Beerbohm, Max, 35, 50–51

Benjamin, Walter: aura and, 46, 61–62; Charlie Chaplin and, 4, 251–56; experience and, 3–4, 9, 135–36, 167, 289n14; innervation and, 2–5, 38–39, 45, 71, 296n46; on the mimetic faculty, 167–68, 277n57; mimetic politics and, 24–25; "negative expressionism" and, 69; optical unconscious and, 3–4, 166–67

Benn, Gottfried, 77

Bennett, Jane, 167

Benveniste, Emile, 152

Bergson, Henri: on comedy, 27, 218, 230–31, 239–42; Lewis and, 27, 59

Berlant, Lauren, 25

Blackmur, R. P., 103–5, 111

Bleackley, J. Arthur, 46–51, 61, 64–66; *The Art of Mimicry,* 24, 35, 40, 46–51

Bloch, Ernst, 10

body: and body politic, 243; Chaplinesque, 258; criticism as embodiment, 141–43; "embodied formalism," 139–41; embodied publicness, 4, 26; extraordinary, 109–16, 124–28; female, 211; gestural, 214; hospitality of, 52; inelastic, 230–31, 242; insubstantiality of, 130–32; materiality of, 209; organic movements of, 72–74; of proletariat, 83–85; sculptural, 109–12; in slapstick, 196–97, 262; spectacular, 137–39, 144–48; suffering, 206–7, 211, 228–29, 236; violence to, 117–20

Bordwell, David, 81

Boone, Joseph, 235

Bourke, Johanna, 117

Brammen, Carrie, 109, 119

Brecht, Berthold, 74, 257

Brennan, Marcia, 139, 148, 285n33

Brennan, Teresa, 36

Breton, André, 27, 199–200

Brown, Bill, 126, 161, 278n1

Buck-Morss, Susan, 105

Bunyan, John, 124

Butler, Judith, 4, 221, 228, 229

Byron, Lord, 106

Caffin, Caroline: *Dancers and Dancing of Today,* 35, 52; "Heterodoxy" and, 35; on mimesis, 24, 33–35, 39–51, 61, 63–66; *Vaudeville,* 33, 35, 40–51

Caffin, Charles, 35

Caillois, Roger, 24, 39

Camera Work, 24, 33

Capra, Frank, 202

Cézanne, Paul, 143

Chaplin, Charlie: Bazin on, 253, 259; body of, 258; decline in reputation, 256–57; as an exile, 256–57, 266; *The Great Dictator,* 257; Kracauer on, 203–4; Lewis and, 59–60, 253–54, 266; *Limelight,* 257; *Modern Times,* 257; *Monsieur Verdoux,* 256–66; *The Pawnshop,* 295n40; progressive politics of, 257–58; queerness of, 255–56; repetition and, 253; significance

for modernists, 251–56; the Soviet avant-garde and, 67–71, 254–56
character: of Chaplin, 259; commodification and, 57–58; consistency of, 252; eccentricity of, 231; frozen, 91, 239–40; inelasticity of, 231; inhuman, 256; in Lukács, 77; performance of, 42–46; social legibility of, 74; vitality of, 219
Chevalier, Albert, 42
Chocolate Dandies, 115
cinema: bourgeois vs. revolutionary, 80; "cinema of attractions," 179–80; early, 169; eventfulness of, 71; expressive movement and, 76; found footage, 187–88; as global vernacular, 251; Lewis and, 13, 58–60, 62; montage and, 170, 178–83; the production of group personality and, 58; vaudeville and, 10. *See also* film
Clark, Suzanne, 104
Codona, Alfredo, 16, 151, 155
Cohan, George M., 41, 202
Cole, Sarah, 122
collectivity: abstraction and, 105; in Cummings, 103–32; desire and, 120; ecstatic, 138; Freud and, 18–19, 123–23; in Lewis, 51–66; ludic, 123; as organic, 81; pictured on film, 80
comedy: animal passions and, 28, 220–21, 230–31, 248–49; biopolitics of, 239–42; in "burlesque" modernism, 108; of Chaplin, 251–66; depersonalization and, 27; humour noir and, 198; in Lewis, 51, 57; masochistic, 244; slapstick, 4, 16, 27; in *Strike*, 75. *See also* laughter; slapstick
community: as ecstatic, 39, 51–54, 248; of the image, 92; of impossible people, 242–49; inhuman, 217–18; intimate, 151–58; limits of, 217; organic, 197; outmoded notions of, 197; secured by sympathy, 199, 215; without identity, 215–18
Conrad, Joseph, 18
contingency: of animal existence, 220, 232; archive and, 154, 170; of detail, 78; lure of, 69, 252; of material world, 200; photographic, 85; slapstick and, 262
Cornell, Joseph: collage trilogy (*Cotillion, The Midnight Party, The Children's Party*),

164, 178–91; eroticism and, 164, 174–78; filmmaking of, 163–64; found footage format and, 187–88; mimesis and, 26; mimesis in, 168–90; mood and, 26, 171–78; public feeling in, 171–78; public intimacy and, 25; repetition and, 182–88; romanticism of, 26, 163, 167, 180; *Rose Hobart*, 182–83; theories of experience in, 26, 163–91; *Vaudeville De Luxe*, 185, 186
Cummings, E. E.: "The Adult, the Artist, and the Circus," 103; comradeship and, 26, 105, 121–23; *Eimi*, 106; *The Enormous Room*, 26, 105, 108, 116–29, 132; eroticism in, 103–5, 114–16, 120–23, 126, 127–28, 175; experiences in World War I, 117–28; *Him*, 105, 128–32; homogeneity and, 109; identification and, 114–16; William James's philosophy and, 106–9; on Gaston Lachaise, 25, 109–12; language of, 103–5, 131–32; liberal individualism and, 106–8; public bodies and, 107–16; public intimacy and, 25, 113–32; radical individualism and, 106–8; the radical left and, 106–8; romanticism in, 105; self-production and, 131–32; sentimentality in, 103–5; on tactility, 25

Dada, 129
Danius, Sara, 21
Darwin, Charles, 220
dehumanization. *See* humanity
Deleuze, Gilles, 94, 115, 184, 248, 253, 256, 271n18
Demuth, Charles, 139
depersonalization: animality and, 27–28; comedy and, 27–28, 217–18; ecstasy and, 53–54; erotic, 159–62; eroticism and, 26; in Jameson, 96; in language, 146, 245; laughter and, 220–21, 256–66; as a strategy of publicness, 24–28, 243–49; sympathy and, 53
Derrida, Jacques: animality and, 238–39, 248; archive fever and, 154; and emotion, 216; on ethics, 299n40; on mimesis, 132; performative in, 188–89
Descartes, René, 93
Dial, 106, 108, 110

Dickinson, Emily, 135
disgust, 115–16, 122
Disney, Walt, 93–98, 114
Doane, Mary Ann, 11, 69, 70, 169, 182
Dos Passos, John, 108, 112
Dove, Arthur, 139
Duchamp, Marcel, 146

eccentric, figure of, 4, 68, 69
Eccentrism, 24, 67–71, 81, 274n7
ecstasy: ambiguity of, 266; community and, 39, 53–57, 300n46; comradeship and, 26; depersonalization and, 18, 54; Eisenstein's theories of, 24, 89, 92; impropriety and, 236; in Lewis, 273n41; in modernism, 96; orchestrated, 148; politics and, 59, 65–66; through public visibility, 245; role in human sociality, 4, 52–54, 56; sociality and, 221, 229; spectatorship and, 153, 159–62; as unfoldment, 174–78, 180; war and, 137
Eisenstein, Sergei: abstraction and, 70, 90; the "attraction" and, 68–69, 72–73, 75–76; on Chaplin, 254–56; on Disney, 16, 93–98; on ecstasy, 24, 70, 76, 89–98; eroticism and, 70, 76, 78–79, 95, 97; expressive movement, 71; "Expressive Movement," 71–72; "Imitation as Mastery," 89; on "inner speech," 89; *Ivan the Terrible,* 95, 254; James-Lange theory of emotion and, 37–38; "Lecture on Biomechanics," 72; modernism of, 70; montage and, 68–69, 75–76, 81, 90–95; "Montage 1937," 90; "Montage 1938," 92; "The Montage of Attractions," 68; "The Montage of Film Attractions," 72; "Notes on Biomechanics," 72; organic nature in, 72–4, 81, 83–85; plasmaticness, 95; *Que Viva Mexico!* 91; on "sensual thought," 89; socialist realism and, 76, 79; *Strike,* 70, 74–89, 90, 94; structuring of emotion and, 24, 70; on theater vs. cinema, 79; "Through Theatre to Cinema," 76, 79; treatment of revolutionary history and, 75; typological thought of, 35, 70, 71; *The Wiseman,* 68
Eisler, Hanns, 257
Eliot, T. S., 9, 11, 21, 41, 46, 106, 146, 222
Ellis, Henry Havelock, 150

emotion: aesthetic, 240–41; in aestheticism, 50; vs. affect, 20, 36, 94; in Barthes, 78; bourgeois protocols of, 9; in burlesque, 196; cognitivist approach to, 22–23, 88; as a complex, 21; contingent, 91; discourse and, 19–20; in Eliot, 225; genuine, 210; incalculability of, 229, 246; inwardness and, 16; James-Lange theory of, 37–38; kinetic, 125; mechanics of, 202–3; mimesis and, 71; nonpurposive, 70; physiological accounts of, 73; poststructuralist theories of, 216; rational telos of, 173; revolutionary, 70; secondariness of, 220–21, 233–42; significant, 21; theatricality of, 211; tools of, 202; uncertain, 196, 213; unstructured, 89; visually perceived, 73; without subjectivity, 216. *See also* affect; feeling
empathy, 73, 75, 115
English Review, 54
event, 69, 71, 81, 94
experience: alterity of, 167; authentic, 123; in Benjamin, 3, 135, 167–69; connoisseurship of, 171–78; in Cornell, 163–64, 166–91; decay of, 197, 199, 204, 217, 244–45; desacralization of, 228–29; as diversion, 135, 148–49; enchantment and, 167; *Erfahrung* vs. *Erlebnis,* 136; eventful, 26, 167–70, 173–78, 180, 190–91; as extension, 183–91; in the Frankfurt School, theories of, 135–36; in Heidegger, 167, 289n12; impurity of, 188–89; poverty of, 213–18; romantic notions of, 25; routinization of, 68; sensory-reflexive dimension of, 160–61; unfoldment of, 174–79; as virtual, 183–84
expressivity: animal, 28, 220–21, 229–42; codes of, 2, 35; crisis of, 220; eccentric, 239–42; evolutionary, 239; facial, 239–42; in Lewis, 56, 58–59, 64–66; romantic, 218; in Soviet theories of acting, 72; in West, 204

Factory of the Eccentric Actor (FEKS), 68
feeling: abstract modes of, 169; asociality and, 225; Chaplinesque, 252; cult of, 198–99, 213; eccentric, 2–5, 7, 16–28, 35, 45, 57, 63–66, 71, 105, 164, 229, 248, 256, 263; exilic, 266; ideational, 17; instrumental, 215–16; in Italian neorealism, 164; locality

of, 228; mechanically produced, 70; modernism and, 1, 5; modern vs. postmodern, 18–19; nervous energy and, 3; outward, 135–39; particularity of, 225; protocols of, 2, 9; publicly mediated, 2–5, 54, 71; purely personal, 128; rationalization of, 171; routine, 171–73; vs. sensation, 103; social, 127; stalling of, 204, 212; vs. thrill, 105; totalizing, 206, 209, 211, 213; true, 20; typicality of, 171–72; undomesticated, 70; universal, 227. *See also* affect; emotion
Feuchtwanger, Lion, 257
Fields, Joe, 27, 202
film: capacity for love, 168, 177–78; cinematographic perception and, 62; Joseph Cornell and, 26; documentary, 76; Eliot and, 9; ethical potential of, 163–70, 177–91; humanism of, 164, 177–78; Italian neorealism, 164–66; Wyndham Lewis and, 62; the life of things and, 203; the optical unconscious and, 166–67; propriety of, 233–42; public feeling and, 3, 58; public recognition and, 4; the variety format and, 9–10. *See also* cinema; technology
Folies Bergère, 25, 112, 115
Ford, Charles Henry, 180
flâneur, 162, 176
Foucault, Michel, 20–21
Frank, Waldo, 139, 141–42
Freud, Sigmund: Cummings's reading of, 117, 119, 120; on fetishism, 78; *Group Psychology and the Analysis of the Ego,* 36–37, 120; on humor, 199–200; on "ideational mimetics," 272n28; innervation and, 3; laughter and, 26; mimetic politics and, 24; on "social feeling," 121–23; social feelings and, 18–19, 25, 26, 121
Frost, Robert, 106
Fuller, Loïe, 180
Fuss, Diana, 121

Genet, Jean, 131
gesture: in Agamben, 214–16; alienated, 204, 217; Brechtian gestus and, 74; of Chaplin, 252; comic, 219–21; compensatory, 219–20; instinctual, 220; mechanical, 230; modernity and, 214–18; organic vs. inorganic, 74, 85

Giddens, Anthony, 25
Goffman, Erving, 25
Gordon, Mel, 72
Gordon, Rae Beth, 37
Great Depression, 258
Griffith, D. W., 92
Guattari, Félix, 115, 271n18
Gunning, Tom, 179

Habermas, Jürgen, 6, 23, 36, 154
Handler, Glenn, 292n6
Hansen, Miriam, 9–10, 38, 160, 168, 198, 289n14
Hartley, Marsden: acrobats and, 16, 133–34, 143–62; *Adventures in the Arts: Informal Chapters on Painters, Vaudeville, and Poets,* 135–36, 139–50, 158; "Concerning Fairy Tales and Me," 135; *Eight Bells Folly,* 287n50; "Elephants and Rhinestones: A Book of Circus Values," 133–34, 149–59; "The Importance of Being Dada," 141; *Indian Fantasy,* 285n25; intimate speech and, 145–47, 150–55; on Lachaise, 109; *Memorial for Hart Crane,* 287n50; militarism and, 136–37; New York Dada and, 134, 139, 148–49; on *Nightwood,* 222, 225–29; *Painting No. 47, Berlin,* 137; *Portrait of a German Officer,* 137; public intimacy and, 25, 105, 134; relationship to the Stieglitz circle, 134, 139–49; sentimentality and, 133–34, 161–62; *Sustained Comedy,* 159; visual eroticism and, 145; *The Warriors,* 137–38, 145; "Whitman and Cézanne," 142; Wilhelmine Berlin and, 134, 136–39, 143
Heidegger, Martin, 167, 172–74, 203, 249
homosexuality: animal life and, 226–29; asociality of, 240–41; as coded in painting, 138–39; emotional particularity and, 210; the German military and, 137; narcissism and, 224; in Nordau, 240–41; in sexology, 134, 150, 226–27; "social feeling" and, 121–22; sophistication and, 142; in the Stieglitz circle, 134, 146–48
Hoover, J. Edgar, 257
Horkheimer, Max, 11–12, 86, 296n43
House Un-American Activities Committee, 264

humanism: Enlightenment, 198, 206; laughter and, 51, 66; mimicry and, 49, 51; notions of community and, 199; universality and, 27, 66

humanity: alienated, 214–18; in Arendt, 14–17; capacity for laughter and, 27, 221; as challenged by satire, 64–66; cinema's love for, 163–66; differentiation of, 177–78; as distinguished from the animal, 28, 93, 220–21; in Eliot, 224–25; finitude and, 178, 190–91; human face and, 91; humanistic imitation of, 271n36; human nature, 202; instrumental violence to, 12, 62–63, 66; limits of, 4, 27–28, 189–90; mediated, 251–52; public recognition of, 221; of realist literature, 77; reification of, 203–4; sensorium of, 12, 66; technology and, 4; vs. things, 203–4, 214; as totality, 177–78; universality and, 12, 42–46; unnaturalness of, 214

Hume, David, 33–34, 272n27

humor: black, 198–200, 255–66; as escape from utility, 254–55; Freudian, 199–200; the "new Humor," 201–2. *See also* comedy; laughter

identification: aesthetic challenges to, 53, 64; in Cummings, 114–16; embodied, 114; emotional mechanisms of, 21, 36–39; Freud's theory of, 121–27; vs. likening, 97; mass politics and, 63; as movement towards an other, 175; stalled, 196, 207

identity: comic undoing of, 159; discursive production of, 65; eccentric feeling and, 25; the face and, 125; fantasies of, 25; of groups, 58–59; humanist notions of, 204; incoherence of, 245; masking of, 139; non-anthropomorphic, 168; performance of, 127; plasticity of, 38, 45–46, 86, 93; politics and, 79; production of sexual, 227; as secondary, 184; totalitarian models of, 23; will to, 132

impersonality: animality and, 27; in Eliot, 223–27; in Hartley, 146, 226–29; intimacy and, 25. *See also* depersonalization; personality

impression, 34, 51, 61

impressionism, 18, 162

innervation, 71, 85, 162, 168, 296n46. *See also* Benjamin, Walter

instrumentality, modernist challenges to, 15–19; publicity and, 6; reason and, 12–13, 15; of the senses, 21–22

intensity, 18–20, 35, 94, 173, 248–49

interiority: Chaplin's adoption of, 259; defended through typage, 57, 61, 64; in Eisenstein, 80, 92; Enlightenment, 198; expressivity and, 64–65; Foucault and, 20; lack of, 220; the "mass in person" and, 63; modernist challenges to, 146; nostalgia for, 204; as a strategy of modernist authority, 161; vs. superficiality, 150; in West, 27

intimacy: anonymity and, 26; as attention to the world, 164–70, 172–78, 180–91; "audience-oriented," 134; collectivity and, 25, 122; comradeship and, 121–23; corporeal, 149; ecstatic, 139; haptic, 111, 125; impersonality and, 25, 53–54; in James, 135; language and, 146–47, 150–55; the life of the feelings and, 1; mediated by beauty, 144; mystical, 157–62; negative affect and, 121; public, 134; publicly mediated, 24–25; stranger, 124–28; in the theories of the Stieglitz circle, 137

Jacobs, Karen, 21, 282n5, 287n54

James, William: on emotion, 37–38, 73; intimacy in, 135, 146; liberal self in, 106–9, 135–36; mimetic politics of, 24; on modern abstraction, 118; on monism, 119–20; *The Varieties of Religious Experience*, 205

Jameson, Fredric, 17, 34, 96

Janis, Elsie, 45

Jenkins, Henry, 40

Johnson, William, 103

Joyce, James, 59

Kant, Immanuel, 105, 116, 125

Keats, John, 106

Kozintsev, Grigory, 68

Kracauer, Siegfried, 12, 136, 152, 203, 244, 295n31, 299n39

Kryzhitsky, Georgi, 68

Kuleshov, Lev, 88

Lachaise, Gaston, 25, 109, 110, 111, 115, 125

Laclau, Ernesto, 65

Lamarr, Hedy, 163, 168
Landru, Henri Desiré, 258–59
Lauder, Harry, 42–43
laughter: animality of, 221, 230–38, 242, 247–48; in Bergson, 213, 216; depersonalization and, 220–21, 255–56; humanity of, 221, 230–38; in *Nightwood*, 227–29; nonpurgative, 216; normative function of, 230–31, 239–42. *See also* comedy; humor
Law, Alma, 72
Lawrence, D. H., 61, 63, 96, 224
Le Bon, Gustave, 24, 36–37, 120
Leitzel, Lillian, 151, 155
Lentricchia, Frank, 106, 107
Levy-Bruhl, Lucien, 89, 97
Lewis, Wyndham: *The Apes of God*, 61–62; *The Art of Being Ruled*, 58; "A Breton Journal," 52–54, 55; caricatures of, 51–52; on Chaplin, 17, 60, 253–54, 266; on comedy, 51, 60; "The Cornac and His Wife," 59–64; critique of amusement, 57; crowd psychology and, 63; early vitalism of, 52–58; on expressivity, 58–59, 64–66; "Inferior Religions," 60; on intimacy, 51; "Les Saltimbanques," 54–57; "The Meaning of the Wild Body," 51; on mimesis, 24, 35; mimesis in, 51–66, 256; on modernity, 57–58, 60, 62–66, 67; on modern politics, 51–66, 58–66, 105, 197, 254; "Paleface," 58, 61; on personality, 58–59; politics, 67; on popular performance, 53–66; reification and, 60, 62–66; "The Revolutionary Simpleton," 58; *Rude Assignment*, 52, 63; on satire, 62, 64; "Some Innkeepers and Bestre," 57–58; on sympathy, 24, 35, 51–66; *Tarr*, 58, 61; theories of publicness in, 51–66; *Time and Western Man*, 58, 59, 62, 67, 253; on type-life, 58–59; on vision and visuality, 62–65; *The Wild Body*, 35, 58–66
Leyda, Jay, 75
Lloyd, Marie, 9, 11, 41, 46
Lippit, Akira, 247
Lipps, Theodor, 73, 90
Litvak, Joseph, 142, 149
Loftus, Cecilia, 45
Loos, Anita, 59
Lukács, Georg, 76, 77, 203

lumpenproletariat, 82, 83
Lyon, Janet, 114

Mandeville, Bernard, 33
manifestoes, 5–6
Marcuse, Herbert, 39–40, 46, 66, 128
Marin, John, 139
Marinetti, F. T., 9
Marks, Laura U., 111, 115
Marx, Karl, 46, 78, 84, 91, 92, 94
mass culture: Fordist, 203; in the Great Depression, 201; modernism and, 8; inauthenticity of, 160; the transformation of vaudeville and, 40–41; the variety format and, 10, 40–41. *See also* technology
Massumi, Brian, 20, 94
Matz, Jesse, 287n58
McCabe, Susan, 300n1
McDougall, William, 36–37, 120
McLane, Maureen, 152, 154
Méliès, Georges, 185
Melville, Herman, 205
Mesmer, Franz Anton, 247
Meyerhold, Vsevelod, 49, 68, 71, 72
Miller, Tyrus, 270n10, 294n30
mimesis: animal feeling and, 240–41; in Benjamin, 167–68, 277n57; in Chaplin, 263–65; cinematic, 164–66, 179–91; constructivism and, 74; idealism and, 132; "imitation-suggestion" theory and, 38–39; through laughter, 230–31; as likening, 97; mimetic contagion, 73; modern art and, 90; normativity and, 16; politics and, 24, 54–66, 70; premodern, 86; of public worlds, 23–24; sensual, 18, 26, 71, 86, 89; social behavior and, 13, 20, 23–24, 38–39, 51–66; technologies of, 49, 58–60, 62. *See also* mimicry
mimicry: animal, 86; emotion and, 74; of movement, 73; in popular performance, 33–35, 39, 71–74; in surrealism, 39; true vs. false, 50, 65. *See also* mimesis
modernism: aesthetic production and, 169; antisentimentality and, 198, 216; attempts to materialize, 6–7; "burlesque," 108; feeling and, 17–23; iconophobia of, 161; the ideology of authenticity and, 160–62; locality and, 201; in Lukács, 78; natural-

ism and, 76; phenomenological vitality of, 22; professionalism and, 22; publicness and, 5–17; realism and, 76; recuperative, 215–18; romanticism and, 64; sensory estrangement and, 66; sentimentality and, 103–5; social alienation and, 65; violent sympathy of, 189; visuality of, 161–62

modernity: of aestheticism, 259; animality and, 221; contingency and, 68–69; disciplining of persons and, 20; ecstasy and, 96; emotional protocols of, 197; the everyday and, 25; expressive movement and, 86; fantasies of, 8; gesture and, 214–18; as groundlessness, 198; as ground of modernism, 8; the hostility to traditional community and, 21; martial, 136; normativity and, 15, 20; the organization of mimesis and, 86; the public world and, 1, 7, 251, 259; rationalization of time in, 169, 252–53; regimes of abstraction and, 97, 107; sensory and experiential dimensions of, 7, 13, 17–18, 66; "sensory-reflexive" dimension of, 160–62; sentimentality and, 134; social abstraction and, 57, 64; social asymmetries and, 23; spectacle and, 214–15; surveillance and, 85

Montagu, Ivor, 75

mood: anxiety, 173, 175; chaste, 175; of enchantment, 167, 172; as an extensive affect, 26; fantasy and, 183; in Heidegger, 172–74; Romantic, 168–69; of "unfoldment," 167, 173–78

Moore, Marianne, 172

de Motherlant, Henry, 77

Musil, Robert, 77

Nancy, Jean-Luc, 300n46

Nathan, George J., 41, 202

National Winter Garden Theater, 112

Newman, J. H., 49

New Masses, 224

Ngai, Sianne, 186, 280n35, 290n24

Nichols, Bill, 79

Nichols, Robert, 122

Nietzsche, Friedrich, 184

Nordau, Max, 239–41

North, Michael, 116, 279n12

O'Keeffe, Georgia, 139

Oliver, Kelly, 175

Ostrovsky, A.N., 68

Owen, Wilfred, 122

Page, Brett, 202

passion: animal life and, 28, 239–39; comedy and, 28, 233–34; compulsive, 220; formalized, 261, 264; passivity and, 220, 247–49; publicity of, 233–34, 236–37; as sign of personality, 220; singularity of, 232–34

performance: mechanistic theories of, 70; politics and, 14–17, 65–66. *See also* acting; popular performance

personality: bourgeois, 252; capitalist modernity and, 25; the carnal body and, 63; of Chaplin, 251–66; coercive determinations of, 19; of the dandy, 259; Eliot's ambivalence toward, 223–26; estrangement of, 124–28; expressive uniqueness of, 64; humanist, 252; on the market, 258, 260; as product of appropriation, 219–20; public legibility of, 227–29; sociality and, 223–29; theatrical projection of, 41–42, 54–66; theatricality of, 220; types of, 21, 35, 41–46. *See also* depersonalization; impersonality

phenomenology: affect and, 22; Arendt and, 14–17; expressive personality and, 64–65; neorealist immanence and, 164–65; publicness and, 7, 11, 14–17, 26, 36

photography: Bazin on, 164–66; Chaplin and, 258; contingency and, 85; human finitude and, 190–92; imitation as, 33, 36, 45, 244–45; subjectivity and, 39; surrealism and, 164–66

Piaget, Jean, 90, 168

Picabia, Francis, 146

popular performance: affect and, 8, 12, 24; biomechanics and, 71–74; historicity of, 11; mimicry in, 33–51; modernist nostalgia and, 8–12; vs. popular culture, 7–8; Soviet Eccentrism and, 67–71; staging of feeling and, 7, 17, 54; variety format and, 9–13, 143–44, 179–80. *See also* acting; performance

postmodernity, 18

potential: animation and, 94; in Lukács, 77; politics and, 83; politics of, 78–79, 83–84, 95–98

potentiality, 15–17, 95

Pound, Ezra, 21, 106, 107, 118, 125

primitivism, 53–56, 63. *See also* race

psychology: bourgeois, 68; experimental, 23, 37; of groups and crowds, 23–24, 73, 120; in James, 107; Marinetti's challenge to, 9; mechanist-materialist vs. vitalist, 72; perceptual psychology and its influence on Benjamin, 3; psychophysiology and, 37, 63; Soviet acting theory and, 67–74; spatialized, 115, 117, 119–20; traumatizing, 116–18

publicity: bourgeois, 6, 14; homelessness and, 266; instrumental, 6; mass publicity, 206; modernist capitulation to, 2; sympathetic, 197; of Whitman, 143. *See also* publicness; public sphere

publicness: advertising and, 5; alternative forms of, 204; in Arendt, 14–17; definition vs. the terms "publicity" and "the public sphere," 1, 7; disqualified, 242–43; ecstatic, 175; embodiment and, 4, 26; emotional pathologies of, 253–54; ethical, 199; as exposure, 229; human recognition and, 4, 28; impropriety and, 221; of language, 103–4; modernist hostility to, 2; as mood, 174; noninstrumental, 15–17, 213–18; nostalgia for, 217–18; as performative, 8, 13–17, 64–66; as a phenomenology, 7, 11, 105; plasmatic, 98; as poetry, 5, 8, 14–17, 64–66, 263; professionalism and, 5; queer, 134; reification and, 39, 60, 62–66; sensational, 244; as sensory horizon, 198; spectacle and, 26; tender, 173–78

public sphere: abstraction and, 206–7; in attempts to materialize modernism, 6; of early cinema, 10; Enlightenment heritage and, 27; in Habermas, 6, 36; heterogenous, 201–3; homosexual intimacies and, 134; humanist, 198; intimate potential of, 105; mimetic-sympathetic, 23, 36–39, 45–46, 51, 61, 62, 67, 70, 96, 244–55, 248; modernist inauthenticity and, 159–62; performative, 86; reified, 97; role of sym-

pathy in, 292n6; as "sensory-reflexive horizon," 159–62; social differentiation and, 42–43; spectacular emptiness of, 213–18. *See also* publicity; publicness

race: impropriety and, 245–46; modernist ideologies, 114; modernist primitivism and, 114–16; racial comedy in vaudeville, 201–2; racial typologies and, 41

Rahv, Philip, 224

Ray, Robert, 78

Reigl, Aloïs, 115

Roach, Joseph, 72, 272n27

romanticism: apostrophe and, 154–55; in Bazin, 166; in Cornell, 26, 163, 167; crowd psychology and, 23, 36–37; in Cummings, 105; excessive personalism of, 158; irony and, 200; Lawrence and, 61; in Lewis, 51–59, 61; mass mediation and, 64; mood in, 168–69; privacy and, 1, 16; as reaction to the Enlightenment, 199; the soul and, 199; surrealism and, 166; sympathy and, 24, 51–56, 61; transcendence of contingency and, 200

Rönnebeck, Arnold, 136, 138

Roosevelt, Franklin D., 257

Rosenfeld, Paul, 146, 148

Rousseau, Jean-Jacques, 93

Royce, Josiah, 106

Sade, Marquis de, 199

Santayana, George, 106, 107, 159

Sassoon, Siegfried, 122

satire, 61–62, 64–66, 230, 256–66. *See also* comedy; humor; laughter

Sedgwick, Eve Kosofsky, 161, 297n53

Seldes, Gilbert, 196

Seltzer, Mark, 25, 39, 63

sensation: of animal life, 221; depletion of, 62; without desire, 105, 108; experiences of diversion and, 136; vs. feeling, 103; irresolute, 228; modern amusements and, 62, 244; modernist poetics and, 105–8; in modern literature, 77; modern sensorium and, 50, 62–63, 66, 68; of Poundian image, 107; primitive, 95, 97; pure, 94; "sensual thought" and, 89; technological mediation of, 21–22; of tenderness, 179; of touch, 105; touch and, 115–16; training of, 48–49, 66; unqualified, 94

sentimentality: asociality and, 104–5; Enlightenment, 199, 216; in the Kantian tradition, 105; in modernism, 161–62; modernist hostility to, 25; violence of, 198

sexuality: discursive inscription of, 227–29; in *Nightwood,* 222; rationalization of, 210–11. *See also* homosexuality

Shaw, Lilian, 42

Shelley, Percy Bysshe, 106

Shklovsky, Viktor, 69, 76, 81, 274n7

de Sica, Vittorio, 164

Simmel, Georg, 25, 98, 124, 126, 127, 136

Sitney, P. Adams, 163

slapstick: contingency and, 262–63; emotional mechanics of, 201–3; identification and, 295n39; materiality and, 195–96, 236; in *Miss Lonelyhearts,* 207–13; in *Nightwood,* 234; rationalization and, 295n31

Smith, Adam, 33–34

sociality: of embodied life, 228, 237; Jamesian, 146; organic, 74; rationalized, 196; sociability and, 98

social world: affective particularity of, 198; alienated, 243; animalized, 230–32, 41; class of, 208; elastic, 230–31, 239–42; as imitative, 38–39; legibility of, 42–46; modern disaggregation of, 13; otherness of, 206; particularity within, 206–7, 209

spectacle, disembodiment and, 134

Spinoza, Baruch, 94

Stallybrass, Peter, 84

Stanislavsky, Constantin, 72, 92

Stein, Gertrude, 59, 106, 135

Stevens, Wallace, 106

Stieglitz, Alfred, 33

subjectivity: ahistorical being and, 77; audience-oriented, 36; authentic, 40, 55–56, 62; as depersonalization, 96; detachment and, 134; dissolution of, 111; imperious, 169; liberal individualism and, 106–8; modernist challenges to, 16, 64–66; monadic, 2, 17–19, 34–35, 64–65; mutable, 95; photographic, 38, 65; queer, 159; self-identical, 38; tender, 168; voracious, 152

surrealism: black humor and, 27, 198–200;

in Cornell, 170, 182; critique of, 292n11; in Cummings, 128; Hartley's opinions on, 286n48; murder and, 258; re-enchantment and, 200; romanticism and, 155; in Nathanael West, 199

Swift, Jonathan, 199

Swinburne, A. G., 224

sympathy: as absent from the public world, 13; as compulsive, 20, 23–24, 36–39; in Darwin, 240; eighteenth-century, 272n27; eighteenth-century theories of, 33–35; in Eliot, 223–25, 228; as experienced collectively, 2, 23–24, 43–46, 49–66; failure of, 213; as a mode of viewing, 44–45; in Nordau, 240–41; physical, 52; primitivism and, 53–57; romantic theories of, 247; as willful, 23

Tanguay, Eva, 45–46, 61

Tarde, Gabriel, 24, 39–39, 45

Taussig, Michael, 86

Taylorism, 68, 72

technology: the appropriation of the senses and, 21–22; first vs. second, 3; incorporation of, 180; mediation and, 17–18, 164–76; mimesis and, 49, 71, 163, 168; political interpellation and, 70; sympathetic manufacture and, 13; visual, 64–65. *See also* cinema; film; vision

Terada, Rei, 220, 297n51

time: anachronistic, 263; of capitalism, 67; capitalist modernity and, 169–70; of Chaplin, 252–66; of collective life, 123; contingency and, 11, 69–71, 79; dead time, 170; disjunctive, 181–82; eccentric feelings and, 8; ephemerality of, 182; the event and, 167; futurity and, 96, 231; the instant, 252; *Jetztzeit* and, 263; of the market, 258, 260; morality and, 240; nonlinear, 187–89; nonsynchronous, 10; repetition and, 182–89; romantic, 254; of the state, 261; of still photograph, 181; untimeliness, 263–66

touch, 105, 111, 115, 120

de Toulouse-Lautrec, Henri, 150

Trask, Michael, 25

Trauberg, Leonid, 68

Tretyakov, Sergei, 72

Trotter, Wilfred, 36, 120

Tsivian, Yuri, 86
typage, 35, 41–46, 51–66, 80, 84, 270n6

de Unamuno, Miguel, 159

Vanderbilt, Gerty, 42
Veitch, Jonathan, 197
Vidler, Anthony, 115, 119
Viertel, Salka, 257
View, 163
virtuosity, 14–17, 28, 65
vision: of Chaplin, 255; cinematic, 280n44; communal, 152; depersonalization and, 26, 245–46; ecstatic, 143; embodiment and, 134; eroticism and, 145–49; ethical, 167–70; haptic, 111, 115; the hypervisibility of race and, 126; identity and, 207; imitation and, 37, 40–46, 62–66; mass visuality and, 65, 214; memory and, 286n38; modernist visuality and, 21–22, 26, 62–66, 161–62; modern transformations of, 13, 62–66; public horizon of visibility of, 227–29; the transmission of affect and, 34–39, 62–66; visionary optics and, 159–62
von Freyburg, Lieutenant, 137, 138–39, 145
Vygotsky, Lev, 89

Wainewright, Thomas Griffith, 259
Warner, Michael, 25, 269n24

Weber, Lou, 27, 202
Weinberg, Jonathan, 284n14
Welles, Orson, 258
West, Nathanael: antisociality and, 195–99, 204, 216–18; critique of community, 197, 213–18; The Dream Life of Balso Snell, 199, 205; the failure of public feeling in, 27–28; the feminine and, 205–6, 211; laughter in, 27; materiality in, 196; Miss Lonelyhearts, 195–218, 236; slapstick and, 16, 195–96, 201–3, 207–13; surrealism and, 27, 199; sympathetic publicity and, 197–99, 201, 205–13
Whitman, Walt, 143, 158
Wilde, Oscar, 259
Williams, Bert, 27, 295n39
Wilson, Edmund, 130, 131
Wolfe, Cary, 107
Woolf, Virginia, 96
World War I, 58, 117, 137
World War II, 170, 258
Worringer, Wilhelm, 90, 91

Yampolsky, Mikhail, 89
Yutkevich, Sergei, 68

Zayas, Marius de, 35
"Zip," 103, 123

The University of Illinois Press
is a founding member of the
Association of American University Presses.

_____

Composed in 10.5/13 Minion
with ITC Kabel display
by Celia Shapland
at the University of Illinois Press
Designed by Dennis Roberts
Manufactured by Sheridan Books, Inc.

University of Illinois Press
1325 South Oak Street
Champaign, IL 61820-6903
www.press.uillinois.edu

Justus Nieland is an assistant professor of English at Michigan State University.